HTML and CSS Web Standards Solutions

A Web Standardistas' Approach

Christopher Murphy
Nicklas Persson

friendsof

DESIGNER TO DESIGNER™

an Apress® company

HTML and CSS Web Standards Solutions: A Web Standardistas' Approach

ISBN-13 (pbk): 978-1-4302-1606-3

ISBN-13 (electronic): 978-1-4302-1607-0

Printed and bound in the United States of America 9 8 7 6 5 4 3 2 1

Distributed to the book trade worldwide by Springer-Verlag New York, Inc., 233 Spring Street, 6th Floor, New York, NY 10013. Phone 1-800-SPRINGER, fax 201-348-4505, e-mail orders-ny@springer-sbm.com, or visit www.springeronline.com.

For information on translations, please contact Apress directly at 2855 Telegraph Avenue, Suite 600, Berkeley, CA 94705. Phone 510-549-5930, fax 510-549-5939, e-mail info@apress.com, or visit www.apress.com.

Apress and friends of ED books may be purchased in bulk for academic, corporate, or promotional use. eBook versions and licenses are also available for most titles. For more information, reference our Special Bulk Sales–eBook Licensing web page at http://www.apress.com/info/bulksales.

The source code for this book is freely available to readers at www.friendsofed.com in the Downloads section.

Credits

Lead Editor	**Production Editor**
Clay Andres	Kelly Winquist
Technical Reviewer	**Compositor**
Paul Haine	Dina Quan
Editorial Board	**Proofreader**
Clay Andres, Steve Anglin, Mark Beckner,	April Eddy
Ewan Buckingham, Tony Campbell, Gary Cornell,	
Jonathan Gennick, Michelle Lowman, Matthew Moodie,	**Indexer**
Jeffrey Pepper, Frank Pohlmann, Ben Renow-Clarke,	Julie Grady
Dominic Shakeshaft, Matt Wade, Tom Welsh	
Project Manager	**Artist**
Beth Christmas	April Milne
Copy Editor	**Interior and Cover Designer**
Ami Knox	Kurt Krames
Associate Production Director	**Manufacturing Director**
Kari Brooks-Copony	Tom Debolski

CONTENTS AT A GLANCE

PART ONE: A SOLID XHTML FOUNDATION

PART TWO: ADDING STYLE WITH CSS

CONTENTS

Chapter 6: Creating Links with Anchors 117

Chapter 7: Getting Your Site Online **145**

PART TWO: ADDING STYLE WITH CSS

Chapter 8: CSS 101 . . . . **167**

Chapter 11: A Two-Column CSS Layout 275

Chapter 12: List-O-Matic. 313

ABOUT THE AUTHORS

Internationally respected digital artist **Christopher Murphy** has been described as "a William Morris for the digital age" (*Creative Review*).

Creatively exploring the potential of the Web since the mid '90s, he is a cofounder of web-based arts publishing organization Fällt Publishing (www.fallt.com) and has worked within the field of audio-related design for over a decade.

Murphy's work has been featured alongside numerous internationally respected designers including Peter Saville, The Designers Republic, Tomato, and Stefan Sagmeister in a variety of design books and magazines, including *Eye* magazine, widely acknowledged as one of the world's leading design journals. A regular speaker at design conferences and workshops worldwide, he also exhibits his work internationally.

In addition to his role as a lecturer in interactive design at the University of Ulster at Belfast, where he has actively promoted a web standards–based curriculum, Murphy runs an established design consultancy and has created award-winning work for clients including Absolut Vodka, Royal Mail, and the British Council.

When not otherwise occupied, he maintains the web site for digital arts collective Fehler:

www.fehlergesellschaftmitbeschrankterhaftung.com

A practicing digital artist since the mid-'90s, **Nicklas Persson** graduated from the University of Ulster in 2000 with a first-class BA (Hons) degree in fine and applied arts. His work has been exhibited internationally at numerous online and offline digital arts festivals worldwide.

On graduation Persson was invited to work for BBC Interactive, a prestigious role he readily accepted. He subsequently moved to a role as senior developer in the well-respected Belfast-based interactive design agency Radar. He now combines work as a lecturer in interactive design at the University of Ulster at Belfast with work as a freelance developer and designer at SL33P (www.sl33p.com) specializing in the design and development of well-crafted web applications.

As a consequence of his commitment to his teaching, he regrets neglecting his obligations to his long-established web site:

www.takete.com

About the Technical Reviewer

Paul Haine is a client-side developer currently working in London for the *Guardian* newspaper. He is the author of *HTML Mastery: Semantics, Standards, and Styling* (friends of ED, 2006) and runs a personal web site at www.joeblade.com.

ACKNOWLEDGMENTS

We're grateful to everyone who has supported us throughout the process of writing this book. We've very much appreciated the support of both our colleagues and our students (not to mention our clients) while we've been knee-deep in paper—thanks for being so understanding. We would particularly like to thank the following people who helped turn this book into a reality.

Clay Andres, our editor, for believing in our original idea and creatively guiding us through the writing process. We appreciate your encouragement and support.

Paul Haine, our technical reviewer, for his meticulous attention to detail. Your insightful suggestions helped improve this book considerably.

Beth Christmas, our project manager, who has kept this book on track and provided inspiration throughout the darker moments! We wouldn't have made it through this process without your boundless enthusiasm.

Ami Knox, our copy editor, who not only improved our text considerably, but also shares our idiosyncratic sensibilities. If we ever write a book again, we'd like you and your eagle eyes on the team!

We've also very much appreciated the hard work of Kelly Winquist, Dina Quan, April Eddy, and everyone at friends of ED, who have worked under relentless pressure (thanks to a few missed deadlines at our end) to deliver this book on time.

Thanks also to Lee Munroe for late-night Twitter support, Michael McCrory (our guinea pig) for his feedback along the way, and Debbie Fraser for her unwavering tolerance (we'll get those projects finished for you now Debbie . . .).

Lastly, thanks to you, for choosing this book. We hope you find it both helpful and inspiring as you embark on your journey as a Web Standardista.

Christopher Murphy and Nicklas Persson

ACKNOWLEDGMENTS

Thanks to Cara for your constant support and understanding over the last few months (and years), and to Ross and Caitlín for being there (when I've been there). Roll on Donegal 2009!

Christopher Murphy

Thanks to Margaret for your enduring support and for holding everything up during the last few months, and to Tiernan and Oskar for still remembering my face.

Nicklas Persson

INTRODUCTION

Why did we choose to write this book? We're both extremely busy—lecturing bachelor's degree and master's degree interactive design students, maintaining our own practice working for clients, and furthering our established careers as artists exhibiting internationally—so the idea of a "how to" book for would-be web designers wasn't arrived at lightly.

That said, we felt the time was right for this sort of book. There are a lot of excellent books that we point our students toward: Dan Cederholm's inspiring *Web Standards Solutions*; Paul Haine's meticulous *HTML Mastery*; and Andy Budd, Cameron Moll, and Simon Collison's indispensable *CSS Mastery*, to name but a few. All are fantastic books and we urge our students to buy every one; however, none of them seemed to cover everything our students needed to embark on a well-grounded, web standards–based approach **in one package**: namely, a solid foundation in well-structured XHTML coupled with a comprehensive introduction to CSS.

Cue Web Standardistas.

A little background

We teach final year bachelor's degree and master's degree interactive design students at the University of Ulster at Belfast, and we're proud of the work that many of them do. We've worked very hard over the last few years to develop a lecture program for our students that covers all of the fundamentals: a solid grounding in XHTML coupled with a strong grasp of CSS. We strive to ensure that when our students leave our courses they're doing web design the right way: creating well-designed web sites built using a web standards approach.

In late 2006 we were invited to write an evening course for absolute beginners, open to all, no previous experience required. We relished the challenge and set about writing a web design course from scratch that covered everything required to set up a web site from start to finish, including registering your own web address and uploading your web site to your own web space—an aspect often surprisingly overlooked in web design books.

The book you're holding in your hands grew out of that course and was designed to help anyone getting started on the Web to get up and running as quickly as possible: low barrier to entry, easy to follow, jargon explained in an easy-to-understand manner.

Who is this book aimed at?

Who is this book aimed at? Anyone! Anyone with an interest in the Web. Anyone with an interest in building and maintaining an easy-to-update web site. More importantly, it's aimed at anyone wanting to set out on the one true path, embracing web standards, to become a Web Standardista.

Even if you're an absolute beginner in web design, this book will enable you to create future-proof web sites that not only look great in all modern browsers, but are also accessible to a wide variety of audiences across a range of platforms—from those browsing on everyday computers to those accessing the Web on the latest, emerging mobile devices.

Across 14 easy-to-follow chapters, we introduce you to the fundamentals of contemporary web design practice. By building progressively, chapter upon chapter, we equip you with a firm knowledge of the fundamentals of web design. In short, everything you need to know to move forward in your lifelong journey as a Web Standardista.

Regardless of your computing platform—Mac OS, Windows, or Linux—we recommend easy-to-master tools that are, in most cases, free and equip you with a knowledge of these tools with a minimum of technical jargon.

Step by step we cover how to build handcrafted web pages using well-structured XHTML markup and how to apply layout and style to these pages using CSS. What this book doesn't require: expensive software or a degree in computer science.

What you'll achieve

As you'll discover in Chapter 1, "homework" forms an important aspect of this book. We've included a series of enjoyable practical assignments at the end of each chapter, exercises for you to follow along with at your own pace.

Following along with the homework will not only ensure that you fully grasp what we cover in each chapter, but also provide you with a well-crafted web site that you can build on once you've completed the book.

It gets better—we're even offering the XHTML and CSS you'll be creating as a part of the book's homework for free, under a Creative Commons license. Complete the homework, and you can use the web site you've built as a framework for your own content, safe in the knowledge that the web site you've created is future-proof and optimized for everyone: from those browsing on everyday computers, to those accessing the Web on the latest emerging mobile devices, as shown in Figure 1.

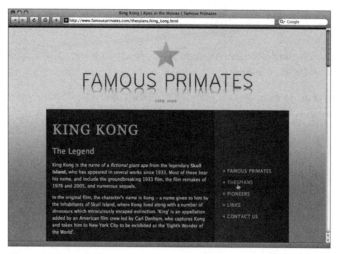

Figure 1. The web site you'll be creating as a part of the book's homework is designed to be displayed across a variety of devices.

By following along with the book's practical assignments, you'll be capable of producing a comprehensive web site that not only looks good in everyday browsers, but also looks great in the latest breakthrough Internet communication devices. You can see the completed web site you'll be creating at

`www.famousprimates.com`

Conventions used in this book

To keep this book as clear and easy to follow as possible, the following text conventions are used throughout.

Important words or concepts are normally highlighted in **bold type**.

Code is presented in `fixed-width` font.

New or changed code is normally presented in **`bold fixed-width font`**.

Menu commands are written in the form Menu ➤ Submenu ➤ Submenu.

Where we'd like to draw your attention to something, or offer some additional supporting material, we've highlighted it like this:

> *Remember, once opened, all tags should be closed.*

Sometimes code won't fit on a single line in a book. Where this happens, we use an arrow like this: ➡.

```
This is a very, very long section of code that should be written all ➡
on the same line without a break.
```

Throughout this book we provide examples of markup in XHTML and CSS. Where we show sections of repetitive markup, we have used ellipses (...) for brevity as follows:

```
<ul>
  <li>King Kong</li>
  <li>Cornelius</li>
  ...
  <li>Cheeta</li>
</ul>
```

Using ellipses allows us to show you the markup that's relevant and that we're specifically referring to, enabling you to focus on what matters.

Accessing the code

All the code examples and homework files used throughout this book are available for download at the book's companion web site. You can access these files along with additional supporting material and links to other resources at

www.webstandardistas.com

Let's get started!

PART ONE

A SOLID XHTML FOUNDATION

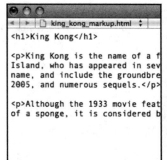

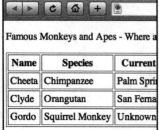

CHAPTER 1

ARE YOU A WEB STANDARDISTA?

Congratulations, you've made it to Chapter 1. This is the point at which we establish a few ground rules and minimum key requirements as we move forward—nothing too challenging beyond a willingness to learn. We're confident you have what it takes. Not everyone can become a **Web Standardista**. We feel optimistic, however, that if you've made it this far, your heart is in the right place and you're ready to join the growing band of web developers and designers that wear the Web Standardistas badge with pride.

Details on getting an actual, real-life, hold-in-your-hands badge are provided at the end of the book. We've hidden those details, however, so don't skip to that part of the book right now; there are a few exercises you have to complete first to earn the right to display your Web Standardista credentials.

Before we embark on the rest of the book, we felt it important to provide a little history of the World Wide Web: who invented it, why it was invented, and how it has changed and evolved.

So, without further ado . . .

A brief history of the World Wide Web

This section provides a contextual overview of web development and introduces some key concepts that lie at the heart of the Web Standardistas' approach, particularly the idea of a return to structured markup and the use of Plain Old Semantic HTML, or POSH. You can find out more about POSH at the Microformats web site:

> http://microformats.org/wiki/posh

At this point you're probably thinking, "This is just the boring background stuff. I want to get my hands dirty." True, some of this chapter deals with history, but we believe that an understanding of how the Web has evolved will help you see where it's heading and, in a rapidly evolving medium, this is useful knowledge to have. It also puts you ahead of the everyday web developer who hasn't availed themselves of the Web Standardistas' approach.

The Web is born

First things first: the Web is *not* the Internet. People often use the terms *the Web* and *the Internet* interchangeably; however, the two terms are not synonymous. The World Wide Web, or Web, is in fact just one of a number of ways information can be exchanged over the Internet, another being e-mail.

The perfect Web

When Tim Berners-Lee and his team at CERN invented the World Wide Web in 1990, they did so with the intention of creating a platform for the free exchange of information. Originally targeted at scientists, the Web was first a somewhat closed community. However, in 1993, Marc Andreessen and Eric Bina at the National Center for Supercomputing Applications (NCSA), a research department at the University of Illinois at Urbana-Champaign, released the Web's first truly easy-to-use browser. The release of Mosaic, the first browser to display images within the browser window, heralded the arrival of the World Wide Web as an information and entertainment medium.

Mosaic, which subsequently evolved into Netscape Navigator, caught the attention of Microsoft, which entered the browser market in 1995 with Internet Explorer. Bundled as part of Microsoft's dominant Windows 95 operating system, Internet Explorer accelerated the expansion of the Web in the public consciousness.

The chaotic Web

Microsoft's entry into the browser market helped to raise the profile of the Web considerably. Unfortunately, competition among browser manufacturers coupled with the growing pains of a rapidly emerging medium quickly led to the creation of proprietary, browser-specific tags and markup. Different companies' browsers adopted different standards, making it extremely difficult to build cross-platform-compatible web sites.

The result was a minefield for web designers: the only way to ensure correct display across browsers and operating systems was to write custom web sites targeting different browsers and operating systems, often doubling and even tripling workload.

This process was extremely inefficient, and it soon became apparent that the solution to the problem of developing web sites efficiently lay in standardizing approaches to web development. Thus the Web Standards Project, or WaSP, was born:

> www.webstandards.org/about/mission

HTML rewind

But let's rewind a little. Before we explore the rise of the Web Standards Project, it helps to clarify what exactly HTML is and what it was intended to do. We'll be demonstrating the use of HTML in this book after all, or at least a variant of it, so you need to have a basic understanding of it.

HTML, or HyperText Markup Language, underpins the Web. The World Wide Web Consortium, or W3C—the nonprofit body responsible for guiding the evolution of the Web and proposing web standards—defines HTML as follows:

> *HTML is the* lingua franca *for publishing hypertext on the World Wide Web. It is a non-proprietary format . . . and can be created and processed by a wide range of tools, from simple plain text editors—you type it in from scratch—to sophisticated WYSIWYG authoring tools. HTML uses tags such as <h1> and </h1> to structure text into headings, paragraphs, lists, hypertext links, etc.*
>
> www.w3.org/MarkUp/

The preceding definition, while accurate, can be a little confusing for the beginner. HTML is a nonproprietary format, HTML can be created by a wide range of tools, HTML can be processed by a wide range of tools, HTML can structure text into hypertext links—what does it all mean? With some experience, the meaning of this is crystal clear, but to the beginner, Douglas Adams' Babel Fish wouldn't go amiss. Cue the Babel Fish.

> *The Babel Fish is a species of fish that can instantly translate any language to any other language.*
>
> http://en.wikipedia.org/wiki/babel_fish

- **HTML is a nonproprietary format.** Translated: HTML isn't owned by anyone. It's open source and free, that is, anyone can use it freely, no royalties payable. This openness is one key to the rapid growth of the Web.

- **HTML can be created by a wide range of tools.** Translated: HTML can be created by anyone. It doesn't require expensive software, and it can be written with the simplest of free, yes free, plain text editors. (We'll explain what a plain text editor is and where to get one later in this chapter in the section "What's your favorite plain text editor?").

- **HTML can be processed by a wide range of tools.** Translated: HTML, when written properly—the Web Standardistas' way—can be read on a variety of devices: your desktop browser, your nearly new mobile phone, and the brand new iPhone you're convincing yourself you really need.

- **HTML can structure text into hypertext links.** Translated: HTML has the ability to convert text (and images) into **hypertext links** or **hyperlinks**, magical portals that transport you from one place to another, not unlike the *Starship Enterprise*'s transporter or the green pipes in Super Mario Bros. Or, in even simpler terms, the links you click to move from one web page to another, that is, the basic fabric of the Web.

HTML evolved

The first documented reference to HTML dates back to 1991, in a page written by Tim Berners-Lee. "HTML Tags" (www.w3.org/History/19921103-hypertext/hypertext/WWW/MarkUp/Tags.html) introduced headers, paragraphs, hyperlinks, and a few other elements that we still use in HTML today. In 1995, the first official specification, HTML 2.0, saw the light of day. In the following few years, as the World Wide Web grew, computers became faster, and browsers more powerful, HTML evolved. The W3C, formed in 1995, released specifications for HTML 3.0, 3.2, and 4.0 in the latter half of the 1990s.

The last valid HTML specification published by the W3C is HTML 4.01, which was released in 1999.

> *In January 2008, HTML 5 was published as a working draft by the W3C. Although still a working draft, certain HTML 5 features are already implemented by some browsers.*

The X in XHTML

XML (Extensible Markup Language) is a language created for the purpose of sharing data between different computers and systems, and is used extensively on the Internet. XML doesn't have a defined set of tags like HTML. Instead, it has a defined structure and strict rules on how this structure is interpreted. XHTML, or Extensible Hypertext Markup Language, is HTML reformulated in XML. Translated, this means that XHTML is HTML with the strict rules of XML added to the mix.

The W3C states the following:

> *The XHTML family is the next step in the evolution of the Internet. By migrating to XHTML today, content developers can enter the XML world with all of its attendant benefits, while still remaining confident in their content's backward compatibility.*
>
> www.w3.org/TR/xhtml1/#xhtml

As if this weren't confusing enough already, XHTML (like HTML) comes in a variety of "flavors": XHTML 1.0 Strict, XHTML 1.0 Transitional, and XHTML 1.0 Frameset. Throughout this book, we'll be using XHTML 1.0 Strict; to avoid confusion for now, that's all you need to know at this point.

Back to the Web Standards Project . . .

A web standards approach

Founded in 1998, the Web Standards Project campaigned (and still campaigns) for a standards-based approach to web design to reduce the cost and complexity of web development, while increasing the accessibility of web pages. Their mission was (and remains) to gain support for web standards recommended by the W3C.

In English, the Web Standards Project has helped to drive forward and underpin a move toward the use of standards in web development, away from the creation of proprietary, browser-specific tags and markup that had taken hold at the height of the "Wild West" browser-specific days of the Web. A noble intention, and one that is paying dividends, but what exactly are standards?

What are standards?

Before we answer the question of what web standards are, it helps to define what standards are in the broadest sense and why we use standards day to day. We can define standards with a dictionary definition (but as you'll see it's a little dry):

> **standard** *–n.* **1** *an object or quality or measure serving as a basis or example or principle to which others conform or by which the accuracy or quality of others is judged . . .* **7** *a document specifying nationally or internationally agreed properties for manufactured goods, etc.*
>
> Concise Oxford Dictionary *(Clarendon Press, 1990)*

In English? We use standards on a daily basis, often without realizing it. When we buy a lightbulb, for example, we know that if we buy a screw-fitting bulb, it will fit our light fitting when we get it home. Standards ensure that the bulb we buy isn't "just a little too large" or "just a little too wide" to fit our light fitting.

Standards enable companies to streamline production and allow consumers to rest easy in the knowledge that what they buy will work when they get it home. Standards are all around us: look at the plugs in your home, the size of the shoes you're wearing, and so on. But what has this go to do with the Web?

So, web standards?

Web standards pick up from the same principle. As browser manufacturers have moved toward embracing standards, the need to write browser-specific markup has diminished.

By using well-structured HTML to mark up content and CSS, or Cascading Style Sheets, to control presentation, we should now be able to design one web site, and it should display consistently across standards-compliant browsers regardless of operating system (Mac OS, Windows, or Linux). Equally importantly, when the same markup is rendered by less-capable, non-standards-compliant browsers—in older, text-based, or mobile browsers—the content should still remain accessible.

Web standards save us time as designers and allow us to sleep at night, safe in the knowledge that our carefully crafted masterpiece is accessible regardless of who's viewing it on which browser and which platform.

As web standards are increasingly embraced by browser developers, a standards-based approach embracing XHTML and CSS—the two key standards this book focuses on—is the right way forward. Web standards pick up from the same principle, i.e., that we should be able to design one web site, and it should display consistently across browsers regardless of operating system.

Why use web standards?

Perhaps a better question to ask would be this one: why ignore web standards? The benefits of adopting a web standards approach are so compelling, why *wouldn't* you use them?

Using web standards cuts down on development time, creates sites that are easy to update and maintain, improves search engine rankings, and, as a welcome byproduct, can improve accessibility, making pages accessible to more people, especially the disabled, some of whom can't use standard browsers.

This is why we built this book around a standards-based approach. In the upcoming text, we run through some of the reasons for adopting this approach in a little more detail. We're confident that by the time you finish reading this chapter, you'll start to see the Web Standardistas' way is the right way.

Separating content and presentation

As the Web evolved, HTML was misused to handle both content *and* its visual presentation and design. The results of this are unfortunately common and are referred to as **tag soup**, where HTML is used to control both how content is structured and how it looks.

This was never the intended purpose of HTML, which was always meant to describe the semantic markup of information, *not* "how it looks within the browser."

This quote from Wikipedia summarizes tag soup nicely:

> Tag soup is characterized by a large number of common mistakes, such as malformed HTML tags, improperly nested HTML elements . . . and the use of presentational HTML elements and attributes in order to create visual effects without respect for their implied meaning (that is, against their semantic purpose). Although often thought of as typifying semi-professional or hobbyist web sites, tag soup is created by many professional web page layout programs, and written by hand by many professional web developers for some of the highest-profile sites.
>
> http://en.wikipedia.org/wiki/Tag_soup

The Web Standardistas' approach is built on a simple concept: we use XHTML to handle the content, structure, and meaning of information; and then use CSS to handle its visual presentation and design. This is by no means a new concept, but is one that is being embraced again and which forms the backbone of the Web Standardistas' approach: using the right tool for the job.

Efficiency through reduced markup

By separating content (the words and images) and presentation (how we style those words and images), we reduce page download times considerably. Less code equals faster download times and easier maintenance and—for a high-traffic web site—lower bandwidth costs.

Separating content and presentation also makes ongoing maintenance much easier. Handling the look and feel of your web site in a separate CSS file centralizes the design aspects of your web site in one location. Change this file, and the whole web site changes.

This is an extremely powerful and compelling feature that assists with ongoing site maintenance considerably.

Let's face it; the Web is a rapidly evolving medium, and the look and feel of web pages changes constantly. Tired of the design you created in 2008? Change the design across your entire web site for a new and improved one by simply updating your style sheet.

Simple. Fast. Efficient. Design changes can be made instantly across your entire site through one, easy-to-maintain file.

Increased accessibility

A major benefit of a web standards–based approach is the issue of significantly improved accessibility for visually or mobility impaired users. As accessibility becomes an increasingly pressing issue with the introduction of legislation to address users with visual and other impairments, you'll find your well-coded pages work well with assistive devices including screen readers or Braille terminals. You can read more about the W3C's Web Accessibility Initiative at its web site:

```
www.w3.org/WAI/Policy/
```

Cross-browser compatibility

In the "Wild West" days of web design, it wasn't uncommon to build multiple versions of the same web site for different users on different operating systems using different browsers. It sounds ridiculous, but there was a time when it wasn't uncommon to build a version of your web site for Windows XP users browsing with IE, another version for Linux users browsing with Mozilla, and yet another version for Mac OS users browsing with Netscape Navigator. Three full web sites—complete with browser-specific quirks—to display the same information on three different computers. This no longer needs to be the case.

Although some web design dinosaurs still cling to these outdated concepts, you as a Web Standardista know better. As browser manufacturers continue to embrace web standards, we can look forward to a time when our single web site—designed for all browsers, regardless of operating system—will "just work."

Nonbrowser compatibility

By using web standards to separate content from presentation, we make it easier to build custom style sheets for nondesktop browsers. Creating a web site compatible with PDAs, mobile phones, and other nondesktop devices is far simpler when using web standards to separate how a web site looks from what it says. With a well-structured XHTML page, we can write a variety of specific style sheets in CSS, for example, to include a print style sheet that produces a well-designed printable page.

The emergence of devices like Apple's iPhone means the mobile web is increasingly a reality, with mobile users no longer forced to navigate web sites on small, cramped screens.

A standards-based approach makes designing for these emerging devices much, much easier.

Forward compatibility

Last, but by no means least, how will your web site look in three, five, or even ten years' time? While no one can guarantee how anything will look an undefined number of years into the future, the road map for future browser development is now clear, and it is underpinned by standards. In recent years, browser manufacturers' attitudes toward web standards have changed, and they are now embracing the benefits of a standards-based approach.

The Web is an ever-changing medium where technologies and trends are in constant motion. Using web standards agreed upon by browser manufacturers helps to future-proof your web site and ensure that it will work and display as intended as browsers evolve.

The Web Standardistas' approach

The first thing you learn when you embark on your voyage into the world of web design is that abbreviations are everywhere: HTML, XML, XHTML, CSS . . . and the list goes on. This book aims to guide you through the abbreviations minefield through a hands-on approach to learning.

As mentioned previously, in this book we focus on two key technologies, XHTML and CSS, the cornerstones of the Web as it is now. An understanding of these forms the backbone of the book.

The Web Standardistas' approach is systematic. It requires learning in a specific, carefully structured, and rigorous way. We expect you to master each chapter before moving on to the next. The urge to want to run before you can walk is understandable. However, throughout this book, we ask you to suppress this urge and trust us as we move forward.

Wax on . . . wax off

In a memorable scene from the classic motion picture *The Karate Kid*, the wise mentor Mr. Miyagi demonstrates the fundamental moves of karate to a young and impetuous student, Daniel-san, by insisting he polish his car—"Wax on . . . wax off."

The moral of this story is that you shouldn't go straight for the fancy moves, but have the discipline to learn and master the fundamental underpinnings of your art.

In other words, don't skip ahead to the "design chapters" of the book in the haste to "make things look nice." In the first half of the book, we're only concerned with basic page structure, we're not focusing on look and feel—styling your web pages comes later. To add style, we'll be using Cascading Style Sheets; however, for the first few chapters, we want you to concentrate solely on learning well-structured markup.

You might wish to dive in and get started with some design, but please don't. If you follow our carefully structured course, the web pages you build will be better, trust us on this. You might think design is all about CSS, but the reality is that well-structured markup in XHTML is an equally important part of the design process.

Why use XHTML?

XHTML has evolved from HTML, and although it has stricter rules than HTML, we feel it is the best choice at this stage in the Web's development as it forces you to write well-formed code.

While adhering to stricter rules might seem daunting at first, in the long run it will serve you better. You will write code that is easier to debug and spot mistakes in, and your web pages will display more consistently in standards-compliant browsers.

The benefits of CSS

Cascading Style Sheets are not new and have been around for a number of years; however, CSS-based web sites have now taken hold in the mainstream. This is largely thanks to a number of high-profile sites embracing web standards and using CSS for presentation and design and increased support for CSS by browser manufacturers.

We begin to cover the implementation of CSS in Chapter 8 because we believe it's important to cover well-structured XHTML markup first. Resist the urge to fast-forward to Chapter 8; the next six chapters will equip you with a solid foundation on which to build.

The Web Standardistas' toolbox

The Web Standardistas' approach encourages you to get to know the different ingredients involved in building web pages and to learn how to put these together to create well-crafted web sites. Like fine cooking, we encourage you to learn about the raw ingredients at the heart of a good recipe; we do not encourage you to go down the processed, everything-out-of-a-jar TV dinner route.

By introducing you to the underlying components of the web pages you are building, we enable you to find examples "in the wild" and learn from them. A 100% WYSIWYG (What You See Is What You Get) approach doesn't give you that understanding. We feel our approach is the best to equip you for long-term learning.

We're not WYSIWYG

As you've probably gathered from what we just wrote, we do not encourage the use of WYSIWYG software in this book. *We're writing markup*.

Why not use WYSIWYG software? It sounds ideal. Drag and drop in a visual environment, click a button, and the software takes care of the rest, writing the markup for you. It sounds perfect. It isn't. The problem with using WYSIWYG software is that you have a lack of understanding of what's really happening behind the scenes because the software is doing everything for you. In other words, WYSIWYG is fine for some people, some of the time, but it will not equip you with a true appreciation of the underlying markup.

The Web Standardistas' approach equips you with a fundamental understanding of web design. Follow our tutorials, and you'll be equipped with everything you need to know to progress as a web designer. You'll not be stuck in a product upgrade cycle waiting for FrontPage Version 12.x, and you'll be saving yourself some money too.

At first glance, the examples might appear a little like a foreign language, but within no time, you'll find everything is crystal clear. Stick with it, and you might even find your friends referring to you as a nerd (which is no bad thing).

After only one chapter of the book, you'll be able to use your browser's View Source menu command to look behind the scenes of other web sites and understand how they are built. We can't stress enough how important this is. Relying on WYSIWYG software won't give you the understanding to deconstruct a web page and work out how it's been coded and learn from it. Embracing the Web Standardistas' approach will.

What's your favorite plain text editor?

This book is intended for anyone with access to a computer (and it doesn't even need to be a powerful computer). The approach we adopt uses free or low-cost tools where possible, eschewing expensive software in favor of freeware or shareware. Why? Because expensive software isn't essential to write the code we'll be covering; all you'll need is a plain text editor.

What is a plain text editor? A **plain text editor** is distinguished from a word processor in that it offers no document formatting capabilities. Unlike Microsoft Word, for example, a plain text editor is used simply for editing text, not for styling it.

We recommend Bare Bones Software's free TextWrangler if you're using a Macintosh or HTML-Kit if you're running Windows. If your platform is a flavor of Linux, you probably already have a favorite plain text editor, maybe Vim or Emacs, or—if you're looking for something less daunting—Bluefish or Komodo Edit.

All of the preceding programs are more than adequate to complete this book. This, in part, explains the phenomenal growth of the World Wide Web: low barrier to entry.

You can find links to all of these applications at the Web Standardistas web site:

    www.webstandardistas.com/tools

Mac OS X, Windows, or Linux?

It doesn't matter which OS you use, this book is written in a cross-platform manner. In fact, the Web—as originally intended by Tim Berners-Lee—is platform agnostic. What type of computer you use doesn't matter. A web standards approach is no different.

Learn to write your web pages using the techniques we recommend, and your web site will be platform independent—no more "This web site only runs in Internet Explorer!" (We loathe those kinds of statements, so you won't be seeing them here.)

Summary

So what have we covered? We've given you a little history of the Web and its development, in particular introducing the transition from HTML to XHTML—the version of HTML we'll be using in this book. We've also introduced you to the benefits of embracing a web standards approach. Lastly, we pointed you in the right direction to get the tools you need. This chapter's homework, which follows, is to get the tools you need to get started and familiarize yourself with them.

In the next chapter we put your freshly downloaded plain text editor to some good use as we dive into the wonderful world of markup, building our very first web pages.

Homework: Set up your work environment

A note on the homework: we'll conclude every chapter with some homework—additional work for you to undertake to ensure you fully understand the principles of what we're covering chapter by chapter. It's important you follow through with this homework. We believe in learning by doing. Following along with our homework projects at the end of each chapter ensures you will hit the ground running in the next one.

It's time to take the first steps toward setting up your work environment—specifically, selecting and installing a plain text editor so that you can work through the examples provided throughout the book and work on the different homework exercises.

1. Research

Research some of the plain text editors recommended earlier. Remember, we've provided a link to some recommended tools at the Web Standardistas web site:

www.webstandardistas.com/tools

Take a look at what each alternative text editor offers. It's worth spending some time researching the different editors at this point, as your text editor will form the backbone of most of the work undertaken in the book.

You might wish to start with one of the free applications from the list of recommended tools, upgrading it for something more powerful as you become more proficient. As the files we're working with are plain text, you'll be able to open them with any editor if you upgrade to paid-for software with more features in the future.

You'll notice that some of the editors offer a feature called **syntax highlighting**. This means that when you save a file as an HTML file, the format we'll be using, the editor colors the markup, which makes spotting mistakes easier.

2. Select, download, and install a text editor

Once you've done your research, select a plain text editor and download it. You'll be using this to complete the homework. Follow the instructions for the editor you've chosen and install it on your computer.

It's worth taking a little time now to explore your editor of choice and get a feel for how it works; this will help pave the way for the following chapter when you start writing markup.

That's it! As you're introducing yourself to the wonderful world of plain text editors, put the kettle on and enjoy a cup of *Darjeeling* as you prepare yourself for the next chapter.

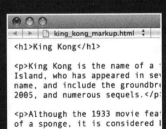

In this chapter, we get started with the hands-on aspects of our Web Standardistas' journey. First, we introduce you to HTML, the language that underpins the World Wide Web. We then build a few basic web pages to give you an understanding of how they are constructed and to introduce you to some fundamental concepts. This will form the cornerstone of the rest of the book, so we spend some time with you working though this systematically to ensure you have grasped a solid understanding of the principles of HTML and XHTML before moving on.

Once you've built your first web page, we show you how to use your browser's View Source command to learn from other designers' web sites by looking at their underlying source code. We also introduce the concept of HTML elements, looking at two key sections of your document: the <head> and the <body>, explaining what their purpose is and how they work.

Along the way, we cover nesting tags, commenting your markup, and the importance of using a well-written <title> tag.

HTML: Tags in action

You briefly met HTML in the last chapter when we covered the evolution of the Web. In this chapter, you get some hands-on use of it. In a nutshell, HTML provides basic formatting for words and images—our **content**—and we use it to build web pages and to give documents structure. HTML is used to describe the different elements that a web page can consist of, for example, headings (<h1>, <h2> . . .), paragraphs (<p>), and lists (<ul>, <ol> . . .). The way we describe these elements and add this structure is through the use of what are known as **tags**.

What are tags?

HTML pages are in essence plain text files with the addition of tags that provide information on how your document is structured. The tags are distinguished from the rest of the content by being enclosed in angle brackets like this: <...>. Everything between the tags is intended for display within the browser; the different tags provide information on how the document should be interpreted and displayed.

A word of warning: we're working with XHTML 1.0 Strict throughout this book, and, as its name suggests, its rules are strict. All tags *must* be written in lowercase (i.e., <h1> is right, <H1> isn't). In addition to this key rule, there are some other important rules that we'll introduce to you when the time is right.

Let's look at an example. In Figure 2-1, we have opened a simple plain text file in our text editor and saved it as an HTML file.

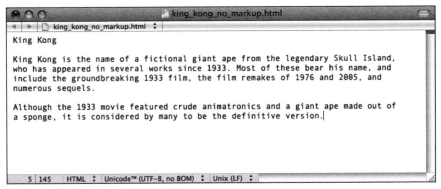

Figure 2-1. Our document, without HTML tags, as it appears in our plain text editor

Figure 2-2 shows the same page as it displays in our browser. Without any HTML tags to inform the browser how to structure the content of the page, the browser has no way of knowing how to display the content, and so simply displays it as a long line of text, wrapping to the width of the browser window. Note that all of the formatting and line breaks in our plain text example are ignored by the browser.

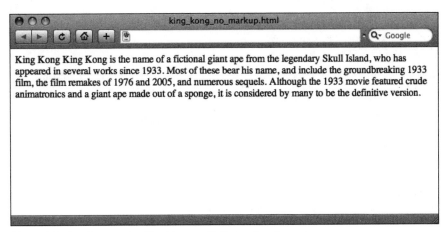

Figure 2-2. Our document, without tags, as it displays in a browser

Compare this to the example in Figure 2-3, where we have added some basic tags to the HTML document. We've marked up the first line—King Kong—to be a header using <h1> tags and marked up the two paragraphs that follow using <p> tags to divide the text into two distinct paragraphs.

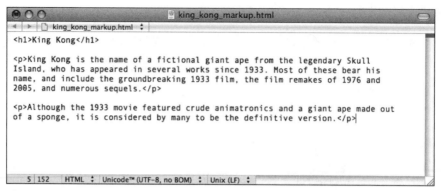

Figure 2-3. Our document, with HTML tags added, in our plain text editor

Figure 2-4 shows how this marked-up version of our document displays in the browser. Note the difference from Figure 2-2: the browser now displays some basic formatting and gives a sense of the underlying document structure.

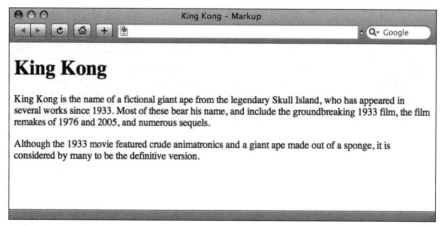

Figure 2-4. Our document, with basic tags added, as it displays in a browser

As you can see, the tags are not directly visible in the browser; instead, the tags inform the browser how the text is structured and how to display the content.

Tags come in pairs, usually

In XHTML, apart from a few exceptions, once opened, all tags need to be closed. Most tags come in pairs consisting of an **opening tag** and a **closing tag** (sometimes called a **start tag** and an **end tag**, respectively). For example, as shown in Figure 2-3 earlier, a paragraph opens with a `<p>` tag and closes with a `</p>` tag (the slash, /, after the opening angle bracket distinguishes the closing tag from the opening tag).

In the earliest days of the World Wide Web, as HTML evolved, browsers were quite forgiving. It was possible to write invalid markup and for the browser to "do its best" to second-guess what you were trying to achieve. However, as web standards become increasingly embraced, writing valid, well-formed markup from the outset makes it easier for browsers to display your pages consistently. Well-formed markup can help to reduce the amount of time spent trying to debug a page that doesn't display the way you intended.

Following the simple rules we introduce in this chapter can save you a significant amount of time—which you would otherwise spend debugging and fixing problems—in the long run. More importantly, it will result in your writing markup that is the envy of your peers. It's not difficult to write well-formed markup; it's simply a matter of diligent attention to detail, something every aspiring Web Standardista should strive for.

The following example shows how to correctly close tags. The `<p>` opening the paragraph has been closed with a `</p>`:

```
<p>I am a paragraph by a well-trained Web Standardista.
I have been closed correctly.</p>
```

In the following example, however, the paragraph has not been closed properly:

```
<p>I am a paragraph by a lazy programmer. I haven't been closed.
```

> Remember, once opened, all tags should be closed.

Getting into the practice of writing well-formed markup—in particular closing all the tags that you open—can help resolve display issues down the line. It is not a difficult habit to get into, indeed, not getting into the habit can result in more difficulty down the line. Follow a few simple rules, and you're well and truly on your way.

It's an element, my dear Watson

The opening tag, the closing tag, and the content within these tags are known collectively as an **HTML element**. Figure 2-5 illustrates the structure of an element. As you can see, the opening tag, the tag's content, and the closing tag *combined* make up the element.

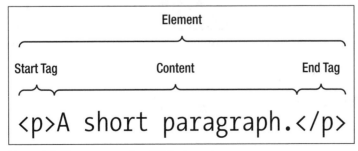

Figure 2-5. The structure of an HTML element

We will regularly refer to opening tags, closing tags, and elements throughout this chapter, so it's worth ensuring that you have an understanding of how an element is constructed.

Your first web page: Hello World!

In this section, you'll build your first web page. Nothing too complicated, but your first web page nonetheless. Although it might at first glance seem a little simplistic, this page will highlight a number of key principles that form the majority of the learning for this chapter.

When learning any new programming language, it's tradition to write a short program to display the words "Hello World!" Our first web page will be no different. It will introduce you to the basic concepts of HTML and provide stage one of your journey through web standards.

Let's get started on your first web page. Launch your text editor and create a new document. Save it as hello_world.html. This will be your first web page.

Before we write the web page, let's take a look at how we've named it. Naming files is important and can cause issues down the line if done incorrectly, so it's worth spending some time on file-naming conventions now. Let's look at the file name we just specified in a little more detail.

The .html part is important: it is a suffix, referred to as an **extension**, that tells the browser the document is a web page. (.html stands for HyperText Markup Language, but then by now you know that, don't you?) An alternative suffix, heralding from the days when certain software could only handle three-letter extensions, is .htm. Some people prefer to name their files using .html, others using .htm. Regardless of which extension you prefer to use, it is best to be consistent. In this book, we're using .html.

The _ (underscore) is also important; we've used it instead of a space, as you can see in Figure 2-6. Spaces, along with a few other characters, are not allowed in URLs. (As you probably know, a **URL**, short for Universal Resource Locator, is the address you type into the browser's address bar when you want to load a specific page on the Web.) Since spaces are not allowed, the browser will convert it to %20, as shown in Figure 2-7.

Figure 2-6. Our "Hello World!" page's URL with an underscore replacing the space is easy to read.

Figure 2-7. Our "Hello World!" page's URL with the space in the file name converted to %20 is confusing.

So the file name that makes sense to you and is easily read as a URL:

```
hello world.html
```

is converted by the browser to the following:

```
hello%20world.html
```

Although the page would still load, the URL will have an unsightly %20 in it. Not only is this rather ugly and hard to read, but it is also a major Web Standardista faux pas. Although we have used underscores in our file names, an alternative is to use hyphens to replace spaces as in the following example:

```
hello-world.html
```

Whether you use underscores or hyphens is largely a matter of taste. Some people prefer the look of underscores, some the look of hyphens. It is worth mentioning, however, that Google tends to interpret hyphens as spaces, so using hyphens might help Google to index your page. Regardless, here is our First Golden Rule:

Don't use spaces in your file names. Ever.

Finally, upper- and lowercase can be interpreted differently on different systems. Windows systems are case insensitive whereas Linux systems are not. The following two file names are seen as different documents by a computer running Linux:

```
hello_world.html
Hello_World.html
```

As such, they'll be treated as different web pages by your browser. It's time to introduce another golden rule so you'll never need to worry about this again. Here is our Second Golden Rule:

Use only lowercase letters when naming files.

Follow this rule, and you won't run the risk of your page not being found because of the difference in upper- and lowercase letters in the file name.

The bottom line is to be consistent, because it will save problems later. We recommend naming all files in lowercase and using _ (underscores) or - (hyphens) instead of spaces throughout. Follow our rules, and you'll save yourself a lot of trouble down the line.

To mark up a web page, you just type

After that brief, but important, digression on file-naming conventions, it's back to your first web page. In your new document, type the following:

```
<html>
<head>
<title>Hello World!</title>
```

```
</head>
<body>
<p>Hello World!</p>
</body>
</html>
```

Save the file and open it within your browser. If you are using a Mac, you can do this by locating your file and dragging it into an open browser window, or by opening your browser, selecting File ➤ Open File, browsing to the hello_world.html file you just saved, and clicking Open. The page will then load into a browser window. (If you are using Windows or Linux, the procedure is similar, but the commands will vary slightly.) The web page is a simple one, but a web page nonetheless. It should look something like Figure 2-8.

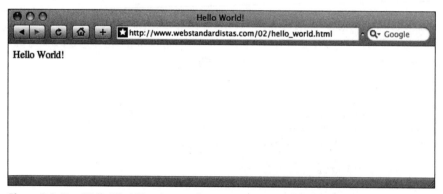

Figure 2-8. Our "Hello World!" web page that we prepared earlier, displayed in a browser

Congratulations! You've just built your first web page. It might not seem like much, but it marks the first step on your journey to becoming a Web Standardista.

The markup makes the web page

Let's look at the preceding markup and break it down a little; doing so will give you an understanding of a web page's basic construction and a solid foundation on which to build as we progress through the chapter. In our "Hello World!" example, we used the following tags: <html>, <head>, <title>, <body>, and <p>.

These tags provide the basic underlying structure:

- The <html> tag tells the browser we're opening a new HTML document; it primes the browser, telling it, "Hey, get ready to receive some HTML goodness!"

- The <head> tag tells the browser we're providing some information *about* the page; this is where we put information like the title of the page.

- The <title> tag tells the browser the title of the page (you'll see it at the top of the browser in your "Hello World!" page).

- The <body> tag tells the browser we're starting information that we want to display on the page itself.
- The <p> tag surrounds our first—admittedly short—paragraph.

That's it. Five tags might not seem like much, but as you can see, they're enough to create a web page, and so begin your journey toward Web Standardista happiness.

Learning from others: How to view source

Now that you have a general understanding of how to use tags to organize and format content, we can start to explore how other designers use tags to structure *their* web pages. The best way to do this is to load up a web page and use your browser's View Source feature to see the original behind-the-scenes code that underlies the page.

At first glance, the source code might look unintelligible, but given time, experience, and persistence, looking at the markup of different web pages will teach you a huge amount about web design and, equally importantly, will enable you to troubleshoot your own web pages when things go wrong.

The wonderful thing about the Web, and what makes it easy to learn from others' Web pages, is the ability to use the View Source menu command in your browser to view the underlying source code for almost any web page. On Safari, the browser we're using, you'll find this command under the View menu (View ➤ View Source) as you can see in Figure 2-9. Most browsers have an equivalent command.

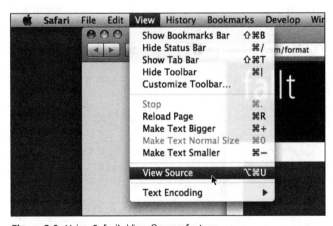

Figure 2-9. Using Safari's View Source feature

Use View Source to take a look at the underlying source code of two web pages we've provided, the URLs of which follow. By now, you should know enough about the structure of HTML to work out what's going on. As you work through the chapters, we encourage you to look behind the scenes of the homework web pages and try and work out what's going on. Experiment by copying and pasting some of our markup into your web pages and seeing what happens. The best way to learn is by doing.

We've uploaded our two example web pages for you here:

www.webstandardistas.com/02/king_kong_junior.html
www.webstandardistas.com/02/king_kong_senior.html

> It is important to stress that although you can look at the source of other designers' web pages and figure out how they are put together and learn from this, it is **not** permitted to copy and paste other peoples' markup and use it as your own, unless the designer has specifically stated that you are allowed to do so.

Every page has a <head> and a <body>

HTML pages are broken into two key elements: the head and body elements, as illustrated in Figure 2-10. Both handle different types of information about the web page itself, and both are essential.

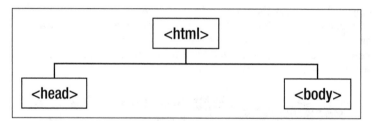

Figure 2-10. The head and body elements are both a part of every HTML page

The head element—everything contained within and including the opening <head> and the closing </head> tag pair—handles information about the document and other data that is not considered part of the document's actual content (i.e., what appears within the viewer's browser window). This includes the page's title, its meta tags (tags which, among other things, can be used to provide information about the page to search engines), its style sheets, and any scripts. In short, anything about or affecting the content of the page itself. Information in the head element isn't seen by the everyday user, only information in the body element is.

The body element—everything within and including the opening <body> and the closing </body> tag pair—is where everything the user will see within the browser is contained. Any text, links, or images you want to be displayed within the web browser reside within it. As we progress through the next few chapters, we'll provide you with additional useful tags to ensure your <body> is well fed.

The importance of using the title element

When you open a book—this one for example—you expect there to be some chapter headings and for the information within the chapters to be broken down into sections with titles and subtitles. Let's face it, it would be difficult to find this book on your bookshelf if it didn't have a title. Web pages are no different.

The head element must contain a `title` element, which is typically displayed in the browser's title bar and, if you are using Windows, in the task bar when the browser is minimized. The `title` is also the name saved when you bookmark a page or save it to your favorites.

If you don't include a `title`, the browser will usually display the name of the file (e.g., `index.html`) in the title bar. This is confusing for the user and certainly embarrassing for any budding Web Standardista.

Spending a little extra time and inserting a proper page title not only improves usability, but also helps improve search engine rankings. Try to use meaningful keywords within your page title; the upcoming examples demonstrate the importance of a meaningful title.

In the following example, the title is clear and informative. It gives us an understanding of the contents of the page.

```
<head>
<title>Burger Flipper | ACME Widgets </title>
</head>
```

The following example is less useful. Which company's product page are we looking at? Is this the Burger Flipper page or another page altogether?

```
<head>
<title>Product Page</title>
</head>
```

How many times have you looked back through your browsing history to try and retrace your steps? Some sites are easy to find, their titles clearly displayed in your history; others are impossible to find—all you can see is Untitled Document, index.html, or Product Page. Providing a well-considered `title` helps resolve this confusion. In the preceding example, `Burger Flipper | ACME Widgets` is clear and unambiguous.

In the next example, we have put the product names, for example "Burger Flipper," *before* the company name, "ACME Widgets." This means that when you have the entire ACME Widgets product catalog open in tabs in your browser, you can see the product names of each page, as illustrated in Figure 2-11. Putting the company name first and product name second might result in tabs reading as follows: ACME Widge . . ., ACME Widge . . ., ACME Widge . . ., again and again and again. Less useful and quite frustrating.

Figure 2-11. The ACME Widgets product catalog, open in tabs

Defining your document type

As we mentioned in Chapter 1, there are several types of HTML and XHTML: HTML 4.01 Strict, HTML 4.01 Transitional, and XHTML 1.0 Strict, to mention but a few.

In order to process your markup correctly, so it displays the way you intend it to, a web browser needs to know which set of rules to use when interpreting your document. For example, if you've created an HTML 4.01 Transitional document, the web browser needs to use different rules than if you've created an XHTML 1.0 Strict document.

But how does the browser know which document type you are using?

It all starts with a DOCTYPE

As we mentioned in the previous chapter, the different versions of HTML and XHTML are defined by the W3C, but they are also defined in something known as a **Document Type Definition**, or **DTD** for short. The DTD is written not for humans, but for tools that process (X)HTML documents. As a consequence, if it looks a little daunting at first sight, it is because it is intended for machines, not people.

The DTD is often referred to as a **DOCTYPE**. The DOCTYPE informs the browser which flavor of HTML or XHTML you're using. Throughout this book, we will be using XHTML 1.0 Strict. The XHTML 1.0 Strict DOCTYPE looks like this:

```
<!DOCTYPE html PUBLIC "-//W3C//DTD XHTML 1.0 Strict//EN"
"http://www.w3.org/TR/xhtml1/DTD/xhtml1-strict.dtd">
```

The DOCTYPE is an additional, but important, part of your web page that tells the browser how to display the page and what language has been used to mark it up. The DOCTYPE needs to come before your opening `<html>` tag, as you'll see later in the section "Hello World!: DOCTYPE edition." Failure to include a DOCTYPE at the start of your web page triggers what's known as **Quirks Mode**, implying to the browser that your web page was written using old-fashioned, invalid, and quirky markup. "What is Quirks Mode?" we hear you ask. Let's take a look.

A short Quirks Mode interlude

Quirks Mode was conceived at a time when browsers were starting to pay proper attention to web standards. Millions of pages out there were created when the implementation of CSS was less than stellar. The authors of these pages had built them to work in older browsers, writing CSS that matched those browser's implementations.

If the new browsers were completely standards compliant, a lot of these old pages—written in the bad old days—would render as broken. As a consequence, browser vendors looked for a solution that would allow old web pages to continue to be rendered using the old rules, and the new pages built with web standards to be rendered using the new, compliant rules. The trigger that would tell the browser to use the compliant, strict mode instead of Quirks Mode was the inclusion of a DOCTYPE. Adding the DOCTYPE to the top of your page was an indication that you knew what you were doing, and that you wanted your pages to be interpreted using the new, strict rules.

As an aspiring Web Standardista, you know how important it is to be standards-compliant. In the next section, we show you where to place the DOCTYPE so that the browsers your markup meets know what to expect, but first a couple of other important additions.

It's all in a namespace

A second attribute that is required when creating valid XHTML Strict web pages is the inclusion of what's known as an **XML namespace declaration**. Essentially, we replace the opening <html> tag from our simple "Hello World!" web page with the following:

```
<html xmlns="http://www.w3.org/1999/xhtml">
```

The xmlns="http://www.w3.org/1999/xhtml" attribute is required when writing web pages in XHTML. Added to the opening <html> tag, it ensures that your page validates.

Just one more thing

As Columbo would say, "Just one more thing . . . "

The last thing we need to add to ensure our pages validate is a character encoding. Like the DOCTYPE and namespace, you don't need to know exactly how this works; you just need to know that you must include it for your web pages to validate. You simply add the following immediately after your opening <head> tag:

```
<meta http-equiv="Content-Type" content="text/html; charset=UTF-8" />
```

The curious among you might want to skip ahead to Chapter 13, where we introduce the wonders of character encoding fully, although this isn't required reading at this point.

You don't have to memorize all this

Don't worry, you won't have to learn or memorize the exact syntax of the DOCTYPE, namespace declaration, or character encoding. For now, you can simply use a template file we've provided for you to ensure your pages validate and render correctly.

To save you a lot of painstaking typing, and to ensure against mistyping, we've uploaded an XHTML file with the correct DOCTYPE, namespace declaration, and character encoding to the book's companion web site, where you can simply download it, and copy and paste it. Use View Source to find it here:

```
www.webstandardistas.com/02/template.html.
```

> Apart from helping your browser determine how to interpret your document, the DOCTYPE also enables you to use tools like The W3C Markup Validation Service (http://validator.w3.org/) to check the syntax of your documents, helping you to ensure that your code is valid.

Hello World!: DOCTYPE edition

Earlier in this chapter, we created a very simple "Hello World!" web page to give you an idea of a web page's basic structure. We'll now develop this by adding the DOCTYPE, namespace declaration, and character encoding as described previously. Let's have a look at our new and improved "Hello World!" web page:

```
<!DOCTYPE html PUBLIC "-//W3C/DTD XHTML 1.0 Strict//EN"
"http://www.w3.org/TR/xhtml1-strict.dtd">
<html xmlns="http://www.w3.org/1999/xhtml">
<head>
<meta http-equiv="content-type" content="text/html; charset=utf-8" />
<title>Hello World!</title>
</head>
<body>
<p>Hello World!</p>
</body>
</html>
```

Although viewing this new and improved version of your web page in a browser will appear to make little difference, trust us, behind the scenes the browser is being informed that you're building standards-compliant pages. The DOCTYPE, namespace declaration, and character encoding are critical parts of every web page you build, and you should include them from now on.

Tags have structure too: Nested elements

HTML elements can be nested, a feature which you have already seen in action in our simple "Hello World!" web page. Figure 2-12 shows the basic structure of this page as a diagram known as a **document tree**.

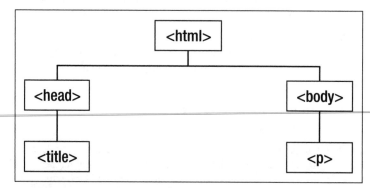

Figure 2-12. A simple diagram of the document tree

Nesting can simply be described as placing one element inside another. In our "Hello World!" web page, illustrated in Figure 2-12, both the head and body elements are placed, or nested, within the html element. The title element is nested within the head element, and the p element is nested within the body.

An easy way to grasp this concept is to think of your web page as an inverted tree. The tree's trunk is the html element; from this trunk have grown two branches, the head and body elements. From each of these branches further elements grow.

An important rule to remember when writing valid XHTML markup is that elements must be nested properly. Think of a Russian nested doll, which is really a set of dolls, each nested within another: tags are no different.

To nest elements in the right order, you need to make sure that you close your tags in the reverse order that they were opened. An easy way to remember this is to use the mnemonic "First In, Last Out." Following is an example of nesting tags in action; in this case, we've added another layer of structure to a paragraph, using <strong> (strong emphasis, by default displayed in bold in graphical browsers) and <em> (emphasis, by default displayed in italics). Figure 2-13 shows this markup in action.

```
<p><strong><em>I am a paragraph, I am not only emphasized,
I am also strongly emphasized.</em></strong></p>
```

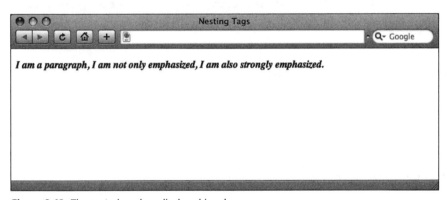

Figure 2-13. The nested markup displayed in a browser

Although web browsers are forgiving and would render the preceding HTML page the same regardless of whether you nested your tags correctly, as mentioned before, making sure your pages are valid is important in the long run. When building more complex pages—and adding CSS to the mix—incorrectly nested tags can lead to inconsistent display of your web page across browsers.

In the following two examples, we show you the right way to nest elements using the First In, Last Out approach. These tags are nested correctly:

```
<p><strong><em>I have been nested properly by a Web
Standardista.</em></strong></p>
```

In the following example, the tags are not nested properly:

```
<p><em><strong>I have not been nested properly, I've probably
been written by the same lazy programmer who didn't close his
tags properly a few pages back.</em></strong></p>
```

Making your markup easier to follow

By now, we've introduced quite a bit of complexity. We're using a variety of tags, we're nesting tags in the right order, we're using DOCTYPEs, and we never, ever forget to use a well-written title element. We're building web pages and using View Source to look at how other designers use XHTML. In short, there's a lot for us to remember as we move forward to the next chapter.

The good news is that we can use both the structure of our code—breaking it over different lines, using tabs and white space—and leave hidden comments within it to make our job that little bit easier.

In this section, we introduce the importance of both commenting your markup—leaving hidden comments within it—and putting some thought into how you format it within your chosen plain text editor—breaking it over different lines, using tabs and white space. This can make your life a great deal easier, especially when you return to a project after some time has elapsed.

Commenting your markup

Not everything we write in HTML displays within the browser. We've already introduced you to the head element, which is largely hidden from view within the main browser window. (X)HTML allows for the inclusion of hidden comments in both the head and body elements that can only be read when using View Source or looking at the .html file in question. Indeed, if you've been using your browser's View Source command to look at other web pages, you might have seen some examples of comments in use.

Comments open with a <!-- and close with a -->; anything included between these markers is not displayed in the browser. This can be very useful for a number of reasons: a comment could serve as a note to remind you why you structured a document a particular way, a note to indicate when you changed the document, a note to a friend working on the same web page, or a means of hiding parts of the document itself. This latter use can be particularly useful when testing, enabling you to switch the display of elements on or off.

The easiest way to show you how comments work is to show you some in action. In the following example, we've included a comment between the first two paragraphs. We've also *commented out* the third paragraph, showing you how you can also use comments to hide parts of your markup.

As you can see in the screenshot in Figure 2-14, our comment between the first two paragraphs is hidden from the viewer, as is the third paragraph.

```
<h1>Comments in Action</h1>
<p>I am paragraph number one, I display in the browser.
The Heading 1 above also displays in the browser.</p>
<!-- I am a comment, I don't display in the browser. -->
<p>I am paragraph number two, I also display in the browser.</p>
<!-- <p>I am paragraph number three, I'm hidden.</p> -->
```

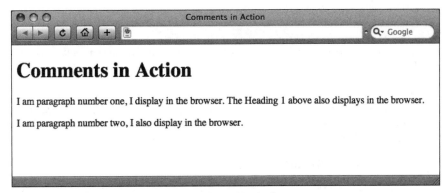

Figure 2-14. Our page with comments, hidden within the browser

Comments aren't restricted to single lines; they can also run over multiple lines. This can be useful when you want to hide a section of a document while you're testing your web pages during development. In our next example, we've hidden a number of lines using comments.

As you can see in Figure 2-15, only the first paragraph is displayed in the browser; the remaining paragraphs are hidden from the viewer.

```
<h1>Getting Clever With Comments</h1>
<p>I am paragraph number one, you met me in the last example.</p>
<!--
<p>I am paragraph number two, I won't display in the browser.</p>
<p>I am paragraph number three, I'm also hidden.</p>
-->
```

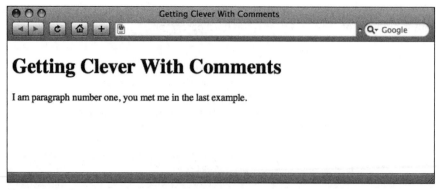

Figure 2-15. The previous example as seen in a browser—only the first, uncommented paragraph is visible.

Although browsers hide everything between comments, your comments are still delivered to the user's browser along with the rest of the page's markup. As you now know, anyone can read these comments using View Source. Comments therefore aren't the best place to hide your secrets. The following, for example, isn't advisable:

```
<h1>Pinocchio - My Darkest Secrets</h1>
<p>I am a child made of wood. My darkest secret was revealed in
Shrek 2.</p>
<!-- I wear ladies underwear. -->
<p>I'm a good little boy.</p>
```

White space

In addition to using comments to assist in the process of writing markup, it's also worth considering the use of white space to enable you to visually indicate your document's structure within your plain text editor. As long as you've written your XHTML in a plain text editor with formatting switched off, you can use line breaks, tabs, and spaces (commonly referred to as **white space**) to separate the sections of your document to make your markup more readable. When viewed in the browser, these white spaces are ignored.

Take a look at the following two examples of our "Hello World!" page. Both display identically in the browser. In the first, we've used no line breaks or tabs:

```
<!DOCTYPE html PUBLIC "-//W3C/DTD XHTML 1.0 Strict//EN"
"http://www.w3.org/TR/xhtml1-strict.dtd">
<html xmlns="http://www.w3.org/1999/xhtml">
<head>
<meta http-equiv="Content-Type" content="text/html; charset=UTF-8" />
<title>Hello World!</title>
</head>
<body>
<p>Hello World!</p>
</body>
</html>
```

In the following example, we've introduced line breaks and tabs. As you can see, this makes the markup much easier to read.

```
<!DOCTYPE html PUBLIC "-//W3C/DTD XHTML 1.0 Strict//EN"
"http://www.w3.org/TR/xhtml1-strict.dtd">
<html xmlns="http://www.w3.org/1999/xhtml">
  <head>
  <meta http-equiv="Content-Type" content="text/html; charset=UTF-8" />
    <title>Hello World!</title>
  </head>
  <body>
    <p>Hello World!</p>
  </body>
</html>
```

You can see both of the preceding examples live here:

```
www.webstandardistas.com/02/no_whitespace.html
www.webstandardistas.com/02/whitespace.html
```

But what if you want to preserve line breaks, tabs, and extra spaces for a web page about poetry or one that is displaying examples of code within the page, for example? Have no fear, we will introduce a tag that specializes in just that in Chapter 4 when we show you how to present preformatted code examples on your web page.

Summary

So what have we covered? In this chapter, we got our hands dirty and started to build some web pages. We focused on the fundamental aspects of a web page's construction and highlighted some dos and don'ts. We also introduced the tricky topic of DOCTYPEs and how they inform the browser behind the scenes that you're a budding Web Standardista. Lastly, we looked at ways of making your code easier to read by using comments and white space.

In the next chapter, we start to add some good, old-fashioned, upper-class POSH markup.

Homework: Create your first space-monkey-themed XHTML page

This chapter's homework is to create a complete XHTML page using the plain text editor you downloaded and took for a test drive at the end of the last chapter. We've supplied some text for you; all you need to do is add some basic markup to this text to create a simple web page along the lines of the ones we've covered in the chapter.

1. Get started

Let's get started. Open your text editor and create a new file. The page you'll be making is about Albert I, the first-ever monkey astronaut. Following the advice on naming files, we suggest you save your new blank file as follows:

albert.html

We suggest you keep all your homework files organized in one place—for now, use a single folder.

> We'll cover organizing files in folders later, as this will have an effect on how your different files relate to each other. At this point please keep all of your files in one location. We suggest you create a folder called homework where you save this and future homework files.

2. A basic web page

By now you should know that the basic, minimal structure of an XHTML document looks like the example displayed here:

```
<!DOCTYPE html PUBLIC "-//W3C/DTD XHTML 1.0 Strict//EN"
"http://www.w3.org/TR/xhtml1-strict.dtd">
<html xmlns="http://www.w3.org/1999/xhtml">
  <head>
  <meta http-equiv="Content-Type" content="text/html; charset=UTF-8" />
    <title></title>
  </head>
  <body>
  </body>
</html>
```

At this point, you have two choices: you can either painstakingly type the preceding markup into your blank albert.html document, or you can go to the Web Standardistas web site and cheat a little by using copy and paste. You can find the preceding markup here:

www.webstandardistas.com/02/template.html

Using your browser's View Source feature, copy and paste the markup into your blank albert.html document and save it.

3. Find out about Albert I

Once you've got the basic markup in place, the next thing to do is to get some content for the page. Following the tradition of the best cooking shows, we've prepared this earlier and supplied you with some text about Albert I at the following location:

www.webstandardistas.com/02/albert.txt

2

4. Add a title

You know the importance of adding a descriptive title to your web pages. We've left this part up to you. After reading the text, add an appropriate title to your page between the `<title>` tags, and save your page.

5. Mark up the content

Copy and paste the text provided into the body of your `albert.html` page.

As our text currently stands, it has no markup or structure. Your task is to add some structure to the page using `<h1>` and `<p>` tags, a process similar to the one covered in Figures 2-3 and 2-4 of this chapter. With such a simple text file, this should be a relatively straightforward process. Add your markup and save the page.

6. Add a comment

Once you've completed the previous stage, add a comment on the page congratulating yourself on creating your very first space-monkey page using XHTML. Do this by leaving a comment in the markup as follows:

```
<!-- Add a comment like this. Well done! -->
```

7. Test your page

Now there's just one thing left to do—test. Save the file and open the page in your web browser to check that everything looks the way you would expect. At this point, we hope all's well; if not, you'll need to check your code thoroughly for any mistakes that may have crept in.

If you do run into problems, some things to consider might be the following: Is the text copied into the body of the page? Have you closed all the tags you've opened? To help you with troubleshooting, we have created a similarly structured page about Cheeta, famous for his role in the *Tarzan* movies. You can refer to this, using your browser's View Source command to see how we've structured the web page, here:

```
www.webstandardistas.com/02/cheeta.html
```

Assuming all's well, put the kettle on and enjoy a cup of *Lapsang Souchong* as you prepare yourself for the next chapter.

This chapter is critical to your evolution as a Web Standardista. Focused on structured markup, the concepts introduced will form a solid foundation on which you will build as we progress through the remainder of the chapters. At the heart of the chapter lies a return to fundamental principles, particularly the idea of embracing Plain Old Semantic HTML (POSH) and using it as a basis on which to build.

First, we introduce the concepts of structured markup and semantic markup and use a case study to explain the idea of using "signposts for reading" to guide the reader. Once we establish the basic principle of structured markup, we introduce you to some fundamental tags: heading tags and tags for adding emphasis. You briefly met one of the heading tags in Chapter 2; now we start to use it and its companions.

It might not seem like much, but with just the tags introduced in this chapter in your toolbox, you'll be able to create well-structured web pages that will be the envy of your less-well-trained peers.

At this point you're probably thinking, "Is that it? A few more tags? Where's the design? Where's the color? Where's the fancy stuff?" The answer is that it's coming, and although you might not realize it, we're already adding design just by structuring the information on our web pages.

Good information design separates the great web sites from the ordinary ones. By the end of this chapter, you'll be creating great web pages with well-structured markup, and that's half the battle.

Adding structure and meaning

Structured markup—sometimes referred to as **semantic markup**—is the practice of using XHTML to define the structure of a document's content. We believe in establishing a firm foundation of structured markup *before* moving on to apply design with CSS. That's why we've devoted almost half of this book to the creation of well-formed XHTML.

As we suggested previously, the process of analyzing a page's content and applying some structure to it is *a part of the design process*. Where the beginning web designer almost always goes wrong is in hurrying too quickly into what they mistakenly believe is the "design phase," which they equally wrongly assume is "only about CSS."

The reality is the design phase in fact encompasses both the creation of well-structured markup in XHTML and subsequently applying style to this with CSS.

Although sometimes used interchangeably, there are some subtle differences between structured markup and semantic markup. The term structured markup *usually refers to the structure of the document: how your headings and paragraphs relate to each other, and arranging your information in a logical and meaningful order. The term* semantic markup *usually refers to adding meaning to your markup, using tags that say something about your content. When you add a heading or a paragraph to your page, however, you are adding both structure and meaning. In fact, structure and meaning are quite closely intertwined.*

What is structured markup?

Structured markup lies at the heart of the Web Standardistas' approach. We believe in using the right tag for the right job. A heading should be within a heading tag; paragraphs should be within <p> tags; a quote should be within <blockquote> or <q> tags. It's simple: look at the content and ask yourself, "Is this a heading?" If it is, then use a heading tag; if it isn't, use a more appropriate tag.

HTML was invented to give structure and meaning to documents. The emphasis was on using tags to describe what they contained. This approach, using semantics to suggest meaning, is fundamental to the Web Standardistas' approach.

The first phase in building any web page should be a careful analysis of the information it contains and identifying its inherent structure.

Take a look at Figure 3-1 and Figure 3-2. The first has no structure at all, but the second is clearly structured.

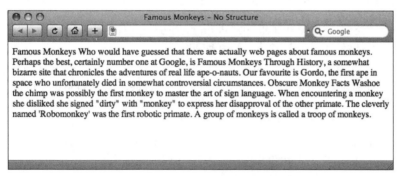

Figure 3-1. A document with no structure displayed in a browser

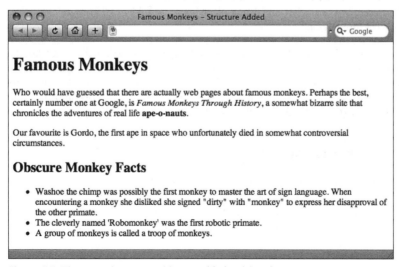

Figure 3-2. The same document with tags added—giving the page structure

41

Looking at these two examples, notice the second one has an implicitly defined structure and a clear information hierarchy. We would argue that *even without style added with CSS* that the document in Figure 3-2 has been "designed." The process of adding this layer of structure or meaning is central to a structured markup approach.

What is semantic markup?

We've mentioned the word *semantic* a number of times, but what exactly does the word mean? A dictionary definition gives us a start:

> **semantic** *–adj. relating to meaning in language.*
>
> Concise Oxford Dictionary *(Clarendon Press, 1990)*

In English? The word *semantic* is derived from the Greek word for *sign*. We use semantics to give meaning to information through the creation of a logical structure. The idea of creating *signposts for reading* is one we introduce later in this chapter. Think of your markup as a series of signs that clearly inform the browser of its purpose, "I'm an <h1>: I'm an important heading. I'm a <p>: I'm a paragraph."

Our emphasis is on semantic markup first and foremost. Is it a list? Then mark it up as a list. Is it a heading? Then mark it up as a heading. We believe code should be meaningful; it should convey some sense and some structure. We believe in using appropriate markup when it's needed, and then styling it later.

Let's repeat that, as it's fundamental to the Web Standardistas' approach: we believe in using appropriate markup when it's needed, and then styling it later.

This is the first hurdle beginners in web design trip over. They look at how big an <h1> is when it renders using the browser's default style sheet and opt instead for an <h2> or an <h3> because they're smaller and "look nicer." "I just couldn't bring myself to use an *<h1>* tag—it's just insanely big!"

This is XHTML + CSS mistake 101. Yes, minus any styling via CSS an <h1> tag is insanely big, but we'll be styling it with CSS, which allows us to design it to be as large or small as we'd like. The bottom line is that, minus the CSS, the information needs to convey meaning. Switch off the users' style sheets, and it's clear that the <h1> is more important than the <h2> and <p> tags beneath it. *The tags convey meaning.* That's the point.

Making markup meaningful

We believe in the use of meaningful markup. Our emphasis is on semantics first and foremost. Before you even open your text editor, look at the content you'll be working with and break it down into its component parts. Give it a hierarchy and try to tease out the meaning of specific phrases. With this knowledge, mark up the document accordingly.

This is design at its most fundamental level: looking at words and working out which tags are most appropriate. If we can convey a document's structure at this level using just XHTML, we're halfway there. The rest, handled with CSS, is just surface gloss and presentational niceness.

POSH and proud

When we talk about being POSH and proud, we're not referring to our gentlemanly lineage, rather we're referring to POSH, which we've previously defined as an acronym for Plain Old Semantic HTML. Coined in April 2007, POSH might sound like a new invention (or an old Spice Girl), but it's not. It is, however, a great way to remember the basics of HTML and what it was first supposed to achieve.

Roger Johansson, a noted advocate of accessible web design, summarizes the appeal of the term nicely:

> POSH is short for "Plain Old Semantic HTML" and is obviously much quicker and easier to say than "valid, semantic, accessible, well-structured HTML."
>
> http://www.456bereastreet.com/archive/200711/
> posh_plain_old_semantic_html/

Rewind two decades. When Tim Berners-Lee first conceived HTML, he intended it to be a language about language, a metalanguage or a means of describing language. POSH markup returns to those original principles, using the right tag for the job, putting meaning and semantics first and adding style later. This is at the heart of the Web Standardistas' approach. Follow our guidelines, and you'll be writing POSH markup in no time; you'll also be the envy of your peers.

Signposts for reading

Whenever we read something—a newspaper or a book, for example—our eyes are guided through the content through the use of established typographic techniques. A headline is styled differently from a paragraph, and different headlines are assigned different levels of importance through relative size and other design aspects, for example, the use of color.

By establishing a basic information hierarchy, such as using <h1> tags for the most important headings and using <h6> tags for the least important headings, we can make the reading process easier; we can also improve the accessibility of the web pages we design (making those pages accessible to, say, visually impaired users using screen readers or high contrast layouts). A welcome byproduct of this improved accessibility is that search engines find indexing your pages easier.

This section covers the relationship of tags to one another. It introduces a core concept that we've already mentioned is key to the Web Standardistas' approach: structured markup.

Creating structure with headings and paragraphs

What's more important, an <h1> or an <h2>? Is an <h3> more important than an <h5>? How does a <p> relate to an <h1>? The answer is simple. In XHTML, there are six headings: <h1>, <h2>, <h3>, <h4>, <h5>, and <h6>. <h1> is the most important, and <h6> is the least. <p> tags indicate paragraphs, which generally sit under one of the heading tags, depending upon where they appear within the document's semantic structure.

In Chapter 2, you saw that you can use more than one set of <p> tags on a page, and heading tags are no different. We can have as many heading tags on a page as we like; the key is to define the structure and apply our markup accordingly.

The W3C states the following:

> Since some users skim through a document by navigating its headings, it is important to use them appropriately to convey document structure. Users should order heading elements properly. For example, in HTML, H2 elements should follow H1 elements, H3 elements should follow H2 elements, etc. Content developers should not 'skip' levels (e.g., H1 directly to H3). Do not use headings to create font effects; use style sheets to change font styles for example.
>
> http://www.w3.org/TR/WCAG10-HTML-TECHS/#document-headers

The following example show a series of headings marked up in XHTML:

```
<h1>Heading 1</h1>
<h2>Heading 2</h2>
<h3>Heading 3</h3>
<h4>Heading 4</h4>
<h5>Heading 5</h5>
<h6>Heading 6</h6>
```

The way the browser displays these headings by default, as shown in Figure 3-3, gives us an indication of the importance of the different headings. The h1 is clearly more significant than the h6. As we mentioned earlier in this chapter, we can use CSS to adjust the style and size of these headings, so by now you know not to be tempted to pick a heading based on its default size.

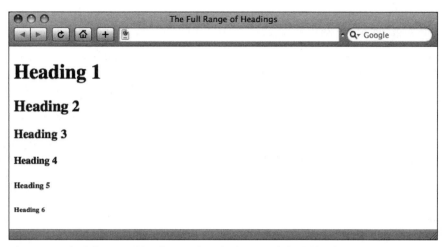

Figure 3-3. The full range of headings as they display, unstyled, within a browser

Applying information hierarchy

When building pages using a Web Standardistas' approach, the first stage in the design process is looking at a page's content and applying some structure to it using the appropriate tags. Once this stage is completed and only then do we move on to style our well-structured markup through the use of CSS.

In Figure 3-1 and Figure 3-2, earlier in the chapter, we showed you two versions of the same page, one *with* and one *without* structure. Let's take a closer look at the text that comprises this document minus markup. By doing this, we can begin to ask some questions about the document's structure and use the answers to those questions to guide our choice of tags when marking up the document.

It might sound obvious, but the first thing we'll do is to carefully read the content. It's important to get a feel for the relationship between the different sections so that we can establish a clear information hierarchy. Our plain, unstructured content looks like this:

```
Famous Monkeys
Who would have guessed that there are actually web pages about
famous monkeys.
Perhaps the best, certainly number one at Google, is Famous Monkeys
Through History, a somewhat bizarre site that chronicles the
adventures of real life ape-o-nauts.
My favourite is Gordo, the first ape in space who unfortunately died
in somewhat controversial circumstances.
Obscure Monkey Facts
Washoe the chimp was possibly the first monkey to master the art of
sign language. When encountering a monkey she disliked she signed
"dirty" with "monkey" to express her disapproval of the other
primate.
```

45

The cleverly named 'Robomonkey' was the first robotic primate.
A group of monkeys is called a troop of monkeys.

After reading through the content, it is time to start marking up our headings and paragraphs. The page is all about famous monkeys, so the first line, "Famous Monkeys," would best be marked up as an h1, the most important heading on the page. Under this heading, we have three sections that we'll mark up as paragraphs. So far, so good. Our document is slowly taking shape.

The line "Obscure Monkey Facts" is destined to become another heading. As it's a subsection and less important than the "Famous Monkeys" heading at the top of the page, we'll mark this up as an h2. Following this heading, we have three obscure monkey facts. Although the first piece of monkey trivia is a little longer than the second and third, this content is still suitable to be marked up as a list. Our final port of call is to add some additional semantic meaning to the page by pulling out some key phrases in this simple example using the <em> and <strong> tags we've already discussed.

The resulting markup looks like this:

```
<h1>Famous Monkeys</h1>
  <p>Who would have guessed that there are actually web pages about
  famous monkeys. Perhaps the best, certainly number one at Google, is
  <em>Famous Monkeys Through History</em>, a somewhat bizarre site
  that chronicles the adventures of real life
  <strong>ape-o-nauts</strong>.<p>
  <p>My favourite is Gordo, the first ape in space who unfortunately
  died in somewhat controversial circumstances.</p>
<h2>Obscure Monkey Facts</h2>
  <ul>
    <li>Washoe the chimp was possibly the first monkey to master the ➡
    art
    of sign language. When encountering a monkey she disliked she ➡
    signed
    "dirty" with "monkey" to express her disapproval of the other
    primate.</li>
    <li>The cleverly named 'Robomonkey' was the first robotic
    primate.</li>
    <li>A group of monkeys is called a troop of monkeys.</li>
  </ul>
```

The result of this process is that we've moved from an unstructured page with no information hierarchy to a well-structured XHTML page with a clear information hierarchy. You'll see as you progress through the book how you can apply style to all of the tags used here to further tease out the document's structure and meaning.

Case study: The Guardian

Looking at an example web page and trying to identify its structure is the best way to learn what structured markup is. At this point, it's over to you. The example shown in Figure 3-4 is taken from www.guardian.co.uk, the web site of the UK national newspaper the *Guardian*. Looking at the example, try to work out which is the most important heading— an h1—and which are the h2 and h3 headings.

Figure 3-4. The *Guardian* home page

In our Famous Monkeys web page that we looked at in the previous section of this chapter, the most important heading, our h1, also happened to be at the very top of the page. Looking at the example in Figure 3-4, however, you can see that there's a lot of information at the top of the page that doesn't seem to fit the "most important heading" description. Sign in? Register? Search? These don't feel like headings, so we need to keep looking.

A contender for the h1 spot is the guardian.co.uk brand, displayed in two shades of blue near the top of the page. This brand is consistently displayed throughout the site, and some might argue that this could indeed be the most important heading on the page. When you pick up a newspaper, however, you're probably more interested in the news headlines than in the paper's branding, which stays the same day in, day out, regardless of what's going on in the world.

As you can see in Figure 3-5, the first news headline on the page is in fact an h1. Following this news story are a number of other headlines, all marked up as h2s. These stories are all considered important; they're not the top story of the day, but they are *all* marked up to be the second most important pieces of information on the page. So a page may have more than one h2; ultimately this depends on the content. Further on, in the right-hand column, less urgent stories about dating and saving are marked up with h3 tags.

Figure 3-5. The *Guardian* home page, annotated to indicate the different levels of headings

It's worth bearing in mind when looking at this example that there may be several different ways to structure our information meaningfully. After all, what is important to you might differ from another's opinion of what should get the highest priority. However, our goal should remain the same: when writing your markup, adding your headings and paragraphs and structuring your page, strive toward adding tags that give clues as to the *meaning* of the content. Not how it should look on the page, but *what it means*.

As a general rule, there are two approaches to applying markup in this first pass: a linear approach, where an h2 is a subsection of an h1 and so on; and a less linear approach, where information is marked up in order of importance (e.g., an h2 isn't necessarily a *subsection* of the h1, but is the second most important item on the page). Which approach you take depends upon the content you're marking up, both on the page itself and throughout the site.

Bear in mind that your web pages don't exist in isolation and will have a relationship to each other. It's worth considering the information hierarchy across different pages in your site as this will also have an impact on how you mark up those pages. At the end of the day, it all depends on the content. Let the content guide your decisions over which tags to use, and you should be fine.

An introduction to phrase elements

We briefly alluded to *elements* in Chapter 2 with a diagram (Figure 2-5) that showed an element consisting of an opening tag, some content, and a closing tag. In this section, we explain what an element is in a little more detail.

What is an element?

You already know what a tag is, and we've briefly discussed elements already. But what exactly is an element? We could have steered clear of elements and simply referred to tags throughout; however, it's useful for Web Standardistas to have a fully functioning vocabulary (you never know which famous web standards evangelist is around the corner, and we want you to be prepared for every eventuality).

Tags, elements? It's not as complicated as it sounds. As we mentioned in Chapter 2, an element is simply a set of opening and closing tags (<p> and </p> for instance) plus the content within these tags, as indicated in Figure 3-6.

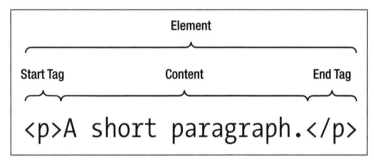

Figure 3-6. The structure of an element

A simple example of an element might be a paragraph of text, like in the following example. This would be referred to as a p element. Note the lack of the < and > brackets—we're talking about *elements* now, not *tags*. The p element in question is *everything* that follows: opening tags, closing tags, *and* content.

```
<p>And now, ladies and gentlemen, before I tell you any more,
I'm going to show you the greatest thing your eyes have ever beheld.
He was a king and a god in the world he knew, but now he comes to
civilization merely a captive - a show to gratify your curiosity.
Ladies and gentlemen, look at Kong, the Eighth Wonder of the World.
</p>.
```

What's important to remember is that elements can contain other elements. In the next example, everything contained within the opening <body> and closing </body> tags, including the tags themselves, can be referred to as the body element.

```
  </head>
  <body>
    <h1>King Kong - The Lost Scenes</h1>
    <p>The original version of King Kong included scenes that later
    were cut to placate the censors. One such scene was only shown
    publicly once during a preview screening in San Bernardino,
    California in 1933. This lost scene featured Kong shaking four
    sailors off a log bridge, causing them to fall into a ravine where
    they were eaten alive by giant spiders.</p>
  </body>
</html>
```

Adding meaning to fragments of text

Phrase elements add meaning to fragments of text. You've already encountered two phrase elements, em and strong, in our example of nesting elements, but there are many more that you can use to improve the structure and meaning of your markup.

In this section, we introduce you to a number of phrase elements to expand your XHTML vocabulary. By the end of this chapter, you'll have an extensive set of elements from which to choose.

Adding emphasis: <em> and <strong>

Poorly trained web designers often confuse <em> (emphasis) with <i> (italics) and <strong> (strong emphasis) with <b> (bold). Given a little guidance, however, we're confident you will never make this glaring error as a Web Standardista. Why? Simply because <i> and <b> are presentational, that is, *they only affect visual display within the browser*, whereas <em> and <strong> suggest *meaning*.

Comparing <i> and <em> should help to clarify this distinction further. <i> deals only with the visual display of text (i.e., it is *presentational*), whereas <em> conveys meaning (i.e., it is *semantic*). This meaning is interpreted by the browser to display as italic; however, it also conveys additional information to assistive devices like screen readers for the visually impaired—where display is, by definition, impossible. When using <em> and <strong>, screen readers will change volume, pitch, or rate to suggest the difference in emphasis.

There are some occasions where using italics might be appropriate, such as to indicate a ship's name, as in the following example (also shown displayed within a browser in Figure 3-7):

```
<p>King Kong travelled to New York in the hull of a ship
called <i>The Venture</i> under Captain Engelhorn.<p>
```

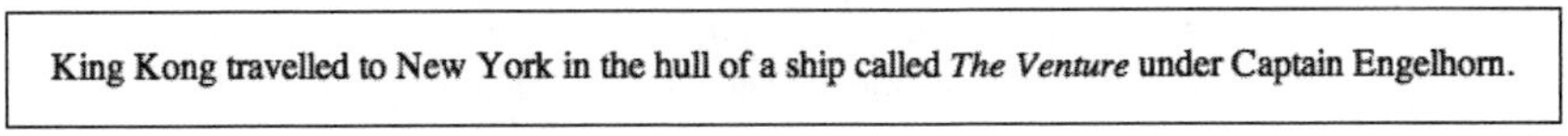

King Kong travelled to New York in the hull of a ship called *The Venture* under Captain Engelhorn.

Figure 3-7. Our italics example as displayed in a browser

Although we would like the ship's name *The Venture* to be displayed in italics in a visual browser, we don't want a screen reader to add emphasis to the ship's name when reading it aloud. This makes an `<i>` tag a more appropriate choice than an `<em>` in this case.

Other phrase elements

Being restricted to only adding emphasis and strong emphasis to your content might become a little bit monotonous after a while, so it's worth getting to know a few other phrase elements. These elements can all be used to add additional meaning to your content. You might end up using some of them all the time, others might be used less frequently, but all are worth knowing about nonetheless.

- `abbr`: Used to identify the enclosed text as an abbreviation or a shortened form of a word or phrase (e.g., Dr.).

- `acronym`: Used to indicate an acronym, a word formed from the initial letters of other words (e.g., NATO).

- `cite`: Used to denote a citation, a reference to another document, especially books, magazines, and articles.

- `q`: Used to mark up short quotations. Standards-compliant browsers will add quotation marks around text marked up with q. Sadly, a lack of consistent browser support has made this element hard to use.

- `code`: Used to denote a sample of program code. By default, code is rendered in the browser's specified monospace font—with this type of font, every character has the same width. This makes the code easier to read and to differentiate from the rest of the page content. Other programming-related elements include kbd (for keyboard commands), samp (for code samples), and var (for code variables).

- `del` and `ins`: Used to indicate deleted and inserted text, useful when revising a document. Deleted text is usually displayed with a line drawn through the text, whereas inserted text usually displays with an underline.

You'll encounter these and other phrase elements again in a little more detail in the following chapter; for now, consider yourself introduced, but not yet intimate.

Block-level and inline-level elements

There are two types of elements in XHTML: **block-level elements** and **inline-level elements**. What's the difference between them? Simply put, block-level elements generally begin rendering on a new line within the document and force a new line when they are closed. You'll have noticed by now that a browser by default inserts a line of blank space above and below an h1 or a p; that is because these are block-level elements.

Inline-level elements, on the other hand, display inline. Adding em or strong elements within a paragraph does not force a line break within the paragraph because these are inline-level elements.

But surely it can't be that easy? Wait, there's more . . .

Imagine a box

Every element within an XHTML document is contained within a "box" that is either block-level or inline-level (the latter is sometimes referred to as **text-level**). The easiest way to demonstrate what this means is to point out some examples in a screenshot.

In Figure 3-8, the first paragraph (contained within <p> tags) occupies its own block-level space. In the second paragraph, both the words *ape* (contained within <em> tags) and the word *monkey* (contained within <strong> tags) are inline-level elements and so display inline. (The paragraph that contains these inline-level elements is also block-level; however, we've resisted the urge to draw a box around it to keep the illustration clearer!)

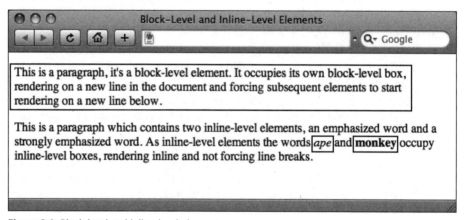

Figure 3-8. Block-level and inline-level elements

The difference between block-level and inline-level elements

As you can see in Figure 3-8, block-level elements generate "breaks" before and after their containing box. Put simply, if we consider a paragraph, we imagine it to be a block of text with space above and below it—it is block level. A word in italics or bold, however, is contained within the paragraph—it is inline.

Some examples of block-level elements include h1, h2, and p.

Some examples of inline-level elements include strong, em, and cite.

In XHTML, block-level elements cannot be nested inside inline-level elements; for example, you cannot have a p element nested within `<strong></strong>` tags. In the following two examples, we show you the right way to nest elements using the First In, Last Out approach.

This example is correct:

```
<p>The strong element nested within the containing p tags in this
paragraph - <strong>me</strong> - is fine.</p>
```

The following example, however, is incorrect, as a block-level element cannot be nested within an inline element:

```
<strong>This is <p>not fine</p>.</strong>
```

It's also worth noting that inline-level elements cannot be placed directly within the body without first being enclosed within block-level elements. Failure to nest inline-level elements within block-level elements will result in pages that fail to validate.

In the next section, we will look at a way to ensure that you've nested your elements correctly and that your document is valid. We'll do so using the W3C Markup Validation Service.

Valid code is browser-friendly markup

By now, you've been introduced to quite a bit of material. If you've been following along with the examples and exercises, and experimenting building your own pages, you should be capable of building pages with quite a bit of complexity.

As with any process, the more complexity you add, the easier it is for errors or mistakes to creep in. These errors might affect the display of your web page within different browsers across different platforms, so it's important you pick them up and correct them.

Wouldn't it be great if there were a service that offered to check all your code for you? A service that highlighted line by line where those errors lie to make your bug-hunting task just that little bit easier? Better still, a service that did all of the above *for free*. Good news, there is. Meet the W3C Markup Validation Service.

The W3C Markup Validation Service

Why use the W3C Markup Validation Service? There are a number of reasons. First, valid pages are Google-friendly pages, and Google-friendly pages are easier to find. Second, valid pages are easier to debug.

When we build a web site, it's inevitable that things will go wrong from time to time. We get distracted, our minds wander, a mistake creeps in. The W3C Markup Validation Service highlights where the errors are, details what those errors are, and points them out line by line, ensuring that they're easy to track down and fix.

3

When your web page displays in an unexpected way, a brief check to see whether your code is invalid or formatted incorrectly can often highlight the problem. Using the W3C Markup Validation Service can save a lot of checking over code line by line by highlighting where any mistakes are. If you've accidentally forgotten to close a tag, for instance, using the validator will show you where you went wrong, saving you hours of looking through your code trying to find the bug yourself.

Use of the validation service is easy, and you don't even need to have your files uploaded to a server to avail yourself of the service (we'll be covering uploading your files in Chapter 7).

Let's give it a test drive. We start off with opening the following page in our browser:

```
http://validator.w3.org/
```

Clicking the Validate by Direct Input tab allows you to copy and paste your markup into the validator. Let's put the markup in the following example through the test:

```
<!DOCTYPE html PUBLIC "-//W3C//DTD XHTML 1.0 Strict//EN"
"http://www.w3.org/TR/xhtml1/DTD/xhtml1-strict.dtd">
<html xmlns="http://www.w3.org/1999/xhtml">
<head>
  <meta http-equiv="Content-Type" content="text/html; charset=UTF-8" />
  <title>King Kong</title>
</head>
<body>
  <h1>King Kong</h1>
  <p>King Kong is the name of a fictional giant ape from the legendary
  Skull Island, who has appeared in several works since 1933. Most of
  these bear his name, and include the groundbreaking 1933 film, the
  film remakes of 1976 and 2005, and numerous sequels.</p>
  <p>Although the 1933 movie featured crude animatronics and a giant
  ape made out of a sponge, it is considered by many to be the
  definitive version.</p>
</body>
</html>
```

As shown in Figure 3-9, we've pasted the preceding markup into the validator. Now it's time for the moment of truth. Click the Check button, and the validator will check our page.

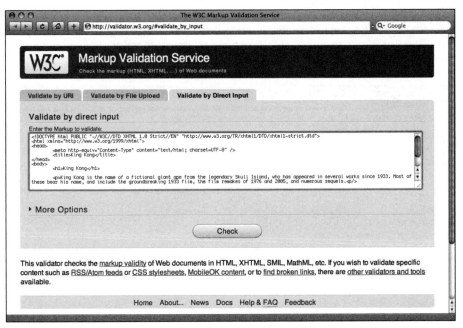

Figure 3-9. We're putting our markup through the test with the W3C Markup Validation Service.

Checking our markup reveals that there's something not quite right with our XHTML. As shown in Figure 3-10, there are a total of six errors, but how do we find out what those errors are so that we can fix them?

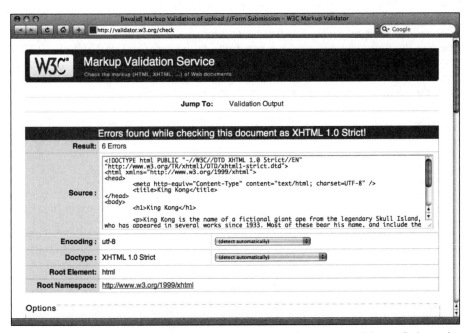

Figure 3-10. The W3C Markup Validation Service shows that our page is not valid. Let's find out why.

This is where the **validation output** comes into play. Scroll down the page, and you will see each error listed, with some helpful, if at first rather perplexing, details. Figure 3-11 shows the first of our six errors. Let's take a closer look at it and try to work out what's gone wrong.

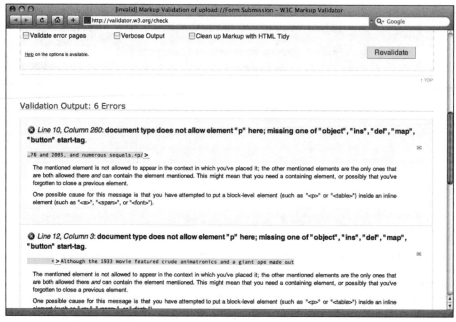

Figure 3-11. The validation output shows the details of our errors.

Let's start from the beginning. The first bit of information, displayed in italic, is telling us where in the document our error has occurred—in this case, on Line 10 of our XHTML document. Most plain text editors have a feature like TextWrangler's Show Line Numbers. If your text editor supports this feature, it's a good idea to turn it on, as this will allow you to quickly identify where to locate any errors, as shown in Figure 3-12.

```
1   <!DOCTYPE html PUBLIC "-//W3C//DTD XHTML 1.0 Strict//EN"
    "http://www.w3.org/TR/xhtml1/DTD/xhtml1-strict.dtd">
2   <html xmlns="http://www.w3.org/1999/xhtml">
3   <head>
4       <meta http-equiv="Content-Type" content="text/html; charset=UTF-8" />
5       <title>King Kong</title>
6   </head>
7   <body>
8       <h1>King Kong</h1>
9
10      <p>King Kong is the name of a fictional giant ape from the legendary Skull
        Island, who has appeared in several works since 1933. Most of these bear his
        name, and include the groundbreaking 1933 film, the film remakes of 1976 and
        2005, and numerous sequels.<p/>
11
12      <p>Although the 1933 movie featured crude animatronics and a giant ape made
        out of a sponge, it is considered by many to be the definitive version.</p>
13  </body>
14  </html>
```

Figure 3-12. Line numbers help you find specific sections of code easily.

The second piece of information, displayed in bold, is probably a little bewildering, as it describes the probable details of your error in very dry, technical terms. Along with the more verbose paragraphs below, expanding on these details, this information is an attempt by the validator to determine the cause of the error for you. In this case, as there could be a number of possible explanations, you're left with the task of deciphering the information and working out which error applies to you.

In simple scenarios, the line of code displaying the markup where your error occurred is the best place to start. In our example in Figure 3-12 earlier, the end of Line 10 looks like this:

```
...film remakes of 1976 and 2005, and numerous sequels.<p/>
```

As you might already have spotted, the error is a simple typo. We've tried to close our paragraph tag, but accidentally written <p/> instead of </p>. Let's fix this typo and revalidate by clicking the Revalidate button. Figure 3-13 shows the result after fixing the error.

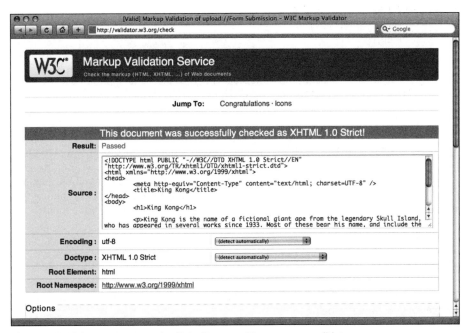

Figure 3-13. Fixing one error made all six disappear. Now our page validates.

Fixing just this one error clearly had a domino effect; the result is that all six errors have disappeared. It's worth revalidating your markup after fixing each error, as one simple mistake can often result in multiple errors being reported by the validator.

One of the reasons to embrace the W3C Markup Validation Service early in your career as a budding Web Standardista is that it can teach you a great deal about how to debug code and resolve web page display issues. The act of debugging a page and trying to get it to validate is extremely educational and, as a welcome byproduct, highlights the importance of well-formed code. The W3C Markup Validation Service is a free tool; it costs nothing but time to use.

If we ensure our pages validate without errors, they should

- Render as we expect in standards-compliant browsers.
- Load faster.
- Be 100% future-proof as the Web evolves.

All good goals to be striving for; all expected of a Web Standardista.

Valid code is not necessarily well-structured code

Passing the W3C Markup Validation Service test doesn't automatically mean that your page is well structured. Imagine that we've marked up the preceding information as follows:

```
...
<p>King Kong</p>
   <h3>King Kong is the name of a fictional giant ape from the legendary
   Skull Island, who has appeared in several works since 1933. Most of
   these bear his name, and include the groundbreaking 1933 film, the
   film remakes of 1976 and 2005, and numerous sequels.</h3>
...
```

Now the most important heading on the page is marked up as a p and the subsequent paragraph has been marked up as an h3. All it takes is a quick glance over this markup to see that something isn't quite right; it certainly hasn't been written by an aspiring Web Standardista. The preceding is perfectly valid, however, and the validator will not find any errors in the markup. Remember, make sure that your page is well structured before you attempt to validate it, or in the words of Gary Larson: "First pants, *THEN* your shoes."

Getting the search mix right

Structured markup is Google-friendly markup, and Google-friendly markup increases the chances of your web site being found.

Let's face it, with an estimated 63 billion web pages in existence (and that was just in June 2008), getting found online is a little like finding the proverbial needle in a haystack, only this is a very big haystack. Using a Web Standardistas' approach helps your web site considerably in the eyes of Google. In this section, we explore why.

By structuring your content in a logical way, using headings, paragraphs, and phrase elements to add meaning to your content, you are not only building the foundations for a POSH site worthy of a Web Standardista, but also helping search engines, which can use your well-structured markup to help them make sense of the contents of your page.

Apart from making sure that your content contains the words or phrases that people are likely to search for, one of the simplest things you can do to guarantee your page is ranked well by Google is to cross-reference the content of your title element and your page's h1 elements and ensure that both feature an intelligent use of words relevant to your web site or web page.

Let's put ourselves in the shoes of someone desperately trying to find useful information about famous primates and take a look at a couple of examples to underline what we mean. In the following examples, we've shown two different versions of the same page. The first tells us—and Google—very little about the page:

```
...
<title>Gordo and Clyde</title>
...
<h1>Furry Forest Dwellers Found Fame</h1>
...
```

Who are Gordo and Clyde? Using our human powers of deduction, we might determine that there was a chance these furry forest dwellers were indeed primates, and since they found fame they would probably also be famous, but it would be very hard for a machine to equate this information with the words *Famous Primates*.

The following example is much better. It's evident from the title element that this page is the one we've been looking for; it also provides Google with a mix of meaningful keywords that also cross-reference with the h1. Perfect.

```
...
<title>Famous Primates presents Gordo and Clyde</title>
...
<h1>Gordo and Clyde - Two Famous Primates</h1>
...
```

Although we can't completely rule out that the somewhat specialist subject matter helped a little, the homework web site we built to accompany this book is an example of how a well-structured page can make it into the top-three position in Google (as shown in Figure 3-14) within only a few weeks of its launch. 3 out of 862,000 isn't bad.

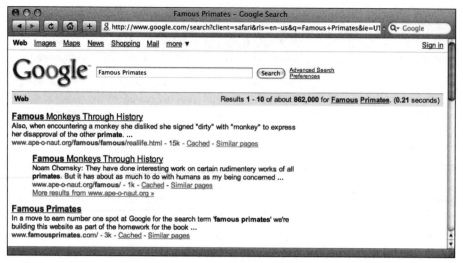

Figure 3-14. After only a few weeks, our page about famous primates reached the third spot in Google.

There are a number of other techniques that help with search engine optimization (SEO); however, what we want to stress here is that search engine–friendly pages are a natural byproduct of the Web Standardistas' approach.

Summary

So what have we covered? Although you might not think we've done any "design" yet, trust us, *we have*. Even without the addition of style with CSS, we've explored the importance of establishing a strong information hierarchy. This process is central to any good piece of design, and hopefully now that you're marking your pages up using the full range of tags at your disposal, you agree.

Along the way we've looked at the W3C Markup Validation Service and considered its importance in ensuring your web pages display consistently regardless of browser or platform. Lastly, we took a look at a byproduct of the Web Standardistas' approach that ensures your web pages are search engine friendly.

In the next chapter we introduce you to lists, the building blocks of web site navigation. We also introduce you to a number of other tags, ensuring that you have a well-stocked web design toolkit moving forward.

Homework: Introducing Miss Baker

In the last chapter's homework, you created a simple web page about Albert I, the first-ever monkey astronaut. In this chapter, we've introduced a number of tags to add additional structure and meaning to your markup. You'll be adding these to another page you'll be creating about Miss Baker, another well-known space pioneer.

Good news: Albert I—now feeling a little lonely in the homework folder—is about to be joined by a lady friend.

As with the last chapter, we'll provide you with all the information you need on Miss Baker; your job will be to add markup to the page to give it some structure. You'll be adding the following: a range of headings from h1 to h4; some additional <p> tags to mark up the paragraphs; and some phrase elements, namely em and strong.

Finally, once you've marked up the Miss Baker page, you'll be validating it using the W3C Markup Validation Service to check that no errors have slipped in during the markup process.

1. Establish an information hierarchy

To undertake the last chapter's homework, we provided you with a very simple page about Albert I, consisting of a single h1 and three short paragraphs. In this chapter, we're increasing the level of complexity.

As before, we've supplied you with a text file that you'll be adding markup to. You can access it here:

www.webstandardistas.com/03/miss_baker.txt

At first glance, the information hierarchy of Miss Baker's page isn't quite as clear as Albert I's page. The first stage in the markup process is simple, but essential: *read everything before you mark up anything*. As you read, your goal is to try to identify an information hierarchy for the text supplied so that you can add effective and meaningful markup in the next stage.

2. Add <h1>–<h4> and <p> tags

Once you've read through the text supplied for the Miss Baker page, try to work out the meaning of the words and the page's information hierarchy. Using <h1>–<h4> and <p> tags, apply some structure to the page.

It's worth noting that there are potentially a number of ways to mark this page up, and the choices you make are in some respects subjective. However, to help you in the process, we have created a similarly structured page about Cornelius, famous for his role in *The Planet of the Apes*. You can refer to this using your browser's View Source command to see how we've structured the web page logically, here:

www.webstandardistas.com/03/cornelius.html

3. Add <em> and <strong>

The next stage in the markup process is to identify any phrase elements that might exist within the text. In this case, you're looking for any words that might benefit from the addition of emphasis. Remember, em and strong are intended for the addition of emphasis to text, not for changing its visual presentation (or look and feel).

Again, you might wish to refer to our Cornelius web page to see where we've added emphasis.

4. Validate your page

Once you've completed adding the markup to your Miss Baker web page, the final stage in the process will be to check it using the W3C Markup Validation Service. Start by opening the following page in your browser:

```
http://validator.w3.org/
```

Click the Validate by Direct Input tab, and copy and paste the markup for your Miss Baker page into the validator. Click Check and wait for the results. If you've been a diligent Web Standardista and written all your markup carefully, you'll be welcomed by the green banner. If you're met with the less welcoming red banner, have no fear, the process of debugging your Miss Baker page will in itself be an educational experience.

Only once you're met with the green banner are you allowed to put the kettle on and enjoy a cup of *Earl Grey* as you prepare yourself for the next chapter!

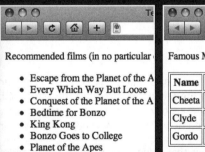

CHAPTER 4

MARKUP THAT ADDS MEANING

In this chapter we look at the topic of adding additional meaning to your markup through the use of a number of new tags we introduce. Our primary focus is to cover a number of methods of organizing and grouping information. In particular, we explore the importance of using lists—unordered lists, ordered lists, and definition lists (don't worry, we'll introduce each of these fully in due course)—to help group together related information. We also introduce tables, often mistakenly maligned, but useful nonetheless for giving form to tabular data.

By the end of this chapter, you'll be ready to build basic lists that will form the backbone of your web site's navigation after we've introduced creating links in Chapter 6. At this point, like your other markup, your lists will remain unstyled, but rest assured you'll style them in good time. You'll also have an understanding of how to use tables to organize tabular data, enabling you to apply structure and meaning to calendars, charts, schedules, and timetables, to give but a few examples.

Finally, and for good measure, we introduce a number of additional tags—bonus tags for every occasion. In a veritable XHTML feast, we supply you with a sizable number of tags that no Web Standardista should be without: tags for quotations—<blockquote>, <q>, and <cite>; tags we're rescuing—<hr />; tags for nerds—<code> and <pre>; tags for writers—<del> and <ins>; and finally, <sup> and <sub>, useful, in particular, for our scientist friends.

Lists: First-level organizers

Lists are everywhere: shopping lists, to-do lists, top ten lists, lists of links, lists of links for navigation, and so on. Lists are semantic: they suggest structure or indicate related groups of information, which is why we're using them.

Look at any well-designed web page, and it's likely that the navigation at the top or the side of the page is a list of links that's been styled with CSS. Lists provide a means of grouping information together and making the separate elements easier to grasp. Lists also give us meaningful tags that we can target with CSS, which we'll cover when we get to Chapter 12, where we show you how to style a variety of lists.

Why use lists?

Look at the following two examples—a list of primate-related films. In the first, we structure the list as an inline paragraph; in the second we structure the list using bullet points. Two different approaches that, as you'll see, have an important impact on how they render in a browser and can have an impact on how they're absorbed as groups of information.

Looking at the two examples, it's clear that using a list to both group and structure the information provides an additional layer of meaning for the information supplied.

Recommended films, version 1 (in no particular order):

Escape from the Planet of the Apes, Every Which Way But Loose, Conquest of the Planet of the Apes, Bedtime for Bonzo, King Kong, Bonzo Goes to College, Planet of the Apes, The King of Kong, Beneath the Planet of the Apes, 2001: A Space Odyssey.

Recommended films, version 2 (in no particular order):

- Escape from the Planet of the Apes
- Every Which Way But Loose
- Conquest of the Planet of the Apes
- Bedtime for Bonzo
- King Kong
- Bonzo Goes to College
- Planet of the Apes
- The King of Kong
- Beneath the Planet of the Apes
- 2001: A Space Odyssey

Looking at the preceding examples, we would argue that certain information lends itself to display in list format. Rendered in the browser as a series of bullet points, the list of films is easier to read than the paragraph with the list of films rendered inline. With each film beginning on a new line and with bullet points clearly indicating each new film in the list, we would argue that the list is easier to read when presented this way. As with the previous chapters, we're using the right tag for the job to indicate the structure and grouping of information to the reader, adding design through the careful use of structured markup.

While it's worth noting that we could use CSS to switch off bullet points and render our list inline as a paragraph (something we'll cover in Chapter 12), the point we'd like to make here is that through the careful selection of appropriate tags, we can amplify the meaning of our raw, unstyled information—no bad thing.

In the next section, we show you how to use the basic components of a list in XHTML; along the way we introduce you to three types of list: **unordered** lists, **ordered** lists, and **definition** lists. We'll focus primarily on the first two types of list, as these will provide you with useful methods of marking up groups of information that you can style later using CSS.

Unordered and ordered lists

We structure unordered lists using two elements: ul and li. The ul element indicates that we are grouping our items in an unordered list, that is, each item in the list is of equal value and the list suggests no inherent order. The li element is used for each item—or **list item**—in the list.

Recall the version 2 example of the recommended films (in no particular order) mentioned previously. Marked up, the list looks like this:

```
<ul>
    <li>Escape from the Planet of the Apes</li>
    <li>Every Which Way But Loose</li>
    <li>Conquest of the Planet of the Apes</li>
    <li>Bedtime for Bonzo</li>
    <li>King Kong</li>
    <li>Bonzo Goes to College</li>
    <li>Planet of the Apes</li>
    <li>The King of Kong</li>
    <li>Beneath the Planet of the Apes</li>
    <li>2001: A Space Odyssey</li>
</ul>
```

The preceding markup, when rendered in a browser, looks like what you see in Figure 4-1.

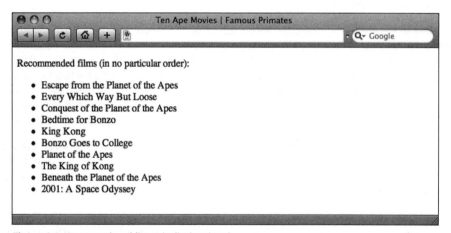

Figure 4-1. Our unordered list as it displays in a browser

We open and close our list with <ul> and </ul> tags, respectively, indicating that what follows is a group of related information. We then list each item in the list within <li> tags.

But what if we want to give our list some order? After all, a top ten list isn't much use if we haven't ordered it.

Enter the ordered list

Perhaps you need to get your lists in order, and an unordered list doesn't meet your requirements. Have no fear, HTML provides a means of doing this. Meet the ol, or ordered list.

In the previous example, we introduced you to a great list of films, but the browser's default bullet points of a ul didn't give us much of a sense of order; in fact, we prefaced the list with the words *in no particular order*. What if you wanted to make a top ten list? Good news, we have an alternative to the ul at our disposal. Enter the ordered list, or ol. Change the <ul> tags in the preceding example to <ol> tags, and we now have a top ten list that looks like the following example (you'll notice our list is now ordered differently—in the authors' order of preference):

```
<ol>
    <li>Bedtime for Bonzo</li>
    <li>King Kong</li>
    <li>Every Which Way But Loose</li>
    <li>The King of Kong</li>
    <li>Planet of the Apes</li>
    <li>Beneath the Planet of the Apes</li>
    <li>Escape from the Planet of the Apes</li>
    <li>2001: A Space Odyssey</li>
    <li>Conquest of the Planet of the Apes</li>
    <li>Bonzo Goes to College</li>
</ol>
```

The preceding markup, when rendered in a browser, looks like the list in Figure 4-2.

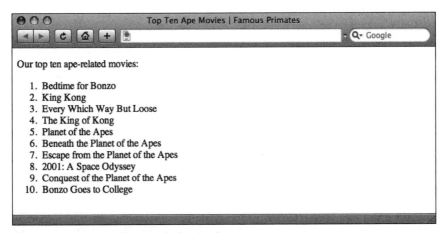

Figure 4-2. Our ordered list as it displays in a browser

The only thing we had to do, apart from putting the films in the order we felt appropriate, was to change the ul to an ol. With just that simple change, the browser takes care of the numbering for us. So, if in the event of a recount we wanted to put *The King of Kong* in at number one, we wouldn't have to renumber the whole list; we could simply move <li>The King of Kong</li> up three lines in our HTML document. Simple.

Another benefit of the ol is that we're not just limited to numerals. As you'll see when you get to Chapter 12, which covers styling lists with CSS, we can exchange our default **1, 2, 3, 4 . . .** (decimal) for

- **A, B, C, D . . .** (upper-alpha)
- **a, b, c, d . . .** (lower-alpha)
- **I, II, III, IV . . .** (upper-roman)
- **i, ii, iii, iv . . .** (lower-roman)

We can even use none, which switches numbering off completely, although why we would want an unordered ordered list is another question altogether.

Nesting lists

Before we add a further layer of complexity to our lists, it's worth noting that both the ul and ol elements are block level and can only contain li elements. No text or other elements can appear in a ul or an ol element unless they are contained within <li> tags.

It's possible, however, to create more complex lists through nesting other elements or even other lists within li elements. This is best demonstrated with an example. Let's take a look at how a nested list is constructed:

```
<ul>
  <li>Famous Apes
    <ul>
      <li>King Kong</li>
      <li>Cornelius</li>
      <li>Cheeta</li>
    </ul>
  </li>
  <li>Famous Monkeys
    <ul>
      <li>Gordo</li>
      <li>Miss Baker</li>
      <li>Albert</li>
    </ul>
  </li>
</ul>
```

As lists become more complex, particularly as lists are nested within lists, it's easy to make mistakes, resulting in pages that fail to validate. The preceding list is perfectly valid; however, the apparent lack of a closing </li> tag on the *Famous Apes* and *Famous Monkeys* list items can be confusing for the beginner. At first glance, these list items appear to open, but not to close; however, they are in fact closed, *after* the ul they contain is closed, a number of lines below.

When nesting a list, the containing list item is not closed until the nested list is closed. The easiest way to get this right is to use indentation or white space to clearly indicate the list's structure within your markup.

The preceding markup, when rendered in a browser, looks like what you see in Figure 4-3.

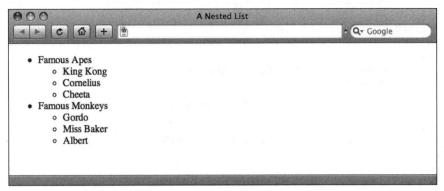

Figure 4-3. The nested list as it displays in a browser

As you can see in the preceding example, as we nest lists within lists, the browser alters the default bullet point to differentiate between the different levels of the nested list. The bullet points your browser uses will depend upon its default style sheet. We'll cover how to control this (and indeed what a default style sheet is) when we get to Chapter 12.

Definition lists

Meet our final list type, the dl, or **definition list**. Definition lists are perfect for lists of definitions, for example, for use in a glossary of terms as might be found at the back of a technical reference. Definition lists consist of three elements: a container—a dl; a definition term—a dt; and a definition description—a dd.

We can demonstrate definition lists best by showing one in action:

```
<dl>
  <dt>Chimpanzee</dt>
    <dd>Chimpanzee, often shortened to chimp, is the common name for
    the two extant species of apes in the genus Pan.</dd>

  <dt>Orangutan</dt>
    <dd>Orangutans are two species of great apes known for their
    intelligence, long arms and reddish-brown hair.</dd>

  <dt>Squirrel Monkey</dt>
    <dd>The squirrel monkeys are New World monkeys of the genus
    Saimiri.</dd>
</dl>
```

The preceding markup, when rendered in a browser, looks like the list in Figure 4-4.

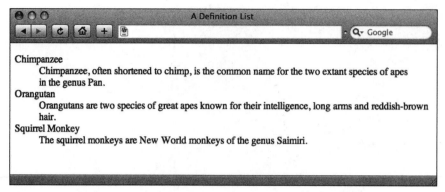

Figure 4-4. The definition list as it displays in a browser

In this example, our dl gathers related terms and definitions together; the dt elements are the **definition terms** (i.e., the terms we're defining); and the dd elements are the **definition descriptions** (i.e., the descriptions or definitions of the terms).

It's possible to use multiple dt or dd elements within a definition list. The following examples show first one definition term with two different possible definitions, and second, two different definition terms with one definition:

```
<dl>
  <dt>monkey</dt>
    <dd>a primate</dd>
    <dd>a mischievous person, esp. a child</dd>
</dl>
```

Or

```
<dl>
  <dt>monkey</dt>
  <dt>ape</dt>
    <dd>a member of the primate family</dd>
</dl>
```

We can also nest block level elements within a definition description (dd), as in the following example. Note, however, that block-level elements *cannot* be nested within the dt element:

```
<dl>
  <dt>Proboscis Monkey</dt>
  <dd>Some facts about the long-nosed monkey:
    <ul>
      <li>Its large, protruding nose can be up to 7 inches long.</li>
      <li>Its nose serves as a resonating chamber to amplify its
      warning calls.</li>
      <li>Its large nose and belly has given it the nickname 'Orang
      Belanda' or 'Dutch Monkey' in Indonesian.</li>
      <li>It is a good climber and a proficient swimmer.</li>
```

```
        </ul>
      </dd>
    </dl>
```

Figure 4-5 shows how this example looks in a browser.

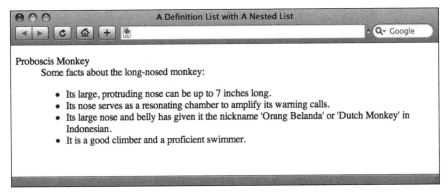

Figure 4-5. A definition term with a number of possible definition descriptions nested as a list

In short, definition lists offer a way to tie together *terms* and *definitions* and, as with all our examples so far, provide an additional layer of meaning or structure to information.

Tables: The good, the bad, and the alternatives

In the "Wild West" days of the interwebs, as HTML evolved, web designers started to push the tags at their disposal far beyond what they were originally intended for, in an effort to make the Web a more beautiful place.

Although many of these designers were incredibly inventive and managed to create some spectacular layouts, their beauty was only skin deep. (The web sites' beauty that is, not the designers', who, as we know, are beautiful people.)

Looking behind the scenes at the code producing these layouts, however, revealed a complex mass of nested table tags with countless rows and columns creating a precarious scaffolding holding the different pages together.

This was never the purpose of the table tag in HTML, which was always intended for gathering together tabular data and giving it structure. Nonetheless, this practice became widespread in an effort to control the look and feel of a rapidly growing Web.

Fortunately for us, browsers evolved, soon developing enough support for CSS to make CSS-based layouts a viable alternative to table-based layouts when designing for the Web. Gone was the need to resort to tables to achieve something they were never intended for.

So, are tables evil, as many early Standardistas believed?

When tables are used for layout purposes, each page includes all the presentational information as well as the content, rather than separating the presentational information into a separate style sheet. As a consequence, table-based layouts result in extra markup that is harder to maintain, and the resulting pages are less accessible to screen readers, mobile devices, and search engines. In short, it's safe to say—when used for layout purposes—tables *are* evil, and many early Standardistas avoided them at all costs.

Used in the right way, however, tables aren't evil and are in fact very useful. Used correctly, tables still have a place in the Web Standardista's arsenal. We know that using tables for layout is strictly off limits, so what do we use tables for? The answer is simple: we use tables for **tabular data**. But what is tabular data?

What is tabular data?

Before we look at an actual table in action, let's rewind just a little and look at some different types of data. First, let's look at a simple list:

```
<ul>
  <li>Cheeta</li>
  <li>Clyde</li>
  <li>Gordo</li>
</ul>
```

This list can be read from the top down, vertically: Cheeta, Clyde, Gordo. In other words, this data is **one dimensional**. But what if our information is a little more complex? Now we're going to step things up a little and add another dimension to the equation.

Consider the table shown in Figure 4-6.

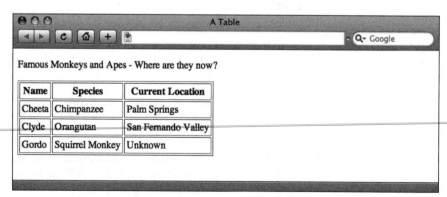

Figure 4-6. A simple three-row, three-column table with table headers. (A table border has been added to reveal the table's underlying structure.)

As you can see, this data can be read in two dimensions: horizontally we can determine that Cheeta is a chimpanzee who lives in Palm Springs. Vertically we can get a list of names

(Cheeta, Clyde, and Gordo), species (chimpanzee, orangutan, and squirrel monkey), and locations (well . . . you get the picture).

Each piece of data can be related horizontally *and* vertically: Clyde is an orangutan who lives in San Fernando Valley. Clyde is also part of a list of names including Cheeta and Gordo. Side to side, up and down. In other words, this data is **two dimensional**. Now we know our two-dimensional tabular data from our one-dimensional list data.

The easiest way to determine whether a table is the right choice for marking up a section of content is to think about whether it could fit into a spreadsheet, like Excel for example. If the grid-like structure of a spreadsheet fits your content like a glove, it's time to roll out the tables.

<table>, <tr>, and <td>

As you've figured out by now, a table consists of rows and columns. We can create a simple table using just three sets of tags, resulting in something like this:

```
<table>
  <tr>
    <td>Cheeta</td>
  </tr>
</table>
```

In this example, we start the table with an opening <table> tag. Next, the <tr> tag starts our **table row**. Between the opening <tr> and the closing </tr>, we have a single table cell, denoted by the opening <td> and the closing </td>. <td> means **table data**; all content in a table is contained inside <td> tags. When all the columns and rows are finished, we have our closing </table> tag, wrapping everything up.

A one-row, one-column table is of course of rather limited use, so let's get a bit more adventurous by revisiting our top ten movies list. If we were to add a little more detail, for example, the film's position in our top ten list, its title, its director, and the year it was made, we'd be heading into table territory. Let's see this in action. (Note: We've added a 1px border—border="1"—to the opening tag to reveal the table's underlying structure in the illustrations. This, however, is presentational and would normally be handled using CSS.)

```
<table border="1">
  <tr>
    <td>01</td> <td>Bedtime for Bonzo</td>
    <td>Dir. Frederick De Cordova</td> <td>1951</td>
  </tr>
  <tr>
    <td>02</td> <td>King Kong</td>
    <td>Dir. Merian C. Cooper</td> <td>1933</td>
  </tr>
  <tr>
    <td>03</td> <td>Every Which Way But Loose</td>
```

```
    <td>Dir. James Fargo</td> <td>1978</td>
  </tr>
</table>
```

The preceding example renders in a browser as shown in Figure 4-7.

01	Bedtime for Bonzo	Dir. Frederick De Cordova	1951
02	King Kong	Dir. Merian C. Cooper	1933
03	Every Which Way But Loose	Dir. James Fargo	1978

Figure 4-7. A simple three-row, four-column table

Although this table has three rows and four columns, it follows exactly the same structure as the simple example that we introduced earlier. First, a <table> tag instructs the browser we're dealing with a table. Each table row starts and ends with a <tr> and </tr> tag, respectively. The cells containing the table data are nested within <td> and </td> tags. Finally, a closing </table> tag ends our table.

It's worth noting that the number of columns must remain the same in each row. That said, there are a number of ways of merging table cells—a topic we've decided to steer clear of in this book to avoid confusing beginners. If you're feeling adventurous, Paul Haine—our technical reviewer—covers advanced tables in his book *HTML Mastery: Semantics, Standards, and Styling* (friends of ED, 2006).

Improving table accessibility

There are several ways to describe the contents of a table, and, in addition to building your table as outlined previously, it's good practice to describe its contents in summary form. This is particularly useful when accommodating nonvisual browsers for the visually impaired, for example.

We have three tools at our disposal to improve the accessibility of tables: the th or **table header**; the caption, which provides an indication of the table's content; and the summary attribute, a means of describing the content of the table in greater depth. Of these, the first two are aimed at *both* visual browsers and screen readers, while the latter is only aimed at screen readers.

You might argue that we could use <td>Species</td> at the top of our Species column in Figure 4-8 (our original table example, repeated here to save you from having to flip back a few pages to find it) to help to visually differentiate the column's header from its contents. However, using <th>Species</th> is better. The th—a table header—achieves the same *visually* but adds a layer of meaning. th is both semantic and, as an added benefit, will be repeated by screen readers as each row of the table's data is read, helping the visually impaired to understand how the table's information is interrelated.

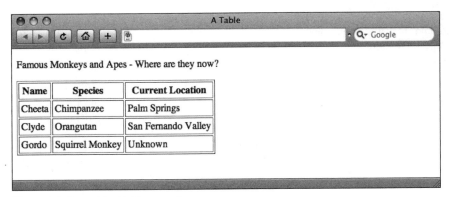

Figure 4-8. Our original table example

A screen reader would read the contents of row three of the table as follows:

Name: Gordo; Species: Squirrel Monkey; Location: Unknown

Now that we've got our table headers sorted, we can give our table a caption. The purpose of the `caption` is to give the table a title, which displays, by default, above the table. In our original example, the caption reads Famous Monkeys and Apes—Where are they now? This adds a further, useful layer of meaning to our table, summarizing at a glance what the table is about.

Finally, we can include a summary attribute, which we'll look at more closely in a moment. For a simple table, table headers and a caption might be sufficient to describe the data they contain. As tables become more complex, however, a well-written summary attribute can prove invaluable to the visually impaired user, browsing the table with a screen reader.

Adding a descriptive summary to a table

Tables are great for condensing information. As you've seen in the preceding examples, they're perfect for drawing together connected information in an easy-to-digest manner. Take train timetables, for example. If you wanted to find out when the next train to Paris leaves, a table is the place to look. The same information displayed in paragraphs or even lists would take up far more space, be harder to cross-reference, and, as a consequence, be harder to digest (remember, it would be *one dimensional*).

But what if you didn't want to take the next train to Paris, but wanted to take the next train to Bordeaux instead? Easy, just glance at the Paris table, determine that this information isn't for you, skip right over it, and find the Bordeaux table. Simple, right?

It's only simple if you're using a visual browser. What if you were blind and couldn't use a visual browser? What if you were using a screen reader? A quick glance over the table's content wouldn't work for you because you were visually impaired.

For anyone who uses a screen reader, listening through each row of a table, column after column, to painstakingly find out whether the table contains the information they need could be a somewhat torturous affair. This is where the summary attribute comes to the rescue.

A table's summary is not rendered in visual browsers, but is especially useful for more complex tables where headers or a caption would not be enough to explain the contents of the table; it's perfect for screen readers and as a consequence should be *high on the accessibility agenda*. A well-written summary should give enough information about the contents and structure of a table to give the users of screen readers an idea of a particular table's usefulness. It should clearly suggest whether it's worth sitting through a table's information or whether it's best to just skip it.

So, let's put our summary attribute into action. Wrapping up, our perfectly formed table—now more accessible than our first version—is listed here:

```
<table summary="The most recent established location of monkeys and
apes made famous by Hollywood and/or NASA.">
  <caption>
  Famous Monkeys and Apes - Where are they now?
  </caption>
  <tr>
    <th>Name</th> <th>Species</th> <th>Current Location</th>
  </tr>
  <tr>
    <td>Cheeta</td> <td>Chimpanzee</td> <td>Palm Springs</td>
  </tr>
  <tr>
    <td>Clyde</td> <td>Orangutan</td> <td>San Fernando Valley</td>
  </tr>
  <tr>
    <td>Gordo</td> <td>Squirrel Monkey</td> <td>Unknown</td>
  </tr>
</table>
```

Although we've only covered the essentials of well-formed and accessibly marked-up tables, we've hopefully given you the basics to create well-formatted tables that not only look good in visual browsers, but also function well for users of screen readers.

Formatting tables using CSS can be complicated for the beginner; however, building on a solid foundation of well-formed XHTML is half the battle. We recommend the chapter "Tables are Evil?" in Dan Cederholm's *Web Standards Solutions: The Markup and Style Handbook* (friends of ED, 2004) for anyone wishing to further their knowledge of using CSS to style well-formed CSS tables.

Quoting text

In this section, we introduce two methods of marking up quotes: the first, using the <blockquote> tag, is block-level and is generally used for substantial quotations; the second, using the <q> tag, is inline-level and is generally used for shorter quotations that are better handled inline. Along the way, we encounter both the cite element and the cite attribute, perfect for citing the source of our quotations.

If you're writing an essay, read this!

What's a <blockquote>?

A <blockquote> is a quote block consisting of one or more paragraphs of text, often accompanied by a cite attribute indicating the source, in the form of a URL, from which the block quote was referenced, as in the following example:

```
<p>The W3C defines HTML as follows:</p>
<blockquote cite="http://www.w3.org/MarkUp/">
  <p>HTML is the lingua franca for publishing hypertext on the
  World Wide Web. It is a non-proprietary format ... HTML uses
  tags to structure text into headings, paragraphs, lists, hypertext
  links, etc.</p>
</blockquote>
<p>Another paragraph here to give the blockquote above context.</p>
```

This renders in the browser as shown in Figure 4-9.

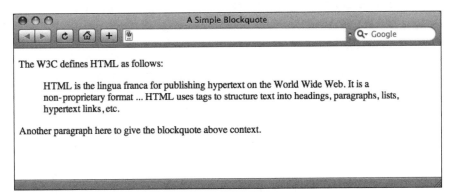

Figure 4-9. A blockquote in action

A blockquote element indents the quote using the browser's default settings (although this can be altered using CSS as you'll see in Chapter 10). The blockquote element adds structure to your document, clearly identifying quotes within your marked-up content.

It's worth noting that the blockquote needs to contain a block-level element, usually a paragraph, to remain valid. This is valid markup:

```
<blockquote>
    <p>So what are you, Mr. Driscoll, a lion, or a chimpanzee?</p>
</blockquote>
```

Whereas this markup would not validate:

```
<blockquote>
    So what are you, Mr. Driscoll, a lion, or a chimpanzee?
</blockquote>
```

Going back to the example displayed in Figure 4-9, we used the cite attribute to reference the source of our quote. Although the cite attribute is not displayed in the browser, it's worth getting into the practice of using it, as it lets you easily track down the source of a quote you've made by looking at the markup of your document. If you want to display this information in the browser, look no further than the cite element, which comes up next.

Citations (or <cite>)

The cite *element*, not to be confused with the cite *attribute*, is used to indicate a citation or reference to another source. Let's jump straight in and look at an example:

```
<blockquote>
    <p>So what are you, Mr. Driscoll, a lion, or a chimpanzee?</p>
    <p><cite>Captain Englehorn</cite></p>
</blockquote>
```

Figure 4-10 shows this example in a browser.

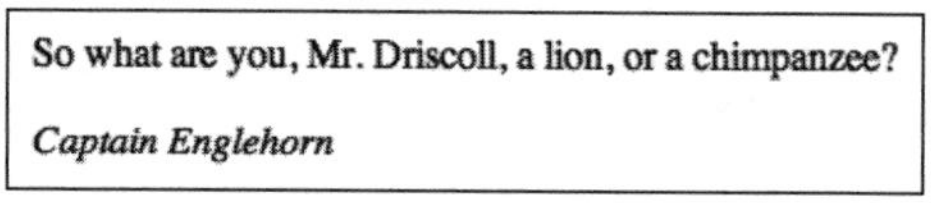

So what are you, Mr. Driscoll, a lion, or a chimpanzee?

Captain Englehorn

Figure 4-10. A block quote with a cite element, by default displayed in *italics*

You can use the cite element anywhere you may need to reference a different source—for example, a book title, the name of a newspaper or magazine, or the title of a movie. As you've already seen, you can also use the cite element to denote the name of the source a quote is attributed to.

The cite element is not confined to being used within a block quote. For instance, you can use the cite element in a paragraph as in the following example:

```
<p><cite title="King Kong (1933)">King Kong</cite> is a film about a
huge gorilla who takes a shine to the blonde star Ann Darrow.</p>
```

Here we have used cite to denote the title of a movie. As you can see, we have added a title attribute within the cite element, providing additional information. If the source you were referencing was to another web page, you might also consider creating a link to that reference using the a element, something we cover in great detail in Chapter 6.

Quotations (or <q>)

A word of warning before we begin: support for <q> tags across browsers is poor at best. However, in the interests of completeness, we're covering them here. Don't say we're not comprehensive.

<q> tags are used to define short quotations that can be included inline, for example:

```
<p>In the words of George Taylor:
<q>Take your stinking paws off me, you damned dirty ape!</q>
</p>
```

This *should* render in the browser as shown in Figure 4-11.

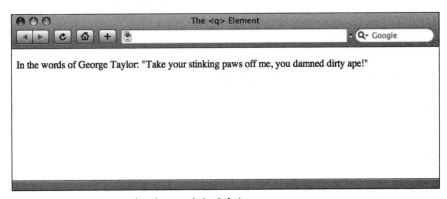

Figure 4-11. A <q> tag rendered correctly by Safari

However, support for the <q> tag is poor, particularly in Internet Explorer, which omits the opening and closing quote marks. This screenshot, taken in Safari, displays the inline <q> as it's supposed to display. (Well done, Safari!)

However, when we nest <q> tags, Safari isn't so hot. What should happen is that the browser should alternate the display of double and single quotes as quotes are nested within quotes, as in the following example, courtesy of Firefox. Safari, however, fails this task miserably, displaying only double quotes. (A little homework for you Safari!) As for Internet Explorer . . . well, let's not go there.

```
<p>Carl Denham: <q>Jack Driscoll does not want just anyone starring
in this picture. He said to me, <q>Carl, somewhere out there is a
woman born to play this role.</q> And as soon as I saw you, I
knew.</q></p>
```

This *should* render in the browser as shown in Figure 4-12.

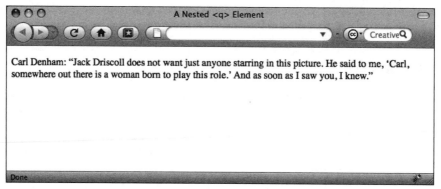

Figure 4-12. A nested <q> rendered correctly by Firefox

In closing, using blockquote and q elements (and including cite attributes) adds additional structure and meaning to your XHTML documents. These elements can be styled using CSS, as we'll cover in Chapters 8 to 13, but first and foremost they are semantic, which we by now know is a Web Standardista best practice.

Other tags in the Standardistas' toolbox

There are tags we use day in, day out—<p> and <h1>, for instance; however, other useful tags exist that, although specialized, can be useful to add specific meaning to your content. In this last section, we take a look at these, which you'll want to add to your Web Standardista's toolbox.

Abbreviations

There are two elements at our disposal when dealing with abbreviations, a shortened form of a word or a phrase. The first is abbr, which is used to identify the enclosed text as an abbreviation, for example, *Dr.*, which is short for Doctor or *abbr.*, short for abbreviation. The second is acronym which, no surprises here, is used to indicate an acronym. An acronym is a special kind of abbreviation formed from the initial letters of other words, for example, NATO.

Although all acronyms are abbreviations, all abbreviations aren't acronyms. You would think it would be safe to just use the abbr element. Unfortunately, earlier versions of Internet Explorer lacked proper support for the abbr element, so in past practice, acronym has often been used for any kind of abbreviation. Looking forward, however, using abbr for all kinds of abbreviations should be the way to go. Let's have a look at abbr and acronym in action:

```
<p><abbr title="Captain">Capt.</abbr> Engelhorn did not have to worry
about the <acronym title="RAdio Detection And Ranging">RADAR</acronym>
as it wasn't invented yet.</p>
```

As you can see, the `title` attribute in each element is used to provide the expanded form of the abbreviation. As shown in Figure 4-13, standards-aware browsers display the contents of the respective `title` attributes as a tooltip.

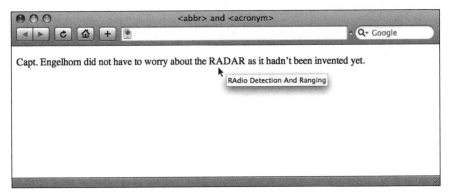

Figure 4-13. The abbr and acronym elements displayed in a browser

It's worth pointing out that the first time you introduce an abbreviation, it's helpful to include the expanded version in the text at least once. Very common abbreviations—Dr. or NASA, for instance—probably won't need this kind of formal introduction. Less common abbreviations—APE (Advocates for Primate Empowerment), for instance—would benefit from an initial explanation.

Making a case for rules: <hr />

The humble `<hr />` or **horizontal rule** gets a bit of an unfair beating at the hands of a number of noted Standardistas. Patrick Griffiths, the acclaimed writer behind the excellent web-based resource HTML Dog (www.htmldog.com), even goes so far as to describe it as a **bad tag**. We, however, beg to differ.

Yes, there are many ways we can create rules or borders using just CSS, but the humble `<hr />` can serve a semantic purpose: as a simple separator of content. Take a look at the example in Figure 4-14, an excerpt from James Joyce's *Ulysses*: essentially this `<hr />` is an example of a lightweight structural section separator.

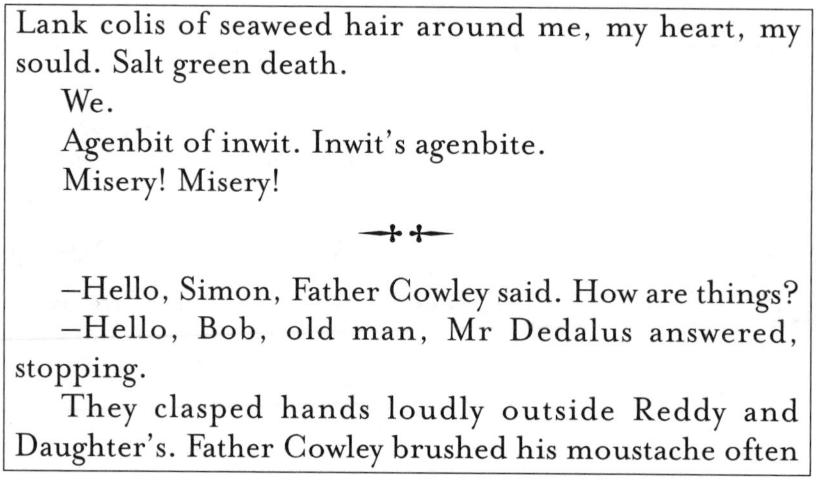

> Lank colis of seaweed hair around me, my heart, my sould. Salt green death.
>
> We.
>
> Agenbit of inwit. Inwit's agenbite.
>
> Misery! Misery!
>
> —+ +—
>
> —Hello, Simon, Father Cowley said. How are things?
>
> —Hello, Bob, old man, Mr Dedalus answered, stopping.
>
> They clasped hands loudly outside Reddy and Daughter's. Father Cowley brushed his moustache often

Figure 4-14. If an <hr /> is good enough for James Joyce, it's good enough for us.

As this example shows, the <hr /> can take a variety of forms, in this case an elegant, decorative separator. As XHTML evolves and new tags are introduced, we hope to see a replacement for <hr /> in the form of a <separator /> element that clearly reflects a more flexible structural use. This would allow, for example, for its use as a vertical separator for languages written vertically, such as Japanese. For now, however, we're happy to use <hr /> where it's appropriate as a section separator.

A note on self-closing tags

As you already know, an element consists of a start tag, some content, and an end tag. You also know that, when writing XHTML, you must close a tag whenever you open it. For example, if you open a <p> to mark up a paragraph, you must close it with a </p> at the end of your paragraph.

There are, however, a few HTML elements that can't hold any content within them and consequently never had a closing tag; some examples include
 (line break), <img> (image), and <hr> (horizontal rule).

With the stricter rules of XHTML, in particular the insistence that all tags must be closed, the elements that didn't have closing tags in HTML are now treated as self-closing in XHTML. We can make a tag self-closing by adding a space and a forward slash (/) to the end of the tag as in the following example:

```
<p>This is a paragraph. It opens and closes like most elements.</p>
<hr />
<p>The tag above is self-closing.</p>
```

Although the space before the forward slash is not required, some older browsers will get confused without it; in addition, it makes the markup a little easier to read, and therefore we recommend including it.

<code> and <pre>

There are a number of phrase elements useful for describing code samples—of particular use when you're a full-fledged Web Standardista and writing your own web pages with examples of coding best practice. In this section, we look at two: code and pre.

In Chapter 2 we briefly mentioned retaining white-space formatting when displaying poetry within a browser; we're revisiting that concept here in the context of writing code. Cue: the <pre> tag.

If we wanted to include a sample of code or markup in a web page, a very simple CSS declaration for instance, we first need to wrap the markup in some <code> tags that tell the browser that the enclosed contents are code. By default, the browser will render anything nested in <code> tags in the browser's default monospace font, helping to identify that text as an example of code. If we also want to retain the formatting—our white space, tabs, and indentations—we then need to wrap the code element in <pre> tags.

This is demonstrated in the following example:

```
<p>In CSS the following have an identical effect, displaying
paragraphs in red:</p>
<pre>
  <code>
    p { color: red; }
    p
    {
    color: red;
    }
  </code>
</pre>
```

This example renders in a browser as shown in Figure 4-15.

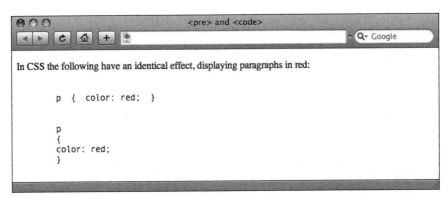

Figure 4-15. An example of code and pre used to display a code example in a browser

Marking up changes with <del> and <ins>

During the process of writing this book, we've made a number of changes as is only natural. One or the other of us writes some text, and then the other finds a better way of phrasing the same thing (or occasionally spots an error). We can use <del> (delete) and <ins> (insert) tags to indicate these changes clearly.

Take a look at the following example, which shows <del> and <ins> in action:

```
<p>Johnny Weissmuller donned Tarzan's loincloth for the last time
in <del>Tarzan and the Leopard Woman</del> <ins>Tarzan and the
Mermaids</ins> after serving 16 years in the role.</p>
```

Figure 4-16 shows how this example displays.

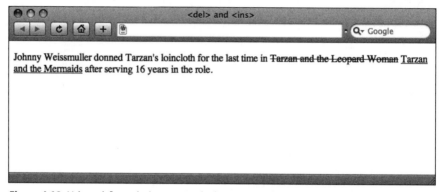

Figure 4-16. Using <del> and <ins> to track changes to a document's content

By default, browsers visually render anything enclosed in <del> tags with a strikethrough or a line through it, while underlining anything enclosed in <ins> tags.

The default underline style that browsers give the ins element is a little bit unfortunate. Most people see underlined text as links and might become frustrated when clicking your perfectly valid <ins> text. A good alternative to underlining is to use CSS to give your ins elements a background color (something that is easily achievable when you have a firm grasp of CSS).

<sup> and <sub>

The <sup> (superscript) and <sub> (subscript) tags have come under fire as being largely presentational; however, there *are* instances where you might wish to use them to add meaning to your markup. In this section, we take a look at some examples that use <sup> and <sub> to convey meaning. If you're a scientist, take note, this section's for you.

First, the superscript. Imagine the Pythagorean theorem without <sup> to supply those all-important squares. Or the classic slasher *Friday the 13th* (not to mention its countless sequels). Or what if you're French and you needed to refer to the abbreviated form of *Mademoiselle*? In all of these cases, <sup> is for you.

```
<p>x<sup>2</sup> * y<sup>2</sup> = z<sup>2</sup></p>
<p>Friday the 13<sup>th</sup></p>
<p>M<sup>lle</sup> Bardot</p>
```

Figure 4-17 shows these examples in action.

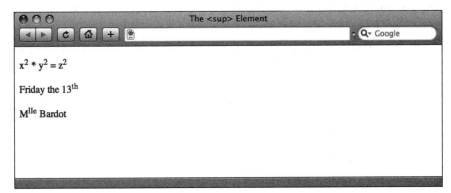

Figure 4-17. Some examples of <sup> in action

Now the subscript. Imagine you're a noted chemist and you're ordering a glass of water using only the language you know. You're really looking for a glass of H_2O, not H2O. Without a <sub>, you're not getting the water.

```
<p>H<sub>2</sub>O is the chemical formula for water. It should
never be confused with H<sub>2</sub>SO<sub>4</sub>.</p>
```

Figure 4-18 shows how this example appears in a browser.

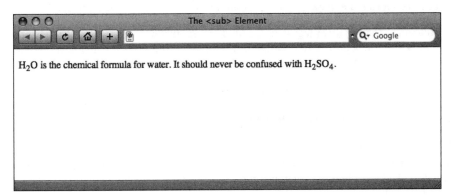

Figure 4-18. Example of <sub> in action

In all of the preceding examples, although the use of <sup> and <sub> is presentational, they convey information more clearly than adding a layer of style using CSS. Equally importantly, using <sup> and <sub> ensures our equations and other examples render as we intend them to, even with styling removed.

Summary

So what have we covered? In this chapter, we've explored a variety of methods of adding additional meaning to your markup. We've introduced two important methods of organizing and grouping information: using lists (unordered, ordered, and definition lists) and tables. The former will prove instrumental when we start to add navigation lists to our web pages and link them together.

Throughout the chapter, we've again stressed the importance of using meaningful markup. Finally, we introduced a variety of additional tags that no aspiring Web Standardista should be without.

We're now at a point where we can build complex web pages that are well formed and marked up semantically. Great news, but everything so far has been text based. By now, you're doubtlessly hungry for some imagery.

In the next chapter that's just what we'll cover. Onward.

Homework: Gordo's Adventure

Last chapter's web page for Miss Baker introduced a little more complexity than the humble web page you built for Albert I in Chapter 2. We've introduced a lot in this chapter and, although we're not demanding you use every single tag we've covered, we'd like you to include some of the important tags in another web page you'll create for noted space pioneer Gordo.

Once again, we'll provide you with all the information you need on Gordo. Your job will be to use the appropriate markup introduced in the chapter as and where you see fit.

In addition to the variety of tags you've added to your two web pages so far, this chapter's homework will include the following: both unordered and ordered lists, covering `<ul>`, `<ol>`, and `<li>`; and adding a quote using the `<blockquote>` and `<cite>` tags.

Once again, we encourage you to validate your web page when you've completed the homework using the W3C Markup Validation Service. Yes, you've guessed it, this is something you should be getting into the habit of doing.

1. Explore the content

As with the previous chapter's homework, we encourage you to read over the content first and get a feel for it before diving into the markup. You'll find this chapter's text file with facts on Gordo here:

www.webstandardistas.com/04/gordo.txt

Again, as you read the text, focus on where it might be appropriate to amplify the text's meaning through the inclusion of unordered lists and ordered lists, and where you'll be including the `<blockquote>` and `<cite>` tags.

Of course, you'll be adding headings and paragraphs, but by now we expect you to do that as a matter of course.

2. Adding unordered lists

We've added a number of facts about Gordo's flight, detailing his reentry speed, his flight's launch time, how long he was weightless for, and his total journey time—a historic 15 minutes. These short lists of facts are the perfect place to introduce unordered lists.

Take a look at the content and, using `<ul>` and `<li>` tags as appropriate, mark up the unordered lists on the Gordo web page.

Once again, we've created a file for you to refer to. Using your browser's View Source menu command, you can look at how we've structured our matching web page for King Kong here:

    www.webstandardistas.com/04/king_kong.html

3. Structuring the references

Our list of references at the bottom of Gordo's page lends itself to being marked up as an ordered list of references using `<ol>` and `<li>` tags. Again, you can refer to our King Kong page for guidance.

It's worth noting that at this point we're simply referencing our sources, as all good students should; we're not including links. We'll add links to these references in Chapter 6 when we introduce links properly.

4. Marking up a block quote

Your Gordo page has a quotation by Donald "Deke" Slayton, one of the original Mercury Seven NASA astronauts. Using the `<blockquote>` and `<cite>` tags, mark this quotation up, citing Deke Slayton as the source.

5. Check for errors

As outlined in the previous chapter's homework, this is a good to time to avail yourself of the W3C Markup Validation Service to check you've got everything right. If as a result of the added complexity of the page you're seeing the dreaded red banner, don't—repeat don't—put it to the back of your mind. Fix the problems and revalidate.

If we're mentioning this again, it's simply to emphasize that using the validator will save you problems later and in the process will add to your understanding.

When you're error free, feel free to put the kettle on and enjoy a cup of *Russian Caravan* as you prepare yourself for the next chapter!

Ever since Mosaic integrated the display of images within web pages in 1993, imagery has been a cornerstone of the Web. They say a picture is worth a thousand words. Good news then: this is the chapter where we introduce a few thousand words through the inclusion of just a few well-chosen images.

This chapter is designed to give you a working knowledge of using images, introducing you to some fundamental concepts. We focus in particular on a variety of means of *compressing* your images for faster download online, an aspect that is once again emerging as an important consideration as we witness the rapid growth of the mobile Web, accessed via increasingly powerful mobile devices.

We'll introduce you to the three main image formats used online—JPG, GIF, and PNG—and explain why you'd select different image formats for different types of imagery. We'll also show you the HTML you'll need to use to include your images, introducing you to some additional image attributes that, though not strictly necessary for your images to display, are de rigueur for any aspiring Web Standardista.

Before we get started, a word of warning. *Contrary to popular opinion, the imagery you find online isn't free for you to copy at will.* It's a common misconception that everything found on the web is free to use because it's freely available. *It isn't.* The chances are that the image you've fallen in love with that you found online belongs to *someone* and, unless stated otherwise, is *copyright protected.* If you're not absolutely certain an image is free to use, don't use it. Simple.

If creating compelling imagery isn't your strong point, don't worry. There are a number of free or low-cost image resources on the Web at hand. We'll introduce you to some of these at the end of the chapter.

So, now that we've got the copyright issue out of the way, let's get started including images in our well-structured web pages.

Introducing the <img /> tag

Including images in your web pages isn't difficult; all it requires is the introduction of one additional tag: the <img /> tag. In this section, we introduce you to this tag and its attributes, starting you on your visual journey on the Web.

The best way to show you how the <img /> tag is used, particularly to underline the aspect of *linking to images,* is to get straight into a practical example and look at how the markup is constructed.

An <img /> tag in action

The minimum markup we need to display an image on a web page is as follows:

```
<img src="king_kong.jpg" />
```

Before we look at this element in a little more detail, it's worth noting that the `<img />` tag, like the `<hr />` tag we introduced in Chapter 4, is a *self-closing tag*. As we've covered before, the closing " `/>`" (space, trailing slash, and angle bracket) are important for our XHTML pages to validate.

> As with all inline-level elements, the `img` element must be nested in a block-level element in order for your pages to validate.
>
> Until your markup options increase we suggest enclosing images within an opening `<p>` and a closing `</p>` tag as you'll see in our reference examples for this chapter.

So, what does the preceding markup do? In a nutshell, it provides a reference to where the image is stored in relation to the HTML file itself. This is a subtle, but important, point to note. Unlike, for example, the text in a p element, which is a part of our HTML file itself, the `img` element is used to add *references to images*, not the *actual images themselves* (i.e., the images are stored separately from the HTML file and referenced by it).

When a browser encounters a web page with links to images, it builds the page by following the links supplied within the `<img />` tag, retrieving the images from the server, and rendering the page in its entirety. So, your web page and the images that are included on it are separate files.

In short, the markup points the browser to the source of the image we'd like it to display. This is referenced in the `src` attribute which, in the preceding example, instructs the browser to look for a file called `king_kong.jpg` and display it. Without the information in the `src` attribute, the browser has no way of knowing where the image file you want to display is.

The example assumes that your image file (`king_kong.jpg`) is in the same folder (or directory) as your web page.

> We will cover how to link to files and images in different folders when we introduce you to linking and organizing files in the next chapter.

Although it's possible to include an image using just the `src` attribute as in the short example earlier, we also need to include an `alt` attribute for our page to validate as in the following example:

```
<img src="king_kong.jpg" alt="The mighty King Kong, a fearsome
giant ape." />
```

Figure 5-1 shows the image of King Kong included on a web page using the preceding markup.

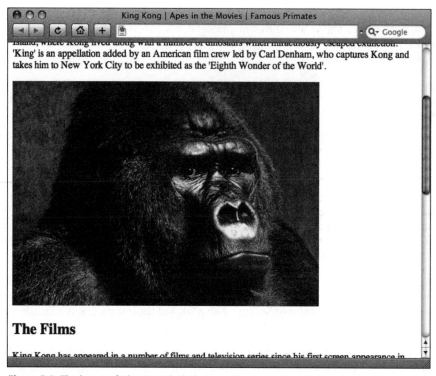

Figure 5-1. The image of King Kong included on our page as displayed in a browser

Although the alt attribute is not required to *display* our image, it is helpful for visually impaired users, and as such you should get into the practice of using it. Supplying an alt attribute is required when creating valid pages and has the added bonus of making your pages more accessible for assistive devices like screen readers. Lastly, the alt attribute provides useful text for search engines to index your page.

The text of your alt attribute is also displayed in a number of browsers when a user browses your web page with images switched off, for example, by someone browsing the Web on a nonbroadband, dial-up connection or over a mobile phone with a slow connection. Your alt attribute will also display in Firefox and some other browsers as the image is being downloaded, useful for images of a large file size that might take longer to download.

It's important to stress that your alt text is intended to be used *instead* of your image, and is not intended to provide additional information about the image. The example in Figure 5-2 shows an alt attribute in action when images have been switched off.

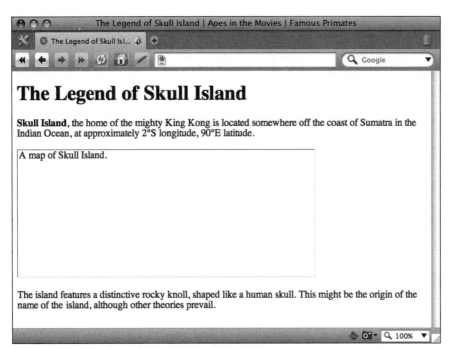

Figure 5-2. Opera, a standards-compliant browser, displaying "A map of Skull Island."—the contents of our alt attribute as an alternative when images are switched off

When writing alt attributes, try to use meaningful language, for example, alt="The mighty King Kong, a fearsome giant ape." is better than alt="Image", and alt="ACME Widgets - Return to Home Page" is better than alt="Logo". This is particularly important in the latter of these two examples, where an image of a company logo is also serving a navigational purpose. Visually impaired users using assistive software like screen readers rely on this information, so ensure you give your alt text some thought.

Put yourself in the shoes of a visually impaired user using a screen reader and try to employ descriptive language that illustrates the images you're using. The bottom line is to ask yourself whether the image is a type of content (in which case you should use a descriptive alt attribute) or only serves a decorative or presentational purpose (in which case an empty alt attribute is better).

There may be occasions where an image serves purely decorative purposes, for example, as a decorative banner, where an alt attribute doesn't contribute much meaning to a visually impaired user. However, in most cases where images serve a purely decorative or presentational purpose, they should be handled with CSS.

If your image *is* purely decorative, it is advisable to use an empty alt attribute, with no space between the quotes, as in the following example:

```
<img src="banner.jpg" alt="" />
```

Although an alt attribute can contain up to 1,024 characters (including spaces), it's best to keep your description short and to the point. Again, consider the impact of your alt text on visually impaired users: listening to a lengthy and over-detailed description might prove frustrating.

So now you know you need to include an alt attribute whenever you add an image to a page. However, there are a number of additional image attributes the true Web Standardista should use. We introduce these in the next section.

Adding width, height, and title attributes to images

In the last section, we introduced you to the minimum markup required to display an image on a web page. As you'll see here, we're now adding to our earlier example to include some additional information about the image:

```
<img src="king_kong.jpg" width="500" height="350" alt="The mighty
King Kong, a fearsome giant ape." title="King Kong contemplates
scaling yet another tall building." />
```

The width and height attributes tell the browser what width and height our image is in pixels. Although these aren't strictly required to display our image, it's good practice to use them. By supplying the browser with the image's width and height, it can allocate space for the image as the page renders, often before the image has fully downloaded; this stops the page from jumping about when loading.

The word pixel *is a 1960s' abbreviation of the term* picture element—*a useful fact worth storing mentally for your next pub quiz.*

The title *attribute* (not to be confused with the <title> *tag* we introduced you to in Chapter 2) is intended for the supply of additional information about our image. In a visual browser, it is usually displayed as a tooltip as in Figure 5-3.

The title attribute is not strictly required, and, if you need to provide additional information about an image, we suggest the use of a caption in a <p> tag beneath the image itself where users can read it without relying on a tooltip. After all, if you're supplying additional information that's important to the understanding of the image, you probably want to make this more accessible within the content of the page itself rather than hidden in a tooltip, which can be read only if a user mouses over an image long enough.

It's important to note that alt and title attributes serve different purposes as outlined previously. The former is intended for the supply of alternative text and is especially useful for accessibility purposes; the latter is intended for the supply of additional information. Don't confuse the two, a mistake beginners often make.

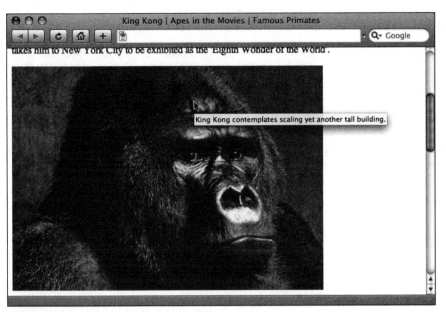

Figure 5-3. A browser displaying the contents of a `title` attribute as a tooltip

Perhaps one reason beginners get confused lies with Internet Explorer, which incorrectly displays the content of the alt attribute as a tooltip unless a `title` attribute is specified. This leads many to believe the alt attribute is for displaying tooltips. It isn't. It's for providing a text alternative to an image. Think "improving accessibility," not "nice little tooltip."

Working with images

In this day and age of low-cost digital cameras and easy-to-use scanners, it's easier than ever to find images for your web site. Plug in your digital camera or fire up your scanner, import your images, and go.

In fact, it's a little more complicated than that. As you'll see in the upcoming text, there are a few stages you'll need to go through to create web-friendly images—images that download quickly and, equally importantly, look good. While these stages are important, nothing's too complicated, and we'll walk you through the process of optimizing your images step by step as we progress through the chapter.

We looked previously at how you add images to your web pages using the <img /> tag and its various attributes. Now we'll explore some practical aspects of working with images, in particular editing them so that they're in the right size and optimized for delivery on the Web. To do this, we'll need to look at some image editors.

Which image editor? (Or how long is a piece of string?)

Which image editor you choose depends upon a number of factors, primarily driven by what you need to achieve. In this section, we suggest some alternatives that range from paid-for software that allows for a more comprehensive approach to image editing to free software with a few limitations. Which option you choose depends upon both what you need to achieve and what you're willing to spend on software.

In the upcoming text, we outline the benefits of three options: Photoshop, Fireworks, and Photoshop Express, before concluding the section with an introduction to GIMP (GNU Image Manipulation Program) and a list of alternative image editors you might also like to try that range in price from free to low cost.

If you're simply importing photographs from a digital camera, scaling them, and making minor adjustments, Adobe's free web-based Photoshop Express is more than ample for your needs and has a very shallow learning curve. It also provides you with an ample set of tools to make basic image adjustments and, equally importantly, to resize and crop photographs and save them at specific sizes.

If, however, you need a more extensive range of tools, in particular the ability to work with type or nonphotographic images—logos or illustrations, for example—Photoshop and Fireworks are better suited to your needs, as they allow for extensive image creation and manipulation.

We've used Photoshop to illustrate some of our examples; however, if you're approaching the book from a position where access to expensive software is an issue, you can still experiment with one of the lower-cost alternatives we recommend at the end of this section.

The bottom line? The basic principles we cover in this chapter are applicable across the range of image editors available. We're focusing on the fundamentals in this chapter; if you're not using the image editor we're using, don't worry, the principles will remain the same.

Photoshop

As long as the Web has been in existence, Photoshop has been one of the leading applications for creating and manipulating imagery for web-based delivery. This is one reason why so many alternative image-editing applications follow the majority of its interface metaphors.

Despite its name, Photoshop is useful for much more than extensive manipulation of photographic imagery. It also features a number of tools for the creation of images from scratch—both photographic and *nonphotographic*.

This becomes important as you start to consider including nonphotographic imagery on your web site. For example, when we needed to create the typographic brand for our Famous Primates web site, we turned to Photoshop.

One drawback of Photoshop is price, but as the old saying goes, you get what you pay for; while its true that Photoshop is expensive, it's also extremely versatile and powerful.

Throughout this chapter, we've used Photoshop to illustrate our examples; however, as we've stated earlier, the basic principles we're covering apply regardless of preferred software.

Fireworks

A less expensive alternative to Photoshop that offers a slightly different approach, but is certainly worth exploring, is Adobe's Fireworks. Formerly developed by Macromedia, but now part of Adobe's stable, Fireworks is a credible alternative for creating graphics for use on the Web and has a loyal following among web developers.

Fireworks takes a hybrid approach, integrating both bitmap and vector tools in one package, allowing you to create and edit both bitmap images and vector objects with tools that are familiar to both image formats in an integrated environment.

Although the focus of this chapter is on raster images (images made up of pixels), in the section "Vector graphics," we give you a brief introduction to this other image type.

Photoshop Express

Throughout this book, we've emphasized an approach that embraces the use of free tools, ensuring a low barrier to entry. With this in mind, we felt it important to include an image editor with a price point set at zero. Luckily for you, you can now tap into Adobe's web-based Photoshop Express, 100% free. That's right, an exorbitant $0.00 (£0.00, €0.00, ¥0.00). Good news indeed. You can access Photoshop Express at

    www.photoshop.com

About this tool, Adobe states "You shot it—now do something to it. Make it pop. Make it impossible to ignore. Upload, sort, polish . . . all for free. Resize, tint, distort, and more—add your mark to all your images."

Believe it or not, this isn't marketing hype; it's true. As broadband has taken off and the Web has evolved, web-based applications like Photoshop Express have emerged as potential competitors to traditional desktop applications.

Despite its nonexistent price tag, Photoshop Express offers a great deal of potential for anyone wishing to experiment with basic image manipulation. Like Apple's iPhoto, the emphasis is on ease of use with one-click options to reduce red eye, adjust exposures, and touch up images. The best way to get a feel for it is to create an account and get started.

It gets better: Adobe has even provided a full set of video tutorials to get you started. You can find these tutorials here:

    www.photoshoponline.com

One key limitation of Photoshop Express is that it is an image *manipulation* program, not an image *creation* program. If you need to create images for your web site from scratch, for example, section headers using custom type, you'll need to use Photoshop or Fireworks, or try one of the other programs listed next.

Bring out the GIMP (and its friends)

Reading the preceding text, you might be mistaken for thinking that Adobe is the only company that offers image editors suitable for web development. Not so. There are a number of alternatives available that are worth mentioning and are also considerably less expensive.

So why have we have used Photoshop to illustrate our examples? The answer is that all of the applications we suggest in this section are built using similar user interface metaphors to Photoshop. All follow very similar approaches to image editing; indeed at first glance their tools and working environments are all very similar.

GIMP, primarily developed for Linux, a platform for which Photoshop was never available, is an open source alternative to proprietary image-editing software. While it has the complexity and many of the features of Photoshop, a number of other image-editing applications offer similar features that are more accessible and beginner friendly.

We've listed a number of these alternatives—for a variety of platforms and potential uses—here. These vary in complexity, features, and price; all are detailed at the respective applications' web sites.

Regardless of the application you choose—free, low cost, or fully featured—we've focused on the basic principles of creating imagery for use on the Web throughout the chapter. At the end of the day, the fundamental principles—image size, image resolution, and compression formats, to name but a few—are the important aspects to focus on.

As free or low-cost alternatives to Photoshop and Fireworks, we recommend Pixelmator or Acorn if you're using a Macintosh, or GIMP or Photoshop Elements if you're running Windows. If your platform is a flavor of Linux, GIMP will probably not intimidate you; however, Pixel is also worth considering.

You can find links to all of these applications at the Web Standardistas web site:

www.webstandardistas.com/tools

Image optimization

While you've seen that it's not too difficult to insert images into your web pages, you first need to convert them to a web-friendly format. If you haven't yet met, welcome to the wonderful world of pixels.

A number of different image formats optimized for web delivery are available to the aspiring Web Standardista, all having different strengths and weaknesses. Picking the right image type for the job is important when designing your web pages. In this section, we guide you through the maze of image types available, highlighting when and where to use different formats (and when and where not to use them).

JPG or, in full, JPEG (Joint Photographic Experts Group), GIF (Graphic Interchange Format), and PNG (Portable Network Graphic)—trust us, you don't need to remember any of these full terms—all have different uses. All, however, share one common feature: they allow for varying levels of image compression, resulting in faster image downloads.

Why compressing your files is important

When delivering images online, compression is important. You've no doubt encountered web pages that take an eternity to download; waiting for the page to load feels a little like watching paint dry. You can help to alleviate this problem, especially when creating a web page that features a lot of images, by using image compression to reduce the amount of information that needs to be transferred from the server to the user's browser. The goal is to reduce the size of your image files as much as possible while retaining as high a quality as possible.

All of the image types we briefly introduced previously allow for varying levels of compression, resulting in faster downloads, and each uses a different compression algorithm suited to a different type of imagery, photographs or illustrations, for example.

The compression of images for delivery online might not seem important now as we enter a phase of broadband delivery, where everything appears to download instantly. However, the web pages we're building in this book are *also* optimized for delivery on nondesktop media, for example, mobile phones and PDAs, where download speeds aren't quite so fast (see Figure 5-4).

Figure 5-4. The same web page delivered to a desktop browser and to an iPhone

Mobile phones—the iPhone in particular—have broadened the appeal of the Web beyond desktop computers, and when delivering to mobile platforms, image compression is important. Imagine this scenario: you love your breakthrough Internet communication device, and you use it all the time. You'd like every page you download to be lean and mean and load as fast as possible. Cue compression.

Take a look at the two images side by side in Figure 5-5. To the naked eye, there isn't much difference between the two; however, one of the images is almost six times smaller than the other.

Figure 5-5. Two images, barely distinguishable; however, the one to the right is a sixth of the size of the other

Both of the JPG images in Figure 5-5 are saved at different levels of compression. The first image is 160K, the second is 28K. Although the images look almost identical to the naked eye, the 28K image will download almost six times faster than the 160K image. If viewed on a mobile phone, with an expensive data contract, the 160K image will cost almost six times as much to download and view. Clearly, you'd rather be downloading the smaller image.

Efficient compression of images isn't just aimed at browsing the Web via mobile phones, however; it's of importance on any platform. Smaller file sizes result in faster downloads, and this makes for a better user experience, something you should strive for.

In the following section, we cover the benefits of the different image compression formats we've mentioned and identify when and where best to use them.

Save for Web

One major advantage that Photoshop, Fireworks, and GIMP offer is the ease with which you can optimize images for delivery on the Web. This feature, known as Save for Web and Devices in Photoshop, is also available as a Save for Web plug-in for GIMP and is built into Fireworks' interface.

As its title suggests, Save for Web is designed specifically for optimizing images for delivery on the Web and makes the image optimization process a simple and relatively painless one. The ability to allow real-time previews of images as you alter image formats and compression settings sets Photoshop, Fireworks, and GIMP apart from most other image-editing applications when optimizing images for web delivery.

Image formats for the Web

Welcome once again to the abbreviation minefield: JPG, GIF, and PNG. All are image formats. All are suited for specific uses. In this section, we cover each image type, introducing you to each format's specific uses.

JPG: Photographs

As Joint Photographic Experts Group, the full term for JPG, indicates, this format is primarily intended for the display of photographic imagery.

JPG is a lossy format, which means that when you save an image as a JPG, the file doesn't store all the data included in the original image. Instead, the compression format tries to discard any information that isn't needed, removing information that is difficult to distinguish by the human eye.

This compression makes the file size much smaller, but it also means that each time you open, edit, and save a JPG file, the quality of your image reduces. This is one of the reasons it's advisable to work from an original file and save your resized or edited images as copies, leaving the original file untouched. If you later need to make some tweaks to your image, you can start again from your high-quality original.

When optimizing imagery for the Web, you always have to make a choice between image quality and file size. A high-quality image that looks great results in a larger file size, which takes longer to download. Saving your image at a lower quality setting, with more compression, results in a smaller file size, which will download more quickly. When saving a JPG through Photoshop's Save for Web and Devices feature, you can experiment with various levels of compression, either by choosing one of the presets (Low to Maximum) or by manually changing the Quality settings as in the example in Figure 5-6.

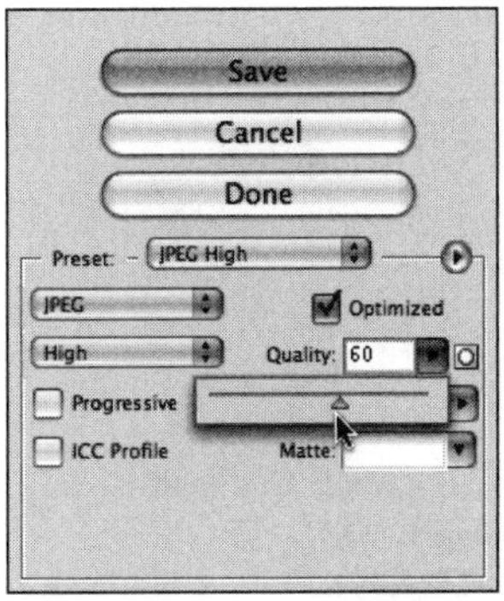

Figure 5-6.
Photoshop's Save for Web and Devices feature (File ➤ Save for Web and Devices)

Photoshop's Save for Web and Devices feature also discards any additional information about the image that isn't absolutely necessary to display it. In particular, this includes any Exchangeable Image File (EXIF) format data—metadata about the photograph, saved when the photograph was taken—including the date and time a photograph was taken, the camera that was used to take the photograph, shutter speed, and other related information.

Using the 2-Up view as in Figure 5-7, you can compare the visual quality of your original image with your optimized version. As you change the Quality setting to a lower value, you will notice how the file size, displayed below the image, is reduced.

Figure 5-7. Photoshop's 2-Up view allows us to compare the quality and file size of our original image alongside the optimized version.

Figure 5-8.
An example of JPG artifacts in a photograph

The trick is to find a good balance between file size and image quality. As each image is different, you will need to use your eye and your judgment to determine where this balance lies. The danger in compressing an image too much is that the compression can become evident through what is known as artifacts—groups of pixels where too much information has been discarded in the compression process—as shown in the example in Figure 5-8.

As we noted earlier, JPGs are perfect for the compression of photographic images. They are not, however, the perfect choice for graphics or type. Let's repeat that because it's important: JPGs are not the perfect choice for graphics or type. If you need to work with type or graphic imagery—a logo or a graphic banner, for example—a far better choice of image type is GIF or PNG. We introduce you to GIFs and PNGs in the upcoming text.

Using the JPG format to compress graphic images, especially type, results in unsightly artifacts—an effect like a halo of pixels—which you can see in Figure 5-9. Not only does this look extremely unsightly, but it's also a definite no-no for the Web Standardista.

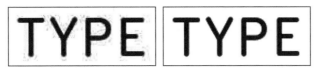

Figure 5-9. The example on the left shows unsightly artifacts when using the JPG format to compress type. The example on the right, saved as a PNG instead, has no artifacts. The images are enlarged for clarity.

GIF: Graphics and type

As the full term for GIF, Graphic Interchange Format, suggests, this format is intended for the display of primarily graphic imagery: type, logos, line drawings, and icons, for example.

The GIF color palette has a maximum of 256 colors (or 8 bits), a much more limited color palette than the JPG color palette, which is capable of displaying up to 16 million colors. However, GIFs are better suited to displaying images containing large areas of solid color and are perfect for compressing and optimizing logos or type.

GIF is a lossless format, that is, no image data is lost when saving images containing 256 colors or fewer. This means it's possible to resave a GIF over and over again without further loss of data.

GIFs are well suited for images with a limited number of solid colors; essentially the algorithm looks for repeated patterns of pixels and compresses this information. One method of reducing the file size of a GIF is to reduce the number of colors it contains. In Photoshop, the Color Table shows how many colors your image contains. You can adjust this number in the Colors drop-down menu as shown in Figure 5-10.

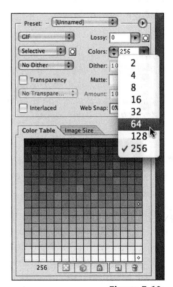

Figure 5-10.
GIF Color Table for Photoshop's Save for Web and Devices feature

Again, how many colors you choose to use is a trade-off between file size and quality. A full-color logo saved as a 256-color GIF might look great, but will result in a larger file size. The same logo saved as a 4-color version will probably look too pixilated and blocky. The best result will probably be to reduce the number of colors to somewhere in between, creating an image that looks great but is also a smaller file. As with JPG compression, the trick lies in getting the balance of compression and image quality right.

GIF also allows for dithering of colors, a method of adding patterned or random pixels to the image, which fools the eye by making it appear that the image contains more colors than are actually in the palette. Using dithering allows you to reduce the color palette further, bringing the file size down even more. However, it's worth noting that if your image contains 256 colors and you need dithering to make the image look reasonable, you might be better off saving the image as a JPG or a PNG-24, which we cover after this discussion on GIFs.

One thing GIFs are not intended for is photographic imagery. With a maximum of 256 colors, photographs do not reproduce well as GIFs. Should you need to compress photographs, use the JPG format.

GIFs have 1-bit transparency, that is, we can pick one color within the image's color table and set it to be transparent, allowing the background on which the image is sitting to show through. However, 1-bit transparency has limitations, especially where we need an image to blend seamlessly with the background as in Figure 5-11.

Figure 5-11. The limitation of 1-bit transparency

If blending an image to the background on which it sits is important, we recommend the PNG-24 format; however, it has some limitations as we outline in the next section.

> *An additional feature supported by the GIF format is simple frame-by-frame animation. The hottest thing on the Web in 1996, the novelty of animated GIFs has now, thankfully, worn off. However, there might be instances where animated GIFs are suitable, for example, for an advertisement banner or animated logo. More complex animations are better achieved using Adobe's Flash, which is beyond the scope of this book.*

So, to summarize, if you're working with graphics, logos, or text set in a particular type-face, choose GIF or PNG, which we cover next.

PNG: The new (old) kid on the block

Meet the new (old) kid on the block: PNG, or Portable Network Graphic. The PNG format, introduced in 1997 as a patent-free alternative to GIF, is suited to the same sort of imagery as the GIF format introduced in the last section. However, PNGs offer a number of distinct advantages over GIFs, notably a larger color palette and advanced transparency features.

As the advanced features of the PNG format have become more widely supported with the introduction of Internet Explorer 7, PNGs are proving a more desirable alternative to GIFs and are certainly worth considering.

PNG-8

In practical terms, a PNG-8 is almost identical to a GIF. It has a 256-color palette and is suitable for the same sorts of graphics covered in the discussion on GIFs (i.e., type, logos, line drawings, and icons).

Why use PNG-8 instead of the GIF format? In some cases, PNG-8 may prove more efficient than the GIF format. You can use Photoshop's Save for Web and Devices feature to compare sizes and select the appropriate format, as in the example in Figure 5-12. The bottom line: use the image format that looks best at the smallest file size.

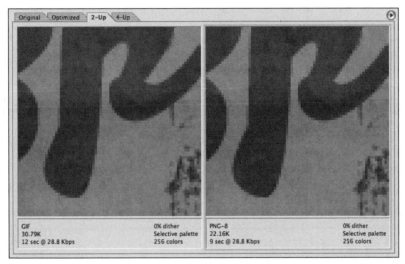

Figure 5-12. These two images are barely distinguishable; however, the PNG is smaller in file size.

PNG-24

Why use PNG-24 instead of PNG-8? The answer is that PNG-24 allows us to display millions of colors compared to PNG-8's limited 256-color palette. It also offers us full alpha transparency. But what exactly is full alpha transparency? Where GIFs or PNG-8s offer 1-bit transparency (i.e., one color is specified as being transparent) PNG-24 allows for more than one color to be transparent, allowing for seamless blends between an image in the foreground and the background of the page.

All this talk of transparency can be a little confusing, so it's best to explain it with an example. Take a look at the two images in Figure 5-13. The image on the left features a PNG-8 image, with transparency limited to a single color. The image on the right features a PNG-24 image, allowing for full alpha transparency. The resulting PNG-24 image allows for a seamless blend between the image in the foreground and the background of the web page.

Figure 5-13. Two images, saved using the PNG format. The image on the left is saved as a PNG-8, the image on the right is saved as a PNG-24.

This can be an extremely useful feature when you want a foreground image to blend into its background to create a particular design effect. However, a word of warning: PNG-24 might look like the answer to your dreams, but it results in files that are much larger than PNG-8s. Of more concern, however, is the fact that Internet Explorer versions 6.0 and earlier do not support full alpha transparency, as shown in Figure 5-14.

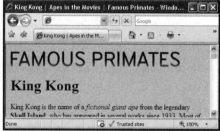

Figure 5-14. A PNG-24 with transparency rendered in Internet Explorer 6 and 7. In IE 6, on the left, the image background isn't transparent.

Given that IE 6 and its previous incarnations are old browsers being superseded by IE 7 and IE 8, this lack of support for transparency in PNG-24 images will hopefully be consigned to the dustbin of history. We felt it important to warn you of this browser shortcoming nonetheless.

A word of warning: images formatted as PNGs can sometimes cause display problems. A number of browsers, Internet Explorer 7 included, will not always exactly match a foreground image in PNG format with a background color specified in the CSS on which they are sitting. The result can prove frustrating with an image and a background color not quite matching up. If this specific scenario poses problems for you, we suggest saving your image as a GIF or JPG instead.

A pixel is a pixel is a pixel

You might have encountered discussion about the relative merits, or lack of, of saving your images for the Web at different resolutions, or dots per inch (dpi). Different authors will sing the praises of 72 dpi over 96 dpi, or vice versa. In fact, the resolution of your images makes no difference onscreen whatsoever. What does make a difference, however, is the dimensions—in pixels (px)—you generate your images at. Most image editors default to 72 dpi when creating new images—it's perfectly safe to leave this setting alone.

Size matters

We've looked at image compression to reduce the file sizes of your images. Another aspect of your images to consider is their actual dimensions—their width and height—in pixels. Although it's possible to resize images using the width and height attributes within the img element, it's not recommended.

Consider the following scenario. We have a JPG image of Cornelius, the noted chimpanzee archaeologist and historian. The original image supplied is 1600 × 1000 px; however, that's too large to fit into the layout we've designed. We really need the image to be 400 × 250 px to fit. In a moment of laziness, we decide not to scale the image down in our image editor and save a new smaller version. We opt instead to scale it down using the width and height attributes as in the following example:

```
<img src="cornelius.jpg" alt="The gifted Cornelius, a noted
chimpanzee scholar." width="400" height="250"
title="Cornelius ponders the meaning of life." />
```

Perfect. But is it? This will instruct the browser to scale down the original, large image and display it at a width of 400 px and a height of 250 px—just the size we want. While this might be convenient, there are a number of obvious downsides to this approach.

Forcing the browser to scale down a large image, while possible, results in longer download times and can also cause images to distort badly in many browsers. A better approach is to resize your images using an image editor so that they're sized to the width and height you need them to display.

Consider again browsing the Web on a mobile device with an expensive data plan. Scaling a 1600 × 1000 px image to 400 × 250 px forces users to download 16 times as much data, 16 times the cost—money they'd rather be spending on a mocha-choco-latte.

> *You might think that the larger image is only four times bigger, but you'd be mistaken. The large image comprises 1600 × 1000, or 1,600,000 pixels of data; the small image comprises 400 × 250, or 100,000 pixels of data, 1/16th smaller.*

The limitations of bitmaps

One of the downsides of using bitmap images that are by nature resolution dependent is the fact that they don't scale up very well. Scaling up bitmap images usually results in a loss of detail and quality. For this reason, when working with images, it's important to work with original images where possible, scaling them down to the size you require them at.

Take a look at the two close-ups of the mighty King Kong in Figure 5-15. The original on the left at 200 × 200 px is fine for use on the Famous Primates web site. When we scale it up to 800 × 800 px, however, it loses detail and quality.

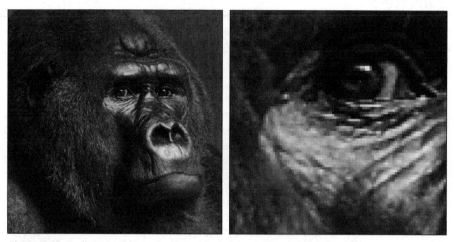

Figure 5-15. Scaling up a bitmap image results in a loss of image quality.

Unlike bitmap images, vector graphics can be scaled independently of resolution, as we cover in the following section.

Vector graphics

Unlike photographs or other bitmap images, vector graphics do not store pixel data; instead they describe images as a series of mathematical formulae using what are known as Bézier curves or paths.

Let's look at a simple example. Imagine you wanted to draw a line from the top-left corner to the bottom-right corner of a piece of squared paper. A bitmap image, which is essentially a grid of pixels, would draw this line using a series of pixels at a specified resolution, as in the example on the right in Figure 5-16. A vector image, however, would simply specify the start and end points of the line, irrespective of resolution.

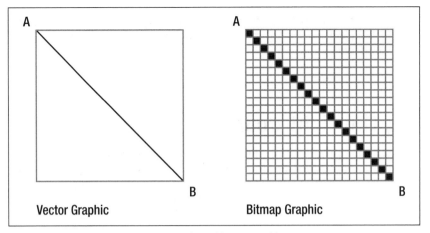

Figure 5-16. A vector graphic compared to a bitmap graphic

One advantage of vector graphics is that they aren't limited to the size they were created at like bitmap graphics are, as shown in Figure 5-17. Simple sets of instructions—draw a line from point A to point B, or connect four points to create a circle—vector graphics, which are resolution independent, can be scaled up or down to your heart's content. The instructions that make up the image remain the same, regardless of the size it is displayed at. As a result, vector images are often smaller in file size than bitmap images.

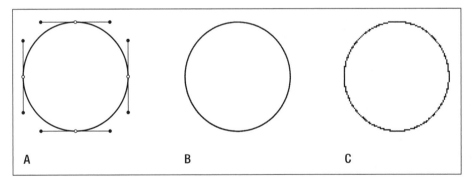

Figure 5-17. Vector images (A) are resolution independent, while bitmap images (B–C) are tied to the resolution they were saved at.

Vector graphics are often used for the creation of illustrations, logos, or typographic headers. Adobe Illustrator is specifically designed for the creation of vector graphics, although both Fireworks and recent versions of Photoshop have support for vector-based image creation.

One point worth noting is that vector images cannot be added to a web page using the <img /> tag; they need to be saved in a rasterized (bitmap), web-friendly format first in order to be displayed as an img within a browser.

> *Scalable Vector Graphics (SVG) is an open standard for displaying vector graphics on the Web. Support for this format is still uneven, with no native support from Internet Explorer.*

Finding the right image

Perhaps your photography isn't the best in the world, or you'd like to use an illustration, but your drawing skills aren't exactly up to scratch. Have no fear, there are a number of low-cost image resources on the Web sure to offer what you're looking for. In this final section, we introduce you to a few, paying particular attention to iStockphoto (www.istockphoto.com) and stock.xchng (www.sxc.hu), both resources we regularly use. Indeed, iStockphoto is the source of all of the famous primates photographs used in this book.

Low-cost images

Companies like iStockphoto and stock.xchng offer a variety of high-quality, but free or low-cost, images, perfect for most needs. If your budget is tight or even nonexistent you're likely to find something at either iStockphoto or stock.xchng that will suit your requirements without breaking the bank.

Allowing emerging photographers and illustrators to share their creative work with others, these sites have built up considerable libraries of images available in a variety of resolutions, ideal for use online. Easy to search and offering a huge variety of styles of photos that are, best of all, free or low cost—iStockphoto and stock.xchng are a perfect first port of call when you're looking for a specific image.

Flickr and Creative Commons

Another option worth considering when looking for images is Flickr (www.flickr.com). Many users of this popular photo-sharing site have licensed their photographs using what's known as a Creative Commons license, which allows you to use them freely under certain conditions.

Creative Commons (www.creativecommons.org), established in 2002, offers an alternative to full copyright, allowing content owners and content creators to offer their works under less restrictive licenses.

What this means in practice is that instead of an image having all rights reserved, making it illegal to use without permission, only some rights are reserved. For example, the creator allows you to use their image as long as you give them credit, or the author allows you to use the image for noncommercial projects only. In essence, Creative Commons offers a variety of different license models designed to expand the range of creative works available for others to build upon and to share legally.

Links to all of the preceding web sites and a variety of other online image resources can be found at the book's companion web site:

www.webstandardistas.com/resources

Summary

So what have we covered? In this chapter we've covered the fundamentals of adding images to the pages of your web site. We've introduced you to the `img` element, which is required to add images to a web page along with its various attributes. We've also introduced a number of image-editing applications and a variety of image formats designed for web delivery. Lastly, we've provided an overview of how to create imagery optimized for delivery on the Web.

In the next chapter we introduce you to links, the elements that make the Web the Web.

5

Homework: A picture is worth a thousand words

Over the last three chapters, you've created three web pages of progressively varying complexity for Albert I, Miss Baker, and Gordo. As you've worked your way through the homework, we've added a variety of elements to enable you to build web pages that have become progressively richer.

This chapter's homework is to add images to your three monkey pioneer pages.

> *We've worked with iStockphoto to enable us to supply you with photographs of all of our famous primates for your homework. Before you download and use these images, here's the small print!*
>
> *Although we're providing you with these images to enable you to undertake each chapter's task, the images remain the copyright of iStockphoto and may not be used for other purposes. iStockphoto is happy for us to offer you these images for educational purposes; however, should you plan on making your Famous Primates web site publicly available, you will need to purchase licenses for the images at a cost of just a few dollars. (Or, alternatively, replace them with images of your own.) We've put a Read Me! file containing the licensing details in the folder with the images.*

You'll be adding two images to each of your three monkey pioneer pages: at the top of the page, above the opening `<h1>`, you'll add the Famous Primates brand, and beneath the text that introduces each monkey you'll add an image of that particular simian.

Do we need to remind you to validate your pages when you're done? We thought not . . .

Once you've added the images to your web pages, the second part of your homework will involve researching some of the image editors we suggested in the chapter.

1. Get the images

As mentioned previously, to make your task a little easier and to save you having to track down all the images you'll need, we've added them all to a folder that we've compressed and zipped for you to download.

You can download the folder here; don't forget to read the Read Me! file:

> www.webstandardistas.com/05/primates.zip

2. Add your img elements

Using the examples provided in the chapter, add the Famous Primates brand and the illustrations of Albert I, Miss Baker, and Gordo to your web pages.

As usual, we've been working on the apes' side of the web site and have created a similarly structured page about King Kong, the Eighth Wonder of the World. You can refer to this, using your browser's View Source command to see how we've included our images, here:

> www.webstandardistas.com/05/king_kong.html

3. Test!

When you've completed the three pages, check them in your browser to ensure everything's working as expected.

4. Research

Research some of the image editors recommended earlier in the chapter. Remember, we've provided a link to some recommended tools at the Web Standardistas web site:

> www.webstandardistas.com/tools

Take a look at what each image editor offers and give Adobe's Photoshop Express a whirl; it won't even cost you a penny.

That's it! After you've explored the wonderful world of image editors, put the kettle on and enjoy a cup of *Chifir'* as you prepare yourself for the next chapter.

CHAPTER 6
CREATING LINKS WITH ANCHORS

Up to this point we've focused on creating well-structured web pages, marking up our content using the right tag for the job. We've introduced you to most of the tags you'll need to include text and images on your web pages. If you've been following along with the homework, you should by now be able to create quite complex web pages using structured markup. All good, but there's something distinctly lacking: **links**.

The Web is all about links; without them there would be no Web. By now you're aware that we're using HyperText Markup Language, but we've yet to create some actual **hypertext** to link our separate pages together. Have no fear; this is the chapter where we introduce you to links to enable you to do this.

The first two initials of HTML stand for HyperText—one word, two initials (because HML wouldn't sound as snappy). The *New Oxford American Dictionary* (Oxford University Press, 2005) states that hypertext "links topics on the screen to related information and graphics, which are typically accessed by a point-and-click method." This chapter introduces you to the point-and-click aspect of web design, or to be more specific, **anchors**.

What is an anchor? Simply put, an anchor is a means of tying together separate pieces of information. We can use anchors to link to other pages or resources on the Web, to other web pages within our web site, and even to different sections of the same web page, which is especially useful if we're creating a web page with a lot of information.

But how do we include anchors on our web pages? The answer is simple: we use the <a> tag, also known as the **anchor** tag, and its necessary attributes, which we introduce next. This chapter will enable you to link your carefully crafted web pages together to create a web site. Let's get started.

Meet <a>

What makes links important? The answer is that without hypertext links the Web wouldn't be the Web, it would simply be a collection of separate, unconnected pages. The W3C states the following:

> HTML offers many of the conventional publishing idioms for rich text and structured documents, but what separates it from most other markup languages is its features for hypertext and interactive documents. Although a simple concept, the link has been one of the primary forces driving the success of the Web.
>
> http://www.w3.org/TR/html401/struct/links.html

Links point the browser to a destination anchor, which can be any form of web resource: for example, an HTML document, a specific part of an HTML document, a link to an e-mail address, or even an image, a video clip, or a sound file. The following example contains a link in its simplest form: it has **link text**, in this case the word *Cheeta*, and a **destination anchor**, which is an HTML document named cheeta.html located at the domain www.famousprimates.com:

```
<a href="http://www.famousprimates.com/cheeta.html">Cheeta</a>
```

The a element instructs the browser we're linking to another piece of information, and the href attribute informs the browser of the location of that information. Without the href attribute, the browser wouldn't know where to look for the information we are linking to. By now you won't be surprised to learn that href stands for **hypertext reference**. It should also come as no surprise that the contents of the href attribute point to, or refer to, the address of the resource we're linking to.

Here is the preceding link again, but this time shown within a short paragraph of text to demonstrate how a browser differentiates ordinary, nonlink text from link text:

```
<p>Tarzan's sidekick,
<a href="http://www.famousprimates.com/cheeta_75.html">Cheeta</a>,
celebrates his 75th birthday, as he retires from the movie business.
</p>
```

The preceding example renders in a browser unstyled as in Figure 6-1.

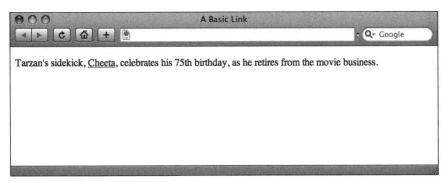

Figure 6-1. Our example link as it renders unstyled in a browser

As you can see, the default style for links in a visual browser is usually blue text with an underline. (As this is a book printed in black and white, you'll have to take our word that the link is, in fact, blue. Better yet, you can take a look at the page in color on the book's companion web site: www.webstandardistas.com/06/unstyled_links.html.) However, as we'll cover in Chapters 9 to 12, when we're adding style with CSS, we can change these defaults using a style sheet, switching off the underlining and changing the color of the link, should we wish to do so. We'll introduce you to how to do this in the second half of the book where we focus on CSS.

Using descriptive link text

As you saw in Figure 6-1, everything contained within the opening <a> and closing </a> tags is highlighted within the browser as a link, in this case the word *Cheeta*.

Our link text can be as long or as short as we like. However, it's good practice to use descriptive language when writing link text so that the user knows what to expect before clicking the link. Writing good link text is an important, yet often overlooked, part of the design process. Taking some time to write descriptive link text results in a more user-friendly site, something you should strive for.

Take a look at the following two examples. The first example doesn't give the user any indication of what they will find if they click the link, as the word *Cheeta* on its own doesn't offer much in the way of clues. It might link to a biography page about Cheeta, an image of Cheeta, or Cheeta's Wikipedia entry.

```
<p>Tarzan's sidekick,
<a href="http://www.famousprimates.com/cheeta.html">Cheeta</a>,
celebrates his 75th birthday, as he retires from the movie business.
</p>
```

The second example, however, uses language that clearly indicates what the user might expect to find at the link's destination, suggesting a page with a gallery of photos of Cheeta celebrating his momentous birthday.

```
<p>Tarzan's sidekick,
<a href="http://www.famousprimates.com/cheeta.html">Cheeta,
here seen celebrating his 75th birthday</a>, as he retires from the
movie business.</p>
```

Descriptive link text also holds significant weight in search engine rankings and is more valuable for search engines than generic phrases like "click here," for example.

Using descriptive link text is also important when the link might break with a user's expectations, for example, a link to a Microsoft Word document or another file type that might not necessarily open within a browser or might launch another piece of software.

Lastly, it's good practice to use clear link text when linking to large files, for example, a movie file. It's helpful to indicate the size of large files as in the following example so that a user has an indication of what they're committing to before clicking the link:

```
<p><a href="http://www.famousprimates.com/cheeta.mov">Watch Cheeta
as he relaxes during his retirement [QuickTime Movie - 8.4 MB]</a>,
on the beach in Florida.</p>
```

Another way of providing more detailed information about links is through the use of a title attribute, which we introduce next.

The title attribute

As with the `<img />` tag introduced in the last chapter, the `<a>` tag has a number of attributes that enable it to work its magic. As you now know, the bare minimum information we need to provide within an anchor is an href attribute, which informs the browser where the information we'd like to link to is located on the Web. We can provide a little more detail about the link, however, with the inclusion of a well-written and descriptive title attribute.

You may recall you met the title attribute in the previous chapter when we introduced adding images. In fact the title attribute can be used with all HTML elements except for a select few; however, it isn't strictly required for any. That this attribute can be used with so many elements—and isn't always—is probably one reason to explain why it's less than clear when to use it and what it's for. The W3C states that a title attribute is meant to offer "advisory information about the element for which it is set" (http://www.w3.org/TR/html4/struct/global.html#h-7.4.3). However, that advice is at best a little vague.

We established in the last chapter that the title attribute wasn't strictly required for our img elements and that, if you needed to add additional information to images, it might be better to include this through the use of a caption in a p element. With links you face a similar conundrum.

First and foremost, it's important to write descriptive link text; however, a well-written title attribute can also provide additional information to the user before they click a link that takes them to a destination they might otherwise not want to go to.

The following example expands on our link about Cheeta's retirement party to include a title attribute that gives the user a little more information about the link before they click it:

```
<p>Tarzan's sidekick,
<a href="http://www.famousprimates.com/cheeta_75.html"
title="Cheeta's 75th Birthday Party Photo Album">Cheeta,
here seen celebrating his 75th birthday</a>, as he retires
from the movie business.</p>
```

Although well-written link text is of more importance when creating links, the title attribute allows for the provision of additional information. In the preceding example, the title attribute clearly indicates the user will be taken to a photo album, information that isn't contained in the link text, but information that's useful nonetheless. The information contained within the title attribute will usually appear within a tooltip when the user mouses over the link as shown in Figure 6-2.

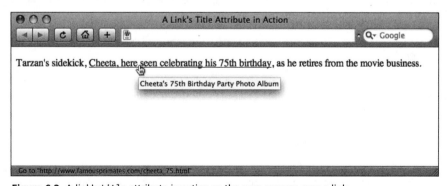

Figure 6-2. A link's title attribute in action as the user mouses over a link

Another important aspect of using the title attribute when creating links is that screen readers for the visually impaired can be set up to read out its contents; however, this is sometimes at the expense of the link text contained within the <a> tags. If you are designing specifically for users with accessibility issues, we strongly recommend a little further reading on this thorny topic. We've provided some links to get you started at the book's companion web site:

www.webstandardistas.com/resources

Let's create some links!

We mentioned briefly that links can be used to link to a variety of destinations. We now introduce you to a variety of examples: **external links** (to other web sites or resources on the Web), **local links** (to other pages within your own web site), **internal links** (links to specific areas within a web page itself), and, lastly, links to other types of resources (an e-mail link, for example).

In this section we introduce a number of different ways of linking to other resources online, showing you how to add links to your own web pages. Good news, we're about to start creating a properly linked-up web site.

External links

Now that you're familiar with the component parts of a link, you know that the address of the page we want to link to is contained within the href attribute. Let's take a look at creating a link to another web site *elsewhere on the Web* on one of our web pages.

> *From this point onward we'll be creating our link examples without* title *attributes. This is to ensure our markup is easier to read.*

If we wanted to link to Wikipedia's monkey page, for example, we can do this by adding the following markup to our web page:

```
<a href="http://www.wikipedia.org/wiki/monkeys">Wikipedia's
monkey page</a>
```

The href attribute in this example contains the full address, or Uniform Resource Locator (URL), of the web site we'd like to link to. Note that the link's address starts with http://— this informs the browser to look for this link on the Web (using the HyperText Transfer Protocol). For external links to other web sites *that we're linking to*, the http:// part is *essential to include*; without it the link will not work.

The preceding example is useful to give you an idea of what one particular example of a link looks like, but let's take it a bit further by creating a list of external links. You can use this to form the basis for a links page for the web site about famous monkeys and apes that you're building as part of the homework.

We'll link to a variety of files, including those for an image, a video, and a web page. Although this adds to the complexity, this will give you an idea of what a typical list of links looks like. While it might appear a little daunting at first glance, there's nothing in the following example that you haven't been introduced to. We're using an unordered list, or ul element, to give our list some added structure.

```
<h1>Famous Online Primates</h1>
<ul>
  <li><a href="http://www.explorepahistory.com/images/➥
  ExplorePAHistory-aOh2z2-a_349.jpg">
  Cheeta - Tarzan's Sidekick</a></li>
  <li><a href="http://www.youtube.com/watch?v= w3TwHW8ItAA">
  Son of Kong fights Giant Bear</a></li>
  <li><a href="http://classicgaming.gamespy.com/➥
  View.php?view=GameMuseum.Detail&amp;id=297">Donkey Kong -
  The Original Gaming Ape</a></li>
</ul>
```

You can see a more complete version of this example that demonstrates a number of external links in action on the following page at the book's companion web site:

www.webstandardistas.com/06/external_links.html

The dreaded ampersand and the validator

When validating your pages, you might at some point encounter an issue relating to URLs in links containing an ampersand (&) character. Including URLs containing ampersands in your links will lead to a frustrating and somewhat obscure error.

The reason is that the ampersand is a **reserved character** in XHTML and therefore needs to be **encoded**—replacing & with &—in order for your page to validate. As a consequence of this, the following markup is not valid:

```
<a href="http://www.webstandardistas.com/the_dreaded_&.html">
The Dreaded Ampersand</a>
```

This markup returns the following error message from the W3C Markup Validation Service: "You used an unescaped ampersand '&': this may be valid in some contexts, but it is recommended to use '&', which is always safe."

You'd be forgiven for wondering what this error message means—and whether or not ampersands are "safe" to use in URLs is another matter; however, if we replace the & with & in the preceding link, the page will validate:

```
<a href="http://www.webstandardistas.com/the_dreaded_&amp;.html">
The Dreaded Ampersand</a>
```

6

It's worth noting that you only need to encode the ampersand within the markup of your page. If you want to type the URL into the address bar of a browser, you should use the unencoded &.

The ampersand isn't the only character you need to encode when writing your markup. You also need to encode < with < and > with > when *not used as part of an HTML tag*. In short, wherever you use these characters when you're *not* creating tags, use their encoded versions as in the following examples.

The following will not validate:

```
<p>Cheeta & Bonzo Combined < King Kong</p>
```

The following, where the & and < are encoded, will validate:

```
<p>Cheeta &amp; Bonzo Combined &lt; King Kong</p>
```

With the < and > characters it's not just a case of passing validation, as some browsers might incorrectly interpret these as the start or end of an actual tag, which might cause rendering issues.

Forgive us for this brief interlude on the intricacies of reserved characters and character entities—now back to business.

Checking your links

Before going live with your web site, it's important to check that all of your links actually work. A simple error when typing in a link—a spelling mistake or a missing piece of punctuation, for example—can easily result in a link not working, which not only proves frustrating to your users, but is also a little embarrassing for the budding Web Standardista.

There are a number of free web-based tools that automatically check all the links on your web site or check links on a per-page basis. Our friends at the W3C, who provide the W3C Markup Validation Service, also provide one such free link-checking tool. We've provided some links to automated link checkers, including the W3C's, at the book's companion web site:

www.webstandardistas.com/resources

The (evil) target attribute

You'll see a number of resources online recommending the use of the target attribute, which can be used to open links to other web pages in a new window as in the following example:

```
<a href="http://www.wikipedia.org/monkeys" target="_blank">
Wikipedia's Monkey Page</a>
```

Including a `target="_blank"` attribute opens a new (blank) window and loads the page you are linking to into it, leaving your web site still open in a window beneath the new window.

Don't be tempted to use the target attribute. Not only is it forbidden in XHTML, but its use is also bad practice as it takes control away from your users. A better approach is to respect your users' wishes and allow them to decide how they'd like to access the links they click.

As tabbed browser interfaces have become increasingly commonplace, users will often choose to open your link in a new tab instead of within the current window. As a consequence, tabbed browsing is to an increasing extent rendering `target="_blank"` null and void, which is no bad thing.

Local links

Now it's starting to get interesting. Having a web page with external links is fine, but a little bit limited. What we really want are a few pages *of our own* all linked together. In other words, a web site of our own.

Imagine we've created a web page titled "Monkeys in Space" to link to all our space monkey pages, and we've named this HTML file monkeys_in_space.html. We've also created another web page that we've named gordo.html with specific information on Gordo. (Does this ring a bell?) To create a link from the Monkeys in Space general overview page to the page specifically about Gordo, we can use the following markup:

```
<a href="gordo.html">All you ever needed to know about Gordo,
one of the first monkeys in space.</a>
```

Assuming both web pages are stored in the same folder or directory, you can see creating the link is as simple as putting the file name of the file you'd like to link to in the `href` attribute. Note that a local link *does not* contain either the `http://` or the full domain name, just the name of the file linked to.

> *We will cover how to link to pages and resources that are not all in the same folder in the "Linking between different folders in our site" section in this chapter.*

You can see a more complete version of the preceding example that demonstrates a number of local links in action on the following page at the book's companion web site:

www.webstandardistas.com/06/local_links.html

Use View Source to get a feel for how the links work to link the separate pages together.

6

Internal links

Although most commonly used for linking *different* web pages together, the a element can also be used to point to specific sections *within a current document or web page*. This can be useful if you've created a long web page with a lot of related information on it.

For example, imagine we've created a long page titled "Apes in the Movies." We might have a section on King Kong, another section on Cheeta, and yet another section on Cornelius. As you can imagine, by the time we include biographical details on our various ape thespians, this page might become quite long.

Using well-structured markup, we've headed the page with an h1 element and headed each of the ape's separate sections with h2 elements. If we give each of these h2 elements an id attribute—a unique identifier that distinguishes each h2 from the other h2 elements on the page—we can link to them within the page's introductory text using internal links, as in the following example, which we explain in full afterward:

```
<h1>Apes in the Movies</h1>
<p>Many famous apes have been featured in the movies.
Some of the most noted include: <a href="#king_kong">King Kong</a>,
<a href="#cheeta">Cheeta</a> and <a href="#cornelius">Cornelius</a>.
</p>
<!-- Imagine a lot of extra content here. -->
<h2 id="king_kong">King Kong</h2>
<p>King Kong is the name of a fictional giant ape from the legendary
Skull Island, who has appeared in several works since 1933...</p>
<!-- Imagine a lengthy section on King Kong here. -->
<h2 id="cheeta">Cheeta</h2>
<p>While inextricably associated in the public mind with
Tarzan, Cheeta as a character was a product of the movies,
never appearing in any of the original <cite>Tarzan</cite> novels by
Edgar Rice Burroughs...</p>
<!-- Imagine a lengthy section on Cheeta here. -->
<h2 id="cornelius">Cornelius</h2>
<p>Cornelius is a chimpanzee archaeologist and historian, appearing
in the original novel of <cite>Planet of the Apes</cite>, and also the
first three installments of the classic movie series of the same
name, from the 1960s and 1970s.</p>
<!-- Imagine a lengthy section on Cornelius here. -->
```

To denote that the links in the first paragraph of the page are internal links, that is, links to another point *on the page we're currently on*, the href attributes start with a # (hash) sign—followed by the section's unique identifier as indicated by its id attribute: in this case either #king_kong, #cheeta, or #cornelius.

These links will cause the browser to jump down to our King Kong, Cheeta, and Cornelius sections when we click their corresponding links within the opening paragraph. This is thanks to the unique identifier, or id attribute, we've added to the opening <h2> tags at the start of each section.

We can give *any* element on the page a unique identifier, or id attribute, allowing us the flexibility to jump from one section of the page to another. Among other things this allows us to create a link at the base of a long page of content that takes the user back to the top of the page as in the following example for the Cheeta page:

```
<h1 id="cheeta">Cheeta</h1>
<!-- Imagine a lot of extra content here. -->
<a href="#cheeta">Back to Top</a>
```

You can see this in action by using View Source at the book's companion web site:

www.webstandardistas.com/06/back_to_top.html

We can also combine internal links with local links, enabling us to link from one web page to a specific subsection of another web page within our site. Imagine we're on the Cheeta web page, but we want to create a link to the King Kong *section* of the Apes in the Movies web page. We can use the following markup to achieve this:

```
<a href="apes_in_the_movies.html#king_kong">Find out more
about King Kong.</a>
```

What this markup does is first tell the browser to go to the Apes in the Movies web page (apes_in_the_movies.html), and then look for the section on that page with the id of king_kong.

Without getting overly complicated—we'll cover the id attribute in greater depth in Chapter 10—each id is a unique identifier meaning that there's only one element on the Apes in the Movies web page with an id of king_kong. The use of unique identifiers allows us, among other things, to create this internal link.

You can see a more complete version of the preceding example that demonstrates internal links in action on the following page at the book's companion web site:

www.webstandardistas.com/06/internal_links.html

E-mail links

You've built your web site and you're happy with it, but you'd like some way for others who browse the site to contact you. One way to achieve this is with a link to your e-mail address. To create an e-mail link is simple, as shown in the following example:

```
<a href="mailto:primates@famousprimates.com">Get in touch
with the primates who run this site.</a>
```

As you can see, the content of this href attribute is slightly different from those that you've encountered so far. Instead of starting with http://, the e-mail link starts with mailto: followed by an e-mail address. When the user clicks this link, their e-mail application is launched with the e-mail address specified in the href attribute already entered in the To: field of the e-mail.

6

> *Spam alert! Putting your e-mail address on your web site can lead to a huge quantity of spam as spambots surf the Web looking for e-mail addresses to add to their databases.*

If you need to insert your e-mail address into a web page, a better approach would be to use a service like Hivelogic's Enkoder, a web-based application that converts your e-mail links into encrypted JavaScript code, which hides them from e-mail-harvesting robots while revealing them to real people. You can read more about the Enkoder at the book's companion web site:

www.webstandardistas.com/tools

Although JavaScript is beyond the scope of this book, if you've been following along with the homework, you should know enough by now to understand how to embed an "enkoded" e-mail link in your web site after you've looked at the preceding page. It's worth pointing out, however, that e-mail-harvesting robots are getting smarter by the day, and the only guaranteed way to ensure that your e-mail address does not end up in their claws is to not include your e-mail address on the page in the first place.

Another approach for allowing users to contact you would be to include a contact form on your web page. This requires a server-side script to parse the data entered on the form and e-mail it to you, a topic that's a little beyond the scope of this book. However, we wouldn't want to leave you feeling short-changed, so we recommend some web-based form creation tools at the book's companion web site:

www.webstandardistas.com/tools

Wrapping up

We've covered four types of links in this section:

- **An external link**: `<a href="http://www.wikipedia.org/monkeys">`
- **A local link**: `<a href="gordo.html">`
- **An internal link**: `<a href="#king_kong">`
- **An e-mail link**: `<a href="mailto:primates@famousprimates.com/">`

The first example, an external link, contains the full path to the file we want to link to on the Web. The second example, a local link, contains the path to the file we want to link to *in relation to the file we're linking from*. The third example, an internal link, links to a specific section of the page that the user is *currently on*. The last example, an e-mail link, allows users to contact us via e-mail.

Absolute vs. relative links

Absolute links or relative links, what's the difference? We touched on this previously, but it can be a confusing topic so we're focusing on it here.

Let's imagine Cheeta's neighbor at the Primate Sanctuary, Bonzo, needs to pass Cheeta's address details on to King Kong. Bonzo uses Cheeta's full address, providing everything needed to contact Cheeta: country, state, city, and so on—as in the following example:

Cheeta
The Primate Sanctuary
Palm Springs
CA
USA

This is similar to an **absolute link** and as a URL it might look something like the following:

```
<a href="http://www.usa.com/ca/palm_springs/➡
the_primate_sanctuary/cheeta.html">Cheeta's Address</a>
```

However, because Bonzo lives next door to Cheeta, he can use a shorter address, expressing Cheeta's location in relation to his own. Cheeta is his neighbor after all, so he uses the relationship between his house and Cheeta's, as in the following example:

Next door

This is similar to a **relative link**, and as a URL it might look something like the following:

```
<a href="next_door/cheeta.html">Cheeta's Address</a>
```

Both of the preceding methods point to the same location, so why use one rather than the other? Clearly the relative link is shorter, which is an added bonus, but the primary reason is that relative links become important as we begin to organize the different files that comprise the web site we're creating, gathering them together in logically structured folders, an exercise we embark on in the next section. As we start to link those files together to create our web site, you'll begin to appreciate the importance of using relative links.

Let's return to our friends Cheeta and Bonzo. But instead of being neighbors at the Primate Sanctuary, imagine they're files for the same web site. We could use absolute links every time we needed to link them together, but as you've seen in the preceding example, the absolute link is much, much longer than the relative link. It's much easier to create links between Cheeta and Bonzo using relative links.

But what if King Kong, from Skull Island, needed to get in touch with Cheeta? He certainly doesn't live next door to Cheeta. If King Kong needed to contact Cheeta, he'd need to use an absolute link.

There are certain situations where you need absolute links, and certain situations where you need relative links. As a rule of thumb, *use absolute links when linking to pages on someone else's web site, and use relative links when linking to pages on your own web site.*

6

The use of relative links will become more apparent as we start to structure our site in the following section.

Structuring your site

By now you should have a number of web pages and image files within your homework folder. Things are—dare we say it—starting to get a little messy.

In this section we focus on some methods of organizing your files that will allow you to plan for future growth. In particular we focus on tidying up your web site by organizing its different files into logical folders and adding an images folder where you'll gather the relevant images you're using for the site.

Keeping all your HTML files and images in one folder works as long as you have only a few files and one or two images in your site. But what happens if you have ten or twenty images and the number of web pages you've created starts to grow? The folder starts to become cluttered, and it can soon become hard to find what you're looking for. This is where a little organization comes into play.

Organizing your files and folders

Before your web site becomes large and complicated, it makes sense to spend a little time considering how to structure it so that you can organize your files and folders as you add them. Until this point, we've been working with all of our files—HTML pages and images—stored in one folder (or directory) as in Figure 6-3.

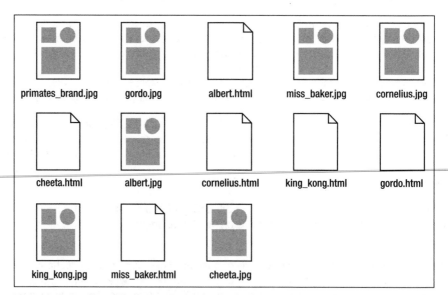

Figure 6-3. Our files as they're currently organized, all in one folder and starting to get a little cluttered

As you can see from Figure 6-3, what we really need now is a little structure to give everything some order. We've left the organization until this point to fit with the structure of the book; however, it's a good idea to consider what your web site might contain and how this information can be logically grouped together **before** you begin developing a web site.

It might surprise you, but at this point in the process, we suggest you turn off your computer and start working with a pen and paper to plan out a site map.

Let's consider what we've created so far. If you've been following along with the homework, you should have created a number of web pages by now. You should have created pages for the following monkey pioneers: Albert I, Miss Baker, and Gordo. Along the way we've provided pages for you to refer to for the following ape thespians: Cheeta, Cornelius, and King Kong. That's quite a few HTML files and images, but we need to add a few more to create a more realistic web site in terms of structure.

With this in mind and to prepare you for this chapter's homework, we'll be providing you with additional files that we have created for you. You'll be organizing and linking these up as part of this chapter's homework.

You'll be aware that there are a number of distinct themes that already suggest some structure, not least the fact that we have two different categories of primates that we could group together. We've covered both monkeys and apes, so we'll create two folders: one where we gather all of our monkey files and a second where we gather all of our ape files.

We could call these folders "monkeys" and "apes," respectively; however, we've also looked at the role of monkeys in the history of space flight and apes in the movie business. So we could give the folders names that reflect that, for example, "pioneers" (for our space-traveling monkeys) and "thespians" (for our apes with acting aspirations).

How we choose to name the folders is important; it has an effect on the character and tone of our web site. Choosing "monkeys" and "apes" as folder titles will result in a web site with a different character and tone than if we choose "pioneers" and "thespians" as folder titles.

Take a look at Figure 6-4, which shows the basic overview of the site we'll be building for the homework with a little structure added. You'll see we've broken the files down into two key sections—pioneers and thespians—which we'll now create folders (or directories) for to keep everything tidy. We've also added a links page, which we'll use to try out some external links for the homework.

6

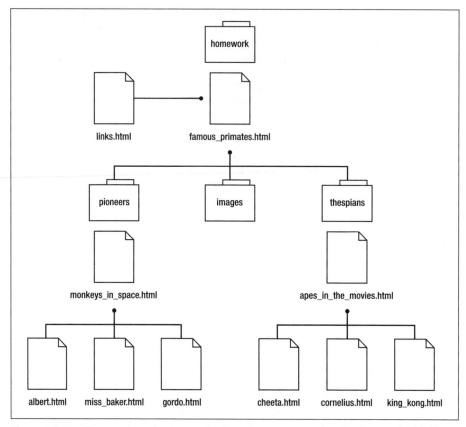

Figure 6-4. Our files as we're going to organize them from now on, using clearly named subfolders

> *Once you've settled on a site structure and uploaded your web site, resist the urge to restructure your site and change your web pages' locations. Bear in mind that others might have already linked to pages within your site, so changing these files' locations will result in broken incoming links.*

One other folder we'd always suggest adding at the start of a project is an images folder where we gather images together, specifically using this for any general images employed throughout the site, for example, branding elements.

The magic index file

When you type www.famousprimates.com/pioneers/gordo.html into a web browser's address bar, you should by now know what is going on: the browser will attempt to display a file called gordo.html located in the pioneers folder. But what happens if you type www.famousprimates.com/pioneers? In this case you don't seem to specify a file for the browser to display; but, as shown in Figure 6-5, a page displays nonetheless.

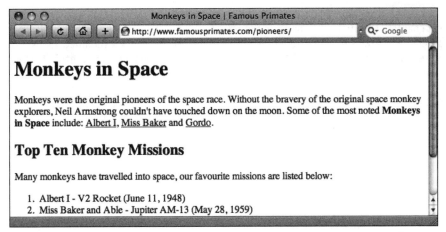

Figure 6-5. Although the URL in the address bar doesn't contain a reference to a specific HTML file, the browser still displays our web page as it will stand after we upload it at the end of Chapter 7.

When you type www.famousprimates.com/pioneers in the address bar, you are telling the browser to look for a folder called pioneers at the `www.famousprimates.com` domain. The reason you don't have to expressly add the file name is that web servers are set up by default to look inside the folder and load a specific file known as the **index file**, in our example a file called `index.html`.

> *On some Windows servers the index file is called* `default.html`.

But what happens if you don't have an index file? Depending on your server, you might get an error message when entering a URL that doesn't contain a reference to a specific HTML file, for example, `www.famousprimates.com/pioneers`. Alternatively, and again this depends on how the server is set up, you might get a listing of all the files in the specific folder like in Figure 6-6.

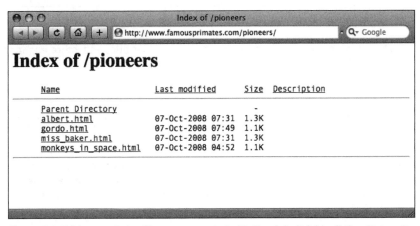

Figure 6-6. Without an index file, we are greeted with the default folder listing. Not pretty.

In preparation for uploading our files to the server on the Web, which we'll cover in the next chapter, we'll make one final amendment to the file structure illustrated in Figure 6-4 earlier. We'll make sure that the files we want to load by default are renamed index.html. Figure 6-7 shows our files and folders after renaming famous_primates.html, monkeys_in_space.html, and apes_in_the_movies.html to index.html.

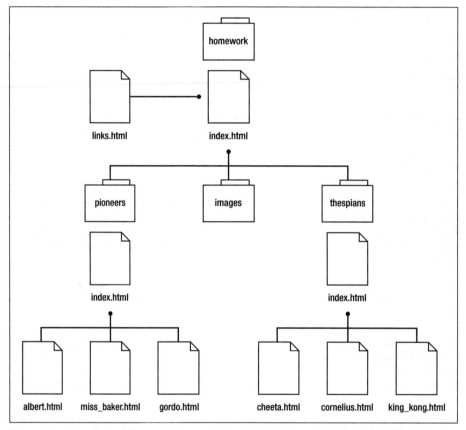

Figure 6-7. Our organized files and folders with the default file in each folder renamed index.html

In the next section we take a look at how the different folder titles and, more importantly, how moving our files into these folders will affect our links.

Linking between different folders in our site

Earlier in this chapter we introduced the concept of *relative links*, noting that links between separate files depend upon the relationship of the files' locations to each other. In the last section we moved some of our files around, organizing them into subfolders. Clearly this is going to have an impact on our files' relative locations, which will have changed to take into account that they're now stored in the folders we just created.

This will mean we need to revisit the links we created previously—another reason to think carefully about the structure of your site *before* you begin building it.

Up until this point all of our web pages have been located in a single folder, so linking to them has been as simple as inserting the file name we'd like to link to in our href attribute when creating a link. We can still use this method for files stored within the same folder, but we'll need to revisit links between files in different folders to take account of their new relationship to each other. This is best demonstrated with some examples.

Linking within a folder

Take a look at our top-level folder; it now contains only two HTML files, as the rest of the files have now been placed into subfolders. To create a link from the main home page, index.html, to the links page, links.html, is as simple as follows:

```
<a href="links.html">Links Page</a>
```

This is because these two files sit alongside each other *in the same folder*, as you can see in Figure 6-8.

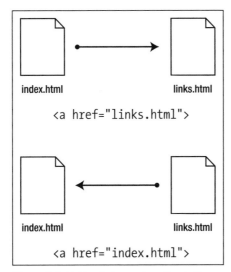

<a href="links.html">

<a href="index.html">

Figure 6-8. Linking between two files in the same folder

Creating a link from the links page back to the home page is equally simple, as shown in the following example:

```
<a href="index.html">Home Page</a>
```

Creating links between files in the same folder is the easiest type of link to create. Let's move to the next stage of complexity, linking from one level of a web site down into a subfolder.

Linking down into a subfolder

Linking down a level, for example, from the main home page, index.html, to the gordo.html page in the pioneers subfolder is slightly different. If you think of the files' relative positions to each other, it should make more sense.

The gordo.html page is now located one folder down from the folder containing the index.html file, that is, gordo.html is located in a *subfolder*. We need to inform the browser of this by giving it the path between the two files as follows:

```
<a href="pioneers/gordo.html">Gordo</a>
```

This is because the file we're linking to is in a folder nested within the main folder as in Figure 6-9. The first part of the preceding href attribute, pioneers/, tells the browser to look into the pioneers folder; the second part, gordo.html, tells the browser to look for the file called gordo.html inside that folder.

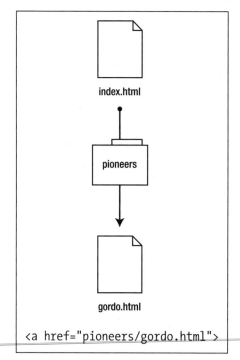

Figure 6-9. Linking to a file in a subfolder

If you've ever typed a typical URL into your browser, you'll have encountered this type of link before, so the structure of the preceding link shouldn't come as a complete surprise.

Linking up into a "parent" folder

For the beginner, linking up into a "parent" folder is probably the hardest concept to grasp, but you should be able to understand the principle if you work through an example. Let's imagine we'd like to create a link from our gordo.html page back to the index.html home page, that is, in the opposite direction to the link explained in the last section.

The gordo.html page is one folder down from the folder containing the index.html page. Somehow we need to inform the browser that we'd like to move out of the pioneers folder and into the next folder up and look for the index.html page.

We inform the browser of the path between the two files as follows (we'll explain it in full in a moment):

```
<a href="../index.html">Home Page</a>
```

The key thing to notice here is the ../ part. This first part of the href attribute acts like a sort of magic escalator to move out of the pioneers folder and up one level. The second part, index.html, tells the browser to look for the file called index.html inside the folder we've just moved into, in this case the top-level folder. This is illustrated in Figure 6-10.

6

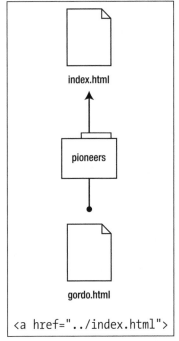

```
<a href="../index.html">
```

Figure 6-10. Linking to a file in a parent folder, we use the magic escalator ../ to move up one level, out of the pioneers folder.

Understanding how to create relative links between files in different folders can be a difficult concept to grasp for the beginner; however, once grasped, the concept will soon fall into place.

> It's worth noting that you can use multiple instances of the magic escalator, ../, to move up more than one level in more deeply nested folders. The following example will move up two levels, linking from a file within a folder that is nested within another folder: `<a href="../../index.html">`.

The best approach to learning this difficult topic is to undertake the exercises in the homework section in which we take you through the relative linking process by moving some files around and asking you to link them together.

Linking up and then linking down

There's just one last thing we need to address now that we've organized all the files . . . our images.

You've seen how to create links between pages in different folders, in particular looking at the escalator—../—which lets you link a file in a subfolder to one in its parent folder. Now that we've organized all of our images by placing them in an images folder, the relationship of the images and the HTML pages we placed them onto in Chapter 5 has changed.

In Chapter 5 we created our image links as follows (we've omitted the alt and other attributes for brevity here):

```
<img src="gordo.jpg" />
```

However, that was when the gordo.jpg image was in the same folder as the gordo.html page. Now these two different files are in different folders, so their relationship to each other has changed. We need to reflect that by updating our <img /> tags.

Taking the gordo.html page as an example, let's see what we need to do to reestablish the link between the gordo.html page and the gordo.jpg image. The gordo.html page is now contained within a folder called pioneers, and the gordo.jpg image is now contained within a folder called images. Clearly this is going to have an impact on how we write our <img /> tags so that they reflect the new folder structure.

In order to reestablish the link between the gordo.html page and the gordo.jpg image, we rewrite the <img /> tag as follows:

```
<img src="../images/gordo.jpg" />
```

Let's break down what this tag is doing. The first part—../—informs the browser to leave the pioneers folder where the gordo.html file now resides and move up into its parent folder. The second part—images/—tells the browser to enter the images folder. The final part—gordo.jpg—tells the browser to display the gordo.jpg image that's now in the images folder. You can see this illustrated in Figure 6-11.

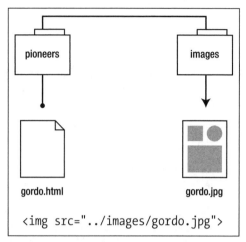

Figure 6-11. Reestablishing the link between gordo.html and gordo.jpg

At first glance, the relationship between links might seem complicated (let's be honest, it is), but practice—as they say—makes perfect. The easiest way to get an understanding of how your different files relate to each other in your newly organized folder structure is to fix the various links that will now be broken as a result of reorganizing your file structure.

In the short term this might seem like a painful process, and the temptation might be to leave everything "organized" in one giant folder. In the longer term, learning about file structure and the relationship between files—in particular the importance of relative links—will stand you in good stead as your web sites grow and expand.

Summary

So what have we covered? This chapter's topic, anchors (or links), is often the biggest obstacle the beginner web designer runs into. Coupling this with the whole topic of organizing files—and the impact that has on links—makes this chapter an important one to grasp.

Understanding relative links isn't easy, and it takes practice through a lot of trial and error. Once the concept is grasped, however, it forms the backbone of the creation of any web site you might build.

After all, a web site wouldn't be a web site without links.

In the next chapter you'll finally take the pages you've created and linked together and upload them to the Web so you can start showing off your work live, worldwide.

Homework: Housekeeping first; links second

In this chapter we've introduced links and their various types: external links, local links, internal links, and e-mail links. We've also introduced the importance of organizing your site by implementing some folder structure to gather your files together in a logical manner.

We looked at how adding a folder structure affected our links, in particular introducing you to the idea of relative links and how they are affected when we restructure our web site and organize its files within folders.

Let's reiterate that point: Relative links are affected as we reorganize our files, so it's a good idea to do the organization *first* and the linking *second*.

This chapter's homework comprises two parts: first, organizing the files you've created so far; second, once that's done, linking up all of the files in your Famous Primates web site.

This is probably the most challenging homework we've set so far and will require some persistence on your part. The topics we've introduced aren't as straightforward as those in the last few chapters, but they *are* important to grasp nonetheless.

1. The content audit

Let's take a look at the files you've created so far. At this point you should have the HTML files albert.html, miss_baker.html, and gordo.html in your homework folder. You should also have the images for these files, along with the ape images (that you haven't used yet). You'll be organizing these files as part of this chapter's homework.

2. Here's one we prepared earlier

Let's face it, for many people organization isn't necessarily a task embraced with relish; however, it's important nonetheless. As a little treat for you, and to make your life a little easier, we've provided a ZIP file for you to download at the book's companion web site that already has the correct folder structure created.

This file also contains all of the additional files you need to complete your homework for this chapter, including a page of primate-related information that will act as a home page (this is the index.html file in the top-level homework folder) and a page of monkey-specific information that will act as the launch page for the monkeys (the index.html file in the pioneers folder). It also contains our ready-made files for the Thespians section of the site.

You can download the additional files for this chapter's homework from here:

www.webstandardistas.com/06/homework.zip

Download and unzip this file, and then move the contents, which should look like Figure 6-12, into your homework folder.

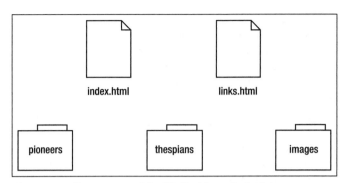

Figure 6-12. The contents of the ZIP file. Move all of this into your homework folder.

3. Move your images into the images folder

We left a little bit of organizing for you to do. Now it is time to put all of the images (monkeys, apes, and the brands we have supplied) into the images folder. After you've done this, try loading the HTML pages that linked to these images. You should see that the images are no longer showing on your pages; this is because the relationship between the images and the HTML files has changed. You will fix that shortly.

4. Move your monkey pages into the pioneers folder

You now have a folder called pioneers. Move your gordo.html, miss_baker.html, and albert.html pages into it. This folder is now the home for all your monkey (pioneer) pages. We have supplied a page of monkey-specific information that will act as the launch page for the monkey pages; this is the index.html file already in the pioneers folder. That's the organizing over with; now it's time to start looking at our links and images.

5. Fix the image references

As discussed toward the end of the chapter, altering the relationship between the HTML files and the image files they refer to will break the links between them. Now it's time to fix these links. Using the ../ (magic escalator) to move up out of the pioneers folder and link down into the images folder, amend the image src attribute to reestablish links from the gordo.html, miss_baker.html, and albert.html pages to their respective images.

To help you with this you can look at the files in the thespians folder to see how these files are linked together. When you've changed the links to reflect the new structure, reload your HTML pages to check that the images display as they should.

6. Add links to the references

Both the Miss Baker and Gordo pages include some references, added in a previous chapter. However, so far these references have not included links. Now is the time to add these. You can get the links for these references in the monkey_links.txt file supplied in the pioneers folder.

Convert your unlinked ordered lists on the Miss Baker and Gordo pages into lists of links. Again, you can refer to our ape pages in the thespians folder to see how this is done.

7. Link your pages together

We've saved the best for last. Now it's time to create internal links from your monkey pages, albert.html, gordo.html, and cornelius.html—each of these pages needs a link to the index.html file in the pioneers folder. Add a short paragraph to each of these pages that says Back to Pioneers and link it up. You'll see a similar link, Back to Thespians, on our ape pages.

When you're done, check that all your links are working as they should.

This has been a complicated chapter. Once you have all your homework files organized and your links working, you'll certainly have earned the right to put the kettle on and enjoy a cup of *Baker Street Afternoon Blend* as you prepare yourself for the next chapter.

What good is a web site if the only person who can see it is you? This chapter covers everything you need to know about finding and buying a domain name (a web address) and buying some low-cost web space to host your web site.

By the end of this chapter you'll have an understanding of what "registering a domain name" means, and you'll also be ready to transfer your files from your computer, where only you can see them, to the Web, where everyone can see them.

We'll introduce some of the principles of File Transfer Protocol (FTP), a method of transferring files from one location to another, and even suggest an improvement to this, SSH File Transfer Protocol (SFTP), which we feel is a better, more secure alternative. This learning will underpin the final stage of the chapter where we walk you through the steps needed to move the various files that comprise your web site from your computer to the Web.

Your address on the Web

In this section we take a look at how to register an address (or a domain name) on the Web. We answer the question, "What is a domain name and what types of domain names are available?" Equally importantly, we look at where you can find out which names are available and where you can register them. Lastly, we outline what registering a domain name entitles you to.

What is a domain name?

Even if you've never heard the expression **domain name**, you've probably seen and used hundreds day to day while surfing the Web: www.google.com, www.wikipedia.org, www.harvard.edu, and www.famousprimates.com—all are well-known examples of domain names, unique names used to locate specific web sites.

Every location on the Web has an address in the form of a number. Let's take Google, for example. Type the following into your browser's address bar and press Return: 72.14.207.99

You should see Google load up just as you'd see it if you were to type in www.google.com. That's because the **human-readable** address www.google.com *maps onto* the **machine-readable** address 64.233.167.99 (also known as an IP, or **Internet Protocol**, address).

Think about it: the verb *google* has now become synonymous with *search the Internet* because it's an easy word to remember. The verb *72.14.207.99* doesn't have quite the same ring to it. (The verb *google* was officially added to the Oxford English Dictionary on June 15, 2006.)

At the time of writing this book, the IP address 72.14.207.99 resolved to www.google.com, however, it is possible that it might not in future. This is due to the fact that domain names are often re-configured to point to different IP addresses to improve server efficiency.

The use of human-readable domain names allows us to easily remember addresses on the Web. It would be very difficult to remember all the web sites we regularly visited if we had to remember them all as complicated clusters of numbers. This explains the popularity of easy-to-remember domain names.

> *Every time you type a domain name into your browser's address bar and press Return, you use the Internet's DNS (Domain Name System) servers, which look up the domain name, identify its matching IP address, and point the browser in the correct direction.*

Every domain name maps onto an IP address and, in the early days of the Web, would have mapped onto a **unique** or **dedicated** IP address. However, as the Web has grown and evolved at an increasingly rapid pace, mapping human-readable domains onto unique IP addresses is now less prevalent. In reality most domain names sit on **shared servers** where one IP address is shared among a number of domain names.

In practical terms, having your web site hosted on a shared server makes no difference. There are a few very specific occasions when a unique IP address is required, and if you should run into one of these in the future, you can still purchase a unique IP address, even on a shared server.

What's a TLD?

Before we point you in the direction of some web-based services that enable you to look up which domain names are and aren't available, it's worth looking at the different types of domain names—or top-level domains—on offer.

A **top-level domain** (TLD) is the last part of an Internet domain name, that is, the letters following the final dot of any domain name as in Figure 7-1. In the domain name `www.amazon.com`, for example, the TLD is com. In `www.bbc.co.uk`, the TLD is uk.

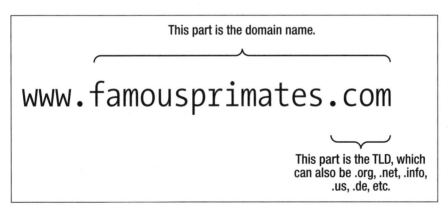

Figure 7-1. The structure of a URL showing both the domain name and the TLD

A number of different domain name levels are available:

- **Top-level domains**: The best known of these are `.com`, `.net`, and `.org`, with `.com` often seen as the most desirable. However, ICANN (Internet Corporation for Assigned Names and Numbers), the nonprofit corporation responsible for overseeing a number of Internet-related tasks, including the management and introduction of TLDs, has created a number of others, which are gaining in popularity.

- **Country-specific domains (ccTLDs)**: A country code top-level domain is a top-level domain generally used or reserved for a country or a dependent territory. All ccTLD identifiers are two letters long. Two examples of this type of domain are `.us` and `.ru`, which stand for the United States and Russia, respectively.

- **Licensed country-specific domains**: A number of the world's smallest countries have licensed their TLDs for world wide commercial exploitation. The best known example of these is `.tv`, which, though commonly interpreted as *dot television*, in fact stands for *dot Tuvalu*, a small Pacific island nation.

When selecting a domain name, your first consideration should be what the different TLDs suggest. For example, `www.acmewidgets.com` suggests a more international company than `www.acmewidgets.co.uk`, based in the UK. However, that does not mean `.com` is necessarily the most appropriate choice.

A novelty leprechaun manufacturer based in Ireland might want to feature the `.ie` TLD for its implicit reference to Ireland, home of a sizable leprechaun population. A nonprofit business might prefer a `.org` TLD, widely held to suggest a noncommercial organization.

The bottom line is to select a TLD most appropriate to your needs.

Think of a name!

When trying to think of a domain name, be inventive. Most short and memorable domains—especially those ending in `.com`—are taken. After all, there are only so many words in existence.

> When creating a domain name, you can use only letters, numbers, and hyphens. Spaces or other symbols are not allowed.

As more and more domain names are registered, you need to be increasingly creative in your thinking. Your first choice might have been registered, so think laterally. Some creative approaches that can prove useful include the following:

- **Combining two or more words to create a memorable name**: `www.simplebits.com`, `www.daringfireball.net`, or `www.superfluousbanter.org`

- **Using a well-known or descriptive phrase**: `www.haveamint.com`, `www.ourspareroom.org`, or `www.mylittlerobot.com`

- **Creative use of a ccTLD**: `blo.gs`, `chronolo.gy`, or `del.icio.us`

- **Inventing a name**: `www.vimeo.com`, `www.odeo.com`, or `www.flickr.com`

If the domain name you really want—`www.pleasantlunch.com`—is taken, try a different TLD. Not every web site address needs to end in .com; perhaps `.org` or `.info` would be better. Alternatively, try a country-specific domain for the country you live in, for example, `www.pleasantlunch.de`.

Be creative, but take a good look at the domain before you click Pay and register it. Check you've spelled everything correctly. (A quick trip to the dictionary now can save tears later.) Also consider how the domain reads. Two consecutive vowels or consonants can make a domain name hard to read, for example, `www.someecho.com`.

When combining words to create a memorable domain, bear in mind that new and unexpected word combinations can appear where words join. For example, *Experts Exchange* probably weren't best advised when they originally registered `www.expertsexchange.com`!

So, you've done some creative thinking and you have a list of names. Is the domain name you'd like available? You can find a number of useful resources online that return domain name availability results instantly, enabling you to quickly identify which names are available. One we use regularly is Instant Domain Search (`http://instantdomainsearch.com/`).

Simply type in the domain name you're looking for and it returns results for the `.com`, `.net`, and `.org` TLDs on the fly.

Congratulations, you've found the perfect name. Now you need to register it.

Registering a domain name

Great, the domain name you've always wanted—`www.roastapigeon.com`—is available. So where do you register it?

In the next section, we'll look at web hosting in detail, but it's worth a brief detour here to introduce the idea that there is a difference between *registering a domain name* and *paying for web hosting*. Both are required.

Although there are a number of companies that focus exclusively on domain name registration *without* offering web hosting, it's worth considering a company that offers both services under one roof. Many web hosting companies also offer free domain name registration as part of their web hosting packages.

So, how much does registering a domain name actually cost? This varies considerably upon the type of domain name you'd like to register. When it comes to registering a country-specific domain, it depends on the country that manages it. Some countries will allow anyone to register a domain name with their two-letter suffix; others impose more restrictions. As always, research is the key. We've listed a number of domain name registration companies at the book's companion web site. You can access these here:

> `www.webstandardistas.com/hosting`

When the Web was first established, registering a top-level domain was an expensive business, costing upward of $100 per year. However, the cost of domain names has dropped

7

dramatically over the last few years, with many companies now offering domains for as little as $4.95 a year.

An important point to note is that when you register a domain name you're not *buying it outright*; instead, you're *buying the right to use it*. Usually you'll pay to register the domain name for a year; however, it is possible to register the domain for up to ten years, saving you the headache of renewing the registration yearly.

Great news, you've identified a domain name and bought it. Now it's time to start thinking about web hosting.

Web hosting

In order to use the domain name you've just registered, you need some web space. We've now established that your domain name is mapped onto a location—or server—where your files are stored. This is where the web hosting aspect comes in.

Think of a web host as a hotel for your domain name. Like any real-world hotel, it can take a number of forms. Perhaps it's of the "pile 'em high, sell 'em cheap" variety: it's a little flea-ridden and there are thousands of rooms, but—a plus point on your tight budget—it's cheap. Perhaps it's a luxury hotel, with all the added benefits: five star, breakfast in bed, and room service only a phone call away. Both offer different levels of quality and service.

In short, expect to get what you pay for. You're not going to get the luxury service in the flea-ridden hostelry. So what should you go for?

> It's worth noting that you can register a domain name with one registrar and host it with a completely different web hosting company. Indeed, with certain country-specific domains, you will need to do this as the country's registrar perhaps only deals with registrations.

Free web hosting?

One thing we *do not recommend* is free web hosting. You might think that a company offering free hosting is the answer to your dreams, but as the old saying goes, "There's no such thing as a free lunch." Ask yourself why you're being offered the hosting absolutely free. What corners are being cut to allow that free "service"?

Bitter experience—our students', not ours—has taught us that free hosting can be fraught with problems: poor, or even nonexistent, service; extremely slow page loading times; hugely restricted bandwidth; or even an insistence on running banner ads all over your carefully crafted web pages.

Trust us, the downsides are too high and experience proves that you'll regret it in the long run.

Getting the balance right

Start by getting something that is affordable and does the job. Initially we'd recommend that you start small. At this point in time you only need the basics; resist the urge to sign up for every feature under the sun. You probably won't use them.

Most hosting companies offer tiered plans, which allow you to scale up your hosting as your needs grow. If your web site *does* take off and generate a huge amount of traffic, don't panic; your web hosting company is more than likely used to this and will allow you to scale up your hosting plan accordingly.

There are a lot of different web hosting companies catering to different types of people; however, finding the right one for you can be a challenge. Finding your way around the web-hosting jungle can often feel a little like learning to speak a foreign language. Hearing that a hosting company offers support for PHP, MySQL, Perl, Ruby on Rails, and Python while allowing full access to the back end is daunting when first encountered.

You may also encounter companies offering to host your web site on a variety of different hardware or software platforms, for example, servers running Windows, Linux, or other flavors of Unix. Because Linux is open source and does not require license fees for its operating system, Linux-based hosting is generally less expensive.

Don't worry, you can afford to ignore most of this. When you're ready for advanced abbreviations (POP, SSL, CGI . . .), you'll know it. Trust us. There are, however, some key things to look for, which we explain in easy-to-understand language next.

7

Things to look for in a hosting company

First things first: everyone is different and every web site is different. What you'll need to look for in a web hosting company will largely be dictated by the type of web site you're creating.

A web site for a record label with thousands of large MP3 audio files and thousands of dedicated fans will have considerably different requirements from a web site for an online music magazine that publishes a small number of text-based reviews read by a dedicated group of followers numbered in the hundreds. The record label will need considerably more disk space and bandwidth, two terms we explain in the upcoming text.

The following list covers the key points you should look for when considering a web hosting company.

Disk space

Disk space is the amount of space you need to store your web site on your web hosting company's servers.

How much will you need? This depends entirely on what your web site is intended for. File sizes vary considerably: a simple HTML page can be as small as a few kilobytes, whereas an MP3 could easily be as large as a hundred megabytes.

Considering the needs of the record label we mentioned previously, thousands of large MP3 audio files will require considerably more storage space than the online magazine whose site is comprised largely of HTML pages and images. Your web site will have its own characteristics; however, most hosting companies will offer more than enough disk space to accommodate your requirements.

Bandwidth

Bandwidth is the amount of actual data transferred from your web site to the browsers of those looking at your web site. In short, anything that is transferred from your server to your visitors' computers is measured and counts toward the bandwidth.

For example, the record label we mentioned previously offers a 100MB MP3 mix for free download, and 500 visitors to the site download it. This is equivalent to 500 $\times$ 100MB, or 50,000MB, or ~50GB. Quite a bit of data. Clearly, if you're offering large files, you will need to consider bandwidth requirements when selecting a web hosting company.

Again, barring exceptional circumstances, most hosting companies will offer more than enough bandwidth to accommodate your requirements.

E-mail

Unless you're building a web site for a Fortune 500 company that needs thousands of e-mail addresses, you'll find that most hosting companies offer more than enough e-mail addresses to support your needs. But then, if you *were* building a web site for a Fortune 500 company, you probably wouldn't be reading this book.

A control panel

A control panel is essentially a form of web-based interface for interacting with your server to change its settings. Control panels can vary considerably, from extremely user friendly to almost nonexistent. Again, this will depend on the hosting company and what it offers.

A good control panel can help take the pain out of adding new e-mail addresses, installing software (for example, blogging software or web-based galleries), or keeping track of your bandwidth usage. A good control panel can make your life considerably easier, and it's worth looking to see whether a hosting company offers one and, if so, what its users think of it.

Support

Remember our hotel metaphor? Support is a little like room service. It's worth taking a look at what types of support a hosting company offers. There's a world of difference between telephone and web-based support. Which you'll need again depends upon what your web site is for.

The bottom line? Do some research and find what's appropriate for your needs. We've created a list of recommended hosting companies at the book's companion web site. As with the other online resources, we'll keep it updated to reflect what's current. You can find the list here:

www.webstandardistas.com/hosting

Moving web hosts

In the "Wild West" days of the Web, hosting companies would launch, grow fantastically, and then crash spectacularly. The resulting chaos would leave you struggling to find an alternative host, often at a moment's notice. You'd sign up with a new company only to find the whole process repeat itself again. They didn't call it the dot.com crash for nothing.

Thankfully, those days are becoming a distant memory. Hosting companies have, by and large, consolidated and become more reliable as a consequence. If, however, you do find yourself having problems with a web hosting company or service provider, don't panic.

Remember, you own the right to use your domain name, and all it's doing is pointing to the server where your web site *is currently hosted*. This server can easily be changed by moving to a new hosting firm and reconfiguring your domain name to point there instead. Although pointing a domain name to a particular server goes beyond the scope of this book, we felt it important to highlight nonetheless.

Uploading your files

You've registered a domain name, you've bought some web space. Now you need to do something with them.

If you've been following along with the homework, you should have a folder with some files organized into subfolders, as shown in Figure 7-2. As things stand the only person who can see these files is you; they're on your computer and so are not publicly accessible.

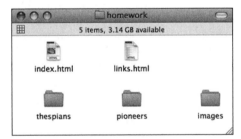

Figure 7-2. The homework files, organized in folders on your computer

It's time to upload your files to the server.

Local vs. remote

What's the difference? Assuming you've been following along with the homework, up until this point you've been working on your own computer. Now you need to transfer your files from your computer to your web hosting company's server, which is possibly located in a faraway country.

As you progress as a Web Standardista, you'll encounter numerous references to a **local** machine and a **remote** machine. The computer you've been working on up until this point is commonly referred to as your local machine. The server, in that faraway country, is commonly referred to as the remote machine.

In the next section we'll be exploring how we create a connection between our local computer and the remote server so that we can transfer our files from one to the other. It's worth mentioning that once we create this connection, we are not restricted to transferring files from the local machine to the remote machine in one direction. We can transfer files in both directions.

So how do we transfer our files to the web hosting company's server so that others can see our web site? Enter FTP. There are a number of protocols for making the connection between your local computer and the remote server. Although FTP isn't the only one, it is one of the most common, and file transfer applications are commonly referred to as FTP clients.

File Transfer Protocol

There are a number of different protocols on the Web. You've already met one: HTTP (HyperText Transfer Protocol)—the `http://` part of any URL. FTP is another protocol that allows us to transfer files, or any form of data, from one machine to another.

> *We'll recommend some FTP clients—programs that allow you to upload your files to your server—in the section "Which FTP client?" later in this chapter.*

Although FTP is probably the file transfer protocol you'll hear about most often, it isn't the only one. A preferable alternative to FTP is SFTP, sometimes called Secure File Transfer Protocol. Unlike FTP, SFTP encrypts both commands and data sent over the network, preventing passwords and sensitive information from being transmitted "in the open."

Why choose SFTP over FTP? Primarily because it offers considerably better security. The difference between FTP and SFTP is the difference between sending an intimate note to your lover as either a postcard or a letter sealed in an envelope. Ask yourself: do you *really* want the postman to read those "romantic confessions"?

In short, FTP sends packets of data, *including your password*, "in the open"; SFTP sends the same information in a much more secure way.

To all intents and purposes, FTP and SFTP work almost identically to the average user, the primary difference being that the latter encrypts any data transferred. If your hosting company supports it, we recommend choosing SFTP over FTP. After all, you don't want all your private information displayed for all to see. A good web hosting company should support SFTP or a secure alternative, so this might be something to consider when choosing your web hosting company.

Propagation

Despite the word *propagation*'s gardening connotation, we're not drifting off into a subsection on the benefits of being green fingered, but rather highlighting an issue you may run into and that is worth being made aware of.

Imagine this scenario. You've worked fast: you registered a domain name, bought some web hosting, fired up your FTP client, and transferred your beautifully designed and carefully crafted web site to the remote machine. The web site's working fine—you checked it locally—and now you can't wait to see it online and show it off to your friends. You fire up a browser and enter www.fatplatterofsushi.com . . .

Disaster! There's nothing there. All you see is something similar to Figure 7-3.

Figure 7-3. Our browser can't find the server www.fatplatterofsushi.com because the domain name hasn't yet propagated.

Don't panic. There's a simple reason for this error. By now you know that the domain name you registered is mapped onto the address of your server. This information—the relationship between domain name and physical (server) location—is stored on a number of DNS servers: giant databases that point browsers in the right direction when looking for web sites (we mentioned them toward the beginning of this chapter). It takes time for the connection between your domain name and the address of the server on which it's hosted to register on these databases, a process known as propagation.

This process can take up to 36 to 72 hours to take effect. Check again in a day or two, and everything should be fine. Patience, our young Padawan.

Tools we're using

As in the previous chapters, we've focused on low-cost, but fully featured applications that enable you to upload your web site to your server space. Although we've used Cyberduck (for Macintosh OS X) for the screenshots in the walkthrough that follows, a number of alternatives are available.

If you're using Windows or Linux, you might want to consider FileZilla, a free FTP client. With tutorials for first-time users available at the FileZilla web site, it's worth trying out:

```
http://wiki.filezilla-project.org/Using
```

The principles of the following walkthrough remain consistent across platform or software used, and you should be able to understand the principles we cover regardless of software.

Which FTP client?

Most file transfer applications support a variety of protocols, including FTP and SFTP. As we've stated, the basic principles we cover in the walkthrough apply regardless of your preferred software.

There are a number of alternative file transfer applications for a variety of platforms and potential uses. These vary in complexity and features, and all are detailed at the respective applications' web sites. We recommend Cyberduck or Transmit if you are using a Macintosh, and FileZilla or Core FTP if you're running Windows. If your platform is a flavor of Linux, FileZilla is a good option; another alternative is gFTP.

You can find links to all of these FTP clients at the Web Standardistas web site. As new software is released, we'll update this list. You can find the most recent version of the list here:

www.webstandardistas.com/tools

Transferring files to the server: A walkthrough

With so many different web hosting companies configured in such a huge variety of ways, it's almost impossible to create a single walkthrough that will satisfy everyone. However, in the following walkthrough we've highlighted the key principles.

Even if you're not using the file transfer application we've used for the walkthrough (Cyberduck) or the hosting company (DreamHost), the principles of creating a basic SFTP or FTP connection from your local computer to a remote server remain the same.

If you're not using the Cyberduck and DreamHost combination, have no fear. Your web hosting provider should have provided some instructions on uploading files and connecting to your server space. There should also be help files for the FTP application you selected. It might sound obvious, but we have to say it: **Read them!**

We also recommend reading through this section before trying the instructions out yourself, to give you an idea of what to expect when first connecting to your web server.

What you need

You'll need to get a number of details from your web hosting company. These will normally have been automatically e-mailed to you when signing up for a web hosting package. There are generally three essential pieces of information, as follows:

1. The address of the server

2. Your username

3. Your password

Let's run through these in order.

The address of the server

This is the address of the web space that you will upload your files to. This address will not necessarily be the same as your domain name. For example, if your domain name is `www.famousprimates.com`, the address to the server could be `ftp.famousprimates.com` or, as in our example, simply `famousprimates.com`. The server address will depend upon how your server is set up. Make sure to get the right details from your hosting company.

Your username

For anyone familiar with the Web, a username shouldn't come as a complete surprise. As with anywhere else online, take care to enter your username using case sensitivity where appropriate (i.e., BaBoon is not the same as babOOn).

Your password

Web hosting companies will often generate a password for you automatically. These can often be quite complicated, for example, LKaQ^L#r. You can usually reset these to a more memorable name; you should ensure, however, that the password remains hard to guess and preferably consists of a combination of numbers, letters, and other characters. Passwords are also case sensitive.

This may seem like common sense, but even for the seasoned web professional careless typing can often be the frustrating cause of a connection not working. Ensuring that you've entered all the details exactly as they were given to you by your hosting company is the first thing to check if something isn't working as it should.

Let's get started

As we've mentioned, in this walkthrough we're using Cyberduck, a free file transfer application available for Mac OS X. You can download it from the following site:

`http://cyberduck.ch`

1. Download Cyberduck and move it to your Applications folder. On launching the application, you should see an empty listings window like the one in Figure 7-4.

7

Figure 7-4. Click Open Connection in Cyberduck to enter your connection details.

2. Click Open Connection in the top-left corner to get started.

Clicking the Open Connection icon in Figure 7-4 rolls out a dialog sheet where you can enter the connection details given to you by your hosting company. The Protocol drop-down menu, as shown in Figure 7-5, lists a number of options, the default being FTP. As mentioned previously in this chapter, if your hosting company allows it, you are advised to use a more secure option such as SFTP.

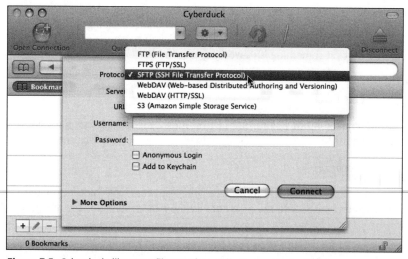

Figure 7-5. Cyberduck, like most file transfer applications, allows other, more secure protocols than FTP.

3. Enter the server, username, and password details in their respective fields, as shown in Figure 7-6. The Port value can usually be left at its default setting unless your hosting company has provided you with specific details that tell you otherwise. Leave Anonymous Login unchecked and check Add to Keychain if you want your Mac to remember your password for you. (If you're not the only one with access to your computer, it might be advisable to leave this unchecked too.) When you've finished, click Connect.

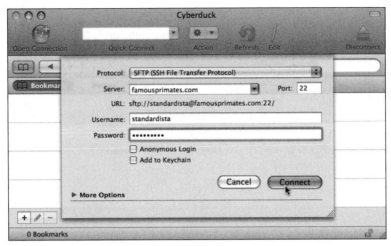

Figure 7-6. Add your server details, username, and password and click Connect.

All being well Cyberduck should now establish a connection to your server. As Figure 7-7 illustrates, Cyberduck displays a listing of the files and folders on the server. Since you haven't uploaded anything to the server yet, you might get an empty listing, or you might get something that looks like Figure 7-7: a collection of folders created automatically on the server when your hosting account was created.

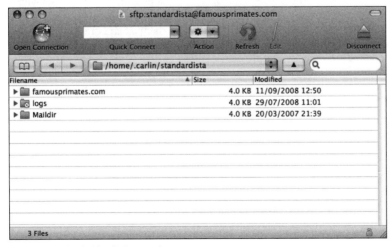

Figure 7-7. The folder listing on the remote server

These folders usually have specific uses: one might contain log files, detailing the visitors to your site; one might contain mail files, where your e-mails are stored; and one is the folder where your web pages need to be placed in order to be viewed online.

In this case, it's easy to deduce that the folder named famousprimates.com is the one to upload your files to. Your hosting company will usually tell you which folder to store your web pages in. This is sometimes referred to as the **path** to your web directory. You can reveal the Path field in Cyberduck by clicking More Options (shown in the bottom of the sheet in Figure 7-6).

4. To move into the famousprimates.com folder, double-click the folder icon. You should be presented with an empty folder listing as shown in Figure 7-8.

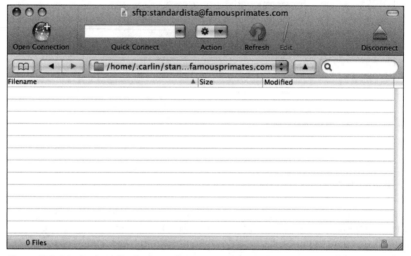

Figure 7-8. Moving into the famousprimates.com folder where our web pages will be stored

5. Switch over to the Finder and open the folder where you have saved all your homework files. It will probably look something like Figure 7-9. The easiest way to transfer these files to your server is to select them all and drag and drop them from the Finder window to the Cyberduck window.

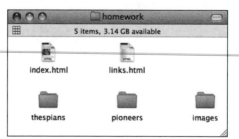

Figure 7-9. Your files are all stored in a folder on your *local* computer.

Dragging and dropping your files from the Finder window to the Cyberduck window, as shown in Figure 7-10, will start the process of transferring your files from your local computer to the remote server. Depending on the number of files, their size, and the speed of your Internet connection, this might take a few moments. Typically uploading files is a much slower process than downloading them.

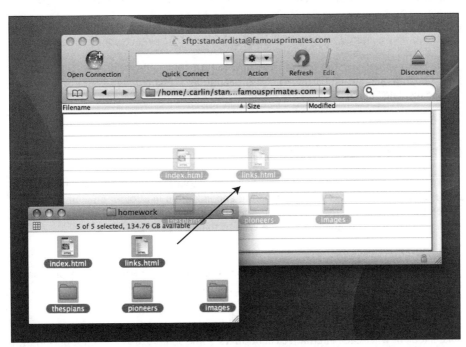

Figure 7-10. Drag the files from your *local* folder to the Cyberduck window to transfer them to the *remote* server.

Having uploaded your files, you can type your domain name into the address bar of a browser; all being well, you should now see your web site in all its (unstyled) glory.

Online walkthrough

We've created a screencast of the preceding walkthrough, which is available to watch at the book's companion web site. It takes you through each of the stages outlined step by step. You can access it here:

www.webstandardistas.com/07/walkthrough

Summary

So what have we covered? We've explored what registering a domain name means and given you some ideas for generating a memorable name for your web site. We've explained how to buy that name and then buy some web hosting so that the domain name has a home (or hotel) on the Web.

Lastly, we've outlined how to transfer your files to your web space. In short, we've shown you how to move everything from your computer (where, until now, it's been stored *locally*) to a server on the interwebs (where, from now on, it will be stored *remotely*).

This is a big step. Up until this point everything you've been working on has been stored locally, so only a limited audience has been able to see it. Now everyone can see it.

In the next chapter, we start to show you how to turn your well-crafted web pages, oozing with semantic and structural markup, into beautifully *presented* web pages using CSS or Cascading Style Sheets.

Homework: Getting your site online

This chapter's homework is all about the process we've covered in this chapter. By now you should have a number of files organized and linked up in a folder on your hard drive. A web site, no less. What we focus on in this chapter's homework is moving that web site from your computer to the World Wide Web so that everyone can see it.

1. Research

Research some of the FTP clients recommended previously. Remember, we've provided a link to some recommended tools at the Web Standardistas web site:

> www.webstandardistas.com/tools

Take a look at what each alternative client offers; some solid research will not only inform you of the differences of what's on offer, but will also help inform you of current best practice.

2. Download and install an FTP client

Once you've done your research, select an FTP client and download it. You'll be using this to complete the homework. Follow the instructions for the FTP client you've chosen and install it on your computer.

Once you register a domain name and purchase some web space, you'll be ready to use your chosen FTP client to upload your web site from your computer to the Web.

3. Register a domain name

Now it's time to purchase your domain name. Bear in mind the suggestions we made earlier about being creative when thinking of a domain name. Remember, this web address could be yours for some time, so put some thought into it. As we did previously, we've provided a link to some recommended domain name tools at the Web Standardistas web site:

> www.webstandardistas.com/hosting

Once you've found a domain name, register it. At this point, it might be worth considering a *combined web hosting and domain name registration* package.

4. Purchase some web space

Now it's time to purchase some web space. Remember the hotel metaphor we mentioned. You don't want somewhere flea-ridden, yet five-star luxury is probably a bit over the top. Start small, and work up.

Again, we've provided a link to some recommended web hosting companies at the Web Standardistas web site:

> www.webstandardistas.com/hosting

> *Since it takes a while for the domain name you registered to propagate, this might be a good time to go on a fishing trip for a day or so.*

5. Connect to your server

Follow the instructions you received from your web hosting provider and enter the details they provided (usually server, username, and password) into the relevant location on your chosen FTP client. At this point you may need to refer again to the help files for the FTP application you selected.

6. Upload your files

Once you've established a connection to your server, upload your files. That's it.

7. Check your web site

Enter your domain name into your browser's address bar and press Return. You should now see your web site. Congratulations.

8. Invite your friends

Let your friends know you've diligently been doing your homework. Relax with a nice cup of *Formosa Oolong Extra Fancy* as you read the congratulatory slew of e-mail from your well-wishers.

7

FAMOUS PRI

King Kong

The Legend

King Kong is the name of a *fictional g*
several works since 1933. Most of the
film remakes of 1976 and 2005, and n

REFERENCES

1. The Lumiere Reader – King K
2. King Kong – An Entertaining
3. Kong is King – The History of

★ FAMOUS PRIMATES

★ PIONEERS

★ THESPIANS

★ LINKS

★ CONTACT US

```
<table border="1" width="480" c
<tr><td width="120"><font face=
color="gray"><b>The Legend</b><

<tr><td><font face="Arial, Helv
is the name of a </font><i><fon
color="black">fictional giant a
Geneva" size="3" color="black">
Helvetica, Geneva" size="3" col
face="Arial, Helvetica, Geneva"
several works since 1933. Most
groundbreaking 1933 film, the f
sequels.</font>
<br> <br>
<font face="Arial, Helvetica, G
film, the character's name is K
```

FAMOUS PR

King Kong

The Legend

King Kong is the name of a *fictional g*
several works since 1933. Most of the:

FAMOUS PR

King Kong

The Legend

King Kong is the name of a *fictional g*
several works since 1933. Most of the
film remakes of 1976 and 2005, and n

We've spent the first half of the book building a solid foundation, teaching you to create markup using well-structured XHTML. Now it's time to add some style to your well-crafted web pages using CSS.

The impatient among you have been waiting for this chapter for some time or have possibly cheated and skipped a few chapters, perhaps because you mistakenly think this chapter marks the beginning of the "design" chapters. If you can recognize yourself in this description, particularly if you skipped the first half of the book because you wanted to dive straight into CSS, please—we urge you—skip back a few chapters.

Why?

Simple. We've been covering design for some time now. All that *structured markup*, all that talk of *semantics*, all that "choose the right tag for the job"—all of that *is* design.

Good design *isn't* choosing this year's color or selecting a typeface that's hot. Good design is much more fundamental than that; it's about taking some information and giving it structure. It's about amplifying meaning by drawing out an information hierarchy and teasing out semantics. In short, it's . . . everything we covered in the first half of the book.

If you're feeling a little guilty—you skipped a few sections here and there, you really wanted to get to "the exciting parts"—**we strongly recommend you skip back** and read the preceding chapters. You'll thank us if you do.

Not guilty? Read on!

This chapter introduces the fundamentals of Cascading Style Sheets (CSS), the presentation part of the *content plus presentation* equation. You'll learn the basic principles of CSS and start applying style to some of the web pages you've created in the first half of the book.

CSS is a language used to control the presentation of documents written in markup language, for example, to style web pages written in XHTML. CSS can be used to define colors, fonts, and a variety of other aspects of document presentation; it can also be used to position elements and control layout.

CSS is primarily designed to enable the separation of a document's content (written in XHTML) from a document's presentation (written in CSS). This separation can improve content accessibility, provide users with more flexibility in accessing content, and allow the same markup to be presented in a variety of different styles for different rendering methods, for example, for viewing on screen and in print or for accessing via a screen reader.

Up until this point our well-structured web pages have been styled using the browser's default style sheet. Although these style sheets vary slightly between browsers, they have common characteristics including black text, blue text for links, and purple text for visited links. By adding your own style sheet, you can override the browser's style sheet, allowing you to style the page as you wish.

By the end of this chapter you'll be ready to start adding additional—visual and presentational—design to your web pages, turning them from well-structured web pages into well-structured *and* well-designed web pages. Good times.

Adding some style

You should by now be capable of building well-structured web pages using semantic markup. You should also know how to upload these to some personal web space as covered in Chapter 7. This is a significant achievement. However, as things stand your web pages aren't too far removed from what the Web was supposed to look like circa 1993. You might find it hard to believe, but that is *not* a bad start.

Now you'd really like to work on the presentation aspect, controlling the look and feel of your web pages to enhance their design. This chapter takes your well-structured web pages and begins to apply some style to them using CSS. Before we embark on this part of our journey, it's worth a quick refresher on what HTML was and, equally importantly, *wasn't* intended for.

HTML: A brief refresher

As we discussed in Chapter 1, when HTML was invented, it was not intended to be a presentational language. The tags that dealt with the visual aspect of text (the choice of typeface, its size and color, for example) were limited and were intended only to introduce a semantic structure to text. We covered this in Chapter 3 when we discussed structured markup, where we used an <h1> to signify "I am more important than an <h2>" and so on.

As web browsers grew more sophisticated, adding support for images and introducing additional—often proprietary—tags, web designers grew more and more adventurous and started to embrace non-semantic markup to create hidden scaffolding for increasingly complicated designs.

The introduction of WYSIWYG (What You See Is What You Get) editors that allowed the user to create HTML by dragging and dropping visual elements on the page, much like in a word processor, created markup of such complexity that it would be almost impossible to create by hand, or to change or edit without access to the program that created the markup in the first place.

Web pages created using WYSIWYG editors (for example, FrontPage or Dreamweaver) took longer to download due to the amount of extra markup they contained, they were harder to update and maintain, and if you wanted to change a visual element on your web site, you had to go through each and every individual page, as the visual style was embedded in the content of the page and not in a separate design file or style sheet.

Working with pages generated in WYSIWYG editors? In a word: nightmare.

CSS offered the possibility to change all that, separating content and presentation, which forms the cornerstone of the Web Standardistas' approach.

CSS isn't new

CSS has been around for over a decade, being proposed as early as 1994 and agreed upon as a W3C Recommendation in December 1996, but it is only in the last few years that browser support has been reliable enough for web designers to depend on CSS for layout and design.

The key advantages of CSS include the fact that it's easy to maintain; it helps in the creation of lean web pages (look at the tag soup example in the next section to understand why this is a good thing); it uses the same XHTML markup for screen and print; and it can be used to improve accessibility, for example, through the inclusion of a high-contrast style sheet for visually impaired users.

Tag soup or lean and mean?

We introduced the concept of *tag soup* in Chapter 1; we'll now show you an example we've reverse-engineered to demonstrate how much smaller a well-formatted web page can become by removing presentational HTML.

In Figure 8-1, we've marked up a section of our King Kong page using <font> tags to style the text and <table> tags to control the layout, as would have been typical before CSS was widely supported by standards-compliant browsers.

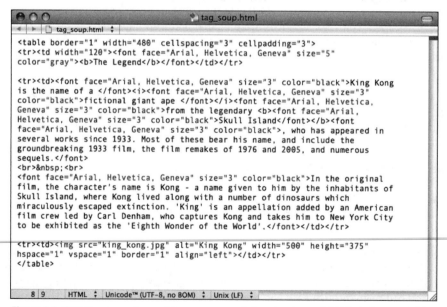

```
<table border="1" width="480" cellspacing="3" cellpadding="3">
<tr><td width="120"><font face="Arial, Helvetica, Geneva" size="5"
color="gray"><b>The Legend</b></font></td></tr>

<tr><td><font face="Arial, Helvetica, Geneva" size="3" color="black">King Kong
is the name of a </font><i><font face="Arial, Helvetica, Geneva" size="3"
color="black">fictional giant ape </font></i><font face="Arial, Helvetica,
Geneva" size="3" color="black">from the legendary <b><font face="Arial,
Helvetica, Geneva" size="3" color="black">Skull Island</font></b><font
face="Arial, Helvetica, Geneva" size="3" color="black">, who has appeared in
several works since 1933. Most of these bear his name, and include the
groundbreaking 1933 film, the film remakes of 1976 and 2005, and numerous
sequels.</font>
<br> <br>
<font face="Arial, Helvetica, Geneva" size="3" color="black">In the original
film, the character's name is Kong - a name given to him by the inhabitants of
Skull Island, where Kong lived along with a number of dinosaurs which
miraculously escaped extinction. 'King' is an appellation added by an American
film crew led by Carl Denham, who captures Kong and takes him to New York City
to be exhibited as the 'Eighth Wonder of the World'.</font></td></tr>

<tr><td><img src="king_kong.jpg" alt="King Kong" width="500" height="375"
hspace="1" vspace="1" border="1" align="left"></td></tr>
</table>
```

Figure 8-1. Our reverse-engineered tag soup example is not only unwieldy, but also uses tables for layout, a Web Standardista faux pas.

Take a look at the paragraphs in Figure 8-1. As you can see, they haven't even been marked up with <p> tags, relying instead on a considerable amount of presentational markup. Every single time a paragraph is encountered, it's been styled with the addition of <font face="Arial, Helvetica, Geneva" size="3" color="black">, setting the paragraphs to display in Arial, size 3, and black (we'll explain why the additional typefaces in the <font> tag are included in Chapter 9). Note how this is added to *every single paragraph!*

As you can see, this could get really messy and hard to read, not to mention hard to write. As if that weren't bad enough, this complex and nonstructured markup is much harder for search engines to index.

Surely there must be a more efficient way to do this. Imagine we have a client who would prefer Times New Roman to Arial and would rather the paragraphs were in red, not black. The client would also like the text size increased just a little. We would have to find *every instance* of <font face="Arial, Helvetica, Geneva" size="3" color="black"> and replace it with <font face="Times New Roman, Times, Georgia" size="4" color="red">. No small task, especially if we had a web site with hundreds of pages.

In the Figure 8-2, we take the same page and remove the presentational <font> and <table> tags, reducing the markup considerably.

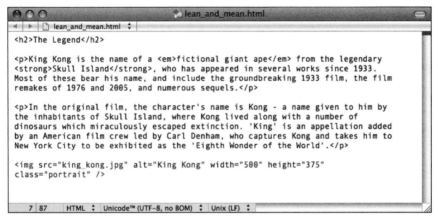

Figure 8-2. Lean and mean, our web standards–based web page is not only considerably smaller, but far more accessible. It's also more search engine friendly.

These contrasting examples go to the very heart of the problem. The use of <font> tags and other presentational markup is inefficient and results in much larger file sizes, which take longer to download and longer to edit and update. The fragment in Figure 8-1 is 1,396 characters long, while the fragment in Figure 8-2 is only 779 characters, *almost half the size.* It will download twice as fast, and we can update its style and presentation considerably more quickly.

So how do we add all the presentational information that's not included in the second example? The answer is using CSS.

CSS to the rescue

Using CSS to add style to your web pages removes the need for all the individual <font> tags encountered in the previous section. By providing a mechanism for selecting specific elements within your markup—for example, all the <p> tags in the preceding example— CSS allows you to target them and style them as you wish. Write one CSS rule and style *every* <p>. This results in web pages that are efficient, much easier to maintain, and faster to download.

While early web authors and designers had little choice but to employ elements in a pre-sentational manner to create visually effective web pages, CSS has largely done away with the need for those methods. Old habits die hard, however, and many authors continue to unnecessarily employ these tag soup hacks rather than embrace CSS. As a Web Standardista, you know better.

Using CSS to control presentation—adding a layer of style to your well-structured XHTML pages—allows you to separate content and presentation. Focus first on the creation of well-structured markup, markup that uses the right tag for the job, before styling that markup and controlling how it displays using CSS. This is a much better approach, and one wonders why it's taken so long for CSS to take a hold.

This all sounds great, but how do we actually use CSS?

Meet CSS

Although XHTML and CSS are two different languages, with different rules, CSS is easy to learn and, once you understand the basic principles of the language, you should be up and running in no time.

Let's take a look at a simple CSS rule. We'll work with a typical piece of markup from the bad old days and demonstrate how you can use CSS to replace the cumbersome <font> tags used. In the tag soup example in Figure 8-1, we showed how <font> tags had been used to style the different paragraphs on the King Kong page. We've simplified the markup here to style just one aspect of the type, its color:

```
<font color="teal">King Kong is the name of a fictional giant ape
    from the legendary Skull Island...</font>
```

In the tag soup days, when we wanted to style a paragraph, we needed to include the additional markup in the <font> tag, *every single time*. With CSS used to style a solid foundation built using structured markup, we can achieve this much more efficiently.

The first step in the process, as you know by now, is to remove the <font> tags and wrap this admittedly short paragraph in <p> tags as in the following example:

```
<p>King Kong is the name of a fictional giant ape from the legendary
    Skull Island...</p>
```

Not only is the inclusion of <p> tags semantic, a good thing as you know, but it also gives us an element we can target with CSS. The result of this is that it achieves exactly the same effect as multiple <font> tags, styling *all* of our <p> elements, using just the following CSS rule:

```
p
{
color: teal;
}
```

Although this might seem a little complicated at first, don't worry, all will soon be revealed as we break down this basic CSS rule in the next section. The preceding CSS rule does exactly same as the <font> tags in the first example, but as we can write one rule to target all instances of <p> on a page, it is a great deal more efficient.

Remember the client who preferred the color red? Simply change the preceding rule as follows, and it will change all occurrences of <p>, styling them red, and the client will be happy:

```
p
{
color: red;
}
```

We'll now introduce you to how the preceding CSS rule is structured, breaking it down into its constituent parts.

8

Anatomy of a CSS rule

At first glance, the rule in the previous example probably appears a little bit cryptic; however, once we've explained it, you'll soon understand what's going on.

CSS rules are comprised of a **selector**, a **property**, and a **value** as follows:

```
selector
{
property: value;
}
```

In Figure 8-3, we've taken this example and rewritten it on one line to illustrate its different components more clearly.

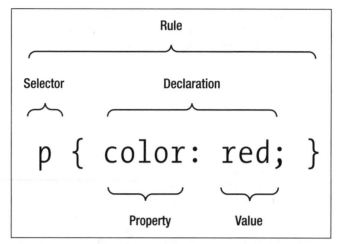

Figure 8-3. The different parts of a very simple CSS rule, styling just one property

Let's look again at this simple rule and break it down into its key components:

```
p
{
color: red;
}
```

- The letter p on the first line targets the p element (i.e., all content within <p> tags on the page).
- Everything between the { and } (curly brackets) is style we're applying to the p elements.
- The declaration color: red; specifies a particular color for those elements.

In CSS a **declaration** is the name given to a property: value; pair. In the preceding example, the property we're targeting is the color, and its value is being set to red. As you'll see in the section "A slightly more complex rule," we can identify a number of property: value; pairs to create more complex rules. The property and value are separated with a colon (:).

It's also worth noting the semicolon at the end of the declaration line. We use semicolons to mark the end of each declaration; we'll need them when we start adding additional declarations to our rules as in the examples in the following section. The semicolon is important and needs to be included; the semicolon, *not* the line break, tells the interpreter that this is the end of the declaration.

A note on formatting

Before we go on it's worth pausing for a moment to talk about how CSS rules can be formatted. If you've been using View Source to take a look at how others' web pages are constructed, you might see a number of variations on how CSS rules are laid out. It's worth noting that the following three examples are all functionally equivalent:

```
p { color: red; }
```

or

```
p {
   color: red;
  }
```

or

```
p
{
color: red;
}
```

Based on our teaching experience, we find the last example to be the easiest layout for beginners to follow as it breaks the selector and property and value pairs onto separate lines. This makes the declaration easier to understand and follow.

A slightly more complex rule

So, now you know what a CSS rule looks like and we've introduced you to a simple rule to style all of our paragraphs red. However, you'd like to do a little more than change your paragraphs to red; you'd like to choose a typeface for them.

We could do this by writing a rule for each aspect we'd like to style as follows:

```
p
{
color: red;
}

p
{
font-family: Arial;
}
```

Although this will work, styling all the paragraphs in red and setting them in Arial, it would quickly become cumbersome, with endless rules styling each element. Good news, CSS allows us to combine declarations as in the following example, which does exactly the same thing:

```
p
{
color: red;
font-family: Arial;
}
```

Figure 8-4 shows an example of a CSS rule with multiple declarations, one per line.

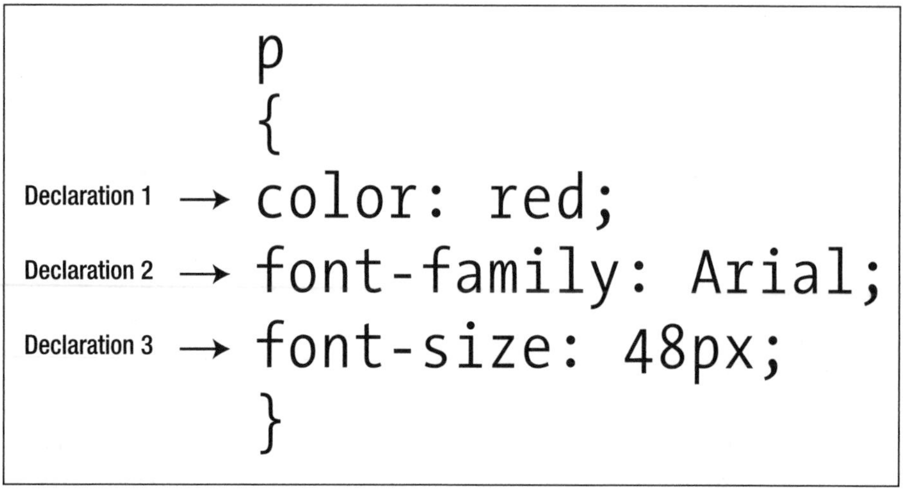

```
p
{
Declaration 1 →  color: red;
Declaration 2 →  font-family: Arial;
Declaration 3 →  font-size: 48px;
}
```

Figure 8-4. A more complex CSS rule, consisting of three declarations, each on its own line

We can add as many declarations as we want to each rule, enabling us to apply specific styles to each element on a page as in the following example:

```
p
{
font-family: Arial;
font-size: 12px;
font-weight: bold;
color: red;
background-color: yellow;
}
```

As you can see, although this example is getting quite complicated, it still follows the basic principles we established earlier. As your CSS rules become more complicated, you'll find them easier to read if you put each declaration on a separate line. Although not strictly necessary, this can help to establish exactly what a specific rule is targeting.

Now that you know what a CSS rule looks like, we need to show you how to add one to a web page. We'll introduce this in the next section, working on our King Kong page to add some basic style to it.

Adding CSS to a web page

Now that you've seen what CSS rules look like, we need to add them to our XHTML pages. There are two primary ways to do this: using either an embedded style sheet, where the style sheet is on the page itself, or an external style sheet, where the style sheet is an external file that is linked to.

While using an external style sheet—one CSS file that controls *all* the pages in our web site—will be our ultimate goal, we'll be focusing on embedded style sheets for the next few chapters.

When embarking on a project, it's often easiest to start with an embedded style sheet to work out basic issues like styling and layout. Having everything—XHTML and CSS—on one page makes developing and fine-tuning a little easier, as everything is located in one place, allowing you to test the effect of your CSS on your markup within a single file. Once you've reached a point at which you're happy with your CSS, it can be offloaded to an external style sheet which, when linked to by each page, will style all the pages in your web site. We'll cover external style sheets in Chapter 13.

One other method—which we'll just mention briefly—is the use of inline styles. Not too dissimilar to the <font> tag we introduced previously, CSS can be used inline to style elements as they occur, as in the following example:

```
<p style="color: red;">King Kong is the name of a fictional giant
ape from the legendary Skull Island...</p>
```

While inline styles can be useful in edge case scenarios, we've chosen not to cover them in this book, focusing instead on embedded and external style sheets.

Adding an embedded style sheet

When embedding a style sheet, we add our various CSS rules within a style element, which we place within the head as in the following example:

```
<!DOCTYPE html PUBLIC "-//W3C//DTD XHTML 1.0 Strict//EN"
"http://www.w3.org/TR/xhtml1/DTD/xhtml1-strict.dtd">
<html xmlns="http://www.w3.org/1999/xhtml">
<head>
  <meta http-equiv="content-type" content="text/html; charset=utf-8" />
  <title>King Kong | Apes in the Movies | Famous Primates</title>
  <style type="text/css">

    p
    {
    color: red;
    }

  </style>
</head>
...
```

The style element is simply another XHTML element, which informs the browser that everything between the opening <style...> and closing </style> tags is CSS. The type attribute is required; it specifies the language of the elements contained within the <style> tags. Put simply, it informs the browser that we're breaking out of XHTML and entering into CSS (text/css). Figure 8-5 visualizes this.

8

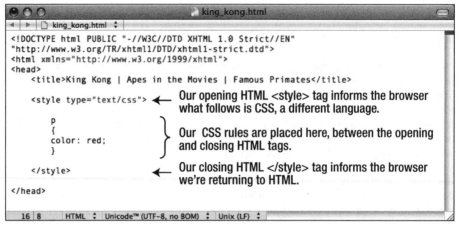

Figure 8-5. Our simple CSS rule, located in an embedded style sheet in the head element

Let's take a look at an actual example—the King Kong page we last worked with in Chapter 6—and see how adding CSS to an unstyled XHTML page works in action. We compare this page unstyled and with some basic style added in Figure 8-6.

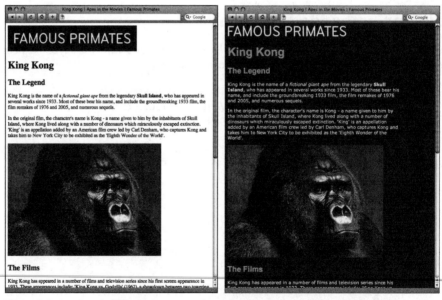

Figure 8-6. Our unstyled King Kong page as it stood at the end of Chapter 6 alongside the same page with some basic style added with CSS

A simple walkthrough

We'll start with the King Kong page that we've been working on in the previous chapters. As the page currently stands it has no style added and so displays using the browser's default style sheet. It's simply an unstyled, but well-structured XHTML page.

In this walkthrough we'll style the body, h1, h2, and p elements to introduce you to the fundamental principles of adding CSS to a web page, but before we get our hands dirty with the CSS, there's just one more thing we need to mention: colors.

Getting colorful

In the preceding examples, we've used keywords to specify our colors, for example, red, teal, and yellow. Although there are a number of additional keywords, there are only 16 original color keywords defined in the HTML 4.01 specification: aqua, black, blue, fuchsia, gray, green, lime, maroon, navy, olive, purple, red, silver, teal, white, and yellow. These 16 keywords are the only ones that are considered valid by the W3C CSS Validation Service.

The world as we see it, however, is not restricted to 16 colors, so why should it be any different in web design? The answer is it's not. We don't need to restrict ourselves to using keywords to specify colors; instead, we can inform the browser we'd like a specific color by using a more specific method of identifying color.

There are a number of methods of selecting colors in CSS; the one we'll be using is **hexadecimal**. "Hexadeciwhat?!" you ask? Good question. Using hexadecimal notation to select colors allows us to access a much broader range of colors, far more than the 16 we've been restricted to so far. But what exactly is hexadecimal?

Think of a paint chart. You can select *Blossom Apple White*, a *human-readable* name; however, it will very likely also have a specific reference or code, for example, *DECT31415*, a *machine-readable* name. Let's take a look at the colors we've introduced previously—teal, red, and yellow—and see how they are specified in hexadecimal.

- teal: #008080
- red: #FF0000
- yellow: #FFFF00

Each code indicates a different color, using a computer-friendly method (computers, unlike most humans, love code). Right now you don't need to know the ins and outs of how and why hexadecimal is used, you can simply use the handy page we've created for you at the book's companion web site to select the color you require:

> www.webstandardistas.com/color

Most image editors, for example Photoshop, allow you to find any color's hexadecimal value, as highlighted in Figure 8-7.

8

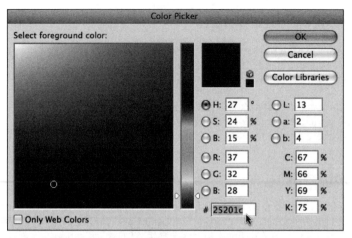

Figure 8-7. Photoshop's Color Picker shows the hexadecimal color value.

> You can find further color inspiration at Adobe's Kuler web site (http://kuler.adobe. com), which offers a number of color palettes submitted by users worldwide. Another excellent source of inspiration is COLOURlovers (www.colourlovers.com).

Styling the <body>

The first thing we'll style is the body; this essentially styles everything that displays within the body element. By now you're probably a little tired of XHTML pages that display as black text on a white background, courtesy of the browser's default style sheet. Good news, this is finally about to change.

First we'll introduce a rule with just one declaration to style the background of the page, in this case displaying it in a dark shade of brown, worthy of a fearsome fictional gorilla. Now that you know you can use hexadecimal color, let's find a nice shade of dark brown for our King Kong web page. After some deliberation, we've chosen #26201C as our perfect shade of brown. Let's have a look at our page with this first CSS rule added:

```
<!DOCTYPE html PUBLIC "-//W3C//DTD XHTML 1.0 Strict//EN"
"http://www.w3.org/TR/xhtml1/DTD/xhtml1-strict.dtd">
<html xmlns="http://www.w3.org/1999/xhtml">
<head>
  <meta http-equiv="content-type" content="text/html; charset=utf-8" />
  <title>King Kong | Apes in the Movies | Famous Primates</title>
  <style type="text/css">

  body
  {
  background-color: #26201C;
  }
```

```
    </style>
  </head>
  <body>
    <p><img src="primates_brand_black.png" alt="Famous Primates"
    width="420" height="80" /></p>
    <h1>King Kong</h1>
    ...
  </body>
</html>
```

The result of adding this simple CSS rule is shown in Figure 8-8.

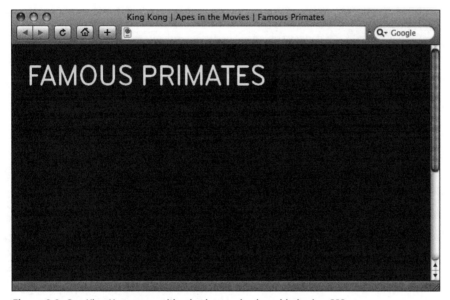

Figure 8-8. Our King Kong page with a background color added using CSS

This is a start, but there's clearly more work to do here. As things stand the text on the page is more than a little hard to read when rendered black on dark brown. It's high time for an additional CSS declaration in our body rule:

```
<style type="text/css">

    body
    {
    color: #F3F1EC;
    background-color: #26201C;
    }

</style>
```

We've added the declaration color: #F3F1EC; to our first CSS rule. This sets the text color of all elements appearing within the body to a shade of creamy white. When specifying a background-color in your CSS, it's good practice to always specify a contrasting text color to ensure that your text remains legible to all.

Another thing we've noticed is that the image displaying the Famous Primates brand would look much better if it matched our fearsome gorilla-brown background color and had some of the space around it removed.

We've taken care of this by firing up our image editor, changing the background color of the Famous Primates brand image to match our CSS background color, #26201C, cropping it slightly, and saving a new image to the images folder. Our King Kong page now looks like Figure 8-9.

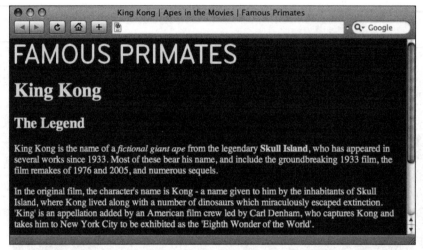

Figure 8-9. The text color is now a creamy white to contrast with the dark brown background color. The brand image background color has also been changed to match the background color of the page.

Much better!

The next thing we'll tackle is the line length. As things currently stand, our paragraphs occupy the full width of the browser window. For anyone using a large monitor this could result in very long lines of text that are difficult to read, as in Figure 8-10.

Figure 8-10. Without a set width, our paragraphs occupy the full width of the browser window.

Adding a simple declaration to the body rule allows us to control the width of the elements within our page. This will be our first small step toward creating a CSS-based layout that we will expand upon over the next few chapters, introducing more versatile alternatives to setting a width on the body element.

Our CSS rule styling the body now looks like this:

```
<style type="text/css">

  body
  {
  color: #F3F1EC;
  background-color: #26201C;
  width: 550px;
  }

</style>
```

> In typography the width of a line of text is known as its **measure**. Too long a measure results in text that is difficult to read. The eye gets to the end of a very long line of text, and then needs to find the beginning of the next line, often getting lost in the process. Equally too short a measure can be frustrating to read with the eye having to jump back and forth as it reaches the end of lots of very short lines.
>
> A look at most books will reveal that there is an optimum measure around which most designers tend to settle. This can vary upon the type of content; however, it is generally agreed to be between 50–60 characters per line. In practice different typefaces will result in different line lengths, especially in an online context where the user can scale text up and down.

Our next step is to look at styling our h1 and h2 headings.

Styling the headings: <h1> and <h2>

Now that we've set the width and styled both the text color and the background color of our King Kong web page, we'll take a look at styling the h1 element. We'll create a CSS rule for it and change its typeface, size, and color.

In the style section of the document, we add a new rule as follows:

```
<style type="text/css">

body
  {
  color: #F3F1EC;
  background-color: #26201C;
  width: 550px;
  }
```

8

```
h1
{
font-family: Arial;
font-size: 36px;
color: #9CC4E5;
}
```

```
</style>
```

This additional rule specifies the typeface Arial for our h1. We've also set the size to 36px (pixels), which is slightly larger than the browser default shown in Figures 8-8 to 8-10. The h1 has also been colored a light shade of blue, specified as the hexadecimal color #9CC4E5. The result of these declarations can be seen in Figure 8-11.

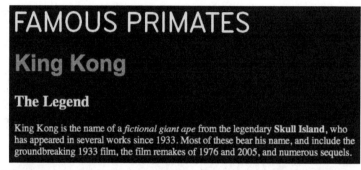

Figure 8-11. The King Kong h1 is now displayed in Arial at 36 pixels in a light shade of blue.

Next we'll add a rule for the h2, almost identical to the h1 rule; it looks like this:

```
h2
{
font-family: Arial;
font-size: 24px;
color: #9CC4E5;
}
```

The only difference between this rule and the previous one styling the h1 is the font-size, which we've set to a slightly smaller size of 24px.

> You'll notice we've used sizes of *36px* and *24px*, setting the sizes in px or pixels. There are a number of options for sizing type, including pixels, %, ems, or keywords. We'll introduce the thorny topic of sizing type in more detail in the following chapter when we look closely at styling text.

As the rules for the h1 and the h2 are largely identical, we can use one of the features of CSS to simplify our style sheet a little. Rather than specifying font-family: Arial; for every single element, we can specify it just once: in the rule styling the body.

The h1, h2, and other elements on the page—which are all nested *within* the body—will *inherit* this style (we'll cover the intricacies of inheritance in the following chapter). Our revised style sheet, with the font-family declaration removed from the h1 and h2 rules and applied to the body rule, looks like this:

```
<style type="text/css">

body
  {
  font-family: Arial;
  color: #F3F1EC;
  background-color: #26201C;
  width: 550px;
  }

h1
  {
  font-size: 36px;
  color: #9CC4E5;
  }

h2
  {
  font-size: 24px;
  color: #9CC4E5;
  }

</style>
```

The result of this revision can be seen in Figure 8-12, which shows the headings and the paragraphs now all being displayed in Arial, all thanks to the power of **inheritance**.

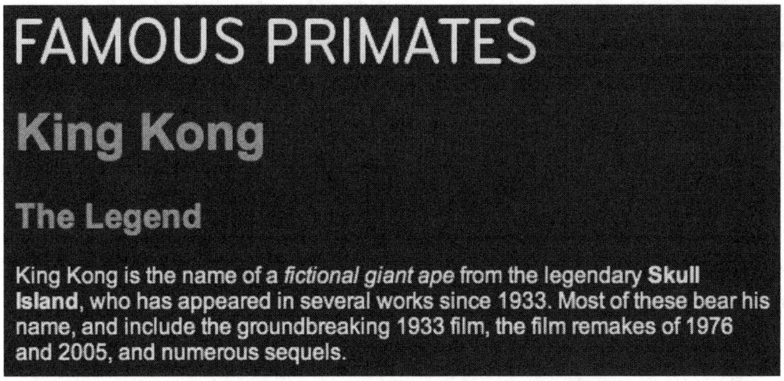

Figure 8-12. Applying the font-family declaration to the body results in our headings and paragraphs all displaying in Arial.

Styling the <p>

But what if we don't want all headings and paragraphs to be displayed in the same type-face? Have no fear, there's an easy solution at hand. Let's have a look at styling our p, changing its typeface from the style specified previously to a different typeface, Verdana. While we're at it, we'll also change the size of the paragraph text.

We add a rule to our style sheet as follows:

```
<style type="text/css">

body
{
font-family: Arial;
color: #F3F1EC;
background-color: #26201C;
width:550px;
}

h1
{
font-size: 36px;
color: #9CC4E5;
}

h2
{
font-size: 24px;
color: #9CC4E5;
}

p
{
font-family: Verdana;
font-size: 14px;
}

</style>
```

Adding the font-family: Verdana; declaration to the p overrides the font-family: Arial; declaration of the body. We'll explain exactly how this works in the next chapter when we discuss the topic of **specificity**.

The result of adding this last rule, styling the p, can be seen in Figure 8-13. As you can see, the rule styles all the p elements on the page, displaying them in Verdana at a size of 13 px.

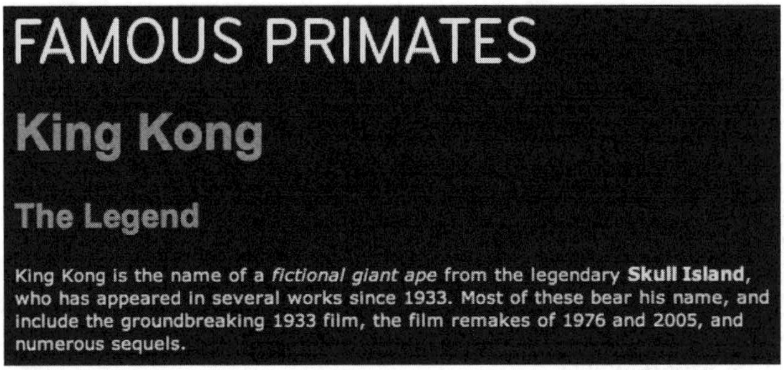

Figure 8-13. Adding a font-family declaration to our p overrides the font-family declaration on the body.

The CSS added to the King Kong page in this chapter is just a start of our journey using style sheets. Although the rules introduced so far are relatively simple ones, they introduce the fundamental principles of CSS. With a little experimentation in your own time, you can try out different typefaces, sizes, and colors and apply CSS to some of the other web pages you've created for your homework.

Commenting your CSS

Just like HTML allows you to use hidden comments within your markup to make notes and selectively hide sections of a web page during the development process, you can also add comments within your CSS, assisting you as you develop your style sheets.

As with HTML comments, CSS comments are useful for a number of purposes: making notes during the development process; commenting out single declarations within a rule; commenting out entire rules; adding structural comments to break your CSS down into logical, grouped sections; and, lastly, giving your CSS a title, useful for keeping a track of the creation date and version number, or noting who created it.

Where HTML uses an opening <!-- and a closing --> to contain your comments, CSS uses an opening /* and a closing */. This is shown in the following two examples so that you can clearly distinguish the syntax. The first example shows an HTML comment; you should be familiar with this by now:

```
<!--
<p>I am a paragraph element that has been hidden from the browser
within comments.</p>
-->
```

The next example shows a CSS comment:

```
/*

The following rule has been hidden from the browser within comments.
```

```
h1
{
font-size: 36px;
color: #9CC4E5;
}
*/
```

As we covered in the introduction to this section, comments in CSS can serve a variety of purposes; let's run through these one by one. Although you're only getting started with CSS and some of these uses will be more relevant when you're writing more complicated style sheets and creating external CSS files, we feel it's useful to gather the examples in one section for easy reference.

As with HTML comments, CSS comments can be useful to keep track of changes or to provide notes for useful reference; following is an example of a note:

```
<style type="text/css">

    body
    {
    background-color: #26201C;
    }

    /* All <h1> instances are set to display in Arial at 36px in a shade
    of blue (#9CC4E5) to contrast with the dark brown background. */

    h1
    {
    font-family: Arial;
    font-size: 36px;
    color: #9CC4E5;
    }

    ...

</style>
```

The ability to comment your CSS can also be very useful throughout the development process. As browsers ignore anything between the opening /* and the closing */, CSS comments can be used to selectively switch on and off entire rules, single declarations within rules, or groups of declarations within rules, as shown in the following examples.

Imagine you're creating a style sheet, and in the process you're trying out a new color for your h1s. You're not 100% convinced that the color's right; perhaps the page looked better before you added the color declaration. Commenting out the declaration, as in the following example, allows you to quickly see how the page looked *before* you decided on chimp vomit green for all your h1s:

```
<style type="text/css">

    ...
```

```
h1
{
font-family: Arial;
font-size: 36px;
/* color: #33FF00; */
}

...

</style>
```

Sitting between comments (or **commented out**), the color: #33FF00; declaration will be ignored by the browser, switching off the chimp vomit green on the h1s. This method makes experimentation easy; if you want to switch the color back on, all you need to do is uncomment the rule.

> *Just like cornflower blue, chocolate brown, and school bus yellow are accepted as "officially recognized" color names, so too is chimp vomit green. Coined by noted web standards advocate Jeffrey Zeldman in his book* Designing with Web Standards *(Peachpit Press, 2006), the term* chimp vomit green *is used to describe a color generated by a Netscape-related browser bug.*

You can use the same method to temporarily disable more than just one declaration in your style sheet, switching off multiple declarations, or even hiding entire CSS rules as in the next example:

```
<style type="text/css">

...

h1
{
font-family: Arial;
font-size: 36px;
color: #33FF00;
}

/*
p
{
font-family: Verdana;
font-size: 14px;
}
*/

...

</style>
```

8

In the preceding example, the comment spans several lines, commenting out the entire p rule. Using CSS comments like this during the development process can be extremely helpful, both when experimenting and troubleshooting.

Although we've only just introduced CSS in this chapter and the style sheets we've shown are quite simple, as your style sheets grow in complexity, you'll find using structural comments to break your CSS down into logical, grouped sections makes the development process easier in the long run. For example, grouping together body and layout sections, typography sections, link styles, and so on can make finding these sections and making changes to them much simpler.

The following examples show some CSS comments used to provide visual breaks within a style sheet, helping to visually separate each logical section. Breaking down a complicated style sheet like this helps finding different sections of the CSS easier:

```
/*
Typography
*/
```

Stylizing these comments a little more can help to visually separate them from your CSS rules as in the following example:

```
/*
Typography
**************************************************
*/
```

Lastly, you can use CSS comments to give your style sheet a title, useful for keeping track of the creation date and version number, or noting who created it. Although we're using an embedded style sheet at this point, CSS comments can be useful to provide you with a quick reference to the status of a style sheet, for example, what version of the style sheet it is and when it was last updated.

The following comment shows a typical example of this that we'll be using at the top of our King Kong web page's CSS as we continue to develop it:

```
<style type="text/css">

    /*
    Famous Primates CSS
    Copyright (C) 2008 Christopher Murphy and Nicklas Persson
    Version: 2.4C
    Last Revision: Thursday, 6 November, 2008 [CM]
    www.webstandardistas.com
    */

    ...

</style>
```

This allows us to keep track of who last edited the CSS and when. In this case we can see the style sheet was last updated on Thursday, 6 November 2008 by CM (the initials of the person who made the last revision).

Summary

So what have we covered? This chapter marked the beginning of our journey into CSS. We've introduced you to some simple CSS rules and covered how to add them to your web pages. Although it might not look like we've changed our basic web page much in the example we've walked through, we've introduced the underlying concept of CSS and how you implement it.

Having followed the preceding examples, you should now know enough to begin adding some style to your well-structured HTML pages that you created as a part of the previous chapters' homework.

In the next chapter we'll take our working knowledge of CSS and expand upon it, enabling you to create web pages that are both well-structured and well-presented. Good times indeed.

Homework: Adding some CSS to Gordo's web page

In this chapter we've introduced CSS, which will allow you to style a number of the elements on the page you've been working on for Gordo. Now it's time for you to give Gordo's page a makeover.

We looked at how CSS rules are written, in particular introducing the idea that one CSS rule could have multiple declarations styling a variety of different properties, for example, font-family, font-size, font-weight, color, and background-color.

We also showed you how to add an embedded style sheet to a web page where, for now, you'll be locating all of your CSS rules. Lastly, we covered the use of comments in CSS and how they can be used to structure and order your CSS rules.

In our King Kong walkthrough, we styled the body, h1, h2, and p elements to introduce you to the fundamental principles of adding CSS to a web page. You'll be applying style to these elements on your Gordo page for this chapter's homework. The process of adding these elements will reinforce the fundamentals of CSS and will form the basis for the following few chapters' homework.

You're embarking on a new language in this homework—writing style sheets. Completing this homework will equip you with a firm grasp of the principles of CSS, something that will prove important as we embark on the forthcoming chapters, which progressively add complexity.

1. Add your <style> tags

Open the gordo.html file in your pioneers folder. In order to add some CSS rules to this page, you'll need to add some <style> tags. In the head section, add an opening <style ="text/css"> tag and a closing </style> tag. You'll be placing all of your CSS rules within these tags.

2. Style the <body>

Referring to the examples in this chapter, style the body element on Gordo's web page. We'd like you to create a rule with three declarations that styles the color and background-color and sets a width for the elements nested within the body.

3. Style the headings

Once you've styled the body, it's time to style the headings. In our King Kong example, we styled the h1 and h2; we'd like you to do the same for the Gordo page. Add new rules to your embedded style sheet for the h1 and h2 elements and style the font-family, font-size, and color of both.

4. Style the paragraphs

The last rule we'd like you to create is for the paragraphs. Create a rule targeting all of the p elements and apply some style to the font-family and font-size to differentiate the paragraphs from the headings.

5. Add a comment

Once you've completed the previous stage, add a CSS comment within the embedded style sheet, giving it a title and a version number (presumably version 1.0), and noting the date you created it. You can do this by leaving a comment at the top of the CSS as follows:

```
/*
Famous Primates CSS
Version: 1.0
Last Revision: Thursday, 6 November, 2008 [CM]
*/
```

To help you with these stages we've created a similarly styled page about King Kong. You can refer to this, using your browser's View Source menu command to see how we've applied our CSS to it, here:

www.webstandardistas.com/08/king_kong.html

6. Validate

You won't be surprised to hear that we'd like you to validate Gordo's new CSS using the W3C CSS Validation Service. Like the W3C Markup Validation Service—for XHTML—that you've been using so far, it offers an option to validate by direct input, allowing you to copy and paste your code into the web page. Alternatively you can enter the URL of your file if you've uploaded it. The W3C CSS Validation Service is available here:

http://jigsaw.w3.org/css-validator/

In the event of errors, the CSS validator offers similar clues to its XHTML counterpart, giving the line number of each error. If you run into errors, debug your CSS and revalidate.

Once you're welcomed with the message, "Congratulations! No Error Found." put the kettle on and enjoy a cup of *Kokei Cha* as you prepare yourself for the next chapter.

8

CHAPTER 9
STYLING TEXT

King Kong

The Legend

The Extravaganza

References

King Kong is the name of a *fiction*
who has appeared in several works
and include the groundbreaking 19
and numerous sequels.

In the original film, the character's
inhabitants of Skull Island, where
which miraculously escaped extinc
American film crew led by Carl Der
New York City to be exhibited as th

REFERENCES

1. The Lumiere Reader – King
2. King Kong – An Entertaining
3. Kong is King – The History o

In the last chapter we introduced you to the basics of CSS, adding a little style to our King Kong web page. In this chapter we go a bit further, styling all of the typographic elements on the mighty gorilla's web page. Cue thunderous roar from the jungle.

We deliberately kept things simple with our King Kong page in the last chapter, styling only a few elements: the body, h1, h2, and p. In this chapter we'll build on what we demonstrated in the last chapter and delve a little bit deeper into CSS, introducing and expanding on some underlying concepts along the way.

This chapter's focus is specifically on styling text, an area CSS is particularly well suited to. By the end of the chapter you should not only have a deeper understanding of how to use CSS, but also have an insight into how powerful it can be in transforming any well-structured XHTML web page into a well-styled, great-looking web page. This chapter also introduces a number of different methods of specifying font sizes in CSS: pixels, ems, and keywords. All have strengths. Unfortunately, all *also* have weaknesses.

We conclude the chapter with a walkthrough of our new, improved King Kong page, along the way introducing a wide variety of ways to make your text more readable and more pleasing to the eye.

Typography on the Web

Working through another pass of the CSS of our King Kong web page will introduce you to some of the fundamentals of typography, including some general typographic principles and a few new terms. It will also highlight how designing for the Web, particularly when it comes to typography, has its limitations, but equally can offer a number of opportunities and advantages.

Before we embark on a look at the specifics of typography on the Web, it's worth defining what exactly typography is.

What is typography?

Typography is often defined in traditional terms referring to the world of print—books, magazines, newspapers . . . in short, anything *printed*. However, typography isn't just appropriate to print, it's also appropriate to everything we create onscreen. In short, anywhere that type is used.

We can define typography as follows:

> **typography** –n. **1** the art or process of setting and arranging types and printing from them **2** the style and appearance of printed matter
>
> *Concise Oxford Dictionary* (Clarendon Press, 1990)

However, this definition implies typography is limited to print, but as you learned hands-on in the last chapter, typography is also used online. After all, we set and arranged some type when we specified both a `font-family` and a `font-size` for the h1, h2, and p elements on our King Kong web page.

Clearly typography is *also* of interest on the Web.

> In traditional typographic terminology, a typeface and a font are not the same. A **typeface** refers to a whole family of type, for example, Times New Roman. A **font**, however, refers to one instance of this typeface, for example, Time New Roman, Italic, 12 pt. This is because historically every typeface would have been comprised of a number of fonts, all cast in metal and set by hand. In a web-based context, however, the terms typeface and font are used interchangeably.

One of the greatest benefits of using CSS to style text is the control it gives us over typography and, equally importantly, its flexibility.

CSS: Our flexible friend

The separation of your content, marked up as well-structured XHTML, and its visual presentation, controlled by your CSS rules, makes for a remarkably flexible and efficient way of applying style to your web pages.

Style is not only easy to apply, but also easy to change: simply alter a rule in your style sheet and *Hey Presto!* your page is displayed using a different typeface at a different size. This enables you to quickly prototype and test design ideas, adjusting your page's typography through nothing more than simple changes and modifications to your style sheet. Herein lies the real power of CSS.

You'll discover this to your delight if approaching a redesign of your XHTML pages. In most cases you can simply take your existing content, marked up semantically, rework the CSS rules in your style sheet, and have a new design ready in an instant.

Making your text accessible

As Joe Clark, a noted accessibility advocate, states,

> Reading is the primary activity of the Web. For people with impaired vision who do not use screen readers, colour choices and, to a far lesser extent, type size become the accessibility issues.
>
> `www.joeclark.org/book/sashay/serialization/Chapter09.html`

An added benefit of CSS, which leverages the separation of content and presentation inherent in the Web Standardistas' approach, lies in the ability to create alternative style

9

sheets for different users. One example would be the creation of a high-contrast style sheet for visually impaired users—easy to create, given the solid foundation of semantic markup that you are now used to creating.

Another advantage of CSS is that it gives a greater level of control to the user, for example, allowing the user to resize text or increase the contrast on the page, making the pages more accessible. While at first this lack of control can appear daunting from a designer's perspective, its important to remember that the primary purpose of the Web as envisaged by Tim Berners-Lee was to make as much information as possible accessible to as wide an audience as possible. A good thing.

Inheritance and specificity

In the last chapter we applied some basic style to the elements on our King Kong page. To refresh your memory, among a few other rules, we specified a font-family and text color for our web page, as shown in the following example:

```
body
{
font-family: Arial;
color: #F3F1EC;
...
}
```

Looking at this rule again you might be forgiven for asking, "Why are we styling a font-family and color on the body element? Why not on the elements themselves? The h1s, h2s, ps, and so on?"

The answer, as we alluded to in the previous chapter, lies in the issue of *inheritance*. Although it can take a little getting used to, the concept of inheritance lies at the heart of CSS and is essential to grasp if you want to create efficient web pages with a minimum of markup. Let's dive right in.

Inheritance

In Chapter 2 we introduced the idea of the document tree, explaining how elements can be nested. You might recall that our simple "Hello World!" web page had a single p nested within the body. Another way of describing the relationship between these elements would be to state that the p element is *descended* from its parent element, the body.

So the p is a child of the body, and conversely, the body is a parent of the p. The important point to note is that *the elements have a relationship to each other*.

Just like children inherit characteristics from their parents in the real world, child elements inherit characteristics from their parent elements in the world of CSS.

If we look at our King Kong web page, we can see that the body element contains the following child elements: h1–h4, p, em, strong, blockquote, cite, abbr, ul, ol, li, a, and img.

Considerably more child elements than the "Hello World!" web page we first built, proof—
if it were needed—of your growing capabilities as a Web Standardista.

In Figure 9-1 we've illustrated a simplified version of the document tree for the King Kong
web page (for the purposes of simplicity, we haven't included *all* of the elements descended
from the body).

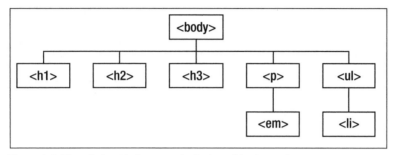

Figure 9-1. The relationship between the body and its descendants

Looking at Figure 9-1, you'll also notice that in addition to all of the elements on the King
Kong page being descended from the body element, there are other elements with child
elements. In our simplified example, both the p and ul elements have children, the former
an em, the latter an li.

The King Kong page we've created also has another element descended from the body
which itself has a number of child elements. The blockquote features two children: two ps,
one of which has a descendent, namely a cite element, as shown in Figure 9-2.

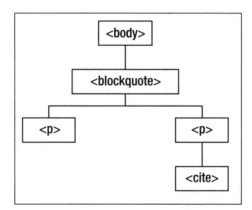

Figure 9-2. Our cite element is a child of a p,
itself a child of the blockquote which, in turn, is
a child of the body. Think of this as a family tree.

Given that all of these elements are descended from the body element, they *inherit* any
rules applied to the body. What this means is that we don't need to write rules for each of
the elements we'd like to style; we can instead rely on inheritance to take care of this for
us, as you briefly saw in the last chapter when we applied some style to our body element.

Bravo! This is going to result in a lot less work down the line. But you might be thinking that this all looks just a little bit too easy . . .

Meet specificity

Now we've ascertained that all the CSS declarations we apply to the body element are inherited by its descendants, let's take a look at this in action. We've created a simplified version of our King Kong web page, removing most of the content so we can focus on the h1, h2, and p elements. We've created a single CSS rule to look at an example of inheritance in action. Our simplified web page looks like this:

```
<head>
...
<style type="text/css">

  body
  {
  font-family: Arial;
  font-size: 14px;
  color: #E0DFDA;
  background-color: #26201C;
  }

</style>
</head>
<body>
  <h1>King Kong</h1>
  <h2>The Legend</h2>
  <p>King Kong is the name of a <em>fictional giant ape</em> from
  the legendary <strong>Skull Island</strong>, who has appeared in
  several works since 1933. Most of these bear his name, and include
  the groundbreaking 1933 film, the film remakes of 1976 and 2005,
  and numerous sequels.</p>
</body>
```

According to the rules of inheritance we introduced earlier, we might imagine that everything on our simple web page would display in Arial at a size of 14 pixels, in cream type against a dark brown background. Let's take a look at Figure 9-3, which shows how this displays in the browser.

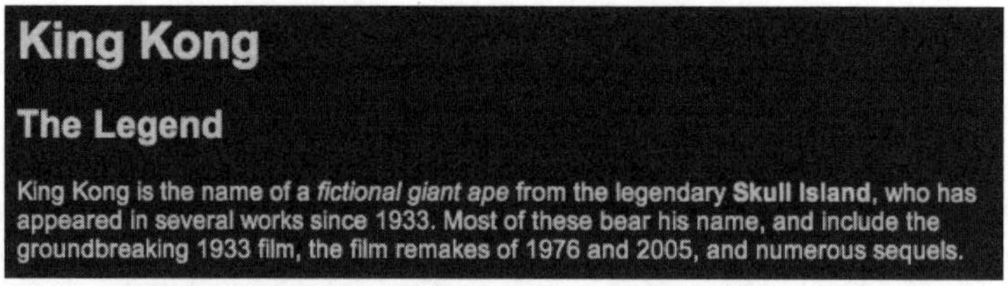

Figure 9-3. Our CSS specified a size of 14px for the body, so why aren't the h1 and h2 inheriting the 14px setting?

We'd hoped *everything* would display in Arial at a size of 14px. Our h1, h2, and p elements are displaying in Arial as we expected; however, the type is clearly not all set to 14px. Why? To answer that question we need to delve a little bit deeper into the complexities of **specificity**.

To explain this riddle, we return to our previous example where we've specified a font-size on the body. This rule should, according to the principles of inheritance, be applied to all of its descendants: the h1, h2, and p.

However, the examples we covered in the previous chapter showed us that if we wanted to change the font-size of a child element, the h1 for example, we could do so by targeting this element with a rule that would be *more specific* and therefore override the less specific rule we applied to its parent, the body.

But in this case there's no rule targeting the h1 in our style sheet—we only applied style to the body. So why is the font-size not 14px? The answer is buried deep inside your browser, in something known as the browser's *default style sheet*.

We've mentioned default styles and the browser's default style sheet previously, but what is the browser's default style sheet? The CSS rules and declarations that apply style to your web pages can in fact come from a number of sources:

Author Styles: The CSS rules we have been writing for our King Kong page are known as Author Styles, as they are style sheets provided by the author of the web page. When we mention style sheets, rules, and declarations throughout this book, we're in fact referring to Author Styles.

User Styles: The user of your web page can also create CSS rules, usually through options in their web browser. These style sheets are applied to all web pages and may override the Author Styles. User Styles might be created to enlarge text or to increase contrast, by a visually impaired user, for example.

User Agent Styles: Finally, User Agent Styles, also referred to as the browser's default style sheet, control the browser's default presentation of XHTML elements. The "unstyled" XHTML pages we worked on in the first six chapters of this book have in fact been styled all along, using the browser's default style sheet. Although these styles vary slightly between browsers, they do share common characteristics.

In the example in Figure 9-3, we used the body selector to assign some style to our page; however, it didn't affect the size of headings. That's because the browser's default style sheet is also assigning style to our page, in particular, controlling the size of the headings.

The browser's default style sheet contains a more specific rule, in this case targeting the h1 and h2 elements directly. In other words, the browser's more specific h1 and h2 rules take precedence over our less-specific body rule.

In CSS, when two or more conflicting rules are controlling the same element, the browser needs to determine which rule to follow. It does this by following a number of basic (but rather complex) rules, as we'll see in Chapter 10. In this case, the browser's default style sheet is winning and overriding the size we set for the headings.

9

Now that we've covered the tricky topics of inheritance and specificity, let's get back to the focus of this chapter: styling text.

Specifying type on the Web

In the last chapter we specified a typeface for our body element using CSS. We deliberately kept things simple, specifying Arial, a typeface most people would be familiar with. However, what if we'd like to use a different typeface? Something a little more exotic perhaps?

As anyone who has ever used Microsoft Word knows, the list of typefaces available is often very large. You might be forgiven for asking, "Why can't I specify one of these other typefaces instead?" The answer is that the display of the typeface you choose depends upon the typefaces installed on your end user's computer, not yours.

When you specify a typeface using CSS, it will only display in that typeface if it is installed on the end user's computer. With so many different operating systems—Windows Vista, Windows XP, Mac OS X, and the various flavors of Linux—all with different preinstalled typefaces, it's difficult to predict with any degree of confidence what typefaces will be on your users' computers.

So, what happens if we specify a font and the end user doesn't have it? Let's take a look. When creating the brand for our Famous Primates web site, we used a typeface called *Bryant*, a lovingly crafted sans serif typeface inspired by mechanical lettering kits used by draftsmen and amateur sign makers, created by the talented Eric Olson of Process Type Foundry (www.processtypefoundry.com). We've rewritten the body rule that specified Arial at the end of the last chapter, to specify Bryant instead, as follows:

```
body
{
font-family: Bryant;
...
}
```

Being conscientious Web Standardistas, we check it in our browser, and it displays exactly as we wanted, as in Figure 9-4.

King Kong

The Legend

King Kong is the name of a *fictional giant ape* from the legendary **Skull Island**, who has appeared in several works since 1933. Most of these bear his name, and include the groundbreaking 1933 film, the film remakes of 1976 and 2005, and numerous sequels.

Figure 9-4. Change Arial to Bryant in the CSS rule and . . . voilà! Everything changes.

Good news. The principle of inheritance is simplifying things considerably. Change the typeface on the body rule and inheritance takes care of the rest, changing the type on the whole page. Not so fast!

Being truly conscientious Web Standardistas, we know better than to check the web page only in our own browsers. We ask a friend to take a look. Disaster. Our friend sends us back a screenshot as in Figure 9-5. No Bryant, just Times New Roman. It turns out he doesn't have Bryant installed on his computer, so the type has reverted to his browser's default text style.

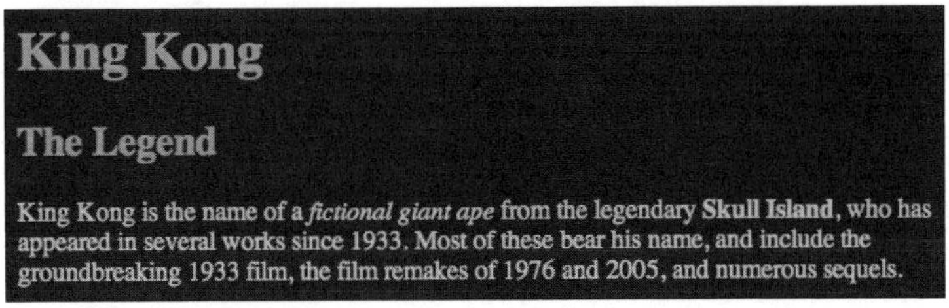

King Kong

The Legend

King Kong is the name of a *fictional giant ape* from the legendary **Skull Island**, who has appeared in several works since 1933. Most of these bear his name, and include the groundbreaking 1933 film, the film remakes of 1976 and 2005, and numerous sequels.

Figure 9-5. No Bryant. No joy.

Needless to say, Figure 9-5 wasn't how we intended this page to display at all. We were happy with it the way it displayed in Figure 9-4. Why has this happened? The answer is simple: we have the typeface Bryant installed, our friend doesn't. Without the typeface we've specified installed on his machine, the font reverts to what is defined by his browser's default style sheet, with the default typeface usually being Times New Roman.

So how can we be sure that a typeface we specify for a web page is available in browsers other than our own? In short, we can't 100%, but all is not lost. Why? Unusually—thanks goes to Microsoft . . .

9

Core Web Fonts

In 1996, Microsoft began a project to establish a standard suite of fonts for the Internet. Released under a generous end-user license, the fonts quickly became established as a cross-platform core font set that could reasonably be relied upon to be installed on most users' computers.

Although this project was discontinued by Microsoft in 2002, the generosity of the original license still allows for distribution and use of the fonts today, with the result being that they still remain prevalent. The full list of fonts available is as follows:

- Andale Mono
- Arial
- Arial Black
- Comic Sans MS
- Courier New
- Georgia

- Impact
- Times New Roman
- Trebuchet MS
- Verdana
- Webdings

As these fonts were optimized for display and legibility on screen, the best way to see how they render is to look at them in your browser. We've created a page displaying all of them here:

www.webstandardistas.com/09/core_fonts.html

Good news: specifying one of the preceding fonts is generally considered reliable as most users have them installed. Better news: we can use the preceding fonts to create a *fallback option* for anyone, like our friend in the example earlier, who doesn't have our obscure, but beloved, typefaces installed. So, how do we establish a fallback font when writing CSS?

Writing more reliable CSS rules to specify fonts

We now know that the fonts we specify in CSS will only display if the user has the same font installed on their computer. We also know that this isn't always the case.

CSS provides a solution to this problem by allowing us to specify more than one font in a CSS rule so that we can provide a list of alternatives or fallback options in the event that the typeface we'd really like is not available on the user's computer.

In the last rule, where we specified Bryant, we supplied it on its own with no fallback option. In the following rule, we'd really like Bryant to display in the first instance; however, we know not everyone has that typeface installed so we've provided a number of alternatives as follows:

```
body
{
font-family: Bryant, Arial, sans-serif;
...
}
```

The browser interprets this list of fonts in order of preference, with the first being your preferred choice. In the preceding example everything in the body will display in Bryant if the user has that typeface installed; if not it will display in Arial, and finally, as a last resort, it will display in the browser's generic sans serif font (unless a different sans serif font has been explicitly set as a *User Style* preference, as mentioned earlier in the chapter).

Let's return to our friend who doesn't have the typeface Bryant; in his browser the revised page now displays as in Figure 9-6.

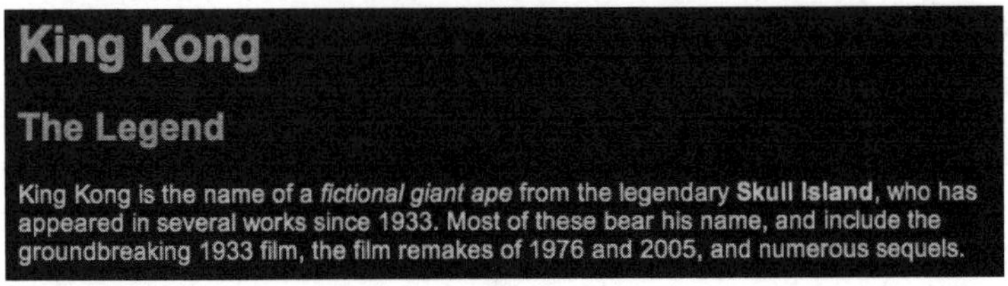

King Kong

The Legend

King Kong is the name of a *fictional giant ape* from the legendary **Skull Island**, who has appeared in several works since 1933. Most of these bear his name, and include the groundbreaking 1933 film, the film remakes of 1976 and 2005, and numerous sequels.

Figure 9-6. The page displayed in our friend's browser. He doesn't have Bryant, so the page displays using our fallback typeface, Arial.

Both Bryant and Arial are sans serif typefaces, and although we may prefer the look of the page displayed using Bryant, the fallback typefaces share the basic characteristics of our first choice. As you've seen from the list of Core Web Fonts, you can also be reasonably assured that Arial will be widely installed. Selecting it as a fallback font has resulted in a page that retains many of the typographic characteristics we were aiming for.

Microsoft's Core Web Fonts were specifically designed for use onscreen and are consequently very readable on most computers. Modern operating systems, Macintosh OS X for instance, however, have made the display of fonts originally designed for print much more viable for onscreen use.

When considering legibility and readability, it's worth considering the best typeface for the job. The Guardian, *which we highlighted in Chapter 3, decided to use Arial as a body font instead of Helvetica because Arial—being custom-designed for the Web—looked better in a wider range of environments.*

So, selecting a carefully considered list of fonts when specifying your font-family can help when a user doesn't have the *exact* typeface you'd like.

Let's take a look at this CSS rule again:

```
body
{
font-family: Bryant, Arial, sans-serif;
...
}
```

You may be forgiven for asking, "What typeface is sans-serif?" Unlike Bryant or Arial, sans serif is not a specific typeface, but a *generic font family*. There are five generic font families built into the CSS language. These are often used as "an option of last resort" when specifying a list of alternative font values.

The five generic font families are as follows.

Serif

Serif fonts are characterized by decorative serifs, or accents, at the ends of various letter strokes. Used widely on the Web, serif fonts are sometimes considered to have a classic, formal style. Examples include Times New Roman, Georgia, and Garamond.

9

Sans serif

Sans serif translates literally as *without serif*. Unsurprisingly sans serif fonts have simpler forms than serif fonts. Also used widely on the Web, sans serif fonts can be seen as having a clean, modern style. Examples include Helvetica, Arial, and Trebuchet.

Monospace

As the name implies, the width of the characters in a monospace font—a, b, c . . . , A, B, C . . . , 1, 2, 3 . . .—are all the same. They are most often specified for displaying examples of computer code, where monospaced characters make the code easier to read. Examples include Andale Mono, Courier New, and Monaco.

Cursive

Cursive fonts emulate handwritten letterforms and have a scriptlike appearance. Their characteristics can vary widely, and most cursive fonts are unlikely to be present on a majority of computers. They should therefore be used with caution. Examples include Bello, Caflisch Script, and Ex Ponto.

Fantasy

Fantasy fonts (who, we ask, came up with the term *fantasy fonts*?) are primarily decorative and usually intended for headings. The junk-drawer of generic families, fantasy fonts don't necessarily share many characteristics, and most are unlikely to be present on a majority of computers. Specifying fantasy fonts is an unpredictable affair, perhaps one reason why these fonts aren't widely used on the Web. Examples include Impact, Critter, and Cottonwood.

Now that we've covered the font-family affair in some detail, let's move swiftly on and talk about another important issue for many: size.

Size matters

In the last chapter we set a font-size for our paragraphs as follows:

```
p
{
font-size: 14px;
}
```

thus setting all instances of p at 14px (or 14 pixels), deliberately keeping things simple. When it comes to setting font-size, however, we have a number of options available, including pixels, ems, and keywords. As we mentioned in the introduction, all have strengths; all also have weaknesses. In this section we focus on two units of measure: pixels and ems. Before we get to those, however, first a word on **keywords**.

CSS includes seven font-size keywords, ranging from xx-small to xx-large, which are relative to the browser's medium setting (where the medium setting is usually interpreted as 16px). In addition to a number of issues in older browsers that require workarounds, the problem with keywords is their lack of precision. Imagine you'd like to buy a T-shirt, xx-large is a little too big, but x-large is just a little too small. Herein lies the problem. That said, if you don't care exactly what size your T-shirt is, maybe keywords are for you . . .

Sizing text with pixels

Sizing your type using pixels is perhaps the easiest method, which explains why we've used it so far; however, it too has its limitations. If you want your paragraphs to appear at a size of 14px, you simply write a CSS rule as we did in the last chapter:

```
p
{
font-size: 14px;
}
```

What if you'd prefer them at 18px? Simply rewrite the value:

```
p
{
font-size: 18px;
}
```

Sizing text in pixels allows you to get consistent font sizing in your web pages without trouble. It's also quite easy to grasp the relationship between different font sizes on your web pages: 10px will be half the size of 20px and so on. Great news, but there's a catch.

The main drawback with sizing text in pixels lies with the issue of accessibility. Internet Explorer 6—rapidly dropping in popularity, but still a widely installed browser—is not capable of resizing text specified in pixels. Where other browsers allow the user to resize text set in pixels, IE 6 has no method of doing so. For people who like their text to be larger (or indeed smaller) than the designer specified in the style sheet, IE 6 and pixels are not a winning combination.

IE 7 goes some way toward resolving this with a feature called **Page Zoom**, which enlarges the entire web page, including images. However, this behavior quickly becomes unwieldy, leading to horizontal scrollbars as your page zooms up. This is better than nothing, but it's not ideal.

If accessibility and allowing the visitors of your web site to resize the text to a size that suits them is important to you, consider ems or keywords instead.

Sizing text with ems

So by now you're really hoping that ems are the Holy Grail. Not quite. (Honestly, are you surprised?) While it's true that ems have a lot going for them, they also have some drawbacks (not least the need to get your head around some, at times complicated, math).

9

An em, not to be confused with the HTML element em, is a relative measure used when sizing type. Ems are *calculated based on the font size of the parent element*. What does that mean in English? Let's look at an example:

```
<body>
  <p><strong>King Kong</strong> is the name of a fictional giant ape
  from the legendary Skull Island.</p>
</body>
```

Imagine you'd like the paragraph in this example to appear at a size equivalent to 14 pixels. You first need to determine the font size of the *parent* element of the p. Now you're thinking, "The parent element? What's that again?"

There's no need to panic; when we introduced the concept of inheritance earlier in this chapter, you met parent and child elements. The parent element of the p in the preceding example is the body, which means we need to establish a size for the body and the p will then be sized relative to that.

If you have a degree in astrophysics, great. If not, brace yourself for a little mathematics.

Most modern browsers have a default paragraph text size that is 16px, that is, unstyled p elements will display at 16px using the browser's default style sheet.

By adding the following rule to a style sheet, we can change the default font size of the page from 16px to anything we'd like by changing the percentage. In the following example we set the default font-size on the body to 62.5%.

```
body
{
font-size: 62.5%;
}
```

Why 62.5%?

62.5% of 16 pixels is 10 pixels. 10 is a nice round number. Setting the base font-size of the body to 10px makes working out relative sizes considerably easier. Using the declaration font-size: 62.5%; sets 1em at 10px. We'd like our paragraphs to display at 14 px. We now size them *in relation to* the body element (1em = 10px, therefore 1.4em = 14px) using the following rules:

```
body
{
font-size: 62.5%;
}

p
{
font-size: 1.4em;
}
```

Let's recap because it's a little convoluted! We've reduced the font size of the body element to 10px in our first rule using a percentage of 62.5% (remember, most browsers have a default font-size of 16px and 62.5% × 16px = 10px). Everything will be sized relative to the body, which is the *parent* element of everything on the page. The second rule is setting the paragraph to 1.4 times the size of the parent element, or 14px. *Voilà!*

Although this is not as straightforward as setting sizes directly in pixels, this method has the advantage of allowing users to resize their text in any relatively modern browser, including IE 6. For accessibility purposes, this is a good thing to strive for.

> *If you're wondering why the font-size in the body element is specified using a percentage instead of using 0.625em, which **should** have the same effect, congratulations, you've just earned five extra nerd points! The answer is that using a percentage works around a bug in IE where the text would resize too much or too little, resulting in super-large or super-tiny text. Redeem your nerd points at the Web Standardistas web site.*

To make the examples in the rest of this chapter easier to follow, we're using pixels from this point on. We'll leave experimenting with the use of ems or keywords as an exercise for the reader.

Writing more efficient rules

Consider the following example, which sets the font-family, respective font-size for our h1–h4 elements, and colors them #9CC4E5 (a light shade of powder blue). We could write the h1–h4 declarations like this:

```
h1
{
font-family: Arial, sans-serif;
font-size: 36px;
color: #9CC4E5;
}

h2
{
font-family: Arial, sans-serif;
font-size: 24px;
color: #9CC4E5;
}

h3
{
font-family: Arial, sans-serif;
font-size: 18px;
color: #9CC4E5;
}
```

9

```
h4
{
font-family: Arial, sans-serif;
font-size: 14px;
color: #9CC4E5;
}
```

In this example each of the rules specifies *identical* font-family and color declarations. If we wanted to change these details down the line, we would have to edit each individual rule. This repetitive task seems somewhat inefficient—surely there's a better solution.

The good news is that CSS allows us a way to group selectors to keep our style sheets leaner and meaner. If we replace the preceding rules with the following, the result will be *exactly the same*:

```
h1, h2, h3, h4
{
font-family: Arial, sans-serif;
color: #9CC4E5;
}

h1
{
font-size: 36px;
}

h2
{
font-size: 24px;
}

h3
{
font-size: 18px;
}

h4
{
font-size: 14px;
}
```

Let's take a look at what's happening here. The first rule is instructing the browser to style our h1–h4 headings in Arial (or a generic sans serif fallback font) and in the color #9CC4E5. We've then written rules for each of the h1–h4 headings that set their size, an additional rule specific to each heading.

The benefits of this are twofold. First, the second set of rules is considerably smaller than the first, and we know that the smaller the file, the faster the download. Second, if we'd like to change the color or the font of our h1, h2, h3, and h4 elements down the line, we can do it in just one location, a more efficient method of making changes.

An understanding of grouped selectors coupled with a knowledge of the principles of inheritance, outlined earlier in this chapter, can go a long way to reducing the size and complexity of your style sheets.

Show and tell: Adding a few more rules

By now you should be quite familiar with adding CSS rules to your web pages, and you should be beginning to grasp some of the principles of CSS. We restricted ourselves in the last chapter to a limited number of CSS properties. We'll introduce a few more in this section to ensure you're getting your money's worth. Value for money is, after all, what it's all about.

Now that we've introduced you to some of the practicalities of handling typography on the Web, we'll finish the process of styling the remainder of the typographic elements on our King Kong page. The process of doing this will introduce you to a variety of CSS properties that you can use to control the look and feel of your web pages' typography.

You can see the effect of all of this chapter's changes combined in our King Kong page, which you'll be referring to as you embark on this chapter's homework: adding additional style to Gordo's page. You can access this page here:

www.webstandardistas.com/09/king_kong.html

Without further ado, let's get started on our typographic journey.

Specifying a typeface

You now know that you can specify a set of typefaces to ensure your typeface selections are more reliable, using alternatives and generic font family names to create a controlled fallback situation in the event that your users don't have your first choice of typeface.

We'd like to display all of the type on our King Kong page in Lucida Grande. A humanist sans serif typeface included with Apple's Mac OS X operating system, we know this won't be available on computers running Windows or Linux by default, so we'll need to specify some fallback fonts for users on other platforms.

We add the following rules to our CSS body declaration, setting the typeface and establishing a base type size for all of the typographic elements on the page. (Remember, elements like our headings will need to be given explicit sizes to stop the browser's default style sheet from overriding our 14px declaration.) We amend the following declarations to our body rule:

```
body
{
font-family: 'Lucida Grande', 'Lucida Sans', Arial, sans-serif;
font-size: 14px;
...
}
```

This sets all of the type on the page to display in Lucida Grande. Users who don't have that typeface installed will get Lucida Sans if it's installed, failing that Arial (a Core Web Font). If that's not available, they'll get their browser's default sans serif.

> *Astute readers will notice that both Lucida Grande and Lucida Sans have quotation marks around them. Why is this? The reason is simple: both typefaces' names consist of more than one word and contain a space. Any font with more than one word and a space—for example, Times New Roman or Courier New—should be enclosed in straight quotes. Note also that the comma needs to follow the closing quotation mark.*
>
> *Quotation marks must not be used to enclose generic font-family names (serif, sans-serif, monospace, cursive, and fantasy).*

You can see the effect of this rule on our King Kong page by following the URL we listed at the start of this section.

Let's lose some weight

As you briefly saw earlier in the chapter when we looked at the issue of specificity, when we mark up headings, the browser's built-in style sheet sets headings to display in bold by default. If we'd like our headings to display in something other than the default weight, we need to explicitly set it using a rule in CSS. We do this using the font-weight property.

We'd like to style all of our headings from h1 to h4 to display in a normal weight (or, if you were a typographer, a *roman* weight). We can do this using one rule, a grouped selector, which takes care of all of our headings by explicitly setting a font-weight. We add the following rule to our style sheet:

```
h1, h2, h3, h4
{
font-weight: normal;
...
}
```

The result of this one rule is that *all* of our headings display in a roman weight. In Figure 9-7 we show the headings before and after the change for comparison.

Using the font-weight property we can set a variety of weights for our type either numerically (100, 200, 300 . . .) or using keywords. The numeric value 400 is equivalent to the keyword normal; 700 is equivalent to bold.

Figure 9-7. Our single rule, using a grouped selector, takes care of all of our headings. On the left our headings as displayed using the browser's default style sheet's font-weight, on the right as they are now styled with our new rule.

Text transform

CSS offers us a variety of powerful methods of altering the text that's included in our markup, enabling us to transform the case in which it's set, regardless of how it appears in our markup. We can use the text-transform property in CSS to visually transform the display of text into uppercase or lowercase, or even to capitalize words using the value capitalize.

In this section we'll use a rule to transform the h4, which sits above our list of references, into uppercase to differentiate it from the other headings on the page. We add the following declaration to our h4 rule:

```
h4
{
text-transform: uppercase;
...
}
```

The result of this declaration is shown in Figure 9-8.

Figure 9-8. Using the text-transform property in CSS, we can magically transforms the visual display of our h4 text into uppercase.

9

Letter spacing

Looking at Figure 9-8, the spacing between the uppercase letters is a little tight; they would look better with a little space inserted between them (a property known to typographers as **kerning**). No problem! CSS provides us with a means of controlling kerning using the letter-spacing property.

We increase the letter spacing of our h4 heading by adding the following letter-spacing declaration to our h4 rule:

```
h4
{
text-transform: uppercase;
letter-spacing: 0.4em;
...
}
```

The result of this is shown in Figure 9-9.

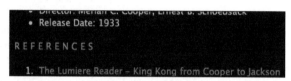

Figure 9-9. Our h4 type is now letter-spaced a little more generously.

It's worth noting that we've specified our letter-spacing in ems to ensure that the amount of kerning is applied in proportion to the text size of the h4.

A word of warning: letter spacing—while useful when styling headings in uppercase letters—is not recommended for lowercase letters. Letter spacing lowercase letters can impede legibility and, unless absolutely necessary, should be avoided.

> The prolific American type designer Frederick W. Goudy went so far as to state, "A man who would letterspace lower case would steal sheep." Trust us, at the time, this was quite an insult. Stealing sheep? Who would even countenance the thought . . . This quote went on to become the title of noted typographer Erik Spiekermann's excellent book Stop Stealing Sheep & Find Out How Type Works (Adobe Press, 1993), which is well worth reading for a comprehensive introduction to the wonderful world of typography.

When setting letter-spacing using CSS, you're not restricted to positive letter spacing values; you can also set negative values, for example, letter-spacing: -0.5em;, although why you might want all of your letterforms to overlap each other to create an illegible mess is beyond us.

CSS also allows you to control the space between words using the word-spacing property as in the following example:

```
p
{
word-spacing: 2em;
...
}
```

We leave it as an exercise for you to add this declaration to your Gordo web page and witness why word-spacing should best be avoided like the plague.

Styling paragraphs

Our page is beginning to take shape. In this section we're going to look at some CSS rules to give our paragraphs some style. We'll introduce some vertical space between the lines within our paragraphs, using a property known as line-height to improve the legibility of our paragraphs.

> In CSS the vertical space between lines of text is called line-height; in traditional typographic terms this would have been known as **leading**. In the early days of typography, strips of lead would have been inserted between lines of text to space them apart, which is where the term leading originates.

Once we've set a line-height, we'll look at the text-indent property to create indents for the first lines of each of our paragraphs. Finally, we'll look at the text-align selector to align our text to both the left and right, to center it, and to justify it.

Setting a line height

Before we embark on adding some line height, let's regroup. The font-size of our p elements is 14px (remember, we set it on the body element, and the p element has inherited this size). However, at present the line-height of all the elements on the page is being dictated by the browser's default style sheet as shown in Figure 9-10.

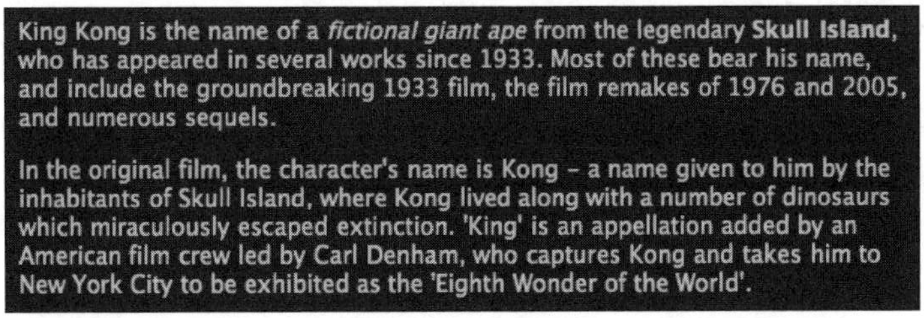

Figure 9-10. The line-height of our paragraphs as it currently stands, styled using the browser's defaults

We'd like to give our p elements some additional line-height, however, to space the lines out a little bit more and improve their legibility. We do this by adding a declaration to the rule targeting our p elements as follows:

```
p
{
line-height: 1.6;
...
}
```

The result of this is shown in Figure 9-11.

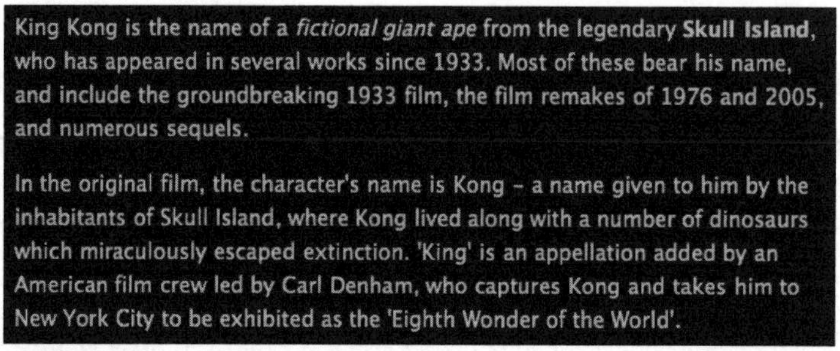

King Kong is the name of a *fictional giant ape* from the legendary **Skull Island**, who has appeared in several works since 1933. Most of these bear his name, and include the groundbreaking 1933 film, the film remakes of 1976 and 2005, and numerous sequels.

In the original film, the character's name is Kong – a name given to him by the inhabitants of Skull Island, where Kong lived along with a number of dinosaurs which miraculously escaped extinction. 'King' is an appellation added by an American film crew led by Carl Denham, who captures Kong and takes him to New York City to be exhibited as the 'Eighth Wonder of the World'.

Figure 9-11. The line-height of our paragraphs set to a value of 1.6—1.6 × 14 px (the paragraph text size)

As you can see, adding the line-height declaration adds a little more vertical space between the lines of our paragraphs, improving their legibility. We can set as much line-height (or as little) as we'd like; however, it's worth bearing in mind that too much (or too little) space between the lines of paragraphs can impede legibility. While we recommend the addition of a little line-height to "loosen the text up a little" when setting large paragraphs of type, we suggest—like extra hot chili powder—it be used sparingly.

When specifying a line-height, we're not using a unit of measure (like px or em); instead we're leaving the line-height value unitless. This way the line-height remains consistent throughout your page. Let's explain this by looking at a simple example:

```
body
{
font-size: 10px;
line-height: 1.5em;
}

p
{
font-size: 20px;
}
```

To make the calculations easier to follow, we've set a font-size of 10px on the body and 20px on our p element. We've set the line-height to 1.5em × 10px, or 15px for the body. The descendent p element will inherit this calculated line-height of 15px.

However, most of the time we'd like the line-height to be consistent across all of our elements. In our example we'd like the line-height of the p element to be 1.5 × 20px, or 30px. The simplest way to achieve this is to remove the unit of measure from our line-height declaration in the body rule as follows:

```
body
{
font-size: 10px;
line-height: 1.5;
}

p
{
font-size: 20px;
}
```

This will achieve our goal of creating a line-height that is *1.5 times* the font-size of each descendant element on our page. The rule of thumb is this: when specifying line-height, leave the unit of measure off, and your CSS will work as expected.

Adding paragraph indents

Now that we've increased the line-height of our paragraphs, let's take a look at another property that CSS allows us to control: text-indent.

As you discovered in Chapter 3, paragraphs are block-level elements, separated by line breaks. As such, the beginnings and endings of paragraphs are easily identified thanks to the vertical space added beneath p elements by default in most web browsers.

In Chapter 10 we'll show you how to reset the vertical space (a property known as margin) that sits between paragraphs, removing the blank lines that separate the paragraphs as they stand on our current King Kong page. However, we'll need to replace this vertical space with something to indicate to the reader that a new paragraph is beginning.

Most novels use indentation to indicate the beginning of each new paragraph within a block of continuous text. We can achieve the same visual effect using the text-indent property in CSS.

Adding the following declaration to a rule styling paragraphs indents the first line of every paragraph by 2 ems:

```
p
{
text-indent: 2em;
...
}
```

The result of this rule can be seen in Figure 9-12.

9

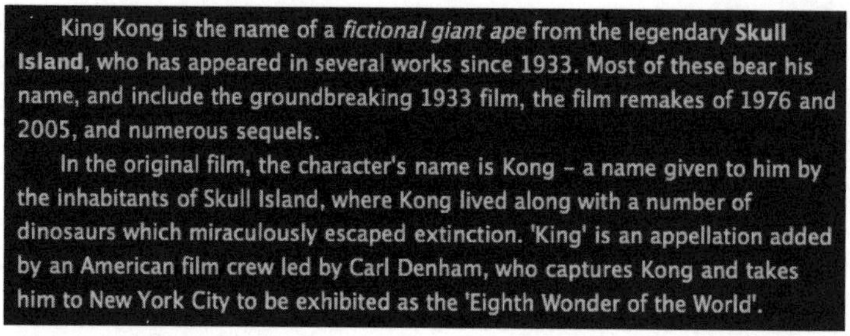

> King Kong is the name of a *fictional giant ape* from the legendary **Skull Island**, who has appeared in several works since 1933. Most of these bear his name, and include the groundbreaking 1933 film, the film remakes of 1976 and 2005, and numerous sequels.
>
> In the original film, the character's name is Kong – a name given to him by the inhabitants of Skull Island, where Kong lived along with a number of dinosaurs which miraculously escaped extinction. 'King' is an appellation added by an American film crew led by Carl Denham, who captures Kong and takes him to New York City to be exhibited as the 'Eighth Wonder of the World'.

Figure 9-12. Using text-indent allows us to indent the initial lines of our paragraphs.

Aligning text using text-align

Our last focus for this section is the question of aligning type. In CSS type can be aligned using the following four principle settings: left, right, center, and justify. The first three are fairly self-explanatory; the fourth comes with a note of caution.

You've seen left-aligned text already on the King Kong page we've been building, as browsers align text by default to the left. With no text-align specified, the browser's default (in the Western world) is text-align: left; and the preceding paragraph examples are all left-aligned. However, we can align text to the right by using a text-align declaration, as added in the following example:

```
p
{
text-align: right;
...
}
```

You can see the result of this declaration in Figure 9-13.

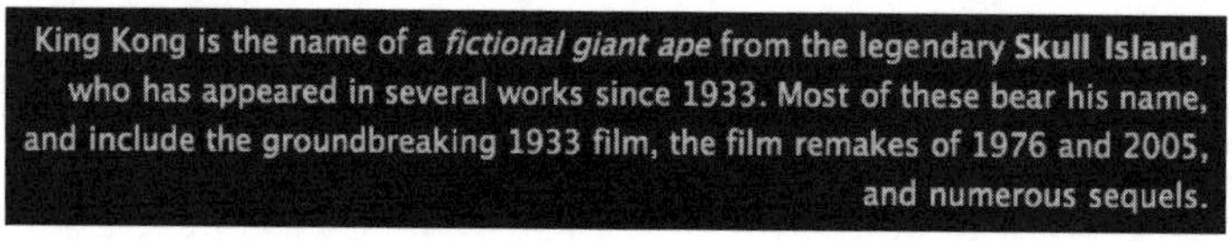

> King Kong is the name of a *fictional giant ape* from the legendary **Skull Island**, who has appeared in several works since 1933. Most of these bear his name, and include the groundbreaking 1933 film, the film remakes of 1976 and 2005, and numerous sequels.

Figure 9-13. Our paragraph is now aligned to the right.

We can also center our text using the center value as in the following example:

```
p
{
text-align: center;
...
}
```

You can see the result of this declaration in Figure 9-14.

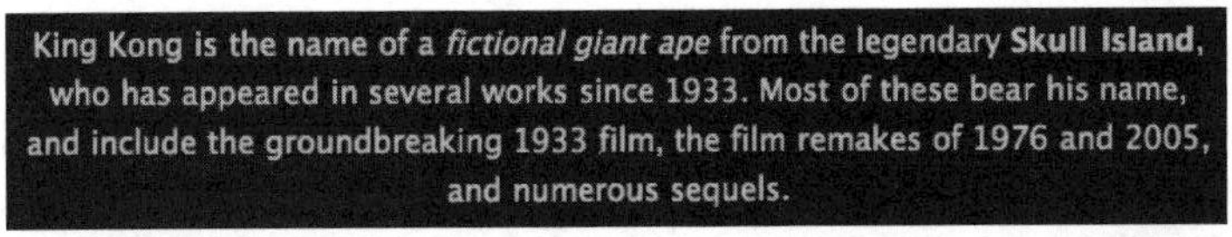

> King Kong is the name of a *fictional giant ape* from the legendary **Skull Island**, who has appeared in several works since 1933. Most of these bear his name, and include the groundbreaking 1933 film, the film remakes of 1976 and 2005, and numerous sequels.

Figure 9-14. Our paragraph is now centered. This can be useful to differentiate type in headings or for centering footer text, for example.

The last `text-align` value we'll consider is the `justify` value as in the following example:

```
p
{
text-align: justify;
...
}
```

You can see the result of this declaration in Figure 9-15.

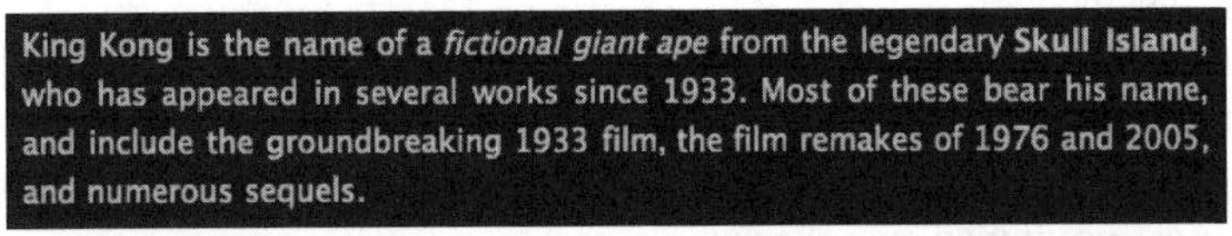

> King Kong is the name of a *fictional giant ape* from the legendary **Skull Island**, who has appeared in several works since 1933. Most of these bear his name, and include the groundbreaking 1933 film, the film remakes of 1976 and 2005, and numerous sequels.

Figure 9-15. Our paragraph is now justified. The browser adjusts both letter spacing and word spacing to justify the text.

Danger, Will Robinson! In certain situations `text-align: justify;` can really add to a design. However, a note of caution: when text is justified in short paragraphs, it can result in large gaps or "rivers" of space between words, for example, between the words *miraculously* and *escaped* in Figure 9-16.

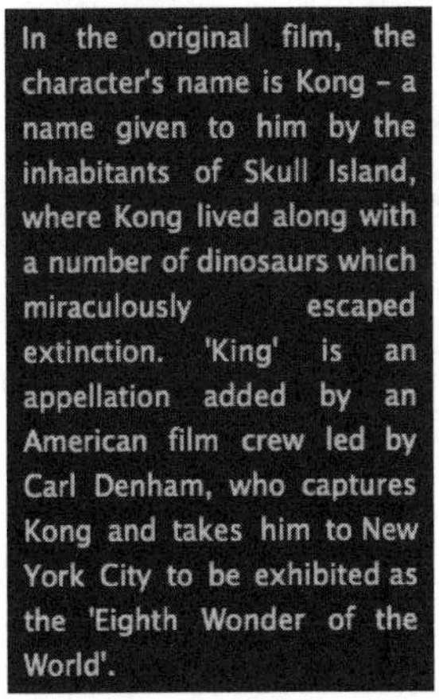

> In the original film, the character's name is Kong – a name given to him by the inhabitants of Skull Island, where Kong lived along with a number of dinosaurs which miraculously   escaped extinction. 'King' is an appellation added by an American film crew led by Carl Denham, who captures Kong and takes him to New York City to be exhibited as the 'Eighth Wonder of the World'.

Figure 9-16.
When used on paragraphs with a narrow measure, justification results in unsightly rivers running through the text.

Justifying text in print is considerably easier than justifying it online. Justifying text in print often involves the use of hyphenation to even out the different lines in a block of text as much as possible, reducing the possibility of rivers of white space. Online, however, where text can reflow as a user increases and decreases the size of their type, this isn't possible.

Styling links

The last typographic element on our King Kong page we need to style are its links. Before we get down to some examples, first a word on styling links in general. How should links be styled? Specifically, *to underline* or *not to underline?*

There are many different opinions on this, and many designers have created great-looking links without an underline in sight. Be aware though that users usually expect links to be underlined (and expect underlined text to be links). However, this isn't to say that links *have* to be underlined. Should you choose to style your links differently, it's a good idea to ensure that they stand out from the body text.

CSS allows us to style links so that they react to a user's interaction with the link itself. We do this by targeting a number of *pseudo-class*es, which relate to the different states a link can be in. These pseudo-classes are as follows:

- link: This is the default state for all unvisited links; left unstyled, this is usually blue and underlined.
- visited: This is the state for all visited links; left unstyled, this is usually purple and underlined.
- hover: This is used to identify when a user is *hovering over* a link (i.e., the user's mouse is positioned over the link).
- active: This is used to identify when a user is activating a link or actually in the process of clicking it.
- focus: This is used to identify when a link has focus, for instance, when a user tabs to the link using the keyboard.

We can style these pseudo-classes to give our users more visual feedback when they interact with links, a topic we cover in the next section.

Using pseudo-classes to style links

We'll introduce classes in a following chapter; for now we'll look at styling your links using the different link pseudo-classes to give your users a richer experience as they interact with your web pages.

Links can be styled at the most basic level through the inclusion of a simple rule in your style sheet, as in the following example:

```
a
{
color: red;
}
```

This rule targets all instances of the a element (our anchors) and overrides the browser's default blue for links, replacing it with a bright red. So far, so good, but not exactly super-exciting. Let's look at links in a little more detail by styling the links in the references section of our King Kong page.

Our page currently stands as shown in Figure 9-17; the links, in the default blue, are very hard to see due to a lack of contrast between the link color and the page's background color.

Figure 9-17. Unstyled, the default dark blue color of our links is hard to read, lacking contrast with the page's background.

We resolve this by setting the links to display in the same powder blue color as our headings, which, being higher contrast, improves legibility. We also switch off the browser's default underlines by setting the text-decoration property of our links to none, removing the underline (we'll add this later using a border). Although this change might seem counterintuitive—switching off an underline to replace it with a border—the border will allow us much more scope for styling as you'll see shortly. Lastly, we give the links their own line-height to space them out a little more.

We add the following CSS rule:

```
a
{
color: #9CC4E5;
text-decoration: none;
line-height: 1.5;
}
```

The result of this rule can be seen in Figure 9-18.

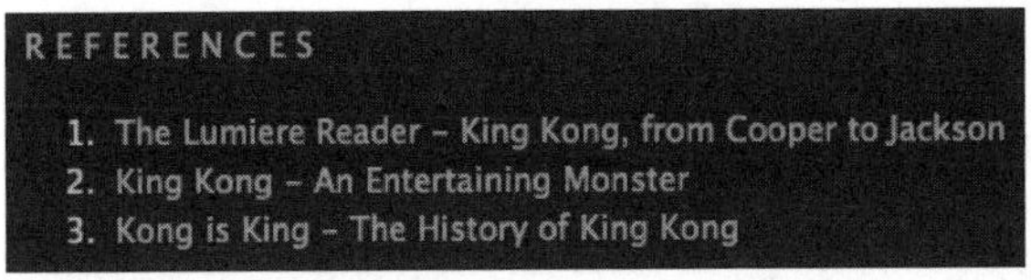

REFERENCES

1. The Lumiere Reader – King Kong, from Cooper to Jackson
2. King Kong – An Entertaining Monster
3. Kong is King – The History of King Kong

Figure 9-18. Our links' color is now set to match the powder blue of our headings. We've also switched off the underlining.

Now our links are styled so they pick up the powder blue theme we've been developing, improving the consistency of our design. However, we switched off the underline in the last stage by setting the text-decoration property to none. This could be confusing to our users who might not realize the references are, in fact, links.

We add a border to our :link pseudo-class to switch the underline back on. Why do this? Simply because the border gives us much more flexibility. We've set the border to be 1px, solid, and powder blue (#9CC4E5). By simply adjusting this declaration, we could increase the weight of our underline to, for example, 5px; we could also use dotted or dashed instead of solid to create, you guessed it, dotted and dashed underlines. We add the following rule to our style sheet:

9

```
a
{
color: #9CC4E5;
text-decoration: none;
line-height: 1.5;
}

a:link
{
border-bottom: 1px solid #9CC4E5;
}
```

The result of this rule is shown in Figure 9-19.

Figure 9-19. Our links are now underlined, this time using border-bottom.

By using a border we have much more control over our link's underlines, allowing us to set the border, for example, to dotted, dashed, solid, double, or groove. We can also accurately control the position of the underline in relation to the link text using padding, as you'll see in Chapter 10.

Now that we've styled our :link state, we'll look at styling the :visited state. Giving it a different style to our :link state will visually inform the user which links they've visited and which they haven't. We add the following rule:

```
a
{
color: #9CC4E5;
text-decoration: none;
line-height: 1.5;
}

a:link
{
border-bottom: 1px solid #9CC4E5;
}

a:visited
{
color: #E0DFDA;
border-bottom: 1px dotted #E0DFDA;
}
```

We've used a dotted border so you can see its effect; we've also set the type and the underline to the same color as the body text on the page, differentiating our visited links from our unvisited links. The result of this can be seen in Figure 9-20.

Figure 9-20. Our visited links are now differentiated from our unvisited links.

Lastly, we style our :hover and :active states to provide some interactivity when the user hovers over the links or clicks them. We do this by adding two further rules to our style sheet:

```
a
{
color: #9CC4E5;
text-decoration: none;
line-height: 1.5;
}

a:link
{
border-bottom: 1px solid #9CC4E5;
}

a:visited
{
color: #E0DFDA;
border-bottom: 1px dotted #E0DFDA;
}

a:hover
{
color: #26201C;
background-color: #E0DFDA;
border-bottom: none;
}

a:active
{
color: #26201C;
background-color: #9CC4E5;
border-bottom: none;
}
```

9

As you can see in Figure 9-21, when the user mouses over a link, the background color changes, giving a clear visual indication that the text is a link.

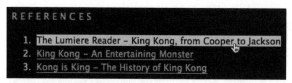

Figure 9-21. Setting a :hover state provides useful visual feedback to the user.

You can see everything we've covered in this section in action at the King Kong web page at the book's companion web site:

www.webstandardistas.com/09/king_kong.html

> To ensure your links are more accessible, it's advisable to include another, lesser-known pseudo-class: a:focus. This pseudo-class is useful for people who might not use a mouse, instead perhaps using their keyboard to navigate through the links on a page. In most instances a:focus can be grouped with the a:hover pseudo-class, using a grouped selector, to easily increase the accessibility of your web page.

We've only scratched the surface of what's possible when styling links. The best way to get a feel for what's possible is to experiment by adding rules to your own XHTML pages and experimenting with changing your own link styles. Trial and error along with some good, old-fashioned use of View Source to look at how links are styled at other web sites will give you lots of inspiration.

LoVe HAte your links

In the last section we added a full set of rules for our links in all of their states (link, visited, hover, and active). It's important to point out that these pseudo-classes need to be written in a particular order in our CSS to behave properly so that one link pseudo-class doesn't override another. This order is as follows:

- a:link (L)
- a:visited (V)
- a:hover (H)
- a:active (A)

An easy way to remember the right order—LVHA—is with the mnemonic: **LoVe HA**te. (Or you could use noted Standardista Dan Cederholm's mnemonic **L**ove **V**egetables? **H**ave **A**sparagus!)

Summary

So what have we covered? This chapter has been a bit of a rollercoaster. We've discussed a great deal, and we'd strongly recommend you read it again, trying out some of the examples as you read along.

We covered some more complicated, but important, aspects of CSS including inheritance and specificity. We also looked at the use of grouped selectors in CSS and how their use can keep our code lean and mean and, as a consequence, easier to maintain as we move forward.

Along the way we looked at typography and how you can use CSS to control it within your documents. In our walkthrough we showed you a wide variety of ways to create great-looking text online. Finally, we explored using pseudo-classes to give a degree of interactivity and user feedback to our links. As with the preceding chapters, follow along using your homework files, comparing them to our examples, and your grasp of styling text with CSS should improve considerably.

In the next chapter we'll introduce the fundamental principles of CSS layout, enabling you to control the position of the elements on your web pages.

Homework: Improving Gordo's typography

In this chapter we introduced you to a variety of methods of styling text using CSS, showcasing the power and flexibility of style sheets when used for handling typography. The topics we covered will enable you to take your Gordo page's typography and raise it to the next level.

Our focus throughout the chapter was on type, and we introduced you to a number of different properties perfect for styling text using CSS, including `font-weight`, `text-transform`, `letter-spacing` and `word-spacing`, `line-height`, `text-indent`, and `text-align`.

We also introduced the concept of inheritance and specificity, explaining how an understanding of these two principles will enable you to write lean and easy-to-maintain style sheets.

In this chapter's "show and tell" we applied all of the preceding properties to our King Kong page to show them in action. Your homework for this chapter will be to apply some of these properties to your Gordo page, enhancing its typography and improving the styling of its text.

The process of adding these new properties will further underline your knowledge and awareness of CSS and, as a byproduct, introduce you to the power of inheritance and how it can be used to improve your style sheets by creating more efficient rules.

9

1. Change your font-family

In Chapter 8 we showed you how to set a font-family on the body and p elements. In this chapter we'd like you to remove the font-family declaration from the p element of your Gordo page and take care of all of the page's typography by setting a declaration on the body and allowing inheritance to take care of the rest.

It's also time to revisit the choice of typeface you're using. In the last chapter we deliberately kept things simple by specifying two widely installed typefaces: Arial and Verdana. In this chapter, however, we introduced you to the concept of fallback fonts and used them to specify values for our King Kong page's font-family property as follows:

```
font-family: 'Lucida Grande', 'Lucida Sans', Arial, sans-serif;
```

We've left it to your discretion to select a typeface of your own choosing for your Gordo page; however, we'd like you to specify a number of fallback fonts to ensure that the page's typography is considered in the event of your first choice of typeface being unavailable.

Once you've made these changes, save your Gordo page and test their effect in a number of browsers.

2. Use grouped selectors

In Chapter 8 we specified the same color for two of our headings (the h1 and h2), writing an identical color declaration for each rule. In this chapter we introduced you to the concept of grouped selectors, which allow you to reduce the number of declarations in your style sheets by targeting more than one element with each CSS rule.

In this chapter we'd like you to style all of your Gordo page's headings from h1 to h4. Set the font-weight of all of your Gordo page's headings to display in normal (overriding the browser's default style sheet bold styling) and set the color of all of your headings to display in the light shade of blue we've been using (#9CC4E5).

Instead of writing duplicate declarations for each heading's rules, use a grouped selector to take care of the common styles that the headings share. You can refer to the example of a grouped selector in this chapter to see how we styled the common declarations on our King Kong page's h1–h4 elements.

3. Style the <h4>

Referring to the examples provided in this chapter, style your h4 element—the "References" heading—using the text-transform and letter-spacing properties.

Experiment with some of the values we covered in the chapter; for example, try setting the text-transform value to uppercase, lowercase, and capitalize and testing the effect of these rules in the browser.

We'd also like you to explore the effect of adjusting your letter-spacing values; try 0.4em, 4em, and 40em. Again, test the effect of changing these values in the browser. (Remember our note of caution: use letter-spacing in moderation, especially when letter-spacing lowercase letters. 40em! What were we thinking?)

4. Style the paragraphs

In this chapter we introduced line-height, text-indent, and text-align—three proper-ties that can be used to great effect to style your paragraphs and improve their legibility. Referring to the examples in this chapter, experiment by setting a variety of values for each of these properties and testing their effects in the browser.

5. Style your links

The last set of rules we'd like you to create is targeted at your Gordo page's links. You might recall that, at the end of the last chapter, the links on your Gordo page suffered from a lack of contrast with the background-color of the page, displaying dark blue on a dark brown background. Good news, you'll resolve this here.

Taking a look at our examples in this chapter, style your Gordo page's links, improving their usability. Using the pseudo-classes we introduced, experiment with setting styles for the following pseudo-classes: a:link, a:visited, a:hover, and a:active.

As usual, to help you with the different stages of this chapter's homework, we've created our own, similarly styled, page about King Kong featuring new, improved typography. You can refer to this, using your browser's View Source menu command to see how we've updated our CSS, here:

    www.webstandardistas.com/09/king_kong.html

Once you've completed Gordo's typographic upgrade, put the kettle on and enjoy a cup of *Ceylon Dimbula Inverness* as you prepare yourself for the next chapter.

9

CHAPTER 10

A ONE-COLUMN CSS LAYOUT

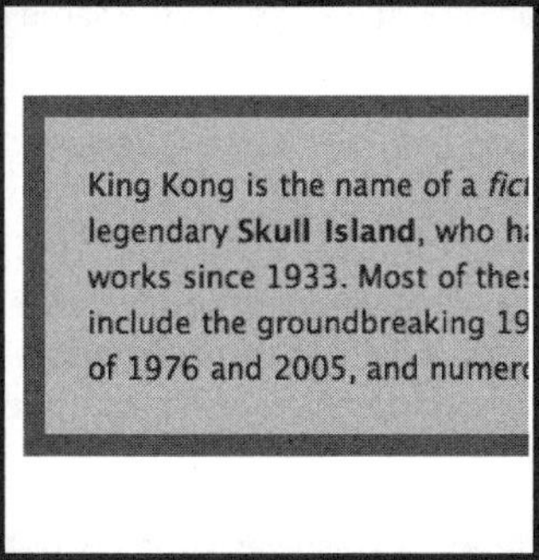

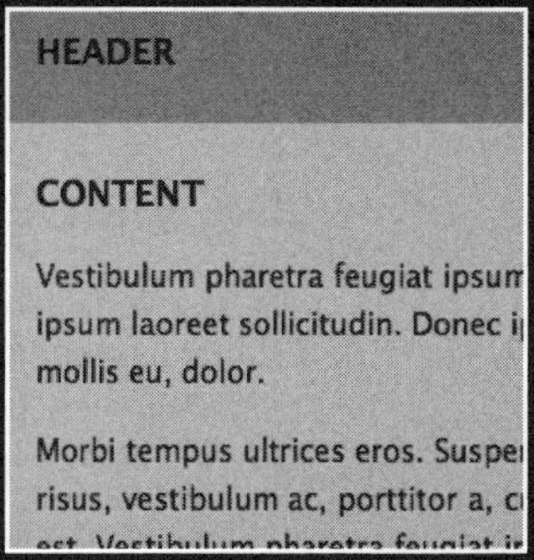

This chapter forms the next stage of our journey to build a well-structured and well-styled web page. As in the previous chapters, we'll be working on our King Kong page and walking you through a variety of practical and hands-on CSS techniques.

In this chapter we'll be adding some additional structure to our document by breaking our King Kong page down into sections or divisions. We'll introduce and use div elements as the basis for creating a simple one-column CSS layout. An understanding of how div elements work is an important part of your Web Standardistas' journey and will form the foundation for creating more complicated layouts in CSS, so we urge you to pay attention throughout this chapter.

Along the way we'll introduce adding margins, borders, and padding, a means of adding borders and space around your elements and, as a byproduct of that, we'll introduce the CSS box model. We'll also look at the humble span, the inline sibling of the div, as well as ids and classes, attributes that allow you to identify and classify individual or groups of elements to easily target them with styles.

Finally, we'll look at CSS background images and how they can be used as a simple but effective means of ensuring your designs are just a little bit more interesting.

We know you're eager to get started and to get your hands dirty, but first, some short messages.

The Cascade in Cascading Style Sheets

Before we get on to the juicy part of this chapter, it's important to introduce a few more aspects of how CSS works. We're reaching a point at which our style sheets can get quite complex, and as a consequence, conflicting CSS rules might have an impact on how our elements display.

Allow us to digress for a moment while we look in a little more depth at the cascade in Cascading Style Sheets. We'll introduce how the cascade works; we'll also take a look at what happens when your CSS contains more than one rule targeting the same element and how the browser resolves these issues.

So what exactly is the cascade?

We've talked a lot about Cascading Style Sheets, but we've yet to touch on the actual topic of **cascading**. As your pages grow in complexity, especially as you start to use internal and external style sheets in combination during the development process, an understanding of the cascading aspect of CSS becomes important.

So what exactly is the cascade? The cascade is how CSS resolves conflicts between different styles, for example, when more than one rule is applied to the same element. The best way to explain how the cascade works is to show you an example.

We mentioned earlier in the book that we'd be working on an *internal* style sheet until we had our design complete. We also mentioned that—when the time was right and we had the style sheet we wanted—we would remove this from the XHTML page itself to create an *external* style sheet that we would link to. We also mentioned the browser's *default* style sheet in Chapter 9. Lastly, we mentioned *inline* styles in Chapter 8, where the various styles are applied within the body of the XHTML page itself, directly to the elements we're styling.

This gives us a total of four potential sources of style for the elements on a page. So what if we have multiple rules targeting the same element? What wins out?

Imagine this scenario: we have a very simple web page with just a single h1 on it. Unlikely, but for the purpose of this exercise, a little easier to follow.

As you know, the browser's default style sheet defines default styles for all the elements on our pages, including our solitary h1. As you saw in the chapters covering XHTML, the browser's default style sheet sets our h1's color to black by default. However, what if we also have an external style sheet with a rule targeting our h1, setting its color to red? (We know we haven't told you how to create an external style sheet yet, but the principle remains.) As if this weren't confusing enough for the poor h1, let's add an internal style sheet too, with a rule for our h1 setting its color to green. Lastly, let's apply a style directly to the h1 itself using an inline style, setting its color to blue.

So, our lone h1 is being styled left, right, and center (and from above too). Which style takes precedence? What color will the h1 display in? The answer is blue, because the inline style wins. Let's find out why.

First, you need to get your head around the concept that before displaying your page, a browser gathers all of the different styles together; these styles then cascade into a new "virtual" style sheet combining all the different styles as visualized in Figure 10-1.

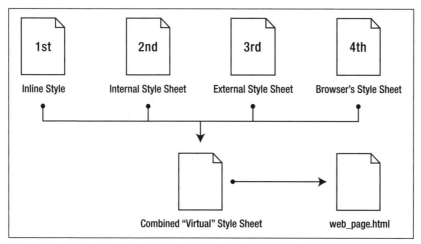

10

Figure 10-1. The browser gathers together the different styles, identifying which rules win in the event of any conflicts, before applying them to our web page.

Which styles "win out" in this new, "virtual" style sheet depends upon a set of complicated rules. We've simplified them here to make things a little easier to understand. The winners, in order, are as follows:

1. Inline styles
2. Internal style sheet (This is the style sheet you're currently using, situated inside the head element.)
3. External style sheet
4. Browser's default style sheet

So, internal style sheets win over external style sheets. Both take precedence over the browser's default style sheet. Inline styles—on the rare occasions you might use them—overrule everything. You can see this in action by looking at the source code of a page we've created for you to demonstrate how our solitary h1 is styled, at the book's companion web site:

www.webstandardistas.com/10/cascade.html

In fact, the rules of the cascade are a little more complicated, but this, in essence, is it. Although you're not using external style sheets yet, you might witness a potential clash between your inline style sheet and the browser's default style sheet. Hopefully an awareness of this will save you tearing your hair out when things are appearing to "go wrong" and you can't work out why.

The order of your CSS rules is important

As your style sheets get longer and more complicated, it's easy to lose track of what you've styled and find yourself writing additional rules lower in your style sheet that clash with earlier rules you've previously written. Take a look at the following example:

```
body
{
font-family: 'Lucida Grande', 'Lucida Sans', Arial, sans-serif;
font-size: 14px;
}

p
{
color: red;
}

/* Imagine another few dozen additional rules here. */

p
{
color: blue;
}
```

You've written a rule for your p elements to display all paragraphs in red as you first intended. However, after writing a few dozen additional rules, you've written another rule for your p elements to display all paragraphs in blue. Perhaps you forgot about writing the first; perhaps someone interrupted your train of thought, and it just slipped in by mistake.

So now there are two conflicting CSS rules targeting your p elements. What color will your paragraphs display in? The answer is blue. The browser takes the rule lowest in the style sheet and uses it to display your paragraphs. *The later a rule appears in a style sheet, the more weight it is given.*

Your style sheets might not be complex now, but they eventually will be, and you'd be surprised how often this happens. When an element doesn't display as you intended, it's worth spending a few minutes checking for duplicate rules in your style sheet(s) as this can often be the source of problems.

Introducing margins, borders, and padding

In Chapter 9 you saw how we could use line-height to give our paragraphs a little more spacing between the lines of text to aid legibility. We can also put space *around* our elements, using margins, borders, and padding to create space *between* our different elements. As we move toward creating more complicated layouts for our King Kong page, an understanding of how the margin, border, and padding properties work is important.

So far we've looked at styling elements in isolation, adding some line-height, and styling the typography of the different elements. In this section we look at how margins, borders, and padding are applied in CSS, affecting the relationship of our elements to each other. An understanding of this will form the basis for creating CSS layouts.

Meet the box model

Before we embark on a walkthrough, adding margins, borders, and padding to a simple paragraph to show how they affect a typical element, we need to cover a little theory.

You already know that all elements on a web page are treated as boxes—some are block-level, some are inline-level (we introduced this concept in Chapter 3). Each of these boxes is comprised of a content area and optional margins, borders, and padding. Up until this point margins, borders, and padding have been set by the browser's default style sheet; however, we can explicitly set them using CSS, overriding these defaults and specifying sizes we'd prefer.

The relationship of an element to its margins, borders, and padding is known as the **box model**. An understanding of the box model and how it works is crucial as we move forward to cover CSS layouts, so, without further ado, let's meet the box model.

Figure 10-2 illustrates the relationship between an element and any added margin, border, and padding. As you can see, the padding sits between the edge of the element and any

10

border added to it; the margin sits between any border added to an element and any adjacent elements.

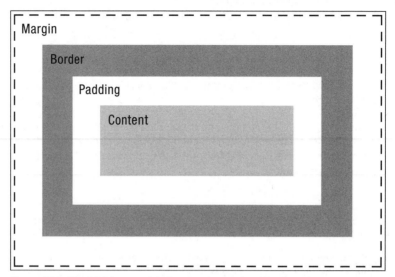

Figure 10-2. The W3C box model, showing the relationship of an element's content to its margins, borders, and padding

When margin, border, and padding properties are all specified, the width of our element—or the space that it occupies within the browser window—is as follows:

```
margin-left + border-left + padding-left + element  width + padding-right +
border-right + margin-right
```

We'll see this in action in the following section when we take a typical element, a paragraph, and add margins, borders, and padding to it, demonstrating the effect that this has on an element within the context of a browser window.

Applying margins, borders, and padding

Now that we've introduced you to the box model and margins, borders, and padding, we need to look at how these are applied to our elements. In this section we add margin, border, and padding declarations to a single p element and demonstrate their effect within a browser. This will give you an idea of how an element's margins, borders, and padding relate to each other and how you can use them together to structure your web page.

To start with we've created a very short web page with a single paragraph. We've written the following two CSS rules:

```
body
{
font-family: 'Lucida Grande', 'Lucida Sans', Arial, sans-serif;
font-size: 14px;
```

```
color: #000000;
background-color: #FFFFFF;
}


p
{
width: 400px;
line-height: 1.5;
}
```

In the preceding rules we've applied some basic styling to a very simple paragraph. We've set a width on our sole p element of 400px to allow us to see the paragraph in context within a browser window and to see how adding margins, borders, and padding affects the overall width of our element within the browser. This renders in a browser as shown in Figure 10-3.

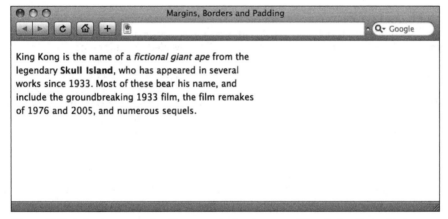

Figure 10-3. A simple paragraph with no margin, border, or padding declarations added

To highlight the block-level nature of our paragraph element, and to enable us to see the effect of adding margins, borders, and padding, we add a declaration to our p rule setting the paragraph's background-color to display in light gray, as follows:

```
p
{
width: 400px;
line-height: 1.5;
background-color: #CCCCCC;
}
```

The result of this is shown in Figure 10-4.

10

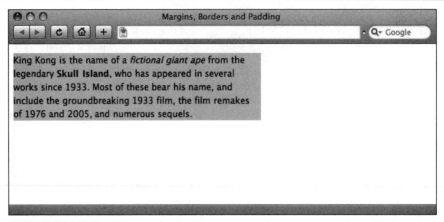

Figure 10-4. Setting a background-color on our paragraph reveals its underlying block-level nature.

Now it's time to add some margins; before we do that, however, we'll begin by removing some margins (this might sound odd, but all will be revealed in a moment).

As you can see in Figure 10-4, our browser's default style sheet is already applying some default margin to both our body element and our block-level p element, adding space above it and to the left of it (there's also space below it and to the right of it, but to all intents and purposes, it's invisible in this example). This is the default margin that the browser applies to our p and body elements in the event of no other style sheet specifying a different amount.

We'll remove the browser's default margin by setting the margin on the body and p elements to 0. We do this by adding the following two declarations to our existing body and p rules:

```
body
{
font-family: 'Lucida Grande', 'Lucida Sans', Arial, sans-serif;
font-size: 14px;
color: #000000;
background-color: #FFFFFF;
margin: 0;
}
```

```
p
{
width: 400px;
line-height: 1.5;
background-color: #CCCCCC;
margin: 0;
}
```

Removing the browser's default `margin` results in the paragraph appearing as shown in Figure 10-5.

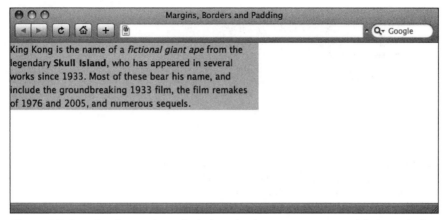

Figure 10-5. Resetting the `margin` on the body and p elements removes any default `margin` from the paragraph that would otherwise be applied by the browser's default style sheet.

By removing the browser's default margins, our paragraph now sits tight to the top left corner of the browser window. Now we're ready to start adding some margins, borders, and padding of our own and see how they affect the paragraph.

We amend the rule styling our p element, changing the value of our `margin` declaration and setting it to 40px:

```
p
{
width: 400px;
line-height: 1.5;
background-color: #CCCCCC;
margin: 40px;
}
```

What this does is set the margin *on all four sides* of the paragraph to 40 pixels as shown in Figure 10-6. Although we've only written 40px once, CSS shorthand is setting this on all four sides of the p element. (Rest assured, we'll be introducing you to the CSS shorthand for margins, borders, and padding shortly.)

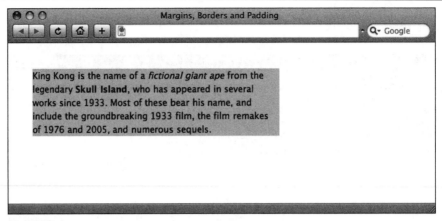

Figure 10-6. Adding 40px of margin to our paragraph moves the paragraph 40px down and 40px to the right. Although you can't see it, 40px of margin has also been added to the right edge and bottom edge of the paragraph.

Now it's time to add a border to our paragraph element. We introduced you to the border property in Chapter 9, when we added a border to our links, so the following additional declaration shouldn't be new to you:

```
p
{
width: 400px;
line-height: 1.5;
background-color: #CCCCCC;
margin: 40px;
border: 10px solid #666666;
}
```

Adding the border declaration results in our paragraph appearing as you see in Figure 10-7.

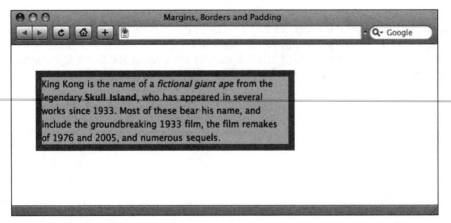

Figure 10-7. Adding a 10px dark gray border to the paragraph

Essentially we're setting a border on the paragraph to be 10px wide, solid, and a darker shade of gray. We now have a border around our paragraph; however, the text of the paragraph is sitting tight to the edge of its block-level box and sitting tight toward the border. It's time to add some padding.

We add a new declaration specifying a value for our padding as follows:

```
p
{
width: 400px;
line-height: 1.5;
background-color: #CCCCCC;
margin: 40px;
border: 10px solid #666666;
padding: 20px;
}
```

Adding this rule results in the layout shown in Figure 10-8.

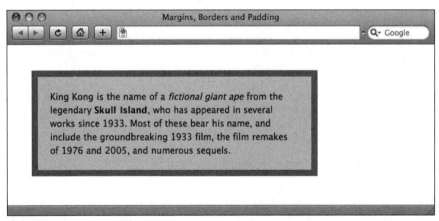

Figure 10-8. Adding some padding to our p element inserts some space between the paragraph and the border.

So now you've seen how an element's margins, borders, and padding relate to each other. Let's take a look at how the preceding additions measure up in the browser.

Understanding how the browser sees this, particularly how it calculates the width the element is now occupying with the added margins, borders, and padding, is important as it will have a bearing on our CSS layouts when we start to place the content of our web pages into divs, assign them a specific width, and set any margin, border and padding declarations.

In Figure 10-9 we've annotated the screenshot in Figure 10-8 to show how the added margin, border, and padding declarations affect the width of our element.

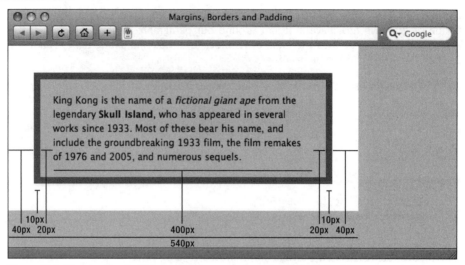

Figure 10-9. The combined width needed for our paragraph is 540 pixels; this consists of all margins, borders, padding, and the width of the paragraph itself.

Looking at Figure 10-9, you can see that when margins, borders, and padding are all specified, the width of our element—or the space that it occupies within the browser window—is as follows:

```
margin-left + border-left + padding-left + element  width  + padding-right +
border-right + margin-right
```

So, in the example in Figure 10-9, our total width is as follows:

```
40px + 10px + 20px + 400px + 20px + 10px + 40px = 540px
```

> *It's worth noting—if only as a historical footnote—that Internet Explorer 5.5 and earlier used a different method of calculating the total width of the box, which used to cause web designers no end of problems. Luckily for you, those days are now, thankfully, a thing of the past. Starting your document with a correct DOCTYPE, as we covered in Chapter 2, instructs Internet Explorer 6 and 7 to use the correct, W3C box model interpretation.*

So, now we know that the browser calculates the width an element occupies on a page by totaling up the width of the element plus any added margins, borders, and padding. It's worth noting that in this example we applied margins, borders, and padding to a p element; we could do exactly the same with a div filled with content, thereby enabling us to control layout.

Using CSS shorthand for margins, borders, and padding

By now you should be using View Source regularly to look at other designers' source code in addition to looking at the source code of the example pages we've been providing for each of the chapters. You might have noticed that CSS rules can be written in a variety of ways, in some instances using what's known as **shorthand** to make rules more compact.

You briefly met some CSS shorthand in Chapter 9 when we introduced the border property to apply a border to the bottom of our links as follows:

```
a:link
{
border-bottom: 1px solid #9CC4E5;
}
```

We can write the same rule in longhand, styling each of the properties separately, as follows:

```
a:link
{
border-bottom-width: 1px;
border-bottom-style: solid;
border-bottom-color:  #9CC4E5;
}
```

Both of these rules style the border-bottom (the border at the bottom of our a:link pseudo-class) in exactly the same way; however, the first is clearly shorter.

Choosing a shorthand method over a longhand method is largely a matter of preference, and it could be argued that a longhand approach allows you to clearly see at a glance exactly what you're styling. However, it's also worth noting that in the preceding example, the shorthand version is half the length of the longhand version. Multiply that over a number of rules, and you're clearly reducing download times and bandwidth requirements.

Let's take a look at another example, from the preceding walkthrough. We added a margin to our paragraph as follows, setting a margin on all four sides of the p element with a single declaration:

```
p
{
...
margin: 0;
}
```

10

We could have also written this as four declarations as follows:

```
p
{
...
margin-top: 0;
margin-right: 0;
margin-bottom: 0;
margin-left: 0;
}
```

The two are functionally equivalent and will result in exactly the same display within a browser. When the value of a property is the same on all four sides, it can be specified once, and the browser will apply this value to all four sides.

> *When specifying zero as a measurement, you don't need to specify a unit of measure;* margin: 0px; *and* margin: 0; *will display identically.*

Let's take a look at a couple of other examples of CSS shorthand in action. In the following example, the values for the top and bottom margin are 20px and the values for left and right margin are 10px:

```
margin: 20px 10px 20px 10px;
```

When the top and bottom, and left and right values are the same, CSS allows us to shorten this even further, as follows:

```
margin: 20px 10px;
```

The first value (20px) styles both the top and bottom, and the second value (10px) styles both the left and right.

It's important to note that, when using shorthand, margins, borders, and padding are defined in the following order: top, right, bottom, left.

> *An easy way to remember the order in which margins, borders, and padding are applied to all four sides is to think of the numbers on a clock:* top = *12 o'clock,* right = *3 o'clock,* bottom = *6 o'clock, and* left = *9 o'clock.*

A longhand approach can prove useful when you're styling an element with different values on each side as follows:

```
blockquote:
{
margin-top: 20px;
margin-right: 40px;
margin-bottom: 60px
margin-left: 10px;
}
```

In this example, our blockquote sits 20px from the base of any element above it, has 40px of margin on the right-hand side, inserts 60px of space beneath it, and has 10px of margin on the left-hand side.

This could, however, also be shortened and written as follows:

```
blockquote:
{
margin: 20px 40px 60px 10px;
}
```

As with everything we've covered, this can be a lot to take in, but practice makes perfect. Use View Source to view others' CSS, and you'll pick up the preceding shorthand in next to no time.

Styling our <blockquote>

We've looked at specifying margin, border, and padding declarations for a simple p element. We've also looked at using CSS shorthand to specify our different rules. Let's combine these two in a real-world example that we'll apply to our King Kong page.

To show margins, borders, and padding in action we'll take our blockquote as it stood at the end of Chapter 9 and apply some style to it, giving it margins, a border (on one side only), and some padding.

As it stood at the end of Chapter 9, our blockquote was styled using only the browser's default style sheet and the rules we had set on the body to style our typography. The result of these combined rules is shown in Figure 10-10.

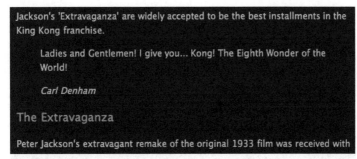

Figure 10-10. Our blockquote as it stood at the end of Chapter 9. The default styling isn't doing it any justice.

We've taught you a great deal over the last few chapters, and we can combine this knowledge to apply a little more style to our humble blockquote, helping to differentiate it from the surrounding text.

Using the margin, border, and padding declarations we covered earlier and adding a few more declarations we introduced in Chapter 9, we'll differentiate the blockquote from the surrounding text, helping to highlight it as a feature within the text. We add the following CSS rule targeting the blockquote:

```
blockquote
{
font-family: Georgia, sans-serif;
font-size: 18px;
```

10

```
font-style: italic;
letter-spacing: 0.1em;
margin-left: 40px;
border-left: 10px solid #E0DFDA;
padding: 0 20px;
}
```

The first four rules should need no introduction, as we covered them in Chapter 9; essentially they set the blockquote in a different typeface from that used on the rest of the page and add a little typographic style, helping to visually highlight the quote.

The margin, border, and padding declarations highlight how we can creatively use these properties to add some style to our blockquote. It's worth noting that we're not restricted to setting the margins, borders, and padding on every side; we can selectively apply these properties as in this example.

Applying a margin-left to the blockquote indents it by 40px, setting it apart from the surrounding text. We also set a border-left that gives a strong visual focus to the left-hand side of the blockquote and creates a more striking effect, visually distinguishing the blockquote from the surrounding paragraphs and headings. Finally, we add some padding to the left and right sides to ensure our blockquote isn't sitting tight toward the left-hand border and to give it an indent on the right-hand side.

The result of our newly added blockquote rule is shown in Figure 10-11.

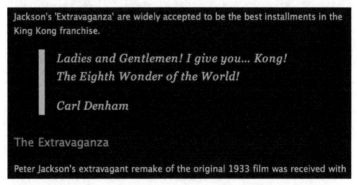

Figure 10-11. Creatively using margin, border, and padding declarations allows us to style our blockquote a little more creatively.

By simply varying the values for our margin, border, and padding declarations, we can apply a great deal of style to our blockquote element.

Dividing up your document

For the remainder of this chapter we'll focus primarily on XHTML's div and span elements and their associated id and class attributes. Used together, these offer us a powerful means of adding further structure to our XHTML documents by enabling us to divide it up into logical sections.

Up until this point we've focused on the use of well-structured and semantic markup. We've been using the right tag for the job. All good. Now we're going to look at various methods for grouping information together into logical sections.

Take a look at any well-designed web page and you'll notice that information is generally grouped into related clusters. For example, a page may have a header, an area where the web page is branded; a content area, where the bulk of the page's information is gathered; a sidebar, for the site's navigation and any supplementary information; and a footer, for copyright and other related publishing information.

XHTML allows us to use div and span elements and their associated id and class attributes to create these document sections. The W3C states the following:

> The div and span elements, in conjunction with the id and class attributes, offer a generic mechanism for adding structure to documents. These elements define content to be inline (span) or block-level (div) but impose no other presentational idioms on the content. Thus, authors may use these elements in conjunction with style sheets . . . to tailor HTML to their own needs and tastes.
>
> www.w3.org/TR/REC-html40/struct/global.html#h-7.5.4

But what does that mean in English? It means we have two additional elements and their associated attributes to introduce. Once we've introduced them, we can begin to break our King Kong page down into logical sections of related groups of information. This will allow us to further style the document's individual sections by allocating them space and creating a CSS layout.

Identifying your document's sections

Let's take a look at our King Kong page. At this point it's one long page with some well-structured and semantic content and some basic typographic styling. A closer look reveals that this content falls into a number of sections that can be logically grouped.

We have a header area, where we have our Famous Primates brand. We have a content area, where the page's primary information is located. Finally, we have a footer area, where we have some copyright information and the date the document was written. You can see our King Kong page's key sections in Figure 10-12.

10

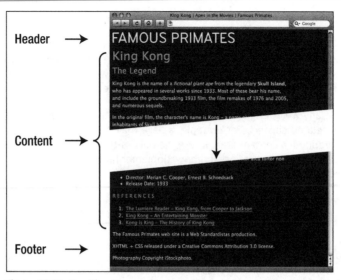

Figure 10-12. Our King Kong web page with some key sections highlighted

As the W3C states, "The div and span elements, in conjunction with the id and class attributes, offer a generic mechanism for adding structure to documents"; as such these are perfectly suited for use to divide up our King Kong page into its header, content, and footer sections.

So now that we've identified some of our web page's key divisions and identified the div element as a possible mechanism for adding some structure to our web page, how do we target the different sections we've identified specifically? The answer is by using a combination of divs and spans, and ids and classes, which we introduce next.

Using div and span elements with id and class attributes

Welcome to the wonderful world of divs and spans, two useful elements for providing additional markup and meaning within your documents. As you saw earlier, the W3C states that these elements are "a generic mechanism for adding structure to documents. These elements define content to be inline (span) or block-level (div) but impose no other presentational idioms on the content." This makes them perfect for adding additional structure to our King Kong page.

Where these elements differ from the ones we've introduced so far lies in the fact that they are *generic*. All the elements we've introduced to this point have had an inherent meaning: a ul is an unordered list, a p is a paragraph, and a blockquote is a quotation. divs and spans are different; they have no inherent meaning and might therefore be described as semantically neutral.

> *As* div *elements are generic elements that impart no deeper semantic meaning to the content nested within them, it's important to ensure that the content you group within your* div *elements is itself marked up using meaningful and semantic elements:* h1–h6, p, ul, li, strong, em, *etc.*

Herein lies their power. As neutral or generic elements, the humble div and span are extremely versatile items in the Web Standardistas' toolkit. We can wrap a div element or a span element around our existing markup and target style at that wrapping element, allowing us to create document sections, for example, the header, content, and footer we identified earlier.

> *Before we introduce* divs *and* spans *properly, a note of caution. It's easy to fall under their spell, wrapping everything in a* div *or a* span *regardless of content.*
>
> *The overuse of* div *and* span *elements—known as* divitis *and* spanitis, *respectively—is itself a minor form of tag soup to be avoided. In the words of Spiderman's Uncle Ben (or was it Stan Lee?):* "With great power comes great responsibility." *Use these elements sparingly and only where necessary.*

Let's take a look at div and span elements and their associated id and class attributes in a little more detail.

div and span elements

You now know that div elements are block-level and span elements are inline-level. Here we'll give you a look at some examples of both, introducing the markup needed to wrap our content in either of these elements.

Let's take a look at two different uses of the div element: the first used to wrap and identify a single section of a web page, the content section; the second used to wrap and classify one of a number of sections of a web page, a number of blog entries.

To identify a unique part of a web page, we wrap its contents in div tags and use an id attribute as follows:

```
<div id="content">
  <!-- This is where the main content of the web page is situated.
  There can be only one div with an id of content on this page. -->
</div>
```

We're not limited to using div elements for main structural sections of a document, however. We can also use div elements to gather together groups of related information that may occur more than once on a page, blog entries, for example. When styling multiple instances of a div, we use a class attribute instead of an id attribute as in the following example:

10

```
<div class="blog_entry">
  <!-- This is where one of our blog entries is situated. We can have
  more than one div with a class of blog_entry on this page. -->
</div>

<div class="blog_entry">
  <!-- This is another blog entry. Notice how we've used the class of
  blog_entry more than once on this page. -->
</div>
```

The first example has an id, the second a class. The id is unique; the class can be used more than once. We'll explain the difference between id and class attributes in a little more detail in the next section, but first let's introduce the span element.

Where span elements differ from div elements lies in their inline-level nature. We can use a span *within* a block-level element to differentiate that section from the surrounding section. For instance, in the following example, we can write a CSS rule targeting the span with the class highlighted to style it differently from the surrounding paragraph:

```
<p>I am a paragraph with <span class="highlighted">some inline
text</span> that is highlighted in a different color.</p>
```

We'll show you some examples of spans in action later in this chapter.

id and class attributes

In the previous section we saw two examples of div elements in action, one used an id, one used a class. What's the difference between the id and class attributes in the examples?

The answer is simple: ids are unique, classes aren't. We can have only one element with a specific id attribute on a page, but we can have multiple elements with the same class attribute on a page. This is an important point to grasp and worth spending some time on.

The id attribute is about *identification*. Think of your identity—your id identifies you and you only. Just like there's only one of you, so too can there be only one element with a particular id on a page.

The class attribute is about *classification*. You can have as many elements with a particular class on a page as you like.

An id is unique; there's only one person with a specific id in a group of people. Within that same group, however, are lots of people who belong to that group: id = one; class = many. In short, an id attribute can only be used once per page, whereas a class attribute can be used multiple times.

Looking at the examples in the section titled "div and span elements" earlier in the chapter, you'll notice we used an id of content when creating our content div, but we used a class of blog_entry when creating our blog entry divs. Think about it—on a page there will very likely be only one content area, but there might be several blog entries.

classes and ids are not restricted to divs and spans. In fact, any HTML element including headings, paragraphs, and images can have a class or an id added. We'll see this in action later when we apply a class to our portrait of King Kong, applying a little style to it. For now, let's return to the examples we introduced earlier.

In our example markup earlier, we identified a div and gave it an id as follows:

```
<div id="content">
  <!-- This is where the main content of the web page is situated. -->
</div>
```

We target this div's id with the following CSS:

```
#content
{
/* This is where the rules styling the content div are situated. */
}
```

Note how we use a # (hash) to indicate that the CSS rule is targeting an id. To indicate that a CSS rule is targeting a class, we use a . (period) as shown in the following example:

```
<div id="blog_entry">
  <!-- This is where each blog entry is situated. -->
</div>
```

We target that div's class with the following CSS:

```
.blog_entry
{
/* This is where the rules styling the blog_entry div are situated. */
}
```

As you'll see in the following sections, the div and span elements and their associated id and class attributes form the building blocks on which we build CSS layouts.

10

It's all in a name

When creating our ids and classes, we're not restricted to set terms like header, content and footer, or blog_entry and diary_entry. In fact, we can choose any names we like. However, when choosing names for ids or classes, it's a good idea to choose names that have semantic meaning, words that can give you pointers when you return to a project after some time has elapsed. Consider the following two class names:

```
<span class="red">Some important content here.</span>
```

and

```
<span class="important">Some important content here.</span>
```

Although the first class name, red, might be presentationally accurate—this year you've decided to highlight important words in red—the second class name, important, is semantically accurate. Ask yourself, what are you *really* highlighting? The fact that the words are in red? Or the fact that they're important?

Next year, after your company's extensive rebranding, important words might be highlighted in blue to reflect your company's new (blue) corporate identity. The following rule won't make quite as much sense:

```
.red
{
color: blue;
}
```

Try to describe the content or function of your elements: primary_navigation is a more meaningful name than right_column, and content is better than box. The point is to use names for ids or classes that are meaningful and semantic; you'll be grateful for this in the long run.

> *When naming* id *or* class *names, we recommend only using the letters a–z in upper or lowercase, the numbers 0–9, and underscores or hyphens. An* id *or a* class *name must always start with a letter. It's also worth noting that* id *and* class *names are case sensitive—to a browser, #Header and #header are different.*
>
> *Keeping your* id *and* class *names in lowercase and making sure they always start with a letter will help to keep you on the one true path.*

Using div elements to create CSS layouts

Earlier in the chapter we ascertained that our King Kong page could be broken down into three logical sections, a header, content, and footer. By creating divs for the different sections of the document and nesting these within a container div, we can begin to create a layout for our King Kong page using CSS. At this point, to create a single column layout, we break our web page down into the key sections shown in Figure 10-13.

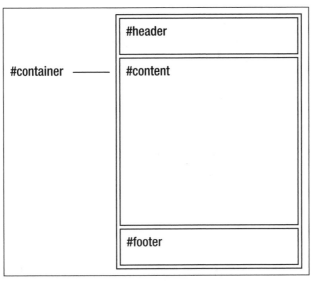

Figure 10-13. The basic div structure that we'll use to create our single column layout

Let's take a look at the markup required to create Figure 10-13. We've created a simplified version of a web page as follows, wrapping the key sections in div elements, adding comments to show where each div closes. (You'll notice the div elements are nested using the First In, Last Out approach we introduced in Chapter 2.) The markup we need is as follows:

```
<body>
  <div id="container">
    <div id="header">
      <!-- This is where the header information is situated. -->
    </div> <!-- Closes the #header div. -->

    <div id="content">
      <!-- This is where the main content of the page is situated. -->
    </div> <!-- Closes the #content div. -->

    <div id="footer">
      <!-- This is where the footer information is situated. -->
    </div> <!-- Closes the #footer div. -->
  </div> <!-- Closes the #container div. -->
</body>
```

Once we've wrapped the key sections of our document in div elements, we can use CSS to apply style to these different div elements just as we would any other element. This includes controlling layout, giving the divs different widths and heights, changing their background color, and positioning them within the browser window.

We'll see div elements in action in the following section when we take the preceding simplified markup and apply basic layout properties to it, demonstrating the effect that this has within the context of a browser window.

10

251

A one-column CSS layout

The first stage in our walkthrough is to create a simple web page with header, content, and footer divs nested in a container div. Although this page's content is simplified, the essential document sections remain, mirroring our King Kong page.

You'll notice the markup that follows is the same as that in the previous example, but with some of the comments removed for the purpose of simplicity. You can see all of the stages in the walkthrough at the book's companion web site:

www.webstandardistas.com/10/walkthrough

Use View Source to look at each of the stages. Let's get started. We create a page with the following basic structure:

```
<body>
  <div id="container">
    <div id="header">
      <!-- This is where the header information is situated. -->
    </div>

    <div id="content">
      <!-- This is where the main content of the page is situated. -->
    </div>

    <div id="footer">
      <!-- This is where the footer information is situated. -->
    </div>
  </div>
</body>
```

We add the following CSS to style some basic properties:

```
body
{
font-family: 'Lucida Grande', 'Lucida Sans', Arial, sans-serif;
font-size: 14px;
line-height: 1.6;
background-color: #FFFFFF;
}
```

```
h1
{
font-size: 16px;
text-transform: uppercase;
}
```

This markup and CSS renders in the browser as shown in Figure 10-14.

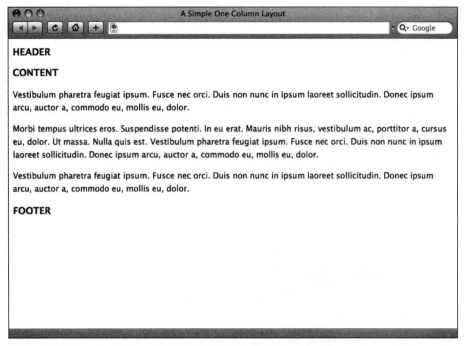

Figure 10-14. Our simplified markup with CSS styling the typography only

Although the content of the web page we're working on for this walkthrough has been simplified, the page is structured identically to our King Kong page with a header, content, and footer section. At the end of this walkthrough, we'll replace the generic content with our King Kong content, resulting in a one-column CSS layout for the page.

We'll now walk through the process of applying some layout to this page using CSS, specifically adding CSS rules to target the four div elements we've added to the markup. We add the following four CSS rules:

```
#container
{
width: 550px;
background-color: #FFFFFF;
}

#header
{
padding: 10px 20px;
background-color: #999999;
}

#content
{
padding: 10px 20px;
background-color: #CCCCCC;
}
```

10

```
#footer
{
padding: 10px 20px;
background-color: #999999;
}
```

These rules set a width on our container div of 550px. Looking again at the preceding markup, you can see that the three remaining div elements—our header, content, and footer—are nested within the container, so setting the width to 550px on the container defines the width of all of our div elements in this example. The other rules we've added set a background-color and add some padding on our other div elements; this is simply to ensure the effect of adding our rules is easier to see.

The result of adding these rules is shown in Figure 10-15.

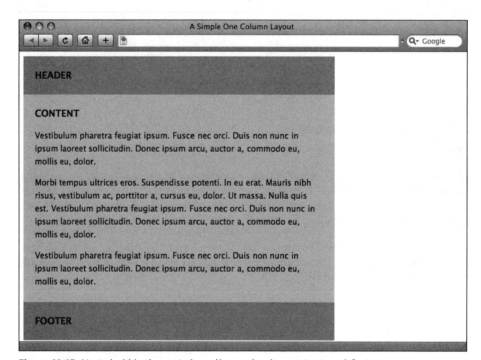

Figure 10-15. Nested within the container div, our header, content, and footer now occupy 550 pixels of horizontal space.

The next step in the process is to add a declaration to the body rule to remove the margin added by browser's default style sheet. We add the following declaration, resetting the margin on the body to 0:

```
body
{
font-family: 'Lucida Grande', 'Lucida Sans', Arial, sans-serif;
font-size: 14px;
line-height: 1.6;
```

```
background-color: #FFFFFF;
margin: 0;
}
```

The result of adding this rule is shown in Figure 10-16.

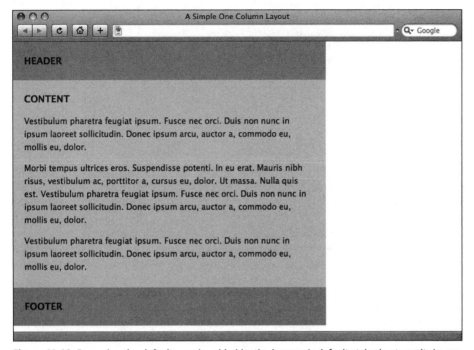

Figure 10-16. Removing the default margin added by the browser's default style sheet results in our container sitting tight toward the top left corner of the browser window.

Now that we've reset the default margin, the next stage is to center the container div within the browser window. We do this by adding a declaration to the rule styling the container. By adding margin: 0 auto; the browser centers the container div, giving it a top and bottom margin of 0px and centering the div as a result of the auto value, which controls the right and left margin.

```
#container
{
width: 550px;
background-color: #FFFFFF;
margin: 0 auto;
}
```

The result of this is shown in Figure 10-17.

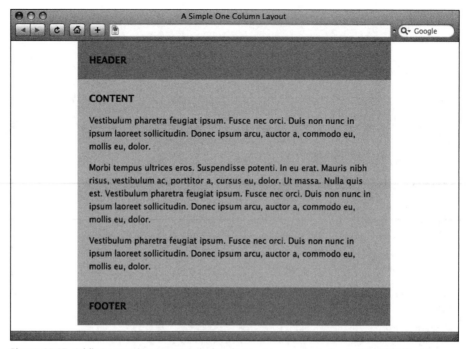

Figure 10-17. Adding a margin: 0 auto; declaration centers our container div within the browser window.

Our page is beginning to take shape. We'll now center the contents of the header and footer by using the text-align property. We add text-align declarations to both the header and footer rules as follows:

```
#header
{
padding: 10px 20px;
background-color: #999999;
text-align: center;
}

...

#footer
{
padding: 10px 20px;
background-color: #999999;
text-align: center;
}
```

The result of adding these two declarations is shown in Figure 10-18.

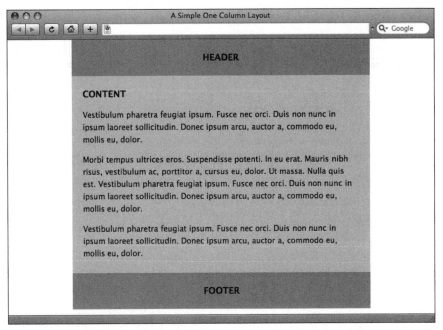

Figure 10-18. Adding a text-align: center; declaration to our header and footer centers the content of these div elements.

The next stage in the process is to change the background-color we set on the header, content, and footer. For the final layout we'd like the content div to form a focal point with a darker background-color and set the background-color of the header and footer to be the same as the background-color of the body.

We change the header, content, and footer background-color values as follows:

```
#header
{
padding: 10px 20px;
background-color: #FFFFFF;
text-align: center;
}

#content
{
padding: 10px 20px;
background-color: #999999;
}

#footer
{
padding: 10px 20px;
background-color: #FFFFFF;
text-align: center;
}
```

10

The result of this is shown in Figure 10-19.

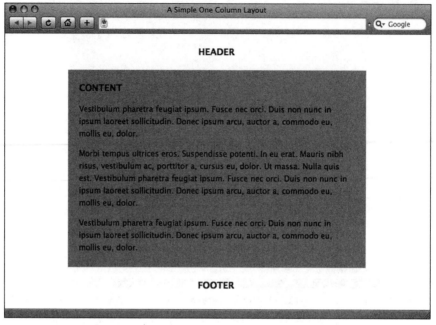

Figure 10-19. Changing the background-color of the header and footer visually distinguishes them from the content div.

The final stage in the process is to add a border to the top of the body and to the base of the container. We do this by adding the following two declarations:

```
body
{
font-family: 'Lucida Grande', 'Lucida Sans', Arial, sans-serif;
font-size: 14px;
line-height: 1.6;
background-color: #FFFFFF;
margin: 0;
border-top: 5px solid #000000;
}

...

#container
{
width: 550px;
background-color: #FFFFFF;
margin: 0 auto;
border-bottom: 5px solid #000000;
}
```

The result of adding these two declarations is shown in Figure 10-20.

Figure 10-20. Note how the border at the top spans the entire width of the body, whereas the border at the bottom spans only the width of the container div.

Note how the border on the body expands to fill the entire width of the browser window, but the border on the container only occupies 550 pixels (the width of the container div).

That's it! It might not seem like much, but once we populate this layout with the content of our King Kong page as it stood at the end of Chapter 9, you can see that things are beginning to take shape. Simply adding the content we styled in the last chapter (and adding a new Famous Primates brand that we'll be supplying for you) results in Figure 10-21.

In just three chapters we've moved from a well-structured web page to a well-styled web page using a single-column layout. Equally importantly, the web page we've been building is accessible and is designed to display across a wide variety of devices, no small achievement.

Figure 10-21.
Our King Kong page as it now stands using the preceding layout

10

Using descendant selectors to minimize markup

Astute readers will notice just one thing wrong with the web page as it currently stands in Figure 10-21. The p elements in our footer are inheriting the color we specified on the body element, a shade of creamy white (#E0DFDA). This is fine for the text in the main content section, which has a dark brown background-color (#25201C); however, against the light background of the footer, the text lacks contrast as shown in Figure 10-22.

Figure 10-22. The text in our footer suffers from a lack of contrast, rendering it very difficult to read.

In order to fix this we need to write a rule that targets *only p elements in the footer*. The good news is we can use this fix to introduce another extremely useful aspect of CSS, namely **descendant selectors** (sometimes referred to as **contextual selectors**).

Before we introduce you to descendant selectors, let's look at one way we could resolve the problem of our p elements that we *don't* recommend. By showing you two ways of achieving the same goal—one that relies on bad practice and one that relies on good practice—we can highlight the better approach.

Earlier in the chapter we mentioned the twin evils of *divitis* and *spanitis*, or the overreliance on div and span elements. Another problem that beginners often fall into is an overreliance on class attributes, using class attributes left, right, and center, resulting in bloated and overcomplicated markup.

We could solve the problem of the footer by styling the p elements that are situated in the footer, giving each of them a specific class as follows (we've removed the markup for the links for the purpose of simplicity):

```
<p class="footer_text">The Famous Primates web site is a➥
Web Standardistas production.</p>
<p class="footer_text">XHTML + CSS released under a Creative Commons➥
Attribution 3.0 license.</p>
<p class="footer_text">Photography &copy; iStockphoto</p>
```

By adding class="footer_text" to each of our p elements, we can then write a CSS rule, as follows, that takes care of all instances of p with a class of footer_text:

```
.footer_text
{
font-size: 11px;
```

```
color: #383330;
}
```

While this will certainly work and will take care of styling the p elements in our footer, differentiating them from the rest of the p elements on the page, it's not the most efficient solution to the problem. As you can see, it relies on us adding class="footer_text" to each of our p elements. Not exactly the most efficient approach to writing lean and mean markup, certainly not the Web Standardistas' way.

Good news, CSS offers us a far better solution, which allows us to selectively target just these p elements based on their context in the footer. We can write a descendant selector that targets all p elements in the footer as follows:

```
#footer p
{
font-size: 11px;
color: #383330;
}
```

Essentially what this does is inform the browser to "look for any instance of the element p within the div footer and apply this rule." This allows us to target *just* these p elements with laserlike precision. This does away with the need for the additional markup—class="footer_text"—on each of our p elements in our footer. The result: less markup = less maintenance = faster downloads. The result of our new rule is shown in Figure 10-23.

Figure 10-23. The p elements in our footer are now styled using a descendant selector, differentiating them from all other instances of p on the page.

Now the paragraphs in our footer are much more legible, and the type is smaller than the main p elements in our content section (which is appropriate given that this is the "small print"). However, the links in light blue need a little more contrast. We'll use a descendant selector to style these differently from the other links on the page. We add the following rule:

```
#footer a:link, #footer a:visited
{
color: #383330;
border-bottom: solid 1px #383330;
}
```

10

By using *descendant selectors* in conjunction with *grouped selectors* (introduced in Chapter 9), we can really minimize our markup, styling multiple elements with a single rule and improving the efficiency of our style sheets considerably.

Essentially the preceding rule targets all instances of a:link and a:visited (i.e., links and visited links) situated in the footer and sets their color to the same as the p elements in the footer, differentiating them from the p elements through the inclusion of a border-bottom. The result of this is shown in Figure 10-24.

Figure 10-24. The a:link and a:visited pseudo-classes are now styled differently, set in the same color as the p elements in the footer.

An understanding of how descendant selectors work can significantly help to reduce markup. Applying style to different elements based on their context reduces the number of CSS rules required and saves peppering your markup with redundant classes. Both things the aspiring Web Standardista should be striving for.

Styling details with the span element

Where div elements are *block-level*, span elements are *inline-level*. Imagine you have a paragraph that contains some content you'd like to style differently from the rest of the paragraph—enter the span. Wrapping a span element around the inline content you'd like to style differently allows you to target your CSS at the span to achieve the effect you'd like.

In the next two sections we'll take a look at this in action. In the first example, we'll use a span to style a specific part of our footer. In the second example, we'll show how noted Standardista Dan Cederholm uses a span to style part of his SimpleBits web site's strapline without needing to resort to image replacement techniques to create an elegant ampersand.

Using a span to style inline content

Let's take a look at a span in action. We'll work with the first line of our footer, which contains our publishing and copyright information. At present it's rendered as in Figure 10-24; however, we'd like to differentiate the words *Famous Primates* in the first line, using the font-weight property to highlight the words in bold and transforming their case to uppercase using the text-transform property. We add the following to our markup (again, we've removed the markup for the link for the purpose of simplicity):

```
<p>The <span class="primate">Famous Primates</span> web site is a
Web Standardistas production.</p>
```

By wrapping the words *Famous Primates* in a span and giving it a class of primate, we can write a rule targeting all instances of the class primate. We add the following CSS rule to our style sheet:

```
.primate
{
text-transform: uppercase;
font-weight: bold;
}
```

Figure 10-25 shows the result of wrapping the span around the words *Famous Primates* and targeting a CSS rule at the span—exactly what we wanted, differentiating the words from the rest of the paragraph.

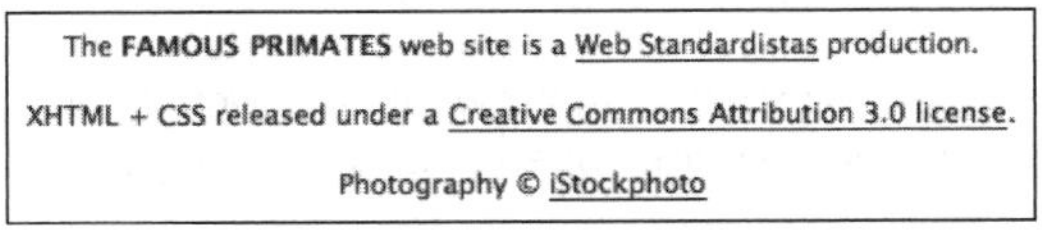

The **FAMOUS PRIMATES** web site is a <u>Web Standardistas</u> production.

XHTML + CSS released under a <u>Creative Commons Attribution 3.0 license</u>.

Photography © <u>iStockphoto</u>

Figure 10-25. The words *Famous Primates* are now styled in bold and uppercase, thanks to the added span.

Where possible it's best to eschew the use of the span element in favor of more meaningful markup; however, in some instances a span is the best option available.

Astute readers will notice one other change in the footer. At the end of Chapter 9, our final line read "Photography Copyright iStockphoto"; in the preceding example, we've now included a copyright (©) symbol. We do this by replacing the word *Copyright* with the character entity for the copyright symbol:

```
&copy;
```

The result is a copyright symbol, more clearly highlighting the fact that the copyright of the photography we're using belongs to iStockphoto.

In the next section, we take a look at another example of a span in action at noted Standardista Dan Cederholm's SimpleBits web site.

Dan Cederholm's illustrious ampersand

One elegant example of a span in action is noted Standardista Dan Cederholm's illustrious ampersand, as featured in the strapline of his SimpleBits web site (www.simplebits.com). Wrapping the ampersand in a span allows it to be differentiated from the surrounding text to create a sophisticated, graceful, and eye-catching feature as shown in Figure 10-26.

10

Hand-crafted pixels *&* text from Salem, Massachusetts.

Figure 10-26. Dan Cederholm's illustrious ampersand, achieved by wrapping the ampersand in a span element

By using a semantically neutral span element, the heading still displays perfectly in a non-CSS environment, as shown, unstyled, in Figure 10-27.

Hand-crafted pixels & text from Salem, Massachusetts.

Figure 10-27. Unstyled, the illustrious ampersand is perfectly displayed in a non-CSS environment.

So you've now met divs and spans, two generic methods of marking up and adding structure to our documents. Of the two, the div is the one you'll be using the most as we move forward. Gathering information together in a div allows us to give that division a size, add some style to it, and apply layout to it by giving it a width and a height.

The ability to create accurately sized divisions within our web pages allows us to embark on layout using CSS. This is another area where CSS can prove powerful.

We're not restricted to using id and class attributes with div and span elements, however. We can apply both to other elements, thereby helping us to avoid the overuse of div and span elements, as you'll see in the following section when we style our King Kong image differently through the use of an added class attribute.

Styling with class attributes

At this point our King Kong web page features two images, the Famous Primates brand at the top of the page and the portrait of the mighty King Kong. In this section we'll look at using a class attribute to give the King Kong portrait its own look and feel.

We'd like our portrait of King Kong to render in the browser with some additional style, using margins, borders, and padding. To do this we need to differentiate our King Kong image from the Famous Primates brand at the top of the page so that we can target our CSS at *just* the King Kong image.

We add a class attribute to the King Kong image as follows:

```
<img src="images/king_kong.jpg" width="500" height="350" alt="The
mighty King Kong, a fearsome giant ape." title="King Kong
contemplates scaling yet another tall building." class="portrait" />
```

By adding a class to the portrait of King Kong, we can now write a rule targeting *any* image with a class of portrait. We add the following rule to our style sheet:

```
.portrait
{
margin: 10px 0;
```

```
  border: 1px solid #FFF7D7;
  padding: 4px;
}
```

You should by now be able to tell that this rule is adding margins (10px top and bottom; 0px right and left), a border (1px solid #FFF7D7;) and padding (4px) to our King Kong portrait. The result of this is shown in Figure 10-28.

Figure 10-28. Our King Kong image with a 1 pixel border and 4 pixels of padding around it

As you know by now, we're not restricted to styling the image in this way; we could have a thicker border, less padding—we could have anything we want—by changing our CSS rule.

10

Enhancing your design by adding background images with CSS

We can use CSS to apply a background-image to almost any element in XHTML including our page's body element (this can be useful for creating page backgrounds to give character to a web page), our div elements, blockquotes, paragraphs, lists, and even inline-level elements.

Creative use of background images can help to break up a page and, as you'll see in this section, help to create more dynamic layouts. In the following section we'll demonstrate how to add a background-image to our body element, in the process introducing you to how to apply background images using CSS. We'll then apply a background-image to our blockquote to further enhance its presentation.

Adding a background image to the body

We'll start with a simplified web page with a single paragraph with 40px of margin applied. We add the following rules to our style sheet to establish some basic style:

```
body
{
font-family: 'Lucida Grande', 'Lucida Sans', Arial, sans-serif;
font-size: 14px;
color: #000000;
background-color: #FFFFFF;
margin: 0;
}


p
{
width: 400px;
line-height: 1.5;
margin: 40px;
}
```

The result of this can be seen in Figure 10-29.

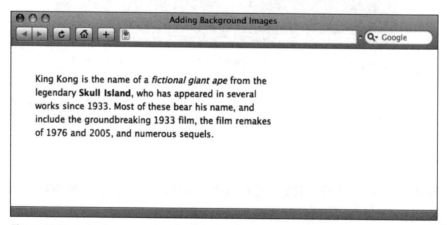

Figure 10-29. A simple paragraph with minimal style added

We create a simple 8 × 8 pixel tile in our image editor as shown in Figure 10-30. This is designed to tile seamlessly, repeating horizontally and vertically across the background of our web page like wallpaper.

Figure 10-30.
We create a simple image in our image editor (magnified here) that we can tile as the background of our web page by setting the image as a background-image on our body element.

We add background-image and background-repeat declarations to our body rule as follows:

```
body
{
font-family: 'Lucida Grande', 'Lucida Sans', Arial, sans-serif;
font-size: 14px;
color: #000000;
background-color: #FFFFFF;
margin: 0;
background-image: url(diagonal_tile.png);
background-repeat: repeat;
}
```

The background-image declaration provides a relative link to the image file we're using, in this case with the relative location of our diagonal_tile.png image file. It's worth noting that the URL specifies the location of the image file in relation to the style sheet. In this case we're using an internal style sheet, so the preceding rule assumes the diagonal_tile. png file is in the same folder as the web page.

The background-repeat declaration instructs the browser to repeat the image along both the x and y axes. (Using repeat-x would repeat the image only along the x axis; using repeat-y would repeat the image only along the y axis; using no-repeat would display the background-image once only, not repeating it.)

The result of adding the preceding declarations is shown in Figure 10-31.

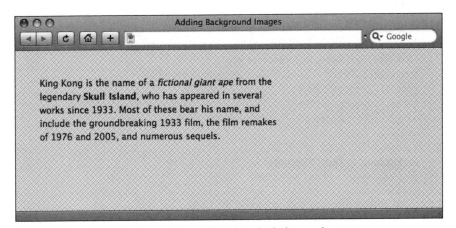

Figure 10-31. A simple background-image tiled along both the x and y axes

Although we've only used a simple, repeating tile in this example, tiling across both the x and y axes, it's possible to creatively use the background-image property to help break up the underlying grid of a simple web page and create layout effects.

One point worth noting is the importance of specifying a background-color *in addition to* a background-image. Although the background-color sits *behind* the background image,

10

its good practice to specify a background-color (and a contrasting text color) when using background images, in case a user is browsing your web site with images switched off.

> It's important to note that using background images in CSS is not the same as adding images to a page using the img element. Images included with the img element are seen as content; images included using the background-image properties of CSS are seen as presentation.

Background images can add to a design considerably. One excellent resource for well-designed background images that are free to use and inspirational is Kaliber10000's Pixel Patterns Collection (www.k10k.net/pixelpatterns/).

Using background images with other elements

In the margins, borders, and padding walkthrough earlier in this chapter, we added a background-color to our p element to highlight the space the paragraph occupied as a block-level element. Although we used this to demonstrate the effects of adding our margin, border, and padding declarations, we could have also employed the background-color property as a design element, perhaps using it to distinguish different parts of our document by setting the background-color to a different color.

Let's take a look at our blockquote again, now setting a complementary background-color to further highlight the quotation. We add the following background-color declaration to our CSS rule:

```
blockquote
{
font-family: Georgia, sans-serif;
font-size: 18px;
font-style: italic;
letter-spacing: 0.1em;
margin-left: 40px;
padding: 0 20px;
border-left: 10px solid #E0DFDA;
background-color: #3E322B;
}
```

The result of adding this rule is shown in Figure 10-32.

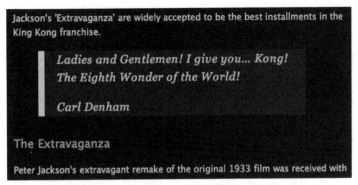

Figure 10-32. Adding a background-color declaration to our blockquote element helps to further differentiate it from the surrounding text.

With CSS we can control much more than background colors for our elements, however. As we mentioned in the last section, we can also add background images to our different elements using CSS to create a variety of presentational outcomes.

Let's take a look at this in action as applied to our blockquote again. We've created an image with a gradient, using the shades of brown employed on the King Kong page; we'll use this to create a background-image for our blockquote.

We add a background-image declaration to our CSS rule as follows:

```
blockquote
{
font-family: georgia, sans-serif;
font-size: 18px;
font-style: italic;
letter-spacing: 0.1em;
margin-left: 40px;
padding: 0 20px;
border-left: 10px solid #E0DFDA;
background-color: #3E322B;
background-image: url(blockquote_bg.png);
}
```

The result of this is shown in Figure 10-33.

10

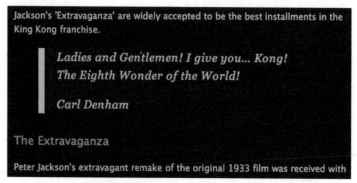

Figure 10-33. Adding a background-image declaration to our blockquote element helps to break up the grid on the page, while still differentiating the blockquote from the surrounding text.

Both of the preceding examples of the background-image property barely scratch the surface. Used creatively, background images can help to break up the grid in a typical CSS layout, resulting in more interesting and innovative layouts.

We've added two background images to our King Kong web page—one on the body, one on our blockquote—to give a glimpse of what's possible using background images. You can see these at the book's companion web site:

www.webstandardistas.com/10/king_kong.html

To give you some experience of the background-image property, you'll be adding background images to your Gordo web page for this chapter's homework.

Summary

So what have we covered? It's been a busy and important chapter, certainly one that's well worth reading again. We've covered a lot of fundamentals including dividing up complex web pages into logical divisions using div elements, an understanding of which forms the basis of creating CSS layouts.

We introduced the CSS box model and looked at adding margins, borders, and padding to our elements with a specific focus on how these properties could be used creatively when applied to our page's different elements. Lastly, we looked at using background images in CSS to help break up our web pages a little.

In the next chapter we'll build on the fundamentals introduced in this chapter, showing you how to create two-column layouts to develop your CSS layout skills considerably.

Homework: Creating a one-column CSS layout

In this chapter we added some additional structure to our document by breaking our King Kong page down into key sections or divisions. The primary focus of the chapter was the creation of a one-column CSS layout to give our King Kong page a little more style and presence. By following along with the examples covered throughout the chapter, you should be capable of creating a single-column layout for your Gordo page in addition to developing the design of its different elements.

We introduced the cascade in Cascading Style Sheets and looked at adding margins, borders, and padding to your elements, introducing you to the concept of the box model. As a by-product of this we introduced CSS shorthand, which will enable you to write shorter and more compact style sheets.

Using our King Kong page as an example, we applied our knowledge of margins, borders, and padding to improve our blockquote, adding a background-image to it also, to further differentiate it from the rest of the page.

The major focus of the chapter was on the introduction of div elements, which we used to break our page down into different sections, which we then positioned and controlled using CSS. Along the way, we looked at how we could use span elements to style details, enabling you to zero in on specific inline-level sections to apply style to. We also introduced the concept of descendant selectors, a powerful means of minimizing markup.

Finally we looked at enhancing your design by adding background images with CSS, both to the body and to other elements.

Your homework for this chapter will be to apply what you've learned to your Gordo page, improving its layout considerably.

1. Add the div tags

If you've been following along with the homework, your Gordo page should feature a similar structure to our King Kong page. For the first stage of this chapter's homework, we'd like you to identify the key sections of your Gordo web page and add div tags where appropriate.

Once you've wrapped your header, content and footer sections in divs, we'd like you to wrap everything in a container div, which you'll use to center your design.

2. Write the CSS

Referring to the examples in this chapter, create rules for your header, content, footer, and container div elements to control the layout of the page.

Once you've taken care of the layout, we'd like you to address the issue of the footer. You'll need to create a rule that styles the text in the footer, overriding the font-size and color declaration inherited from the body rule. Write this rule using a descendant selector to minimize your markup.

10

3. Upgrade the Famous Primates brand

As with the previous chapters, we've created everything you need to complete the home-work. This includes an all-new-and-improved Famous Primates brand, in addition to two pre-baked gradient images to use as a background-image for your Gordo page and your blockquote. You can download the assets here:

www.webstandardistas.com/10/assets.zip

Once you've downloaded these files, transfer the images to your images folder and upgrade the Famous Primates brand.

4. Style the blockquote

Styling the blockquote is a two-stage process. Firstly we'd like you to apply margins, bor-ders, and padding to distinguish the blockquote from the surrounding text. Once you've achieved that, we'd like you to specify the image we supplied as a background-image for your blockquote.

5. Style Gordo's image

Style your image of Gordo by creating a class to differentiate it from the Famous Primates brand and create margin, border, and padding declarations for the image. We added a 1 pixel border with 4 pixels of padding; you might like to experiment with an alternative, for example, try adding a 5-pixel border with no padding in the light shade of blue we've been using (#9CC4E5) as follows:

```
.portrait
{
margin: 10px 0;
border: 5px solid #9CC4E5;
}
```

Remember, you'll need to add a class="portrait" attribute to the markup of your Gordo image for this rule to take effect.

6. Add a background-image

The last part of the homework is to add the background-image we've supplied. This image needs to be repeated along the x axis, which will tile it horizontally. You'll also notice from our King Kong example page that we've included an additional declaration background-attachment: fixed;. The background-attachment property sets whether a background-image is fixed or scrolls with the rest of the page. Try commenting out this declaration and testing its effect on the background-image within a browser.

As usual, to help you with the different stages of this chapter's homework, we've created our own, similarly styled, page about King Kong featuring all of the enhancements we covered in this chapter. You can refer to this, using your browser's View Source menu com-mand to see how we've updated our CSS, here:

www.webstandardistas.com/10/king_kong.html

Once you've completed the rollout of your one-column CSS layout for Gordo, put the kettle on and enjoy a cup of *Robert Fortune Blend 41* as you prepare yourself for the next chapter.

10

CHAPTER 11
A TWO-COLUMN CSS LAYOUT

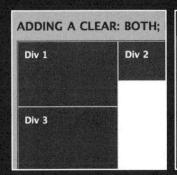

In this chapter we create a slightly more complex, two-column layout. Building upon the one-column web page we created at the end of Chapter 10, we'll add a second div to sit alongside the content div. We'll use this to contain some additional sidebar content, which could be anything: some supporting content, a navigation list, or any number of other elements.

For the purposes of this chapter, and to keep the focus on layout, we'll keep the content of the sidebar div simple. Inside it we'll place a single <h2> followed by a short paragraph containing links to our Cheeta and Cornelius pages. In the next chapter we'll replace this sidebar content with a styled list of links, creating the navigation for our Famous Primates web site.

As with the other chapters, we'll be working with our King Kong web page, and you'll be working along with your Gordo page for the homework. By the end of the chapter you should have a working knowledge of two-column layouts, floating elements, and the importance of clearing floats.

The fundamental concepts discussed in this chapter will provide a solid foundation on which you can build, providing the building blocks for more complex layouts down the line.

A float-based CSS layout

There are a number of ways to create multicolumn layouts using CSS. These include floating, absolute positioning, and using negative margins. We'll be focusing on a float-based approach as we find this the most flexible method, as well as being easy for beginners to understand.

> *Although we've focused on float-based layouts in the book, we have featured a roundup of other layout methods, including absolute positioning and the use of negative margins, in the periodical section of the book's companion web site where we have also provided links to a number of additional resources that deal with CSS-based layouts.*

To get started with float-based layouts, we need to introduce the idea of floating elements and removing them from the document flow. But what exactly do we mean by the *document flow*?

Looking back at the XHTML web pages we created earlier in the book, you know that web pages are linear by nature. The elements of your web pages flow down the page starting with the first element at the top of the page and finishing with the last element at the bottom of the page. Elements can be either block-level (forcing a line break) or inline-level.

In Western languages a paragraph of text starts at the top left corner of the page and works its way down toward the bottom right corner of the page. When writing, each word is placed just to the right of the preceding word until there is no more room on the line; the next word is then placed at the very left of the next line.

Similarly, all elements on an XHTML page have a natural tendency to sit as close to the top left of the page as possible. This is the natural flow of web pages (in the Western speaking world) and is known as the **document flow**.

Using the float property in CSS allows us to remove elements from this flow, enabling us to position them on the page. A floated element is taken out of the normal top left to bottom right flow and moved as far as possible to the left or right (depending upon the CSS rules written to target it). This will become clearer to grasp when we introduce some examples in this chapter.

Before we introduce you to some examples of floats in action, by floating some divs, let's see what the W3C has to say about floats:

> *A float is a box that is shifted to the left or right on the current line. The most interesting characteristic of a float (or "floated" or "floating" box) is that content may flow along its side (or be prohibited from doing so by the "clear" property). Content flows down the right side of a left-floated box and down the left side of a right-floated box.*
>
> *A floated box is shifted to the left or right until its outer edge touches the containing block edge or the outer edge of another float. If there's a line box, the top of the floated box is aligned with the top of the current line box.*
>
> www.w3.org/TR/CSS21/visuren.html#floats

While that might sound a little confusing just now, it should all become apparent as we walk through some practical examples demonstrating how floats work, which we'll do in the following section. Using some simplified web pages we apply floats to our different elements and show you how the floats we add affect the normal document flow.

Floating divs

We know from Chapter 10 that divs are block-level elements; this means they force a line break after they close. We can, however, use the float property to alter their relationship to the natural document flow of a web page.

To demonstrate how floats work, we've created a basic web page with a container div and three nested div elements. We've numbered the divs so that you can see exactly how the different div elements are affected as we apply floats to them. Our markup looks like this:

```
<h1>No Floats</h1>
<div id="container">
  <div class="box"><h2>Div 1</h2></div>
  <div class="box"><h2>Div 2</h2></div>
  <div class="box"><h2>Div 3</h2></div>
</div>
```

11

We give the container a width and height of 400px and give the three divs nested inside it a width and height of 100px; lastly we've added 1-pixel borders and background colors on all of the div elements and the body element to make our divs easier to see. We do this using the following CSS:

```
body
{
margin: 20px;
padding: 0;
font-family: 'Lucida Grande', 'Lucida Sans', Arial, sans-serif;
background-color: #CCCCCC;
}

#container
{
width: 400px;
height: 400px;
border: 1px solid #000000;
background-color: #FFFFFF;
}

.box
{
width: 100px;
height: 100px;
border: 1px solid #CCCCCC;
background-color: #333333;
}
```

The preceding markup renders in the browser as shown in Figure 11-1.

As with all div elements, our three smaller divs are block-level; as such they force a line break so that our three divs sit one on top of the other. At this point, the three nested divs are in the normal document flow with the first box at the top and the last box at the bottom.

Let's now apply float: left to the div elements with the class of box and see how this affects the layout. We add the following additional declaration to our CSS:

```
.box
{
float: left;
width: 100px;
height: 100px;
border: 1px solid #CCCCCC;
background-color: #333333;
}
```

The result of adding this declaration is shown in Figure 11-2.

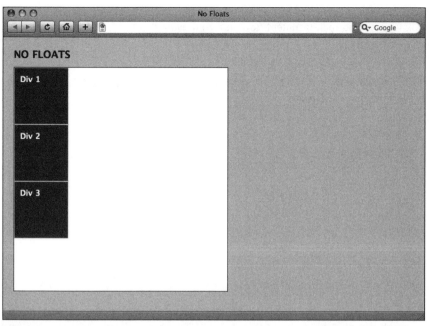

Figure 11-1. Our three nested div elements, each with a class of box as they render nested within the container. No floats are added at this point.

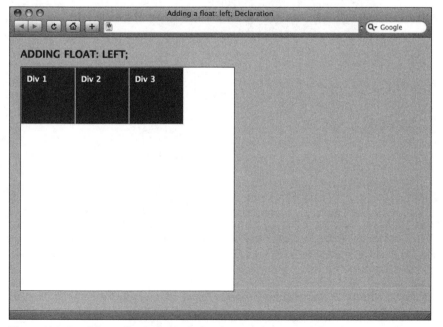

Figure 11-2. By adding a float: left; declaration, our three nested div elements, each with a class of box, are now removed from the normal document flow.

As you can see, the addition of a float: left; declaration removes all divs with a class of box from the normal document flow, in turn moving them as far left as possible within their containing element (in this case the container div). The result is that the three nested div elements display horizontally and are aligned—or floated—to the left.

Let's now apply float: right to the same div elements and see how this affects the layout. We amend our CSS as follows:

```
.box
{
float: right;
width: 100px;
height: 100px;
border: 1px solid #CCCCCC;
background-color: #333333;
}
```

The result is shown in Figure 11-3.

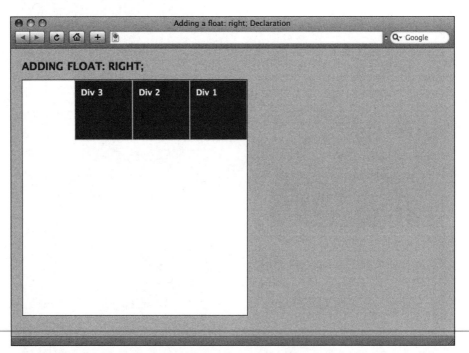

Figure 11-3. Changing our float value from left; to right; alters the relationship of our nested divs to the container div.

Looking at Figure 11-3, you might be forgiven for wondering why the order of the divs is now Div 3, Div 2, Div 1.

At first glance this might appear confusing; however, the explanation is simple. The browser is rendering Div 1 as far to the right as it will go, in this case aligning it to the top right edge of the container div it's nested in. It's then rendering Div 2 in the markup, and then Div 3. This is due to the float: right; declaration, which takes the divs with the class of box out of the normal document flow and floats them to the right.

This might be confusing to start with, but it's important to get an understanding of how floats remove elements from the normal flow of the document, as this will form the basis of the layouts we'll be creating later in this chapter.

Before we get on to applying this knowledge to our two-column layout, let's take a look at what happens when not all of our div elements are floated. To do this, we've adjusted and added to our markup as follows, introducing a different class for the first of our three smaller boxes:

```
<div id="container">
  <div class="boxspecial"><h2>Div 1</h2></div>
  <div class="box"><h2>Div 2</h2></div>
  <div class="box"><h2>Div 3</h2></div>
</div>
```

We now have two different classes—box and boxspecial. We alter our style sheet as follows, removing the float property from the box class, and adding a rule targeting the new boxspecial class we've just created:

```
.box
{
width: 100px;
height: 100px;
border: 1px solid #CCCCCC;
background-color: #333333;
}

.boxspecial
{
float: right;
width: 100px;
height: 100px;
border: 1px solid #CCCCCC;
background-color: #333333;
}
```

Let's try and anticipate what's going to happen. Div 1 has a class of boxspecial, so it's going to be floated to the right. Div 2 and Div 3, however, have no float specified, so they're going to sit within the normal flow. Let's take a look at how this renders in the browser, as shown in Figure 11-4.

11

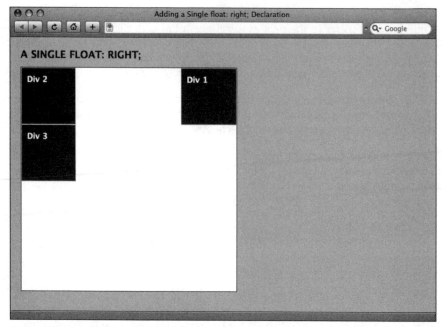

Figure 11-4. By specifiying `float: right;` for Div 1, and specifying no float for Div 2 and Div 3, Div 1 is removed from the normal flow of the document. Div 2 and Div 3, still within the normal document flow, ignore it completely.

As you can see, Div 1 has been floated to the right and *removed from the document flow*; this results in Div 2 and Div 3 occupying the space (at the top left) that Div 1 no longer occupies. Div 3 is dropping below Div 2, because it is no longer floated and is block-level.

If you return back to the idea that floated boxes are *removed from the document flow* and that boxes with no floats applied are *still within the normal document flow*, this should make sense. Div 2 and Div 3 are essentially ignoring Div 1 because it has been floated and removed from the document flow.

The preceding examples all deal with divs that are the same size. In reality, however, our different div elements are likely to be different sizes (as they will be when we deal with our two-column layout). Let's see how three divs of different size relate.

In the following example, we've amended our markup to give each div a different class (box1, box2, and box3), and we've written three rules, one for each class, that we add to our style sheet as follows:

```
.box1
{
float: left;
width: 160px;
height: 100px;
border: 1px solid #CCCCCC;
background-color: #333333;
}
```

```
.box2
{
float: left;
width: 160px;
height: 60px;
border: 1px solid #CCCCCC;
background-color: #333333;
}

.box3
{
float: left;
width: 160px;
height: 140px;
border: 1px solid #CCCCCC;
background-color: #333333;
}
```

We've now changed the size of all three divs; all are also now different heights. As in Figure 11-2, all have a float: left; declaration, so they are removed from the normal document flow. Figure 11-5 shows the result of our changes.

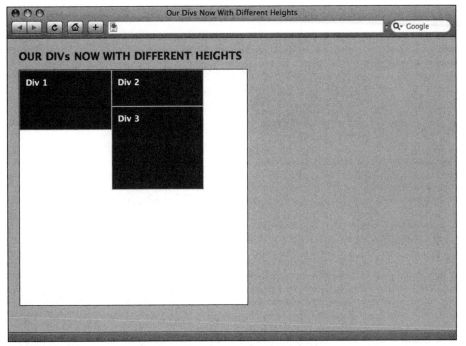

Figure 11-5. Div 1, Div 2, and Div 3 are now 160px wide, so they will not fit side by side within the 400px container div. Note how Div 3 occupies the first available position in the document flow, as far to the top left as it can go.

As we increased the width of our three divs to 160px, they no longer fit side by side in the 400px container div. The result is that Div 3 drops down to the next available space within the document flow, positioned as far to the top left as it can go. It's worth noting that this *isn't* below Div 1, but below Div 2, due to the space available beneath Div 2.

What if we'd like to drop Div 3 down so that it starts afresh on a new line and sits below Div 1? The answer is we use the clear property to clear the floats of Div 1 and Div 2 and instruct the browser to display Div 3 below them. (We'll use this technique in due course to clear our footer when we create the two-column layout for our upgraded King Kong page.)

We amend our CSS as follows:

```
.box3
{
float: left;
width: 160px;
height: 140px;
border: 1px solid #CCCCCC;
background-color: #333333;
clear: both;
}
```

The result of adding the clear property is shown in Figure 11-6.

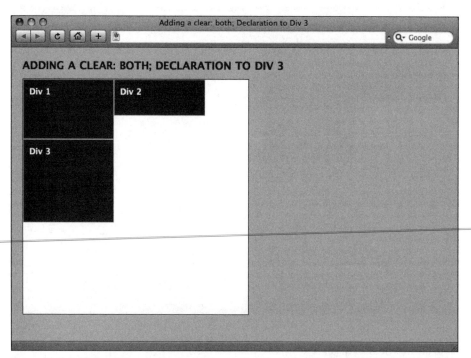

Figure 11-6. Adding a clear: both; declaration to the rule styling Div 3 clears both the Div 1 and Div 2 floats, dropping Div 3 beneath them.

Although all of our divs have been removed from the normal document flow by being set to float: left;, the addition of a clear declaration to Div 3 clears the above floats and positions Div 3 below Div 1 and Div 2.

In the next section we put the preceding examples into practice as we begin to build our two-column CSS layout using floats.

Applying floats to layouts

In the previous chapter we created a one-column layout and, in the process, subdivided our content into a number of divisions or divs. For the purposes of our one-column layout, we created header, content, and footer divs and nested them within a container div to hold everything together.

In this section we'll introduce a further div to our layout, a sidebar, which we'll use to gather some additional content to sit alongside our content div.

Simplified, we adjust our markup as follows, adding a sidebar div:

```
<body>
  <div id="container">
    <div id="header">
      <!-- This is where the header information is situated. -->
    </div> <!-- Closes the #header div. -->

    <div id="content">
      <!-- This is where the main content of the page is situated. -->
    </div> <!-- Closes the #content div. -->

    <div id="sidebar">
      <!-- This is where the sidebar of the page is situated. -->
    </div> <!-- Closes the #sidebar div. -->

    <div id="footer">
      <!-- This is where the footer information is situated. -->
    </div> <!-- Closes the #footer div. -->
  </div> <!-- Closes the #container div. -->
</body>
```

We now know that we can use CSS to float elements to the left or to the right. Because floated elements float until their outer edge meets the containing block they're situated within, or the outer edge of another floated element, we can nest our header, content, sidebar, and footer divs inside our container div and build a layout.

Figure 11-7 illustrates what we'll be building as we work through the examples in our two-column layout section. We'll float our content div to the left and our sidebar div to the right.

11

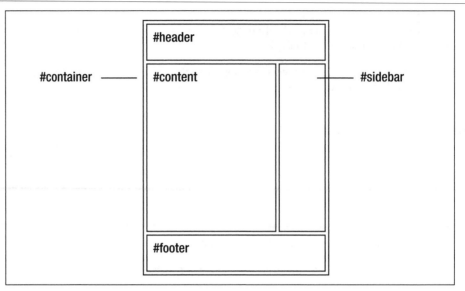

Figure 11-7. How our divs relate to each other once we add a sidebar div into the mix

It's worth noting, however, that, *regardless of the order our content appears in our markup*, we can float the content and sidebar divs in *either* direction, changing the visual order and display of the content and sidebar as we wish.

This allows us to organize our markup in the best way possible, putting the most important content first in the markup. As our divs can be floated in *either* direction, this means we can position the content div *before* the sidebar div in our markup, but use floats to visually position the sidebar div *before* the content div if we'd like to.

We write our markup in the optimum order, putting the content—which is more important than the sidebar—first in the markup order, as follows:

```
<body>
  ...

  <div id="content">
    <!-- This is where the main content of the page is situated. -->
  </div> <!-- Closes the #content div. -->

  <div id="sidebar">
    <!-- This is where the sidebar of the page is situated. -->
  </div> <!-- Closes the #sidebar div. -->

  ...
</body>
```

We can then control how these display in the browser by using floats. By floating the content div to the left and the sidebar div to the right, the content comes first in the visual display in the browser as in Figure 11-8.

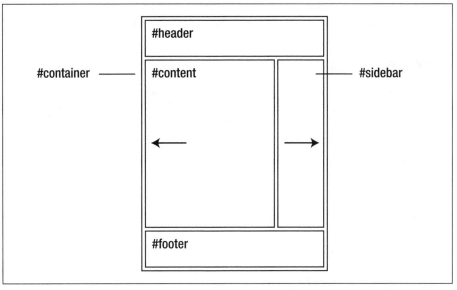

Figure 11-8. Floating the content div to the left and the sidebar div to the right changes the order our divs display in in the browser.

By simply changing the float values, we can float the sidebar to the left and the content div to the right, *without changing the order of our markup* as in Figure 11-9.

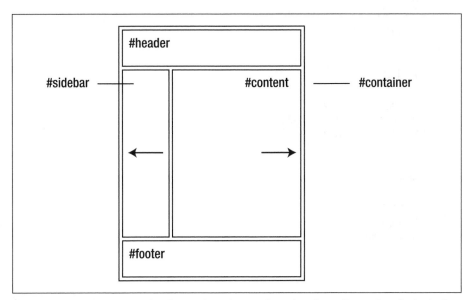

Figure 11-9. Simply switching the float values changes the order of our divs as they display in the browser.

11

In the next section, as we walk through the creation of our two-column layout, we'll show you how easy it is to switch our floats. Let's start building the two-column layout.

Creating our two-column CSS layout

We'll now take our markup with our header, content, sidebar, and footer divs nested within the container div and add some CSS to control our layout. This walkthrough develops the one-column layout we created in Chapter 10 and gives us a basic layout upon which we can build as we move forward.

We add the following rules to our style sheet:

```css
body
{
font-family: 'Lucida Grande', 'Lucida Sans', Arial, sans-serif;
font-size: 14px;
line-height: 1.6;
color: #000000;
background-color: #FFFFFF;
margin: 0;
}

#container
{
width: 790px;
background-color: #CCCCCC;
margin: 0 auto;
}

#header
{
padding: 10px 20px;
background-color: #333333;
text-align: center;
}

#content
{
width: 510px;
padding: 10px 20px;
background-color: #999999;
}

#sidebar
{
width: 200px;
padding: 10px 20px;
background-color: #666666;
}
```

```
#footer
{
clear: both;
padding: 10px 20px;
background-color: #333333;
text-align: center;
}

h1
{
font-size: 16px;
text-transform: uppercase;
}

#header h1, #footer h1
{
color: #FFFFFF;
}
```

With no floats applied, our document, as structured here, with our header, content, sidebar, and footer divs nested in a container div, will render using the browser's normal document flow; that is, each div will display one after the other, each forcing a line break. You can see the result of this in Figure 11-10.

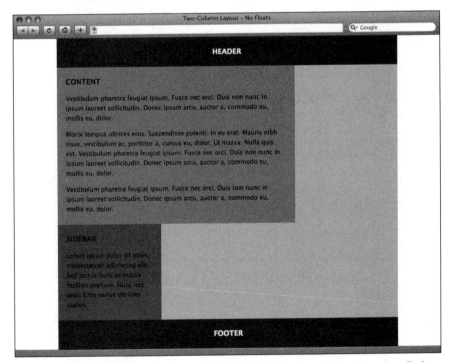

Figure 11-10. With no floats, our four nested block-level divs force line breaks and so display on separate lines.

Clearly this isn't what we want; we'd like our content and sidebar divs to float beside each other, with the content div floated to the left and the sidebar div floated to the right, as indicated in Figure 11-8 earlier. To do this we need to inform the browser to float the content and sidebar divs, and as you know from the preceding examples we can use the float property of CSS to align our content and sidebar divs to the left and right, respectively, effectively positioning them where we need them.

We do this by adding the following declarations to the content and sidebar rules in our style sheet:

```
#content
{
width: 510px;
padding: 10px 20px;
background-color: #999999;
float: left;
}

#sidebar
{
width: 200px;
padding: 10px 20px;
background-color: #666666;
float: right;
}
```

The result of adding these floats is shown in Figure 11-11.

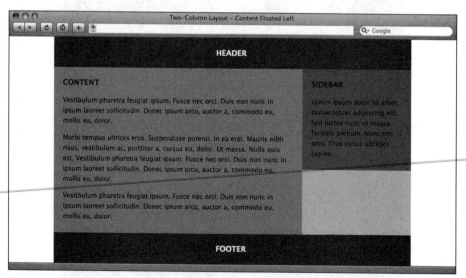

Figure 11-11. Adding float declarations to both the content and sidebar divs positions our div elements as we'd like.

What we've done is float our content to the left. Left-floated elements will move as far to the left as possible until they are in contact with the edge of the containing element (or another floated box); in this case the containing element is our container div.

Next, we've floated the sidebar to the right-hand edge of the container. Following the same principal as the left float, this pushes the sidebar as far to the right as possible, until it touches the edge of the container. As seen in the CSS markup earlier, we have explicitly specified widths on both the sidebar and content divs.

> It's important to specify widths on floated elements. In theory a floated element without a specific width should shrink to be as wide as the content within it; however, how this is interpreted can vary between browsers. As a rule of thumb: always specify a width on floated elements. The only exception to this rule is when floating images, which, by their nature, already occupy a specific width.

Imagine, however, that we'd like the sidebar div to display *before* the content div. We don't need to adjust the order of our markup; all we need to do is change our floats as follows:

```
#content
{
width: 510px;
padding: 10px 20px;
background-color: #999999;
float: right;
}

#sidebar
{
width: 200px;
padding: 10px 20px;
background-color: #666666;
float: left;
}
```

The result of changing the float value on the content and sidebar divs is shown in Figure 11-12.

11

291

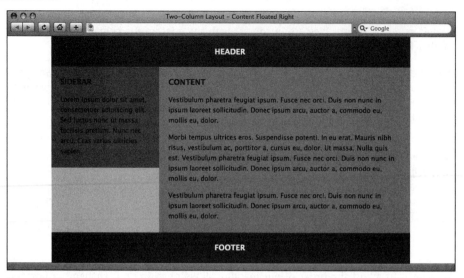

Figure 11-12. Changing the content and sidebar float values changes the order the divs display in within the browser.

Simply changing the values of the floats changes the visual display within the browser. This is a useful point to note as it allows us to create our markup in the most logical (and useful) order and then control the order of its display using CSS.

Another thing to note in our examples is the height of the sidebar div. We haven't specified a height for the sidebar div, and as you can see in Figure 11-12, the sidebar is only as tall as it needs to be to accommodate the content within it. This is the natural behavior of block-level elements: unless a height is specified, a block-level element will only ever occupy as much height as it needs.

As a consequence of this, the background-color of our container div, inside which our four other divs are nested, shows through below the sidebar div. We'll cover a workaround for this later in this chapter when we introduce the concept of **Faux Columns**, a term coined by noted Standardista Dan Cederholm while writing for *A List Apart* in 2004.

One final point to note: by default, elements following other floated elements will try to wrap around them, much like a paragraph of text wrapping around an image in a newspaper article. As we want our footer (which has no width set on it) to display *below* both the content and sidebar divs, we apply a clear: both; CSS declaration to the footer rule. This moves the footer div below all of the preceding floated elements on our page.

It's worth noting that floats can be applied to other elements, not just divs like our content and sidebar. Later in the chapter, in the section "Applying a float to an image," we'll take a look at this in action and see how we can use floats to control the display of images on our web pages. But first, a little mathematics . . .

Calculating the width of your elements

As we move on to two-column layouts, one thing worth noting is the importance of calculating the total width our elements occupy when floated side by side to ensure that they fit within their containing boxes. This once again brings us to the box model.

We touched on the box model—how we calculate the width of boxes in CSS—in Chapter 10, but it's worth a short refresher here in the context of our new two-column layout. Now that we're dealing with our content and sidebar divs sitting side by side nested in a container div, a recap of the box model is well worth including.

A short box model recap

Let's revisit the box model briefly; it has a bearing on two-column layouts (and more advanced multicolumn layouts) so we want to ensure you fully understand how nested divs relate to the divs they may be nested within.

As illustrated in Figure 11-13, the total width a box occupies in CSS is calculated by adding the declared width of the element and adding any margins, borders, and padding.

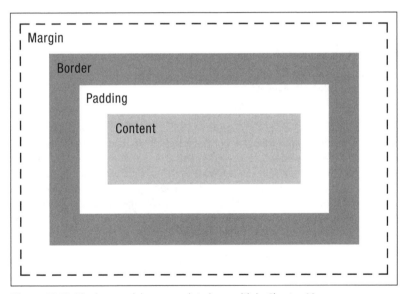

Figure 11-13. The box model we acquainted you with in Chapter 10

Calculating the total width boxes occupy is the point at which beginners often stumble. They give a div a width, and assume that this is the *total width* the div occupies, forgetting to add any margins, borders, and padding.

Let's apply the box model theory we introduced in Chapter 10 to our two-column layout. Cue a little mathematics.

We'd like our content and sidebar divs to sit side by side within the container div. To do this we need to allow enough room in our container div to accommodate these divs. Let's take a look at the figures. First let's look at the container, content, and sidebar rules in our CSS, in particular the relevant measurements. These are as follows:

```
#container
{
width: 790px;
background-color: #CCCCCC;
margin: 0 auto;
}

...

#content
{
width: 510px;
padding: 10px 20px;
background-color: #999999;
float: left;
}

#sidebar
{
width: 200px;
padding: 10px 20px;
background-color: #666666;
float: right;
}
```

Our container div is 790px wide. Our content and sidebar divs (with any added margins, borders, and padding) need to fit within this div, so we need to ensure their combined width is less than 790px. Our content div is 510px wide with 20px of padding on the left and right (remember our CSS shorthand—padding: 10px 20px;—establishes a padding-top and padding-bottom of 10px, and a padding-right and padding-left of 20px). Our sidebar div is 200px wide with 20px of padding on the left and right. Figure 11-14 shows how these measurements add up.

Let's take a look at the measurements. The value of our container width is 790px. Our content and sidebar divs have no margins or borders; this has the added benefit of making our calculations a little bit easier. We need the content and sidebar divs to fit inside the container div.

The total width the content div occupies is as follows:

padding-left + element width + padding-right or 20px + 510px + 20px = 550px

The total width the sidebar div occupies is as follows:

padding-left + element width + padding-right or 20px + 200px + 20px = 240px

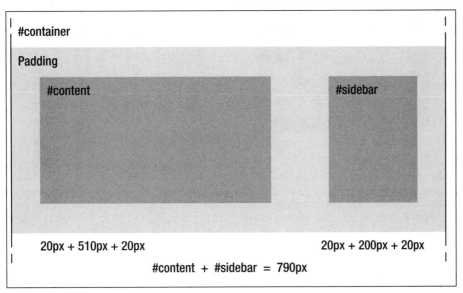

Figure 11-14. Calculating the actual widths of our content and sidebar divs, including any applied margins, borders, and padding, gives us the total width of 790px that we need to allocate for our container div.

This gives us a combined width for our content and sidebar of 790px, so the value of our container width is perfect. In the following section we'll show you what happens if the divs we're nesting occupy more space than the element that contains them, demonstrating the importance of getting your calculations right before you begin building your layouts.

What happens when your elements are too wide?

What happens when the div elements we're nesting occupy more space than the divs they're nested within? Let's take a look.

We've created two pages; both have a container div with a width of 790px. On the left we've repeated Figure 11-11 where the combined width of our content and sidebar divs fits neatly within the container div they're nested within. On the right, however, we've increased the width of our sidebar from 200px to 240px, increasing the combined width of the content and sidebar divs to 830px, too large for our 790px container div.

The result is that the sidebar div drops beneath the content div and is floated to the left as specified in the rule that is controlling it. You can see the two results in Figure 11-15.

11

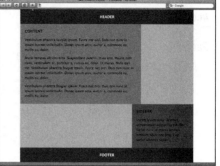

Figure 11-15. On the left our content and sidebar divs fit within our container div. On the right the combined width is too large to fit side by side, forcing the sidebar to display below the content div.

Let's take a look at the CSS behind the example on the right, simplified for brevity:

```
#container
{
width: 790px;
}

...

#content
{
width: 510px;
padding: 10px 20px;
float: left;
}

#sidebar
{
width: 240px;
padding: 10px 20px;
float: right;
}
```

Again, we need the content and sidebar divs to fit inside the container div. Let's take a look at the figures. The total width the content div occupies is as follows:

padding-left + element width + padding-right or 20px + 510px + 20px = 550px

The total width the sidebar div occupies is as follows:

padding-left + element width + padding-right or 20px + 240px + 20px = 280px

This gives us a combined width for our content and sidebar of 830px, so the value of our container width—specified as 790px—is too small.

The result is that the sidebar, which we'd like to float to the right of our content, floats to the right, but *beneath* the content. When a floated box is taken out of the normal flow of the document, it will move as far to the left or right as possible, remaining in the same position horizontally. However, if there isn't enough space to accommodate the floated box, it will move downward line by line until there is room for it—in this case, sitting beneath the content div.

You can take a look at the source code for both of the preceding web pages at the Web Standardistas web site:

> www.webstandardistas.com/11/container_perfect.html
> www.webstandardistas.com/11/container_too_small.html

Throughout the last section we looked at the importance of calculating widths when creating layouts. In the next section we'll look at the measurement of heights, in particular introducing you to the topic of collapsing margins.

Collapsing margins

One aspect of CSS-based layouts that can prove a little confusing for the beginner is the concept of **collapsing margins**. To explain what collapsing margins are and how they work, let's revisit the example we created in Chapter 10 to show how margins, borders, and padding work when applied to elements.

You might recall that the example we created in Chapter 10 demonstrated the effect of applying margins, borders, and padding to a single paragraph. We'll expand upon that example now and use two paragraphs to see how they interrelate, looking in particular at how the vertical margins between them interrelate.

To start with we've created a very short web page with two short paragraphs. We've written the following two CSS rules:

```
body
{
font-family: 'Lucida Grande', 'Lucida Sans', Arial, sans-serif;
font-size: 14px;
color: #000000;
background-color: #FFFFFF;
margin: 0;
}


p
{
width: 400px;
line-height: 1.5;
background-color: #CCCCCC;
margin: 20px;
}
```

11

Our two paragraphs styled with these simple rules are displayed in Figure 11-16.

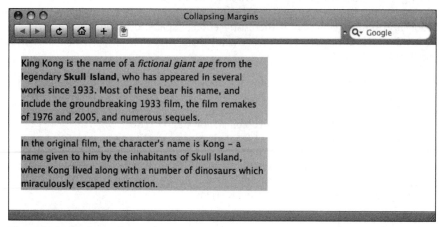

Figure 11-16. Note the distance between the top edge of the browser and the first paragraph (20px). You might be forgiven for wondering why the margin between the two pararaphs is 20px and not 40px.

In the rules we established earlier, we set a `margin: 20px;` on our p elements. As we know from Chapter 10, this CSS shorthand sets a margin on *all four sides* of our p elements of 20px. However, as you can see from Figure 11-16, the distance between the top left edge of the browser and the first paragraph appears to be 20px, yet the distance between the two paragraphs appears to be the same, also 20px.

Surely, if we've set a margin on *all four sides* of our paragraphs of 20px the distance between the two paragraphs should be 40px? (20px `margin-bottom` on the first paragraph plus 20px `margin-top` on the second paragraph equals 40px.) Why is the space between the two paragraphs only 20px?

The answer to this conundrum is that we are witnessing collapsing margins in action. Put simply, when the top and bottom margin of two elements within the normal document flow touch vertically, the smaller of these margins collapses to zero, leaving only the larger of the two margins separating the elements.

But why do collapsing margins collapse in the first place?

The reason this feature was implemented is that on most occasions, collapsing margins make perfect sense from a design perspective, making your style sheets easier to write, saving you from having to carefully calculate the top and bottom margin on each of the elements of your page in relation to each other to achieve consistent margins between the different elements in your layout.

Let's expand on our preceding example to illustrate why collapsing margins can be helpful when creating layouts. We've created two web pages in which we've added some additional elements to our previous example, adding an h1 element to both and including a couple of additional paragraphs. We've set a `margin: 20px;` on both the h1 and the p elements.

In Figure 11-17, the example on the left shows how collapsing margins should work, resulting in even spacing between our elements. In the example on the right we've added an additional class to override the collapsing margins and demonstrate how the same web page would look if the margins didn't collapse. The doubled-up margins between the elements result in too much vertical space separating the elements.

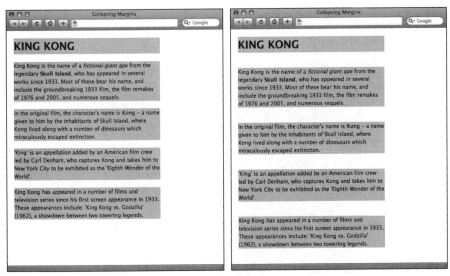

Figure 11-17. The example on the left shows how collapsing margins work normally, improving the visual consistency of the design. The example on the right shows how the page would look if the margins didn't collapse.

Collapsing margins can be a difficult topic to grasp at first, but hopefully these examples will give you some basic understanding of the principles. We recommend the chapter "Visual Formatting Model Recap" in *CSS Mastery: Advanced Web Standards Solutions* by Andy Budd (friends of ED, 2006) for anyone wishing to earn a black belt in advanced CSS visual formatting models.

11

Applying a float to an image

In the section "Creating our two-column CSS layout" earlier in this chapter, we promised we'd show you how to apply floats to elements other than div elements. In this section we'll look at applying floats to images.

In the earlier examples in this chapter, we floated our content and sidebar divs. In this example, we've created a simple page layout where we've added an image to our content div; we'll use a float to control the relationship of the image to the remainder of the content within the content div. Before we look at how this image displays in the browser, let's take a look at the markup we're using. Our simplified markup is as follows:

```
<div id="content">
  <h1>Content</h1>
  <img src="tall_squirrel_monkey.jpg" width="150" height="350"
  alt="Gordo prepares to meet Miss Baker." />
  <!-- This is where the remaining paragraphs are situated. -->
</div><!-- Closes the content div -->
```

By default the image is positioned within the normal document flow as shown in Figure 11-18.

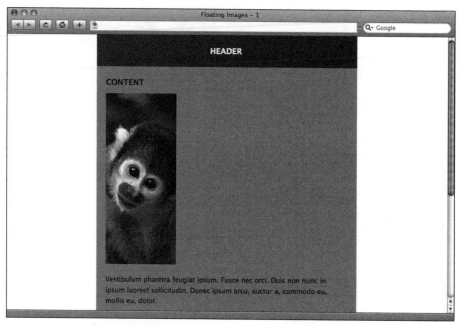

Figure 11-18. With no floats our image is placed within the normal flow of the document.

By default the image is positioned within the normal document flow with our paragraphs appearing immediately after it. However, what if we'd like to wrap our text around the image? Good news—we can do this by applying a float to our image.

In Chapter 10 we introduced a class of portrait for our primates' different portraits; in this example we have a tall, tightly cropped image. We'll create a class for any tall primate images like this one, by adding the following CSS rule:

```
.tallprimate
{
float: left;
padding: 10px 10px 10px 0;
}
```

We then add the class to our markup as follows:

```
<img src="cropped_squirrel_monkey.jpg" width="150" height="350"
alt="Gordo prepares to meet Miss Baker." class="tallprimate" />
```

What this rule does is target any images on our web page with a class of tallprimate and float them to the left. As you can also see, we've added 10px of padding (to the top, right, and bottom) of our tallprimate class to create some space between the image and the paragraph text that will now flow around it.

You can see the results of adding these rules in Figure 11-19.

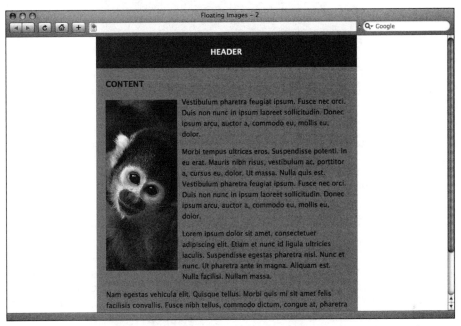

Figure 11-19. Applying a float: left; results in our image being removed from the normal document flow and the text wrapping around it.

Perfect, the paragraph text is now wrapping around the image just as we'd like. However, what happens if the floated element, in this case our image, is taller than its containing element? In other words, what would happen if we would remove half of our paragraphs? Let's take a look.

We remove all but two of our paragraphs from our content div. The result of this is shown in Figure 11-20.

11

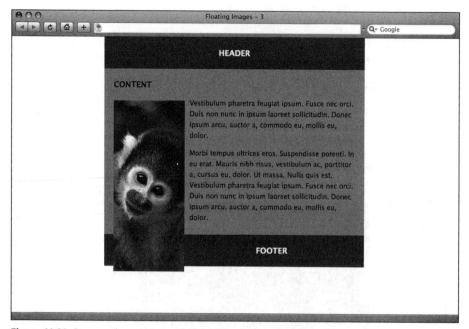

Figure 11-20. By removing our img with the tallprimate class from the normal document flow, it is not counted when the height of the containing element is calculated, which is now only tall enough for the two paragraphs.

Needless to say, this isn't so great. Why is the image breaking out of the layout?

The first thing to note is that our image is placed inside our content div. The height of the content div is determined by the height of the content inside it (unless we have specified a height for the element in the CSS). Since we've floated the image by specifying float: left in our CSS, this image is taken out of the normal document flow and as a result is not taken into account when the browser calculates the height of the content div. Instead, the height of the content div is determined by the two paragraphs of text, which have no floats applied.

The end result is that our floated image element now breaks out of our content div and into the footer. This is clearly not what we want, so we need to add a few additional declarations to our CSS to solve the problem.

Earlier in the chapter we introduced you to the clear property, which we can use to clear floats. By adding a clear declaration to the footer div, we're taking care of our footer problem. We add the following declaration to our footer rule:

```
#footer
{
...
clear: both;
}
```

Adding this rule results in the changes shown in Figure 11-21.

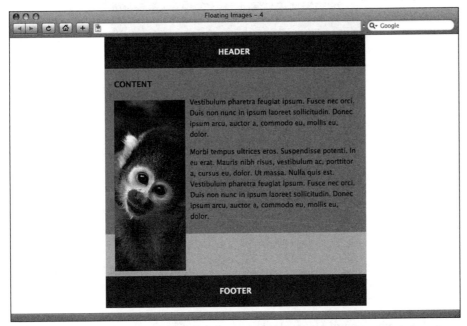

Figure 11-21. Adding a clear: both; declaration drops the footer beneath the content above it.

Applying a clear: both; declaration to an element moves it below all preceding floated elements. This results in our image no longer breaking into the footer div; however, our image is still breaking out of its containing element, the content div. We'll resolve that issue next . . .

The clear: both; declaration that we applied to the footer won't help us here as the clear property moves an element to a position *below* the preceding floated elements, and our image is placed not *above* but *inside* the content div.

This looks like a sticky situation, and over the years many solutions involving advanced CSS trickery and extra XHTML markup have been devised to crack this particular nut. There is, however, one easy way of solving this problem. Applying one simple CSS declaration to the containing element (in this case our content div) will ensure that the floated element no longer breaks out of its container. We add the following declaration to our content rule:

```
#content
{
...
overflow: auto;
}
```

Figure 11-22 shows how our page looks after applying this declaration to our content div.

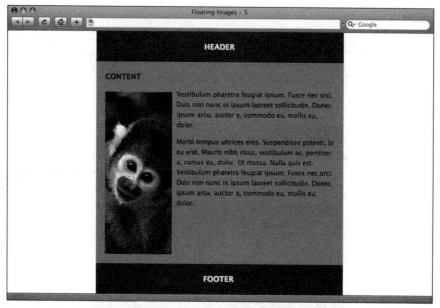

Figure 11-22. Applying overflow: auto to the content div ensures our floated image no longer breaks out of it—perfect.

That's it, a combination of float: left; to float our image to the left, clear: both; to clear the footer, and overflow: auto; to ensure our content div allows for the image being larger than the paragraph text in the content div solves the problem.

> *The CSS* overflow *property determines how content inside a* div *or other block-level element should be displayed if its width or height exceeds that specified for the containing element. The* overflow: auto; *declaration serves the primary purpose of instructing the browser to add scrollbars if the dimensions of the containing element are less than the declared dimensions of the content within. As a side effect, applying this declaration has the benefit of solving our issue with a floated element breaking out of its container.*

Faux Columns

One of the frustrating aspects of creating multicolumn CSS layouts is the fact that our columns only expand to fill the content that they occupy. In Figure 11-23, we've created two typical web pages, one that has a long content div and a short sidebar div, and a second that has a long sidebar div and a short content div.

Ideally we'd like the backgrounds of the shorter columns to extend down so that they occupy the same vertical space as the longer columns. As things stand the divs only occupy as much space as the content within them. There is, however, a deceptively simple solution to the problem using a technique known as Faux Columns (a term originally coined by bon vivant Dan Cederholm in a 2004 article for *A List Apart*).

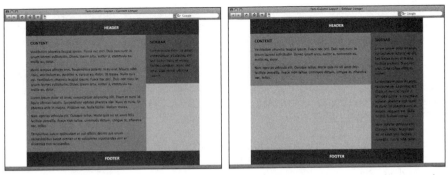

Figure 11-23. The backgrounds on the shorter columns only occupy as much vertical space as the respective columns' contents.

By defining a background-image for our container div that we tile vertically behind the two columns, we can create the illusion that both columns are the same height. This is best demonstrated with an example.

With no background-image defined on our container div, our page displays as shown in Figure 11-24.

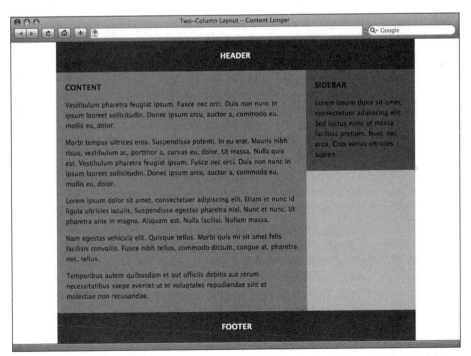

Figure 11-24. Our layout with no background-image applied to the container div. The result is that the columns are of unequal height.

The first thing we need to do is to create a background-image that is 790px wide (the width of our container div) and that visually indicates the two columns. We've created a 790px × 10px image as shown in Figure 11-25.

Figure 11-25. Our background-image, which we'll tile vertically within the container div, gives the illusion of two columns.

We adjust our container, content, and sidebar divs as follows, adding the background-image to the container and removing the background-color on both the content and sidebar divs:

```
#container
{
width: 790px;
background-color: #CCCCCC;
margin: 0 auto;
background-image: url(container_bg.png);
background-repeat: repeat-y;
}

...

#content
{
width: 510px;
padding: 10px 20px;
float: left;
}

#sidebar
{
width: 200px;
padding: 10px 20px;
float: right;
}
```

The result of amending our container, content, and sidebar rules is shown in Figure 11-26.

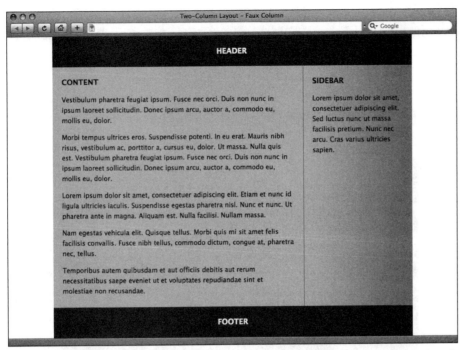

Figure 11-26. Our background-image tiles vertically within the container div, giving the illusion of two columns of equal height.

That's it. Simply adding a background-image to the container div and tiling it vertically using the background-repeat property gives the impression of two columns of equal height.

Wrapping up with King Kong

By tying together the different elements we've covered in this chapter, we can create a two-column CSS layout for our King Kong page, using floats to control the layout of the content and sidebar divs. In Figure 11-27, we've combined the two-column CSS layout walkthrough with our Faux Columns walkthrough to create a two-column version of our of King Kong web page. By applying a background-image to the container div that features a subtle gradient effect, we've distinguished both the content and sidebar divs, visually differentiating them. All of this is built on a solid foundation of well-structured and well-formed markup.

11

Figure 11-27. By drawing together the different topics covered in this chapter our King Kong page is really beginning to take shape.

Our King Kong page is now really coming together and, as you'll see in the next chapter, we'll repurpose our sidebar div to act as the perfect location for our Famous Primates web site's navigation, adding the web site's one missing ingredient.

Summary

So what have we covered? In this chapter we introduced you to two-column CSS layouts, demonstrating how we can use the float property to remove elements from the ordinary flow of our document. We used a float-based approach as the basis for creating a two-column CSS layout.

We also refreshed your memory of the box model, particularly looking at its importance when working out widths when nesting div elements. Building on our walkthough from Chapter 10 on adding margins, borders, and padding, we introduced the topic of collapsing margins, demonstrating how they can make the layout process a little easier.

Finally, we covered the topic of Faux Columns, showcasing how we could creatively use a background-image to visually distinguish our content and sidebar divs.

In the next chapter we'll build on this layout by replacing the h2 and p elements in our sidebar with a navigation list styled using CSS. This will form the backbone of our Famous Primates web site's navigation. Good times.

Homework: Adding a second column to Gordo's web page

In this chapter our primary focus was the creation of a two-column CSS layout. Building upon the one-column CSS layout we created in Chapter 10, we introduced you to floats, explaining how they can be used to remove elements from the normal document flow. Once we'd demonstrated how floats worked, we showed you how to create a two-column float-based layout and used Faux Columns to create the illusion that your content and sidebar divs were of equal height.

This chapter's homework is to add a second column to your Gordo web page and include some content we've provided you to temporarily occupy the sidebar until we repurpose it in Chapter 12. Once you've added your second column, we'd like you to add Faux Columns to your container div to tie together the content and sidebar divs of your Gordo page.

1. Add a sidebar div

The first change we'd like you to make to your Gordo page is to add a sidebar div to your XHTML markup. Add this after your content div and before the footer div as demonstrated in our King Kong example in the chapter.

As with the previous chapters we've created everything you need to complete the homework, including providing some ready-made content for your brand-new sidebar div so you can focus on creating the two-column layout. You can download the assets here:

www.webstandardistas.com/11/assets.zip

11

Once you've downloaded the preceding files, transfer the Faux Column image we've supplied to your images folder, you'll be using it shortly. Add the content we've provided to your new sidebar div; we'll leave it as an exercise for you to add the links to the Albert I and Miss Baker pages where appropriate.

2. Add a sidebar rule to your style sheet

Now that you've created a sidebar div for your Gordo page, you'll need to add a rule to apply some style to it in your style sheet. We'll fill the rule with some declarations shortly. First we'll need to pause for a little mathematics.

3. Measure up the divs

In the last chapter, when we were creating our one-column layout, we only needed to set a width on our container div; the other divs nested within the container expanded to fill the available space within it. In this chapter, however, we'll need to consider the relative widths of the container div to the content and sidebar divs.

As you'll have noticed from our example in this chapter, you'll need to widen your container div and set a width on both the content and sidebar divs, ensuring that the container div is wide enough to accommodate your two columns. We could ask you to take a look at the figures from our example earlier in the chapter, but we'll save you some time and provide them for you.

The first thing you'll need to do is widen the container; remembering it needs to fit the content and sidebar divs, increase its width to 790px. You'll now need to add a width to your content and sidebar rules. Add a width: 510px; declaration to the content div and a width: 200px; declaration to the sidebar div.

4. Add the floats

In our example we floated our content div to the left and our sidebar div to the right. Add float declarations to both your content and sidebar rules and float them to the left and right, respectively.

You might also like to try floating the content to the right and the sidebar to the left and refreshing the page. This should help underline that the order of your markup can be changed visually with your CSS.

5. Add padding to your sidebar

Once you've floated your content and sidebar divs, we'd like you to add a declaration to your sidebar rule to adjust its padding. Pay particular attention to the padding at the top of the sidebar to ensure the h2 in the sidebar lines up with the h2 in the content div. You might like to refer to our example as you do this. You'll also notice from our example that we've added 20px of padding to the left and right of our sidebar; this is to ensure everything adds up to fill the new 790px-wide container div.

6. Add the Faux Columns

As with the previous chapters we've provided an image for you to use to create your Faux Columns. Following along with our example in the chapter, set the image provided as a background-image on your container div and use a background-repeat: repeat-y; declaration to repeat the image vertically within the container div. This will act as a background image to create the illusion that your content and sidebar divs are occupying the same vertical height.

As usual, to help you with the different stages of this chapter's homework, we've created our own, two-column CSS layout for King Kong featuring our newly added sidebar div and Faux Columns background-image. You can refer to this, using your browser's View Source menu command to see how we've updated our CSS, here:

www.webstandardistas.com/11/king_kong.html

Once you've created your two-column CSS layout for your Gordo web page and added the Faux Columns background-image we provided, put the kettle on and enjoy a cup of *Java Malabar* as you prepare yourself for the next chapter.

11

CHAPTER 12
LIST-O-MATIC

- ★ Famous Primates
- ★ Pioneers
- ★ Thespians
- ★ Links
- ★ Contact Us

- ★ FAMOUS PRIMATES
- ★ PIONEERS
- ★ THESPIANS
- ★ LINKS
- ★ CONTACT US

SITE MAP

- Famous Primates
- Thespians
  - King Kong
    - King Kong (2005)
    - King Kong (1976)
    - King Kong (1933)
  - Cheeta
    - Tarzan, The Ape
    - Tarzan Escapes (1
  - Cornelius

As you might have guessed by the title, this chapter is all about lists. Why focus on lists? Simple. As designers have moved toward adopting web standards they've learned to embrace the humble list, turning lists from unstyled but semantically rich XHTML lists, styled with the browser's default style sheet, to well-styled lists that use CSS for design and presentation.

One area where XHTML and CSS lists come into their own is for the creation of web site navigation, and one of the primary focuses of this chapter will be on marking up and styling a list to create the Famous Primates web site's navigation.

Before we get started though, credit where credit's due. The title for this chapter is an homage to Max Design's excellent Listamatic:

```
http://css.maxdesign.com.au/listamatic/
```

Listamatic is an invaluable resource that's well worth a visit. Designed to showcase what's possible with CSS, Listamatic shows the power and flexibility of CSS when applied to a single, simple, well-structured list. By styling an identical XHTML list in a variety of ways, Listamatic demonstrates how CSS can be used to completely change the look and feel of lists, just by changing the CSS.

Once you've read this chapter, we strongly recommend you visit Listamatic to get a feel for what's possible when styling lists with CSS. You'll find a variety of inspirational approaches there that you might also like to experiment with.

In the last chapter we introduced a second column to our King Kong page's layout, creating a sidebar div. At that point our primary concern was to introduce basic layout principles. As a consequence the content of our sidebar div was a humble affair, a simple paragraph sitting under a lone h2; it served its purpose linking from our King Kong page to our Cheeta and Cornelius pages.

This was fine for the purposes of Chapter 11, but if you've been diligent and worked along with the homework, you'll be aware that our Famous Primates web site is a little more substantial than this . . .

We have a number of sections. Each section has its own "launch pad" page, providing the reader with some useful ape and monkey facts—our primates are thespians and pioneers after all. Each of these pages links to a number of additional primate-specific pages: homes for King Kong, Cheeta, Cornelius, Gordo, Miss Baker, and Albert. Finally, we have our Links and Contact Us pages.

In short, we have a great deal more content to link to. That content has an implicit structure and, as you'll see at the end of this chapter, we can use nested lists to give that content some additional semantic meaning, creating a well-styled site map for the Famous Primates web site.

In this chapter we'll replace the sidebar content we introduced in Chapter 11 with a list that we'll use to link to the different sections of the Famous Primates web site. This list will act as the navigation for our finished web site.

We'll use the background-image property, which we introduced in Chapter 10, to replace the browser's default bullets with our own custom star images, fitting for our ape thespians and monkey pioneers, creating a visually engaging home for our web site's navigation. Lastly, as we promised in Chapter 4, we'll take a look at styling ordered lists.

So, now that you know what we're covering, let's get started.

Styling lists

A long time ago in a galaxy far, far away . . . (in Chapter 4) we introduced you to the humble list. By now you're familiar with lists—both unordered and ordered—as we've included examples of both on the King Kong and Gordo web pages. This chapter is where we begin to style these lists using CSS.

As before, we'll use a step-by-step approach. We'll start by adding an unordered list to our sidebar, listing the main sections of the Famous Primates web site. In the first pass we'll style this list using CSS, showing you how to turn a humble but well-structured XHTML list into a well-designed and well-styled CSS list, add custom bullets to the list, and replace our browser's default bullets.

Once we've walked you through adding custom bullets, we'll add some links into the mix; these will form the backbone of our web site's navigation and will give us an opportunity to further style our list. Let's get started.

Styling a simple list

The first step in the process is to amend our sidebar content, replacing the content we added in Chapter 11 with an unordered list, listing the key sections of our Famous Primates web site. We replace the h2 and p elements in our sidebar with an unordered list as follows:

```
<div id="sidebar">
  <ul>
    <li>Famous Primates</li>
    <li>Pioneers</li>
    <li>Thespians</li>
    <li>Links</li>
    <li>Contact Us</li>
  </ul>
</div>
```

12

Without any additional CSS, this list renders in the browser as in Figure 12-1. This list will form the basis of our Famous Primates web site's navigation.

Figure 12-1.
Our unordered list as it appears in our sidebar with no additional CSS added

Although this list could benefit from some additional styling, we now have an unordered list in the sidebar that we can use as the basis for creating the navigation for our Famous Primates web site.

One thing you'll notice is that, as it stands, our list items could do with some additional line-height. You might recall we added some line-height to the p elements of our King Kong page in Chapter 9. Although this took care of the line-height on our p elements, the browser's default style sheet is applying a different line-height for our ul elements. We override this by adding the following rule to our style sheet, which targets all the unordered lists on our King Kong page:

```
ul
{
line-height: 1.8;
}
```

The result of adding this rule is shown in Figure 12-2.

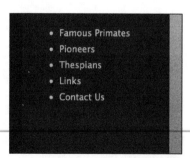

Figure 12-2.
Adding some line-height to all ul elements on the page inserts a little more vertical space between our unordered list items, giving them a little more breathing room.

A welcome by-product of this additional rule is that it takes care of *all* unordered lists on the page, including the two unordered lists beneath each of our King Kong films (listing the respective directors and release dates).

By simply adding this one rule, we've added some line-height to *all* the unordered lists on the King Kong page. You can see the result of this rule on one of these unordered lists in Figure 12-3.

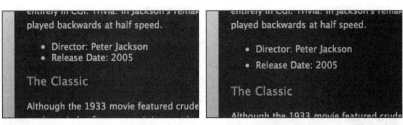

Figure 12-3. On the left our `ul` elements as they stood at the end of Chapter 11, a little tight. On the right, as they now stand, a little more `line-height` added makes a big difference.

The benefit of applying the `line-height` to the `ul` element on our King Kong page is that it uses inheritance to take care of *all* of the unordered lists on the page. This allows us to take care of all of the unordered lists in one pass and later apply more specific rules to those lists we'd like to style differently.

In the last pass we specified a `line-height` for *all* the `ul` elements on our King Kong page. As we move forward, however, we'd like to target the changes we're making to the unordered list in our sidebar only. In order to do this, we need to identify this specific list, singling it out for the changes we're about to make.

In Chapter 10 we introduced you to `id` and `class` attributes and covered how we could use these to target specific elements of our web pages. We'll now add an `id` to our `sidebar` `ul`; this will allow us to write additional rules that target *just this list*.

We add an id to our markup as follows:

```
<ul id="nav">
  <li>Famous Primates</li>
  <li>Pioneers</li>
  <li>Thespians</li>
  <li>Links</li>
  <li>Contact Us</li>
</ul>
```

Now that we've identified this specific list, we can write rules targeted *at this list only*, enabling us to specify properties for this list alone.

Before we move on to adding our own custom bullets to our `sidebar` list, it's worth noting that we can also use CSS to style the bullets of our unordered lists using any of a variety of generic browser styles, including `none`, `disc`, `circle`, and `square`. We do this by simply adding a rule to our style sheet targeting the `list-style` property as follows:

```
#nav
{
list-style: circle;
}
```

Adding this rule replaces our default, unstyled list items' bullets (styled with the `disc` value) with the `circle` value, as you can see in Figure 12-4.

Figure 12-4.
By adding a rule targeting the ul with the id of nav, we can change the default list-style to circle instead of the browser's default disc.

This is a good start; however, we can go further than this by defining a background-image in CSS to specify custom bullets that relate to our site's theme a little more closely. In order to do this, we first need to switch off the browser's default bullets.

We do this by amending our previous declaration as follows:

```
#nav
{
list-style: none;
}
```

The result of changing this rule is shown in Figure 12-5.

Figure 12-5.
By changing our declaration to list-style: none; we can switch off the bullets of the browser's default style sheet. This is the first stage in replacing these generic bullets with our own.

Although we've switched off the default bullets of the browser's default style sheet, the default indentation for list items remains. This is due to the fact that, by default, unordered lists have a certain amount of padding or margin (depending on which browser you're using) to accommodate the bullets. Before we apply our own bullet using a background-image, we'll switch off the default padding and margin by adding the following declaration:

```
#nav
{
list-style: none;
padding: 0;
margin: 0;
}
```

The results of removing the browser's default padding and margin can be seen in Figure 12-6.

Figure 12-6.
Removing the browser's default padding and margin turns off our list items' indentation.

Now that we've removed the default bullets and removed the indentation, it's time to add our own custom bullets using a background-image specified in our style sheet. We could do this using the list-style-image property in CSS; however, this produces inconsistent results with our bullets' vertical positioning. A better approach is to use a background-image on each li element.

We add the following rule, which targets only the list items in the ul with the id of nav; note how we're using an id to differentiate the ul in our sidebar from the other ul elements on the page:

```
#nav li
{
background-image: url(../images/star.png);
background-repeat: no-repeat;
background-position: 5px center;
padding: 7px 0 7px 20px;
}
```

Adding this rule results in the changes shown in Figure 12-7.

Figure 12-7.
By using the background-image property to add a new, custom bullet made from a star image, we can create a list that's more in keeping with our Famous Primates web site.

What we've done with the last rule first of all is to specify a background-image for all of our sidebar list items, targeted at the ul with the id of nav. We've set the background-image to be a PNG we've created called star.png, which is located in our images folder. We've then set the background-repeat property to no-repeat, instructing the browser not

12

319

to tile the background-image. We covered both of these properties in Chapter 10 when we introduced background images; however, in this example we've introduced a new background-related property, background-position, which we'll introduce properly now.

The background-position property allows us to position background images in relation to the elements we apply them to. When no background-position is specified, the browser will default to background-position: 0 0;, which sets the background-image to the top left edge of the element (the first value specifies the position from the left, and the second value specifies the position from the top).

In this case we've used a background-position of 5px center to position our star.png custom bullet 5 pixels from the left of each li element and to center the image vertically in relation to each list item.

Lastly, we've set some padding on each list item to allow our 9 × 9 pixel star.png image to show through completely, giving it 7 pixels of space at the top and bottom and 20 pixels of space on the left-hand side. Without this padding on the left, our list item text would sit on top of the background-image. The amount of padding you add to the left-hand side of the li will depend on the size of your custom bullets.

The final stage in the process is to apply a little typographic style to the text of our list items, a small but important touch. We add the following declarations to our #nav li rule:

```
#nav li
{
...
text-transform: uppercase;
letter-spacing: 0.1em;
}
```

Figure 12-8 shows the results of adding these two declarations.

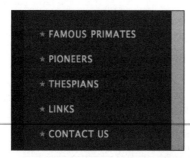

Figure 12-8.
To differentiate our unordered list in the sidebar from the other unordered lists of the page, we use the text-transform property to transform our sidebar list into uppercase and we add a little letter-spacing.

This transforms the list items in the sidebar into uppercase and adds a little letter-spacing, both properties covered in Chapter 9 when we covered styling text.

That's it. Although we've not added any links yet, the preceding walkthrough covers everything you need to know to transform your well-structured XHTML lists into well-styled lists using CSS. By experimenting with the bullets you apply using the background-image property, you can achieve a variety of striking effects while still creating well-structured lists that will display perfectly when CSS is switched off (as it might be in a nonbrowser context).

All we need to do now is to add some links to the unordered list in our sidebar, and we're on our way to creating some much-needed navigation for our Famous Primates web site.

Styling a navigation list

In the last section we used CSS's background-image property to create custom bullets for the list items in our sidebar, switching off the browser's default bullets in favor of an image that we defined using CSS. The one thing the last list was missing, however, was links.

In this section we'll add links to the unordered list in our sidebar. Before we do that, however, let's regroup and refresh where we are, as we'll be building on our existing XHTML markup and CSS as we move forward. Our sidebar list is currently styled with the following rules:

```
ul
{
line-height: 1.8;
}

#nav
{
list-style: none;
padding: 0;
margin: 0;
}

#nav li
{
background-image: url(../images/star.png);
background-repeat: no-repeat;
background-position: 5px center;
padding: 7px 0 7px 20px;
text-transform: uppercase;
letter-spacing: 0.1em;
}
```

12

We showed you the result of these rules in Figure 12-8; we're repeating the screenshot here in Figure 12-9 as this is the starting point from which we'll build as we move forward, adding links into the mix.

Figure 12-9.
Our unordered list as it stood at the end of the last section. This will form the foundation on which we build moving forward.

Before we add links to our unordered list, we'll put in place a little advance groundwork, adding some borders above and below our different list items; this will help to further differentiate the Famous Primates web site's different sections. We add the following declarations to the rules shown previously:

```
#nav
{
list-style: none;
padding: 0;
margin: 0;
border-top: 1px solid #39322D;
}

#nav li
{
background-image: url(../images/star.png);
background-repeat: no-repeat;
background-position: 5px center;
padding: 7px 0 7px 20px;
text-transform: uppercase;
letter-spacing: 0.1em;
border-bottom: 1px solid #39322D;
}
```

Adding these two border declarations results in the changes shown in Figure 12-10.

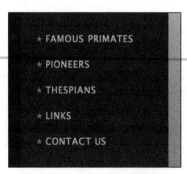

Figure 12-10.
By adding a border to the top of the unordered list in our sidebar and to the bottom of each of our list items, we can help to draw out the structure of the navigation list.

The two previous rules have added a border (1px solid #39322D;) to the top of our unordered list in the sidebar, targeted at this list's unique id of nav; it's also added a border with the same specifications to the bottom of every li element in this particular list. This helps to distinguish the different navigation sections of the Famous Primates web site.

We'll now complete the process of building the navigation list by adding links to our sidebar list. We add the following relative links to our sidebar's list items:

```
<ul id="nav">
  <li><a href="../index.html">Famous Primates</a></li>
  <li><a href="../pioneers/index.html">Pioneers</a></li>
  <li><a href="index.html">Thespians</a></li>
  <li><a href="../links.html">Links</a></li>
  <li><a href="../contact.html">Contact Us</a></li>
</ul>
```

Figure 12-11 shows the results of adding these links to the unordered list in our sidebar.

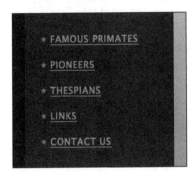

Figure 12-11.
Adding the links to the list in our sidebar gives us a navigation list for the Famous Primates web site.

Adding the links to our unordered list adds a border-bottom to the list of links (this is inherited from the rule we wrote in Chapter 9 targeting our a:link pseudo-class).

The next stage is a subtle one, but we'll reap the benefits of it in a moment. We change the selector targeting our sidebar list items (#nav li) to a selector targeting anchors located in our sidebar list items (#nav li a).

By using a descendant selector, we're targeting only a elements that are li elements in the ul with an id of nav. (You might want to read that again, but it makes perfect sense—essentially we're targeting just these links with laserlike precision.) We covered the use of descendant selectors to target specific elements based on the context in Chapter 10; essentially we're only targeting links that are list items in our sidebar list.

We do this by changing the selector for our existing rule as follows:

```
#nav li a
{
background-image: url(../images/star.png);
background-repeat: no-repeat;
background-position: 5px center;
```

12

```
padding: 7px 0 7px 20px;
text-transform: uppercase;
letter-spacing: 0.1em;
border-bottom: 1px solid #39322D;
}
```

Changing the selector results in what you see in Figure 12-12.

Figure 12-12.
In Figure 12-11 we used a selector of #nav li; we're now using a more precise selector of #nav li a.

The anchor elements that we're now targeting are inline-level and so occupy less vertical space than the block-level list items; however, we'll resolve this in a moment by setting our anchors to display: block;.

Although this change to our selector has resulted in the vertical space between the links being reduced, we'll resolve this now. Making this change allows us to more accurately target the links within our sidebar list, which will prove useful in a moment. We add the following to our rule:

```
#nav li a
{
background-image: url(../images/star.png);
background-repeat: no-repeat;
background-position: 5px center;
padding: 7px 0 7px 20px;
text-transform: uppercase;
letter-spacing: 0.1em;
border-bottom: 1px #39322D solid;
display: block;
}
```

Adding display: block;, coupled with a more precise selector targeting the anchors in the sidebar list, instructs the browser to display our sidebar links as block-level elements as shown in Figure 12-13.

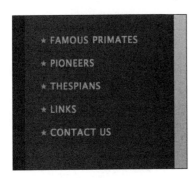

Figure 12-13.
Adding display: block; to the a elements in our sidebar list forces them to display as block-level elements, taking up the vertical space previously occupied by the block-level list items.

By setting our a elements in the sidebar to display: block;, they will display as block-level elements as opposed to inline-level elements; this forces them to occupy the entire vertical space that each block-level list item previously occupied, increasing the rollover area of our links. The result of this is shown in Figure 12-14.

Hovering over these block-level a elements now gives us a larger a:hover state, resulting in a more generous rollover area in our sidebar links.

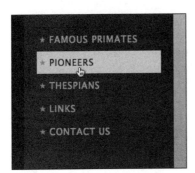

Figure 12-14.
Setting display: block; gives us a more generous rollover state.

With the changes we've made to this rule, when we hover over the links, the background-color is the same as that set on the links in our content div (#E0DFDA). We could leave this as is, but we'll add one other twist by creating an additional rule for the a:hover pseudo-class of our sidebar links.

By setting the background-color and color (the text color) on the a:hover pseudo-class of our sidebar links, we can create a more compelling hover effect. We add a new rule as follows:

```
#nav li a:hover
{
background-color: #39322D;
color: #88B4DB;
}
```

By simply changing the background-color on the a:hover state on our sidebar links, we can create the effect of our link's background-color fading into the background-color of

12

the sidebar, with the text of the links on the a:hover state set to the pale blue we've been using for our links. The result of this change is shown in Figure 12-15.

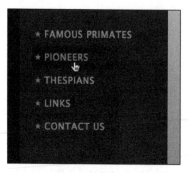

Figure 12-15.
The addition of this one extra rule gives our sidebar links an elegant fading a:hover effect.

With just a few additional rules we've created a well-styled, but equally well-structured, navigation list for our Famous Primates web site in the sidebar.

Creating horizontal lists

In the first half of this chapter, we enabled you to add custom bullets to your lists using CSS, allowing you to add to the design of your web pages. There are a number of other presentational aspects, however, that we can also control with CSS, not least taking lists—which are often imagined to be vertical—out of the normal flow of the document and, as a consequence, creating horizontal lists.

We can achieve a horizontal list in one of two ways: using either float: left—which you now know removes the list items from the normal document flow—or, alternatively, setting the list items, which are block-level elements, to display: inline, instructing the browser to display them as inline-level elements.

In this section, we'll explain how to use display: inline to change a simple unordered list of links into a "breadcrumb trail" of links, enabling the user to see at a glance where they are on the Famous Primates web site.

The first step is to create the list itself. We'll do this by adding some additional markup to our King Kong page, where each of our list items represents a level within the Famous Primates web site, allowing you to easily traverse back up through the levels of the Famous Primates web site using the links in the breadcrumb trail.

We add the following list to our King Kong web page (note the magic escalator we introduced in Chapter 6):

```
<ul id="crumbs">
  <li><a href="../index.html">Famous Primates</a></li>
  <li><a href="index.html">Apes in the Movies</a></li>
  <li>King Kong</li>
</ul>
```

We've given the ul an id of crumbs, which allows us to target this specific list with its own set of rules. Before we start adding the CSS, the list looks as shown in Figure 12-16.

Figure 12-16. Our unordered list with links to the Famous Primates home page and the Apes in the Movies section page. As we are on the King Kong page, there's no need to link to it.

This gives us a solid foundation on which to build and some markup to apply our CSS to. Let's get started with the process of turning this into our horizontal breadcrumb trail. The first stage in the process is to remove the default bullets, margins, and padding using the following rule:

```
#crumbs
{
list-style: none;
margin: 0;
padding: 0;
}
```

The result of this change—which should come as no surprise—is shown in Figure 12-17.

Figure 12-17. Removing the default bullets, margins, and padding is the first step in the process of creating our horizontal list.

The real magic resides in the following rule. Short, but to the point, it instructs the browser to display the list items in our list as inline-level elements rather than block-level elements. We add a rule styling all list items in the ul with the id of crumbs; this styles just these particular list items.

```
#crumbs li
{
display: inline;
}
```

As a result of adding this short rule, the default block-level line breaks above and below these specific li elements are removed, and the list is now horizontal instead of vertical, as shown in Figure 12-18.

12

Figure 12-18. Setting our list items to display: inline; creates a horizontal list.

We'll now begin to fine-tune our design a little, starting by removing the border-bottom we set on our links in Chapter 9. We do this by adding a descendant selector, targeting only anchors within list items in the unordered list with the id of crumbs:

```
#crumbs li a
{
border: 0;
}
```

Figure 12-19 shows the result of adding this rule.

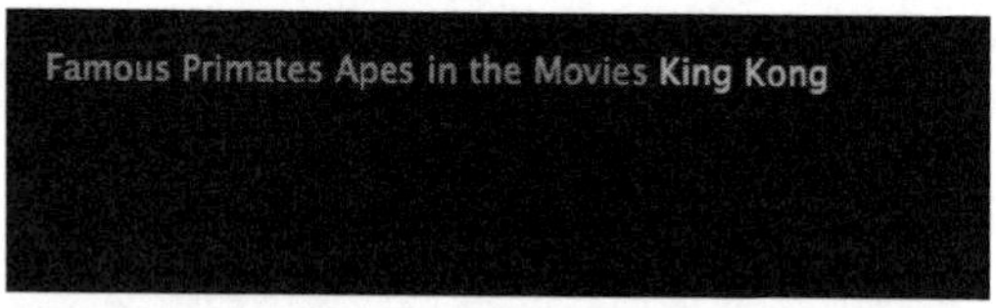

Figure 12-19. We remove the border-bottom we set on links in Chapter 9 with a rule targeting just this list.

Our breadcrumb trail is taking shape, but would benefit from some horizontal space between the list items, which, at this point, are sitting tight against each other, separated only by a blank space. We'll once again leverage the power of margins and padding, combined with a carefully chosen background-image to insert some arrows into our horizontal list to give the breadcrumb trail some style.

We add the following declarations to our #crumbs li a rule:

```
#crumbs li a
{
border: 0;
padding-right: 20px;
margin-right: 5px;
background-image: url(../images/arrow.png);
background-repeat: no-repeat;
background-position: right center;
}
```

Adding these additional declarations results in the changes you see in Figure 12-20.

Figure 12-20. Using an arrow as a background-image and adding some margins and padding draws out the structure of the breadcrumb trail.

Let's have a look at what the declarations we've added are doing. First we've added 20px of padding to the right-hand side of our a elements; this makes room for the background-image, which we position to the right of the links and center vertically using background-position: right center;. We also set the background-image to display just once, using background-repeat: no-repeat;. We use margin-right; 5px; to create 5 pixels of space to the right of the arrow image; this inserts space between the arrow and the next list item.

By using a descendant selector to target *just the anchors in this list*, our arrows are applied only to the right of the links. Note that the words King Kong don't get the arrow, as they're not acting as an anchor element. Perfect. Figure 12-21 shows the list in action.

Figure 12-21. Our breadcrumb trail allows users to retrace their steps back up the levels of the Famous Primates web site, improving usability.

That's it—targeting these three simple rules using an id allows us to differentiate this list from the others on our King Kong page, creating a useful navigation breadcrumb trail that improves our web site's usability.

Lists are not only semantically the right choice when marking up lists of items, but are also extremely versatile when it comes to styling them with CSS. The ability to change a list's direction from vertical to horizontal makes the list a versatile and useful tool in any self-respecting Web Standardista's tool box.

Styling nested lists

Although we've focused on the King Kong and Gordo web pages in our walkthroughs and homework, you should by now have an awareness of the entire Famous Primates web site's structure. In this section we'll look at using nested lists to create a site map for the Famous Primates web site.

12

Nested lists are the perfect choice for a site map, indicating a site's logical structure and different sections' and pages' relationships. Admittedly our site—with an extensive eleven pages—is a little small to merit a full site map; however, the principles we discuss here can be scaled up and applied to larger sites with more pages, making this is a topic worth covering to prepare you for your ongoing journey as a Web Standardista.

Styling a site map with a nested list

In the following example we've added some additional, fictitious content to our Famous Primates web site to give us a little more to material to work with. Our King Kong and Cheeta entries now feature further nested lists, where we've added some imaginary subsections covering various films starring these two renowned ape thespians.

For the purposes of simplicity, we've restricted ourselves to just a handful of the films these two ape thespians starred in; however, you can see a more extensive version of this site map at the book's companion web site:

www.webstandardistas.com/12/site_map.html

We're focusing on styling nested lists, particularly looking at using descendant selectors to target lists nested within other lists. With all of this nesting, things can get quite complicated, so to keep things simple, we're not adding links to our list items. With everything we've covered so far, however, you should be more than capable of combining our different examples to create nested navigation lists of some complexity.

To give us some material to work with, we create the following nested list (for a refresher on nested lists you might like to refer back to Chapter 4):

```
<ul>
  <li>Famous Primates</li>
  <li>Thespians
    <ul>
      <li>King Kong
        <ul>
          <li>King Kong (2005)</li>
          <li>King Kong (1976)</li>
          <li>King Kong (1933)</li>
        </ul>
      </li>
      <li>Cheeta
        <ul>
          <li>Tarzan, The Ape Man (1932)</li>
          <li>Tarzan Escapes (1936)</li>
        </ul>
      </li>
        <li>Cornelius</li>
    </ul>
  </li>
  <li>Pioneers
```

```
    <ul>
      <li>Gordo</li>
      <li>Miss Baker</li>
      <li>Abel</li>
    </ul>
  </li>
  <li>Links</li>
  <li>Contact Us</li>
</ul>
```

We now have a reasonably long nested list that we can add some style to using CSS. Figure 12-22 shows how the preceding markup renders in a browser using our existing style sheet.

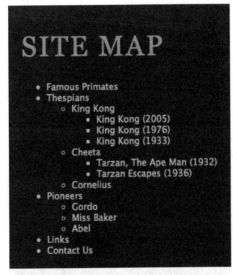

Figure 12-22. With our existing style sheet, our nested list is displayed with the browser's default bullets.

Even without any additional CSS our Famous Primates web site's structure is clearly indicated, with the hierarchy of pages obvious. As it stands, however, this is looking a little bland. We can use CSS to draw out the hierarchy further, highlighting the top-level pages in the site—Famous Primates, Thespians, Pioneers, Links, and Contact Us—differentiating them from the subsections and their related pages.

The first thing we need to do is give our unordered list an id so that we can target our CSS at this specific list without affecting any other lists on the page. We apply an id of sitemap to the containing ul as follows:

```
<ul id="sitemap">
  <li>Famous Primates</li>

  ...

</ul>
```

We can now write a rule targeting the `sitemap` id, applying some general style to the list. We'll then use shades of color to differentiate the different levels of our list, using a lighter shade for the top-level list and progressively darker shades for the nested lists.

We add the following rule to take care of some basic styling:

```
#sitemap
{
font-weight: bold;
color: #E0DFDA;
line-height: 1.8;
}
```

This displays in the browser as shown in Figure 12-23.

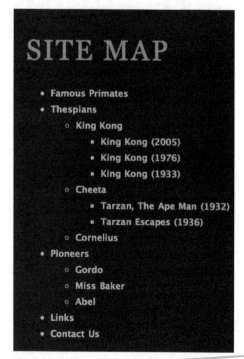

Figure 12-23. Adding some line-height to our nested list gives the list a little more breathing room. We've also set the list items to display in a bold weight using the `font-weight` property.

Setting the `font-weight` property to bold and adding a little `line-height` is the first stage in the process of styling our list. We're also setting a color for the list items to #E0DFDA (the light creamy text color we've been using). We'll overwrite this in a moment for darker shades on the nested list items.

We now amend our #sitemap rule as follows and add a second rule to remove all of the list items' bullets:

```
#sitemap
{
font-weight: bold;
color: #E0DFDA;
line-height: 1.8;
padding: 0;
margin: 0;
}

#sitemap li
{
list-style: none;
}
```

This displays in the browser as shown in Figure 12-24.

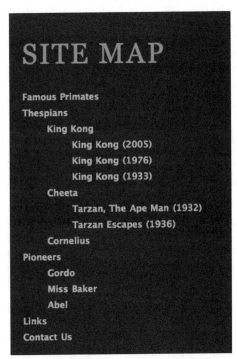

Figure 12-24. With the list-style: none; declaration, we switch off the browser's default bullets; we also remove the indent on our first level list.

One point to note here is that resetting the margin and padding on the top-level list (with the id of sitemap) only resets the margin on *this* list. Remember, there are other lists

12

nested inside this list with their own default margin and padding. We're leaving the margin and padding on the nested lists untouched to reveal the hierarchy of the web site.

The second key point here is that our list-style: none; declaration is taking care of *all* list items in the nested list. Essentially, the selector #sitemap li instructs the browser to "look for any list items in the list with the id of sitemap and remove the bullets."

Now that we've removed the browser's default bullets, we'll add our own on the second- and third-level lists, adding stars in keeping with the design we've created. We'll target these at the nested list items.

We add the following additional rules:

```
#sitemap ul
{
color: #C0BDB8;
margin: 5px 15px;
padding: 0 15px;
}

#sitemap ul li
{
background-image: url(images/star_first.png);
background-repeat: no-repeat;
background-position: left 6px;
padding-left: 15px;
}
```

This displays in the browser as shown in Figure 12-25.

What's important to note here is that we're using our knowledge of descendant selectors (targeted at specific elements) coupled with the use of inheritance to take care of the styling.

The first of the two rules we've added targets any unordered lists nested in the ul with the id of sitemap (that's all the nested lists at the second and third level) and sets their color to a slightly darker shade of brown (#C0BDB8) to differentiate them from the list items at the top level. We also add some additional margin and padding to give our site map a little more breathing room.

The second of the rules uses inheritance to apply a background-image to our nested list items. We've created a star image that's the same color as the color we set in the last rule (#C0BDB8). In the next, and final, stage we'll create a more specific rule that takes care of the third-level list items, differentiating them further.

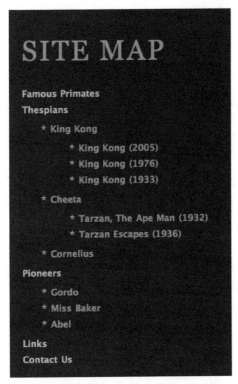

Figure 12-25. Adding custom bullets to our list items using a variant of the star image we used for the `sidebar` navigation list ties this list into our design.

We do this by adding the following rule, which targets our third-level lists with laserlike precision:

```
#sitemap ul ul li
{
color: #8D8984;
background-image: url(images/star_second.png);
font-weight: normal;
}
```

This displays in the browser as shown in Figure 12-26.

12

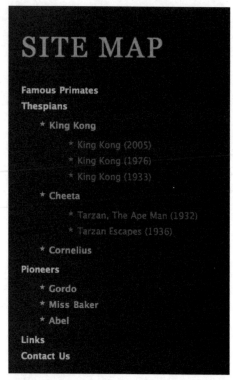

Figure 12-26. Changing the text color and setting the font-weight of our third-level list to normal differentiates it from the lists above it in the hierarchy.

In the final stage of the process we've differentiated our third-level lists from the lists above it in the hierarchy. Changing the color of the text and the associated color of our custom bullet in addition to using the font-weight: normal; declaration has helped to further underline the hierarchy of our site map.

As with the previous stages in the walkthrough, we're progressively targeting the elements we want to style: in this case all instances of li nested within a ul, nested within another ul, nested within the ul with the id of sidebar. That might seem a little complicated, and in this case it is, but it's completely logical!

Let's take a look at our finished CSS with comments added to indicate which level of the list the rules are targeting:

```
/* First-Level List */

#sitemap
{
font-weight: bold;
color: #E0DFDA;
line-height: 1.8;
padding: 0;
```

```
margin: 0;
}

#sitemap li
{
list-style: none;
}

/* Second-Level List */

#sitemap ul
{
color: #C0BDB8;
margin: 5px 15px;
padding: 0 15px;
}

#sitemap ul li
{
background-image: url(images/star_first.png);
background-repeat: no-repeat;
background-position: left 6px;
padding-left: 15px;
}

/* Third-Level List */

#sitemap ul ul li
{
color: #8D8984;
background-image: url(images/star_second.png);
font-weight: normal;
}
```

Styling nested lists can take a bit of getting used to and is certainly not a beginner-level topic. Dealing with inheritance in nested lists can be a little like a baptism of fire, but as ever, practice makes perfect. (Remember Mr. Miyagi? "Wax on . . . wax off.")

12

Styling an ordered list

In Chapter 4 we promised we'd introduce you to some of the alternative values we can use when styling ordered lists. Good news, this is the section where we cover this in action.

To give this some context, let's take a look at the references on our King Kong page where we've used an ordered list. At present this list is styled using the browser's default style sheet, which gives each list item a numeral (using a default value of decimal on the list-style property). This displays as shown in Figure 12-27.

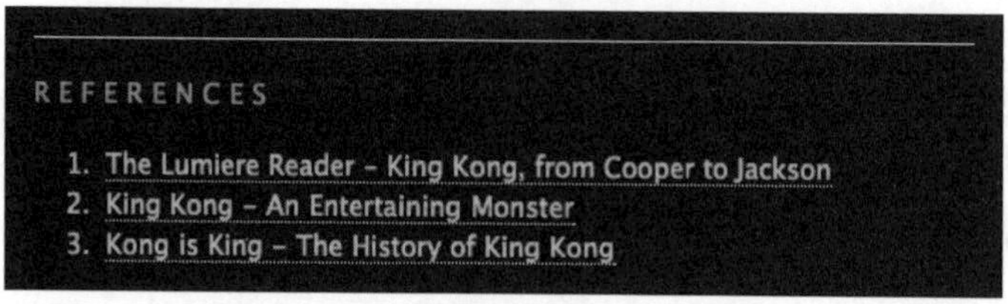

REFERENCES

1. The Lumiere Reader – King Kong, from Cooper to Jackson
2. King Kong – An Entertaining Monster
3. Kong is King – The History of King Kong

Figure 12-27. Our references as they are currently styled, with the browser's default style sheet specifying a `list-style` value of decimal

However, as we indicated in Chapter 4, we're not restricted to numbers for our list items; we can also use, among others, upper-alpha and lower-alpha (to change the numbers for letters), or upper-roman and lower-roman (to change the numbers for Roman numerals).

Let's take a look at these in action. If we'd like to change our list markers from sequential numbers to sequential letters (A, B, C . . .), we simply add the following rule to our style sheet:

```
ol
{
list-style: upper-alpha;
}
```

This results in the changes shown in Figure 12-28.

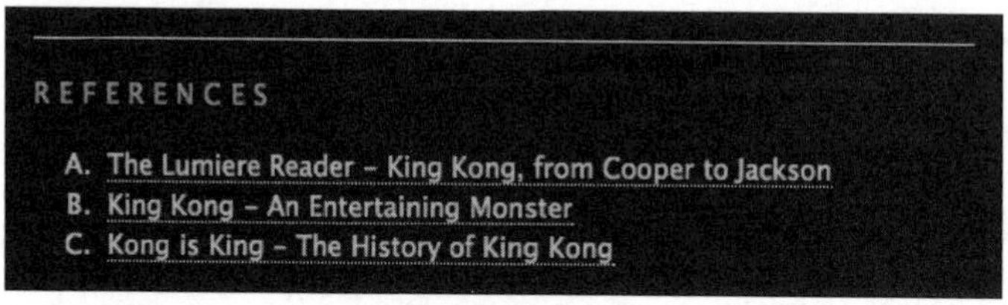

REFERENCES

A. The Lumiere Reader – King Kong, from Cooper to Jackson
B. King Kong – An Entertaining Monster
C. Kong is King – The History of King Kong

Figure 12-28. Our references are now ordered with sequential letters in uppercase.

Our list-style declaration is similar to the one we used previously to turn off the bullets on our unordered lists earlier in this chapter, in this case replacing our numbering with an ordered list of letters.

If we'd prefer a more Roman flavor, we can simply change the value of the list-style declaration to, for example, lower-roman as follows:

```
ol
{
list-style: lower-roman;
}
```

Figure 12-29 show the results of this change.

Figure 12-29. Our references are now numbered with lowercase Roman numerals.

Although this barely scratches the surface of styling ordered lists, it should get you started on your ordered list journey. There are a number of even more exotic ways to display ordered lists, including Greek, Armenian, and katakana list markers.

Noted CSS and web standards advocate Eric Meyer has a comprehensive test page at his web site that lists (pun intended) all available markers:

```
http://meyerweb.com/eric/css/tests/css2/sec12-06-02a.htm
```

Summary

So what have we covered? In this chapter we've looked at a number of the ways you can use CSS to style lists. We've looked at adding custom bullets to your lists by using the background-image property, and we've created both vertical and horizontal lists of links, creating block-level rollovers for the navigation we added to the sidebar of our Famous Primates web site.

We also looked at styling nested lists to enable you to create well-structured and well-styled site maps. Lastly, we briefly looked at some ways we can style ordered lists, introducing a variety of alternatives to plain old decimal.

An understanding of this chapter will enable you to create navigation lists (and other lists) for the web sites you build that are not only well-structured using semantic markup, but also well-styled with CSS. Combining the techniques we've covered will give you a flexible array of list styles to apply to your projects. As usual, experimenting with your own lists will help you develop your abilities further.

In the next chapter we'll introduce you to the benefits of using external style sheets, where a web standards approach really comes into its own. We'll also introduce you to a number of useful troubleshooting tools and techniques to serve you as you continue on your journey toward Web Standardistas' nirvana.

12

Homework: Adding the Famous Primates web site's navigation

Over the last five chapters we've progressively added to your knowledge of CSS to enable you to create well-styled web pages that are built on a solid foundation of well-structured markup. This is the backbone of the Web Standardistas' approach and one we'll conclude in the following chapter when we create an external style sheet for your Famous Primates web site, tying all of the web site's separate pages together.

In this chapter we showed you how to use CSS to create well-styled vertical and horizontal lists; we also showed you how to add custom bullets to these lists to improve their look and feel. We replaced the placeholder content we added to our sidebar div in Chapter 11 with a list of links to form the Famous Primates web site's navigation.

This chapter's homework is to create the navigation list for the sidebar of your Gordo page, once again following along with our King Kong page as an example. Once you've added your navigation list to your Gordo page, we'd like you to implement the navigation across the remainder of your Famous Primates web pages.

Lastly, we'd like you to explore the different ways you can style the ordered list of links in your Gordo page's references section by creating a rule to change the default decimal style with something a little more interesting.

1. Add the ul to the sidebar

In the last chapter we added some placeholder content to the sidebar div when we created our two-column CSS layout. In this chapter we'd like you to replace this content with an unordered list. This list will form the basis of your Famous Primates web site's navigation.

Following along with our King Kong example, give your sidebar ul an id of nav. This will allow you to create rules targeting this specific list on the page while leaving the other lists on your Gordo page untouched.

2. Add the custom bullets to your sidebar list

As with the previous chapters we've created everything you need to complete the homework. You can download the assets here:

www.webstandardistas.com/12/assets.zip

Once you've downloaded the preceding files, transfer the images to your images folder. You'll be using the star images we've supplied for you to replace the bullets of the browser's default style sheet with images more in keeping with Gordo, your space-traveling friend.

Following along with our King Kong example earlier, remove the bullets of the browser's default style sheet; reset your margins and padding; and specify the stars provided as background-images on each of the list items in your sidebar ul.

3. Add the links to the nav ul in the sidebar

Taking care to ensure your relative links are correct, add links to each of the list items in the navigation list in the sidebar div.

Following along with the second part of our King Kong navigation list walkthrough, use a descendant selector to target only the a elements that are li elements in the ul with the id of nav; that is, you'll be creating a rule for the following:

```
#nav li a
{
...
}
```

This is a moving into slightly more complicated territory, but if you've followed along, you should be ready. Before you embark on this aspect of the homework, you might want to re-read the second part of our navigation list walkthrough along with the introduction to descendant selectors in Chapter 10, to see how you're using descendant selectors to target these specific a elements with laserlike accuracy.

4. Style the ordered list in the references section

The final part of this chapter's homework is to style the ordered list in your references section. We set the list-style on our ol to upper-alpha and lower-roman—why not try something different? You might like to refer to Eric Meyer's comprehensive list of all available list-style markers here:

http://meyerweb.com/eric/css/tests/css2/sec12-06-02a.htm

As usual, to help you with the different stages of this chapter's homework, we've created our own, similarly styled, page about King Kong featuring our newly added sidebar navigation list. We've also styled the references section, changing the default list-style to decimal-leading-zero. You can refer to this, using your browser's View Source menu command to see how we've updated our CSS, here:

www.webstandardistas.com/12/king_kong.html

Once you've added the navigation list to the sidebar of your Gordo web page and styled the references, put the kettle on and enjoy a cup of *Keemun Orchid* as you prepare yourself for the next chapter.

12

CHAPTER 13

HARNESSING THE POWER OF EXTERNAL STYLE SHEETS

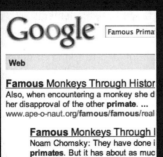

We're almost there! This is our last practical, hands-on chapter, and we'll use it to introduce some quite advanced topics; but if you've been a diligent Web Standardista and done your homework, we're confident you're ready.

At this point we have a well-structured and well-presented King Kong page; however, there are still a number of fundamental ways in which we could improve it. Not least by introducing you to the power of using external style sheets, where the real benefit of a web standards–based approach becomes clear.

We'll use the contents of a typical head element to form the basis of the majority of this chapter's journey, introducing a number of useful new tags and elements into the head that allow you to really get the most out of the Web Standardistas' approach. In particular we'll cover the use of <meta> tags, looking at what they're useful for and exposing a few myths about them along the way. These are the tags and elements that will really set you apart from your less well-trained peers.

The primary focus of the chapter will be to look at the benefits of using external style sheets: taking the style sheet we've created for our King Kong page, removing it from the King Kong page itself, and linking to it as a separate file. Doing this will allow us to link *all* of our ape and monkey web pages to the same style sheet, allowing us to focus our efforts on a single style sheet that styles *all* of the Famous Primates web site's pages, improving efficiency and ensuring consistency across the site. This is where the real power of CSS lies. We'll also show you how to create a separate print style sheet so your web pages look fantastic in print too.

Lastly, we'll cover testing and troubleshooting, two aspects essential to the Web Standardistas' approach. Without further ado, let's get started.

The head elements that make it all happen

According to the W3C's recommended standard, only a few elements are legal inside the head element: base, link, meta, title, style, and script. You've encountered some of these elements before, not least the meta, title, and style elements with which you're now well and truly acquainted, but the remainder are probably new to you.

Now that we're getting toward the end of the book and this kind of detail is no longer intimidating to you, we're going to take a look at a typical head element that you might encounter on a web page "in the wild." We'll break it apart and look at what each element is doing. This will introduce some important new concepts that will form the closing part of our Web Standardistas journey.

One element we're not going to focus on is the title element; you're well acquainted by now and we don't need to reveal any more of its secrets to you. We will, however, look at the style element where, up until this point, we've been locating our CSS.

We'll examine the style element in relation to the link element, showing how you can use it to offload your CSS to an *external* style sheet so that all of your documents are linked to one, easily updated style sheet stored in a central location. This is where the real power of a combined XHTML and CSS approach lies: using a *single* CSS file to style *all* of your web pages.

Once we've covered that, we'll run through the remainder of the elements you'll find in the head section, introducing you to each, one by one. This will give the chapter some structure around which we can build, as we introduce each new element and its purpose.

The following example shows some markup that you might expect to find on a typical web page. We've expanded upon our King Kong page to tie it back into the process we've been working through for the last few chapters. Many of these elements are new; however, we'll walk through them one by one and introduce you to them.

```
<!DOCTYPE html PUBLIC "-//W3C//DTD XHTML 1.0 Strict//EN"
"http://www.w3.org/TR/xhtml1/DTD/xhtml1-strict.dtd">
<html xmlns="http://www.w3.org/1999/xhtml">
<head>
  <meta http-equiv="Content-Type" content="text/html; charset=UTF-8" />
  <title>King Kong | Apes in the Movies | Famous Primates</title>
  <meta name="description" content="King Kong is a fictional giant ape
  from the legendary Skull Island. A renowned ape thespian he is
  unquestionably a famous primate." />
  <meta name="author" content="Web Standardistas" />
  <link rel="stylesheet" type="text/css" href="../css/screen.css"➥
  media="screen" />
  <link rel="stylesheet" type="text/css" href="../css/print.css"➥
  media="print" />
  <!--[if lte IE6]>
  <link rel="stylesheet" type="text/css" href="../css/iehacks.css" />
  <![endif]-->
  <link rel="shortcut icon" type="image/ico" href="../favicon.ico" />
  <script type="text/javascript" src="../js/primates.js"></script>
</head>
```

Clearly the preceding is a little more complicated than the web pages we've been creating up until this point. At first glance all these extra elements in the head might appear a little intimidating; however, as we introduce each of them to you, you'll become familiar with them in no time.

The importance of meta tags

13

The first element we're going to introduce properly is the <meta> tag and its attributes. You first met a <meta> tag in Chapter 2 when we introduced character encoding, and if you've been using the template file we provided for you, you should be used to seeing it by now. In this section we'll formally introduce you, revealing its secrets. <meta> tags are used for much more than character encoding, however; let's take a look at them in a little more detail now.

In computing terms, **metadata** is data that describes other data and, as you'll see, one use of the <meta> tag is to describe the contents of a web page. In this section we'll look at some uses of the <meta> tag and its various attributes in action.

To save you constantly referring back to our introductory example, we'll include the relevant lines of code from the head element as we introduce each section. In this section we'll be looking at the <meta> tags as follows:

```
<meta http-equiv="Content-Type" content="text/html; charset=UTF-8" />
...
<meta name="description" content="King Kong is a fictional giant ape
from the legendary Skull Island. A renowned ape thespian he is
unquestionably a famous primate." />
<meta name="author" content="Web Standardistas" />
```

You might have heard of <meta> tags in discussions about Google and search engine optimization that possibly express the importance of "using keywords in meta tags" and the benefits of using <meta> tags to provide a description for search engine purposes.

In fact Google relies less on <meta> tags for keywords now, looking instead at the actual content of a page to establish search rankings. This is largely due to the manipulation of keywords, where less-than-scrupulous search engine optimization (SEO) consultants would fill the keywords attribute with content often of no relevance to the page in an effort to boost search engine rankings (a tactic known as keyword stuffing). As search engine robots—the programs that index your web pages—have become more sophisticated, the value of keywords in <meta> tags has declined considerably.

Although meta keyword tags are no longer really relevant, meta description tags are still relevant and can be used to provide the description that the search engine will use in its listing of your site as shown in Figure 13-1.

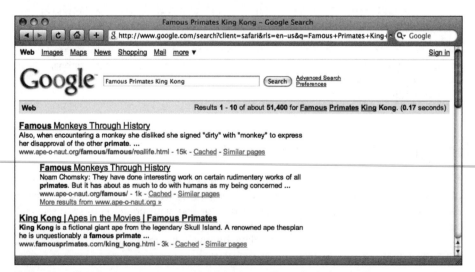

Figure 13-1. The King Kong page's meta description attribute displaying as a description of the page in Google

<meta> tags aren't just for search engines, however, as the example of a typical head element earlier in the chapter showed. We've included two other <meta> tags; the first contains a character encoding that we introduced in Chapter 2, but will explain in detail in a moment:

```
<meta http-equiv="Content-Type" content="text/html; charset=UTF-8" />
```

The second specifies the authors of the specific page:

```
<meta name="author" content="Web Standardistas" />
```

As the three examples in this section suggest, <meta> tags can be created for almost anything. There are a number of initiatives, not the least the Dublin Core Metadata Initiative (DCMI), that are developing metadata standards. The DCMI (www.dublincore.org), established in 1995, is dedicated to creating a simple and standardized set of metadata conventions for describing documents online in ways that make them easier to find. Microformats (www.microformats.org), a more recently emerging set of markup principles, is also aimed at exploring metadata and information markup.

It's all in a name

<meta> tags have four types of attribute: http-equiv, name, content, and scheme. You met the name attribute earlier, when we introduced the description attribute. In fact there are a number of potential values for the name attribute, one of which is included in our typical head element example:

```
<meta name="author" content="Web Standardistas" />
```

No prizes for guessing that this is used to identify the authors of the particular page (in this case the authors of the book you're now holding). The following are a few other name attributes:

- keywords: As we already mentioned earlier, Google and other search engines no longer place any emphasis on keywords in <meta> tags. You should instead ensure your web page's content has a rich mix of keywords marked up within the h1, h2, and p elements on the page itself.

- copyright: This attribute is useful for including copyright declarations and information.

- robots: This attribute is useful for informing search engines which pages you would like to be indexed (and equally importantly, which pages you wouldn't).

There are a number of other potential values for the name attribute. We've covered these and the topic of the <meta> tag and its attributes in greater depth at the book's companion web site:

www.webstandardistas.com/periodical

13

Speaking a foreign language

You first met the http-equiv attribute in Chapter 2 when we briefly introduced you to character encodings. The following <meta> tag provides information to the browser about how to interpret the contents of our XHTML page. Let's take a look at it more closely now to see how it works its magic:

```
<meta http-equiv="Content-Type" content="text/html; charset=UTF-8" />
```

The parts we're interested in are the values in the content attribute: the first value, text/html, informs the browser that the document should be treated as text/html, and the second instructs the browser to use a character set (charset) of UTF-8. Lost yet? Resist the urge to skip this section; we encourage you to stick with us to the end as the UTF-8 character set is important.

UTF-8 (which stands for 8-bit Unicode Transformation Format) supports a large character set allowing you to, for example, include words with umlauts and accents on your web pages.

The easiest way to explain the benefits of using UTF-8 is to show two examples in action: one web page with UTF-8 specified as a character set and one without. We'll use an invented but very foreign-looking word—Iñtërnâtiônàlizætiøn—that uses a variety of unusual characters in two different web pages and look at how the character encoding, or lack of, affects the display of the characters in the browser.

The following very short page has no character encoding specified:

```
<!DOCTYPE html PUBLIC "-//W3C//DTD XHTML 1.0 Strict//EN"
"http://www.w3.org/TR/xhtml1/DTD/xhtml1-strict.dtd">
<html xmlns="http://www.w3.org/1999/xhtml">
  <head>
    <title>Iñtërnâtiônàlizætiøn - No Character Encoding</title>
  </head>
  <body>
    <p>Iñtërnâtiônàlizætiøn</p>
  </body>
</html>
```

This page displays in the browser as shown in Figure 13-2. Note the page's title and the p within the body. Disaster. With no character encoding specified, the web page doesn't display what we'd like it to. Clearly we need to fix this.

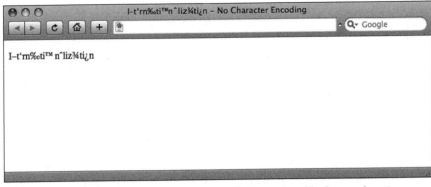

Figure 13-2. Our web page with no character encoding struggles with obscure characters.

Now take a look at the same page, with our character encoding specified as UTF-8:

```
<!DOCTYPE html PUBLIC "-//W3C//DTD XHTML 1.0 Strict//EN"
"http://www.w3.org/TR/xhtml1/DTD/xhtml1-strict.dtd">
<html xmlns="http://www.w3.org/1999/xhtml">
  <head>
    <meta http-equiv="Content-Type" content="text/html; ➥
    charset=UTF-8" />
    <title>Iñtërnâtiônàlizætiøn - Encoded Using UTF-8</title>
  </head>
  <body>
    <p>Iñtërnâtiônàlizætiøn</p>
  </body>
</html>
```

This page displays in the browser as shown in Figure 13-3—perfect. By specifying UTF-8 as a character set, our web page can now support a wide variety of characters, allowing us to create pages that are internationally friendly.

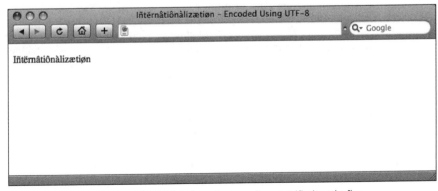

Figure 13-3. Our web page with UTF-8 character encoding specified works fine.

Character encoding is a tricky topic, and we've barely scratched the surface here. We'd strongly suggest that anyone involved in working with an international character set reads up further on this. To help with this, we've provided additional resources at the book's companion web site:

www.webstandardistas.com/resources

External Style Sheets

Next on our quest to unravel the head is the link element. As we briefly alluded to earlier, we'll use the link element to enable us to offload our style sheets and link to them. Up until this point all of our style sheets have been written on the pages we've been working on and embedded within them; now we'll separate our XHTML pages (the content) and CSS files (the presentation).

This section is where the real power of CSS comes into play in full effect.

Although it's useful during the development phase to work with all the XHTML and CSS in one file, we've now reached a point with our King Kong page that it's nearly finished. This is the stage at which we take all the information we've developed in the embedded style sheet and offload it to an external style sheet, creating a single, external style sheet that all of our documents link to.

Before we show you the relevant markup, we'll pause for a moment and consider the pros and cons of embedded style sheets as opposed to linked style sheets.

Embedded vs. linked style sheets

As we've mentioned, throughout the previous chapters we've used an embedded style sheet to develop our King Kong web page. The benefit of using an embedded style sheet *during the development phase* is that it allows you to tightly control and test your web page as it evolves from within one easy location.

However, there are a number of downsides to using embedded style sheets. Unless every single page on your web site is different—an unlikely event—linking to a single CSS file is a better approach for a number of reasons.

First, by linking all of the web pages in your web site to a single CSS file, your users' browser will only need to download the CSS file once, after which it will be accessed from the browser's cache. This speeds up download times considerably and reduces bandwidth requirements. With embedded CSS every time a page is downloaded, the CSS is downloaded, an inefficient and bandwidth-intensive process. Not only will a page with an embedded CSS file take longer to download, it will also place a heavier load on the server.

Another reason to link all your files to a single CSS file to control presentation is to improve consistency and reduce the number of files that need to be updated. Imagine every single page in your web site has the same embedded CSS. If you need to make just one change, you'll need to update all of the web pages. Clearly a single, linked, external style sheet is a better approach.

Linking to an external style sheet

The relevant part of our head element that handles the link to our external style sheet is the following line:

```
<link rel="stylesheet" type="text/css" href="../css/screen.css"➥
media="screen" />
```

Let's take a look at this in detail and work out what's going on. The first attribute, rel, defines the relationship of the linked document with the current document, in this case highlighting that the link is to a stylesheet. The second attribute, type, specifies the style sheet language: text/css. The href attribute, which you're familiar with, specifies a URL pinpointing where the style sheet can be found and what it's called, in this case a file named screen.css in a folder called css. Lastly, the media attribute specifies the intended rendering medium or media, in this case screen.

In the preceding example we've set the media attribute to screen, but there are a number of other media attributes we can use.

Media types

CSS supports a wide variety of media types, although support for a number of them is inconsistent. The following media types are supported as specified by the W3C's CSS 2.1 specification (http://www.w3.org/TR/CSS2/media.html):

- all: Suitable for all devices
- aural: Intended for speech synthesizers
- braille: Intended for Braille tactile feedback devices
- embossed: Intended for paged Braille printers
- handheld: Intended for handheld devices
- print: Intended for printed material and for documents viewed on screen in print preview mode
- projection: Intended for projected presentations, for example, using data projectors
- screen: Intended primarily for color computer screens
- tty: Intended for media using a fixed-pitch character grid, such as teletypes, terminals, or portable devices with limited display capabilities
- tv: Intended for television-type devices

In this chapter we'll be focusing on screen and print styles, the two you are likely to find yourself using most.

13

It's worth noting that many of these media types are not supported by any devices at all and possibly may never be, for example, tty and both Braille types (which is perhaps no bad thing given the specialist knowledge that would be required to create effective Braille style sheets).

Using @import

An alternative method to using the link element to link to our style sheet is to use an @import rule instead as in the following example:

```
<style type="text/css">
@import url(../css/screen.css) screen;
</style>
```

Essentially what this does is inform the browser to look for a CSS file called style.css, import it, and use it to style the document. This was a popular method of importing styles as support for web standards evolved.

The original motivation for the @import rule was to hide CSS from old browsers that didn't understand CSS very well, most notably Netscape 4 (a browser you're highly unlikely to encounter in this day and age). The idea of the @import rule was to serve a simple style sheet or no style sheet at all to CSS-challenged browsers, while sending a full style sheet to standards-aware browsers. However, since these browsers are over a decade old, supporting them should become less and less of a concern.

One area where the @import rule has an advantage over the link element is that its use is not restricted to the head element of a web page; it can also be used within an external style sheet.

This allows us, for example, to link to a separate CSS file that contains a number of @import rules pulling in other, additional style sheets. When dealing with multiple style sheets, this approach enables you to easily manage importing external style sheets, while keeping the head of your XHTML files neat and tidy. We cover this in greater depth at the book's companion web site:

www.webstandardistas.com/periodical

In this day and age, whether to use @import or the link element to link to your style sheets is largely a matter of taste; both methods work, and all modern browsers understand either.

Creating our external CSS file

The creation of our external CSS file is simple and should take only a few moments. We create a new plain text document in our plain text editor and save it as screen.css. The .css extension, like the .html extension, identifies the file type to the browser, in this case indicating it is a Cascading Style Sheet.

We open our King Kong web page and select everything between the opening <style type="text/css"> and the closing </style> tags (but not the <style> tags themselves). We simply copy all of our CSS rules (and any relevant comments) and paste them into the screen.css document we just created and save it.

Like the images folder we created in Chapter 6 to organize our images, it's a good idea to create a css folder to store your style sheets in. Although at this point you only have one style sheet, later in the chapter we'll create a print.css style sheet to style printed pages. Storing these separate style sheets in one location will make the management of our web site easier as it grows.

The next stage is to create a link from all the XHTML pages we'd like to style with this style sheet using the href attribute. This process is identical to creating any other link (to an image for example). Bear in mind the path to the CSS file will be relative to the different web pages we're linking from. Our example in the typical head element follows:

```
<link rel="stylesheet" type="text/css" href="../css/screen.css"➥
media="screen" />
```

In this example our screen.css file is located within a folder called css sitting in a folder above the file we're linking from.

That's it. Now we can delete any internal style sheets from any XHTML documents we've linked to this external style sheet; the link element will now take care of the link to the CSS, styling the pages. One file, styling everything. Once we've deleted our <style> tags we load our page in a browser and test it. The result is shown in Figure 13-4.

One thing worth noting is that when you transfer your screen.css file into your css folder, you'll need to check and amend the relationship of any images you have used in your style sheet, ensuring their relative links are fixed to take into account the relative locations of the style sheet and the images specified.

For our Famous Primates home page we've specified three background images in our style sheet. If we take one as an example, and see the effect of moving the screen.css file into the css folder, it should help you understand the principle. We take the original rule, as follows:

```
background-image: url(images/body_bg.png);
```

and change it to the following:

```
background-image: url(../images/body_bg.png);
```

13

This step is essentially the same as the one you took in Chapter 6 when you fixed the links to your images after putting them into the images folder.

Figure 13-4. Our King Kong page with the linked style sheet displays exactly the same as it did when the style sheet was embedded.

The real power of CSS

By moving all of our styles to an external style sheet and linking *all* of our Famous Primates web pages *to this one file*, we can style everything from one central location. This is where the real power of CSS lies.

Using linked style sheets will save you a significant amount of time in the long run and considerably cut down the amount of time and effort it takes to make changes to the presentational aspects of your web site. **Change the one CSS file, and the entire web site is updated automatically.** Good times!

But it gets better; we can build multiple style sheets for different purposes, all styling the same well-structured markup. For example, we might build a print style sheet for printed pages or a high-contrast style sheet with larger type for visually impaired users. The flexibility is the key.

In the next section we demonstrate this by building a print style sheet, showing how we can completely alter the look and feel of the King Kong page just by changing the style sheet.

Adding a print style sheet

One of the beauties of CSS lies in its flexibility. Having built a solid foundation of well-structured semantic markup, we can now quickly and easily restyle the very same markup to create a print style sheet that is tailored to the world of the printed page.

Clearly, printed pages have different characteristics from pages viewed onscreen. Screen and print are two different media with two distinctive sets of requirements. It makes sense to provide a print style sheet for your users that is optimized for the medium of print. Some key aspects to consider when designing a print style sheet include the following:

- Hide elements that aren't useful in print. It makes sense to hide certain aspects of your markup when developing the print style sheet, for example, navigation (after all, a user can't click links on a printed page!). CSS allows you to use display: none; to switch off the elements you'd prefer not to show in print, perfect for this purpose.

- Create a print-specific logo. If you've used subtle gradients for onscreen purposes that might not print well, include a version of your logo and hide it in the screen style sheet, but show it in your print style sheet.

- Ensure your print style sheet works in black and white and high contrast. When setting white text on a dark background color, bear in mind that background images and colors do not print by default. Some browsers will print just the text—*in white*—and no background; the resulting printed page will be a challenge to read!

- Ensure the sizes you specify work in print. A #container set at 760 pixels for screen is better set in inches (or centimeters, for countries that have embraced the metric system). Consider the width of the printed page and design accordingly.

- Use points for font sizes. In print—as with any common word processors—you'll notice type is set in points, usually 10 pt for legible body copy. When designing your print style sheet, use sizes geared toward the world of the printed page for the best results.

Building the print style sheet

Let's get started. In our example of a typical head element earlier, we have the following link element, specifying a link to a print style sheet:

```
<link rel="stylesheet" href="../css/print.css" type="text/css" ➥
media="print" />
```

We'll now walk you through the process of creating this style sheet. The first step in the process is to open a new file in our plain text editor and save it as print.css; we'll save it in the css folder to keep all of our CSS files organized.

13

Style the body

We add our first rule as follows, styling the body so that it's perfect for print:

```
body
{
font-family: Georgia, serif;
font-size: 10pt;
color: black;
background: white;
width: auto;
margin: 0 10%;
}
```

By now you should know enough about CSS to have a clear understanding of what's happening here. We've specified Georgia, a serif font, for our print style sheet. We could have used Lucida Grande as we specified in our screen.css style sheet; however, serif fonts are generally considered easier on the eye on paper (and Georgia is a beautifully designed typeface).

You'll notice we've set the font-size to 10pt, using points as a unit of measure instead of pixels. Pixels are perfect for screen; points are perfect for paper. We've set the page to print black on white, not the dark background-color of our screen style sheet; think how much toner that would eat up!

Lastly, we set the width of the page to auto, filling the page to use less paper, and set a margin of 10% on the left and right, adding a little space around our content.

Hide unnecessary content

Onscreen and in a browser our list of links in the sidebar is perfect, enabling us to navigate throughout the site. In print, links aren't clickable, so printing them is of no benefit to the user. We hide the sidebar using the display property of CSS, setting the display to none as follows:

```
#sidebar
{
display: none;
}
```

Style the headings

The next stage is to style the headings and add a little padding to space out our paragraphs a little to aid our printed page's legibility. We do this by adding the following rules:

```
h1
{
font-size: 18pt;
}

h2
{
```

```
font-size: 16pt;
}

h2
{
font-size: 14pt;
}

h4
{
font-size: 10pt;
text-transform: uppercase;
letter-spacing: 0.4em;
margin-top: 10mm;
padding-top: 5mm;
border-top: solid 1px black;
}

p
{
margin: 0 0 5pt 0;
}
```

Style the links

Although we switched off the links in our sidebar by using display: none;, we'd like to display our links in our references section and the copyright information and links in our footer. We use a grouped selector to target both our a:link and a:visited pseudo-classes, styling them black and switching off the links' default text-decoration (we'll indicate that they're links by including the URLs in a moment):

```
a:link, a:visited
{
color: black;
text-decoration: none;
}
```

The last thing we do, which we're introducing here for the first time, is to use CSS's :after pseudo-class, which will enable us to write a rule that displays the URLs of our links *after* the link text. This will be useful for anyone reading the King Kong page and wanting to find out a little more about the mighty ape online. We add the following:

```
a:link:after, a:visited:after
{
content: " (" attr(href) ") ";
}
```

What this declaration does is to write some content to the page after our a:link and a:visited elements in standards compliant browsers. Essentially it writes the following: a space and an opening bracket, the href attribute, and a closing bracket and a space.

13

We add the following two declarations to our rule to style the URLs in a light shade of gray to reduce their prominence and set their font-size to 80%.

```
a:link:after, a:visited:after
{
content: " (" attr(href) ") ";
color: #CCCCCC;
font-size: 80%;
}
```

Click Print and check the results

That's it, we're finished. Simple. The only thing we need to do now is check the results when printed. Figure 13-5 shows the results of printing out our page. Perfect!

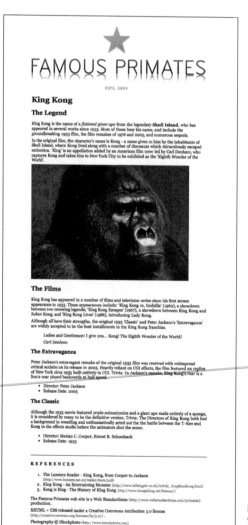

Figure 13-5. Our King Kong page restyled for the wonderful world of paper

Conditional comments for Internet Explorer

Conditional comments only work in Internet Explorer and provide a mechanism for targeting specific versions of the browser. The conditional comment in our head example looks like this:

```
<!--[if lte IE6]>
<link rel="stylesheet" type="text/css" href="../css/iehacks.css" />
<![endif]-->
```

The conditional comment starts with a `<!--` and ends with a `-->`, so to all browsers other than IE the conditional comment will look just like one of the comments you met in Chapter 2 and be ignored. However, IE 6 and earlier versions of the browser will see the main style sheet we've linked to (`screen.css`) *and* the linked style sheet within the conditional comment (`iehacks.css`), which contains additional rules specifically written for IE that override the main style sheet.

It's worth noting that the reason the IE-specific rules in the `iehacks.css` style sheet override our `screen.css` style sheet is due to the fact that the `iehacks.css` link is below the `screen.css` link in our markup and so overrides any styles set in the `screen.css` style sheet. (To refresh your memory about this topic, you might like to revisit the section titled "The order of your CSS rules is important" in Chapter 10.)

As older versions of Internet Explorer notoriously suffered from shortcomings in the interpretation of CSS compared to browsers with better standards compliance, several methods of targeting CSS specifically at IE were developed. Known as **CSS hacks**, these workarounds took advantage of known bugs in different browsers' CSS interpretations to target rules to specific browsers.

One of the best-known CSS hacks is Tantek Çelik's box model hack, used to work around Internet Explorer 5's box model bug. To illustrate what a CSS hack looks like, we've included an example of this hack here:

```
#content
{
width: 400px;
voice-family: "\"}\"";
voice-family: inherit;
width: 300px;
}
```

The first declaration in the rule specifies a width for IE 5/Windows of 400px. What follows is designed to bamboozle IE 5 with a set of obscure rules that effectively force it to throw its hands in the air and give up on attempting to parse the remaining declarations. Smarter browsers, however, continue parsing and get the correct width of 300px on the last line of the rule. In a nutshell, IE 5 sets the width of the content to 400px, while smarter browsers set it to 300px.

If this looks complicated, it's because it is. As we said at the start of the example, this was a hack—a workaround web designers were forced into, as support for standards in older

13

browsers evolved. While there might be times you're forced to use hacks, they should be avoided unless absolutely necessary.

Although a proprietary extension of regular HTML comments by Microsoft, conditional comments offer us a method of serving specific CSS to specific versions of Internet Explorer (arguably the number one culprit for browser bad behavior). Conditional comments allow us to write "good" CSS for all browsers and then add an additional set of amended rules for IE only.

This allows us to keep our main style sheet clean of obscure hacks and separate the IE-specific workarounds into a separate file. You can target specific versions of Internet Explorer using this method; in our example, in the typical head element we've used `<!--[if lte IE 6]>`, which targets versions *less than or equal to* IE 6 (lte).

The following example would target all versions of Internet Explorer 5 and above (conditional comments were introduced in IE 5, so they are supported from IE 5 onward):

```
<!--[if IE]>
<link rel="stylesheet" type="text/css" href="../css/iehacks.css" />
<![endif]-->
```

If we just want to target IE 5 and IE 5.5, we could use the following, which targets versions of IE lt (less than) IE 6:

```
<!--[if lt IE 6]>
<link rel="stylesheet" type="text/css" href="../css/iehacks.css" />
<![endif]-->
```

We can also use gt (greater than) and gte (greater than or equal to) as in the following example, which targets all versions of IE from 5.5 onward:

```
<!--[if gte IE 5.5000]>
<link rel="stylesheet" type="text/css" href="../css/iehacks.css" />
<![endif]-->
```

In the following section we'll look at a conditional comment in action as we use it to target a style sheet at IE 6 and earlier.

A conditional comment in action

In Chapter 10 we specified a 24-bit PNG image with a transparent background as part of our King Kong page. In the main style sheet (which we're now linking to) we've linked to this image. Unfortunately IE 6 doesn't natively support alpha transparency, resulting in unpredictable rendering. We can, however, use the conditional comment from our head element example to point IE 6 and below to `iehacks.css`, a style sheet built just for IE 6 and earlier where we address this problem:

```
<!--[if lte IE6]>
<link rel="stylesheet" type="text/css" href="../css/iehacks.css" />
<![endif]-->
```

We'll use this style sheet to set the transparent PNG used for all well-behaved browsers to a less pretty, but still workable, GIF image with a solid background color for IE. So, all other browsers will get `transparent_background.png` via the main style sheet:

```
/* Our main style sheet (screen.css) for well-behaved browsers. */

#header
{
background-image: url(../images/transparent_background.png);
}
```

The conditional comment will ensure IE 6 and older gets `solid_background.gif` via our IE hacks style sheet:

```
/* Our hacks style sheet (iehacks.css) for badly behaved browsers. */

#header
{
background-image: url(../images/solid_background.gif);
}
```

It's worth stressing that conditional comments, like hacks, should be used as a last resort; it's much better to find CSS solutions that work across all browsers. However, conditional comments are better than CSS hacks that rely on browser bugs; one reason for this is the ability to remove browser-specific CSS from your main style sheet, another is that any workaround rules are guaranteed not to have an impact on browsers other than those intended.

Adding a favicon

Adding a favicon (short for favorites icon) is by no means necessary; it is, however, the sort of attention to detail that the true Web Standardista should aspire to. Favicons appear in a number of places, including address bars, tabs, bookmarks, history, and browser tool-bars. They provide an instant visual cue to the user, especially useful when scrolling back through browsing history, in addition to providing a valuable branding opportunity (admittedly small at just 16 × 16 pixels).

We add a favicon to our site using a `link` element as shown in the following example:

```
<link rel="shortcut icon" type="image/ico" href="../images/➥
favicon.png" />
```

Like the `link` elements we used for linking to our external style sheets, our link to our favicon contains a number of attributes and values: first, a `rel` attribute with a value of `shortcut icon`; second, a `type` attribute with a value of `image/ico`, informing the browser that the file being linked to is a favicon; lastly, an `href` attribute with a path to where the favicon is located in relation to the web page.

An example of a favicon is shown in Figure 13-6, at the Web Standardistas web site, where the URL is accompanied by a tiny gold star.

13

Figure 13-6. Our Web Standardistas' favicon as it displays in Safari's address bar

Originally favicons had to be saved in an ICO format; however, a majority of browsers now support PNGs and GIFs too. You can even make animated favicons, although their support is limited at present.

Adding scripts

Although adding JavaScript to your page is beyond the scope of this book, we felt it important to introduce you to a script element so that you would know one when you encountered it on a typical web page when using View Source. Unsurprisingly, JavaScript is referenced using the script element as follows:

```
<script type="text/javascript" src="../js/primates.js"></script>
```

This example, from our typical head element introduced at the start of the chapter, shows a link to a JavaScript file called primates.js located in a folder called js.

It's worth noting that JavaScripts don't always need to be linked to; they can also be added between the opening and closing <script> tags as in the following example:

```
<!DOCTYPE html PUBLIC "-//W3C//DTD XHTML 1.0 Strict//EN"
"http://www.w3.org/TR/xhtml1/DTD/xhtml1-strict.dtd">
<html xmlns="http://www.w3.org/1999/xhtml">
<head>
  <meta http-equiv="Content-Type" content="text/html; charset=UTF-8" />
  <title>JavaScript Hello World!</title>
</head>
<body>
  <script type="text/javascript">
    document.write("Hello World!");
  </script>
</body>
</html>
```

This page, when loaded in a browser, will display identically to the very first "Hello World!" web page we created back in Chapter 2.

Contrary to what many beginning web designers mistakenly think, JavaScript is not Java and Java is not JavaScript. Both were initially developed in 1995, but both are different.

Java, developed by Sun Microsystems, is a full-fledged object-oriented programming language that can be used to create stand-alone applications in addition to mini applications, called applets.

JavaScript, developed by Netscape, is a smaller programming language commonly used to extend XHTML documents to provide levels of interactivity beyond what is possible with typically static XHTML pages. JavaScript is not used to create stand-alone applications or applets.

Testing and troubleshooting

We would be remiss if we didn't include a section on testing and troubleshooting. Both are important topics, and both will have an impact on your day-to-day progress as a Web Standardista.

By now you're well aware of the importance of testing your web pages using the W3C Markup Validation Service and CSS Validation Service, but by the very nature of the Web, and with the rapid emergence of the mobile Web, your web pages are likely to be seen in a variety of contexts, so testing in browsers is an equally important part of the testing process. The browser you're using isn't necessarily the browser your user is using, and as a consequence of this a thorough testing process should lie at the heart of your approach. A failure to test your web site can result in unexpected errors or worse, inaccessible content, a glaring Web Standardista faux pas.

Thoroughly testing your web pages invariably highlights issues that will need troubleshooting if their cause isn't immediately apparent. To help you with this, we've highlighted a number of troubleshooting techniques in this section, a checklist if you will, that you can run through, prelaunch, to ensure any errors have been picked up and resolved.

Testing

The golden rule when developing and designing web sites is *test, test, test!* When you consider that your carefully crafted web site, overflowing with XHTML and CSS goodness, might be seen on anything from a laptop running Mac OS X using Safari, to a desktop running Windows Vista using Internet Explorer, to a tablet running Linux using a Mozilla-based browser, the potential for browser-related display issues becomes clear.

Mac OS X alone supports a variety of browsers including Safari, Firefox, Opera, and Camino (not to mention Lynx, which has reemerged as a Universal Access web browser for the visually impaired). One operating system, a variety of browsers. Windows and Linux are no different, supporting an extensive array of browsers from popular, well-established browsers to niche browsers.

13

Figure 13-7 shows a typical range of browsers as displayed in Shaun Inman's popular web site analytics program Mint (www.haveamint.com). Clearly the list is a long one with some of the usual suspects: Firefox, Internet Explorer, and Safari. However, it also includes a variety of lesser-known suspects: Camino, Konqueror, and Lynx, all clocking in at less than 1%.

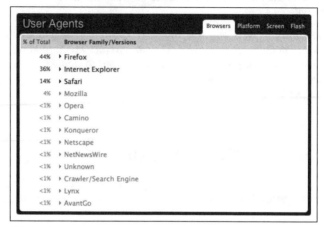

Figure 13-7. A typical list of user agents (or browsers) as shown in Mint

As you can see in Figure 13-7, not only do we need to factor in a variety of browsers when testing, we also need to consider screen size, not to mention the color depth of our users' screens. Testing for all of these eventualities is almost impossible, of course, so how do you test your web site across a variety of contexts? One answer lies in web-based browser test services, which allow you to see your web site through the eyes of another platform and browser.

Web-based browser test services

There are a number of web-based browser test services that, like the W3C validators, offer you a way of testing your web site. Essentially tools that allow you to see how your web site displays across a variety of operating systems and in a broad range of browsers, these range from paid-for services to open source initiatives that allow you to quickly test your web site in a variety of browsers. One that's well worth exploring is Browsershots. The description on the Browsershots web site describes it best:

> *Browsershots makes screenshots of your web design in different browsers. It is a free open-source online service created by Johann C. Rocholl. When you submit your web address, it will be added to the job queue. A number of distributed computers will open your website in their browser. Then they will make screenshots and upload them to the central server.*
>
> www.browsershots.org

Essentially, Browsershots uses an open source, distributed computing approach to create browser screenshots, splitting the workload across a number of distributed computers. Typically, the results take a few minutes to arrive upon submitting a URL; however, what you get over that few minutes is an extensive snapshot of how your web pages are looking in a variety of contexts.

Another service worth mentioning is Litmus (`www.litmusapp.com`)—a subscription-based browser and e-mail client test service. Through an elegant interface, shown in Figure 13-8, Litmus shows you exactly how your web site designs look on every platform, across every popular web browser. It also tests rich, HTML e-mail campaigns across a variety of different e-mail clients. Better still, once you've finished testing, a single click publishes a full compatibility report ready for review.

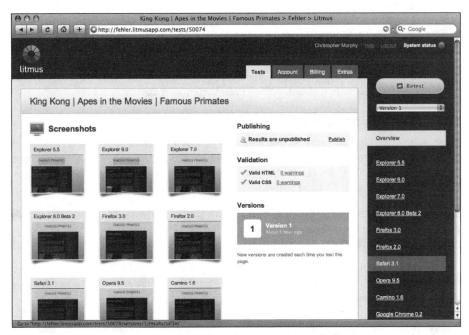

Figure 13-8. Litmus returns screenshots of the web page we've tested, allowing us to see how it looks across a variety of browsers.

Although these web-based browser test services are convenient and useful, they do, however, have one drawback. What they return is a static image, essentially only testing one state of your page and showing you the results. By their nature they can't show you how your web site loads and is displayed *over time*.

As you evolve as a Web Standardista and begin to embrace more advanced topics, for example, adding animation and scripting, or including dynamic, user-interface effects on your web pages, a service that returns a static image can't give you any insight into how these elements of your page are working.

There is a solution at hand, however: building a **guerilla testing suite**.

13

Building a guerilla testing suite

Given the focus of this book's homework on the Famous Primates web site, you might be forgiven for thinking a guerilla testing suite is one manned by a staff of apes. We can't be sure what you call your friends, but we do not call our friends apes (except under extreme circumstances). A guerilla (not gorilla) testing suite is a great way to build a low-cost, high-feedback testing suite for checking your web site.

Essentially an ad hoc testing service, manned by friends and fellow designers and developers using different platforms, a guerilla testing suite allows you to use your network of contacts to test out pages in a variety of situations.

Built on a trust-based model—if you test my pages, I'll test yours—this approach offers you a much deeper level of feedback: "Your dynamic, JavaScript-driven image rotator took forever to load!" or "There's a real problem with your images. There are far too many and they're far too large—I was able to boil the kettle and enjoy a pleasant cup of *Orange Pekoe* while I waited for the page to load."

This kind of critical and objective feedback is invaluable and is something that screenshot-driven services just don't offer. Even better, all it costs you is time.

Graded browser support

After reading the last few sections, you might be forgiven for wondering if you really need to support absolutely every possible combination of platform, operating system, and browser out there. The answer is that—in practical terms—you don't, especially if you embrace the concept of **Graded Browser Support**.

We have Yahoo! to thank for the concept of Graded Browser Support—essentially a broader and more encompassing definition of the word *support* coupled with the idea of grades of support. Yahoo! states the following about this concept:

> In the first 10 years of professional web development, back in the early 90s, browser support was binary: Do you—or don't you—support a given browser? When the answer was "No", user access to the site was often actively prevented. . . . By contrast, in modern web development we must support all browsers. Choosing to exclude a segment of users is inappropriate, and, with a "Graded Browser Support" strategy, unnecessary.
>
> http://developer.yahoo.com/yui/articles/gbs/

Essentially browsers are graded. Figure 13-9 shows Yahoo!'s current A-grade browser list. There are three grades: A-, C-, and X-grade, defined as follows:

- **A-grade**: A-grade support is the highest support level. By taking full advantage of the powerful capabilities of modern web standards, the A-grade experience provides advanced functionality and visual fidelity.

- **C-grade**: C-grade is the base level of support, providing core content and functionality. It is sometimes called **core support**. Delivered via nothing more than semantic XHTML, the content and experience is highly accessible, unenhanced by decoration or advanced functionality, and forward and backward compatible. Layers of style and behavior are omitted.

- **X-grade**: X-grade provides support for unknown, fringe, or rare browsers. Browsers receiving X-grade support are assumed to be capable. (If a browser is shown to be incapable—if it chokes on modern methodologies and its user would be better served without decoration or functionality—then it is considered a C-grade browser.)

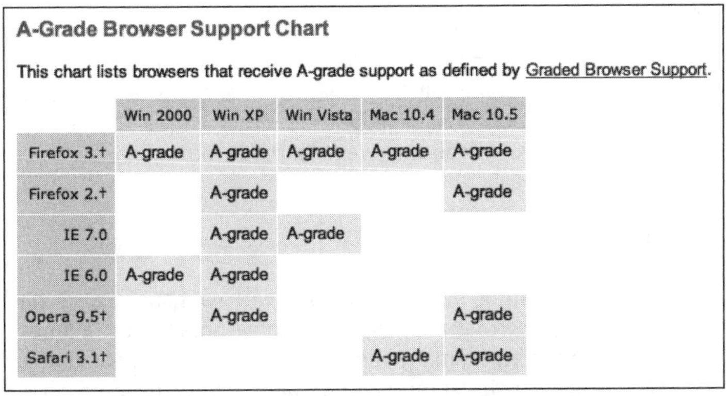

A-Grade Browser Support Chart

This chart lists browsers that receive A-grade support as defined by Graded Browser Support.

	Win 2000	Win XP	Win Vista	Mac 10.4	Mac 10.5
Firefox 3.†	A-grade	A-grade	A-grade	A-grade	A-grade
Firefox 2.†		A-grade			A-grade
IE 7.0		A-grade	A-grade		
IE 6.0	A-grade	A-grade			
Opera 9.5†		A-grade			A-grade
Safari 3.1†				A-grade	A-grade

Figure 13-9. Yahoo!'s list of browsers that receive A-grade support

One important aspect of a Graded Browser Support strategy is to understand that not everyone gets the same experience. Expecting two users using different combinations of operating system and browser to have an identical experience fails to acknowledge the very essence of the Web, namely its diversity. Further, requiring the same experience for all users creates a barrier to participation—accessibility should be our key priority, as we've stressed throughout this book.

What does this mean in the context of troubleshooting and testing? Essentially, not everything will display as you expect it to all of the time, but that's to be expected. The Web is evolving, as you know by now, and things change. Quickly. Designing for the Web has always been a delicate balancing act between *progressive enhancement* and *graceful degradation*.

When designing for the Web, it's important to make an intelligent and informed decision about what you will support and what you won't. This is not a question of stating, "This web site is best viewed at 1024 × 768 or higher resolution with Microsoft Internet Explorer 6 or newer." We shudder when we read these declarations, and so should you. Tim Berners-Lee summarized this nicely in 1996 when he stated the following:

13

> *Anyone who slaps a "this page is best viewed with Browser X" label on a Web page appears to be yearning for the bad old days, before the Web, when you had very little chance of reading a document written on another computer, another word processor, or another network.*
>
> www.anybrowser.org/campaign

A far better approach is to point people in the direction of web standards, informing and educating them, an approach that lay at the heart of the WaSP's successful Browser Upgrade Campaign (www.webstandards.org/action/previous-campaigns/buc/), which began in 2001.

As a Web Standardista, you can do a great deal of good for the Web, helping to ensure that the road for future development is fundamentally standards based. At the end of the day, this book has been about enabling you to create sites that look fantastic in standards-compliant browsers. Spread that web standards message.

Troubleshooting

Yes, troubleshooting is frustrating, but isn't it helpful when a manufacturer has put a little thought into what might go wrong and suggested some possible techniques for turning those wrongs into rights? How many times have you returned home with your fresh-from-the-shop, shiny new breakthrough Internet communication device, only to discover it isn't quite working as you'd expected it to, right out of the box? You look for the instructions in frustration, hoping—praying even—that you'll find the word *Troubleshooting* on the contents page.

Good news, this is that section of the book (and we've even neatly listed it, clearly labeled "Troubleshooting," in the book's table of contents for future reference). This is the page you should be turning to when things are going wrong and you just can't even begin to work out why.

When something goes wrong, there's always a reason, of course, and finding it can be made a lot simpler by adopting a systematic approach using a few tried and tested techniques, which we introduce now.

Validate, validate, validate!

In Chapter 3 we introduced you to the W3C Markup Validation Service. When things go wrong, this should usually be your first port of call. Of course, if you've been a diligent Web Standardista, you should by now be using this validator as a matter of habit. Did you stray from the path? (Guilty? You know who you are!) If you did, learn to love this validator all over again. It is your friend.

Yes, the language used by the validator is a little dry and technical (and we'd love to meet the person who wrote "character "&" is the first character of a delimiter but occurred as data"), but, as we demonstrated in Chapter 3, the validator is the perfect tool for pinpointing any mistakes with laserlike precision:

Line 56, Column 8: character "&" is the first character of a delimiter but occurred as data.

Knowing that the possible source of the problem lies in Line 56 is a lot more helpful than knowing that the possible source of the problem lies in one of, say, 1,816 lines of markup.

It's also worth noting at this point that the W3C Markup Validation Service isn't the only free validation service the W3C offers. It also offers a CSS validator, which you've already seen, in addition to a number of others. If your web pages are passing the W3C Markup Validation Service, but still posing problems, test them by using the W3C CSS Validation Service. Like the W3C Markup Validation Service, the W3C CSS Validation Service helps you narrow down the potential source of problems, making the troubleshooting process easier. You can access the W3C CSS Validation Service here:

```
http://jigsaw.w3.org/css-validator/
```

Leanr to spel

Again, our next bit of advice sounds obvious and you should by now be used to this type of error, but spelling mistakes and accidental typos can often cause your carefully crafted web page to display in an unexpected manner. When writing markup by hand—a good thing as you now know—it's possible for the occasional error to creep in here or there; we're only human after all.

Checking your spelling can often highlight the cause of problems—again, the W3C's validators are great tools for highlighting these issues.

The following is invalid:

```
a
{
text-decaration: underline;
}
```

The following is valid:

```
a
{
text-decoration: underline;
}
```

In this case a simple spelling mistake, decaration instead of decoration, has caused the problem. An easy mistake to make, but one that is often overlooked. Looking on the bright side, writing your markup and CSS by hand in a plain text editor will improve your spelling and attention to detail, and that's no bad thing.

Another spelling-related issue that can occur from time to time—again an easy mistake to make—is when a word is spelled correctly in HTML, for example, `<div id="content">` but spelled incorrectly in the corresponding CSS, for example, `#contnet {color: red;}` or vice versa. Again, the result is an error; frustrating, but understandable when you find it. Case sensitivity can also be an issue, for example, `#Content` and `#content` are not the same.

13

Finally, it's worth mentioning that mistakes can also crop up even when you've diligently checked all of your spelling. The following example, where the HTML id doesn't match up with the CSS id, might cause a few sleepless nights. This HTML:

```
<div id="nav">
```

will obviously not be styled by this CSS:

```
#navigation
{
...
}
```

The bottom line when mistakes occur is to check everything carefully, using the validators to help you find the needles in the haystack.

Adopt a lurid palette

Another useful technique, especially when troubleshooting CSS layout issues, is to temporarily adopt a lurid palette of background colors to clearly highlight the different sections or divs within your document. Using a distinctive color scheme, setting background colors to bright, easily distinguishable colors—for example aqua, fuschia, lime, red, and yellow—allows you to clearly indicate the areas your different divs are occupying and their relationship to each other.

This can also be a useful approach for other elements as well, for example, applying a background-color to text elements to highlight them and clearly indicate how much space they occupy on the page. (We used this technique in Chapter 10 when we introduced margins, borders and padding on a simple p element.)

Check for repetition

In Chapter 10 we explained how rules lower in a style sheet override rules targeting the same element that occur above them. This might not seem to be a likely occurrence in a short page, but as your style sheets get longer and more complex, it's an easy mistake to make. The h1s in the following example will appear red, as the rule styling h1s in red appears lower than the first rule, which styles the h1s in blue.

```
h1
{
color: blue;
}
```

```
/* Imagine lots of additional rules here. */
```

```
h1
{
color: red;
}
```

Using your plain text editor's Find command can help pick these sorts of mistake up quickly.

Reduce to deduce

When all else fails: *reduce to deduce*. Simplify your XHTML and CSS by selectively removing parts of your code from the picture, and then refresh your web page in the browser. Removing CSS rules one by one will usually help identify the causes of any problems. Before embarking on this process, however, it's a good idea to make a backup copy of the file you're testing.

An easy way to achieve this is through the use of comments to selectively switch off aspects of your XHTML or CSS (a process known as **commenting out**). The following example shows a rule styling our h2s that has had the line-height commented out:

```
h2
{
font-size: 24px;
/* line-height: 0.6em; */
margin: 0;
padding: 26px 0 10px 0;
}
```

Commenting out the line-height in this example and refreshing the page in the browser allows us to quickly test the effect that this declaration has on our markup.

XHTML rule reference

To assist you with your troubleshooting, we've included a ready reference of XHTML rules in this section.

Remember that adopting XHTML Strict forces us to use stricter rules that are easy to forget. Your mind wanders, a mistake creeps in, and as a consequence your page throws up a glaring error. Although we've covered these rules throughout the book, we've listed them again here for easy reference:

- Ensure you've opened with the proper DOCTYPE and namespace (if you've been working from the file we provided at the book's companion web site—www.webstandardistas.com/02/template.html—you should be fine).

- All markup must be written in lowercase: <p>...</p> is valid, <P>...</P> isn't.

- Every tag you open must close. "Empty" elements—<img ... />, <br />, <meta ... />, and <link ... />, for example—must be closed with a space and slash—" />".

- Nesting must be symmetrical. Remember the First In, Last Out rule: <p><strong>pioneer</strong></p> is valid, <p><strong>pioneer</p></strong> isn't.

- Encode all <, >, and & characters. Less than or more than signs—(<) and (>)—that aren't part of a tag must be encoded as < and >, respectively; likewise ampersands (&) must be encoded as &.

13

- All attribute values must be enclosed in quotes: width="500" is valid, width=500 isn't. You also need to separate attributes with spaces: width="500" height="375" is valid, width="500"height="375" isn't.

- Don't put double dashes within comments: <!-- Bananas --> is valid, <!-- Fruit -- Bananas --> isn't.

Summary

So what have we covered? In this chapter we've tied up a lot of loose ends. The most significant thing we've covered is how to move from an embedded style sheet, useful during the design, development, and build phases, to an external sheet that maximizes the real benefits of a CSS-based approach: strength, power, and flexibility.

We've also looked at the contents of a typical head element, introducing you to <meta> tags, exploring how they can be used to provide additional information about our web pages; the link element, looking at how it can be used to link to external style sheets and to include a favicon for our web pages; and lastly the script element, acquainting you with it and briefly showing an example of JavaScript in action to create a simple JavaScript "Hello World!" page.

Finally, we took a look at the importance of testing and troubleshooting, giving you a troubleshooting checklist that you can refer to if things go wrong.

In the next chapter we ask, "Where to from here?" and answer that question with some pointers—a few suggestions for what you might focus on after you've completed this book.

Homework: Linking to external style sheets

In this chapter we introduced you to the typical contents of a head element to highlight some additional head elements you might encounter as you use View Source to view web pages "in the wild."

We used our journey through the head to introduce you to a number of elements you might find useful, not least the <meta> tags we introduced. We also used this journey to demonstrate the power of putting external style sheets to work, introducing you to style sheets for both screen and print media.

As we had reached the culmination of the design process, we took our completed internal style sheet and showed you how to use it as the basis for creating an external style sheet. This will allow you to take full advantage of the benefits of using a *single* style sheet that you can link *all* of your web pages to. We also introduced print style sheets that allow you to create perfectly printed web pages optimized for the medium of print.

Along the way we introduced you to favicons, explaining how they can prove useful as a usability aid. Finally, we introduced you to a number of techniques and tools that can prove useful in troubleshooting your web pages.

Your homework for this chapter will be to apply what you've learned to your Gordo page, adding to its head element and creating an external style sheet that you can then use to style all of your Famous Primates pages.

1. Add some <meta> tags

Using the meta description tag we created for our King Kong web page as a guide, create a meta description tag for your Gordo page. We've left it to your discretion to write the contents of the description attribute; however, bear in mind that the first words you use are the important ones. Search engines will often truncate longer meta descriptions, so make your first words count.

You can find out a little more about writing good-quality meta description tags here:

> http://tinyurl.com/mrgoogle

Once you've added your meta description tag, add a meta name tag and insert your name in the content attribute, as in the following example:

> <meta name="author" content="Your Name" />

2. Create an external style sheet

In your plain text editor, create a new document and save it as screen.css; you'll transfer the rules you've written up to this point on your Gordo page to this document. Referring to the examples covered in this chapter, remove the rules you've written for your Gordo page and add them to your screen.css file.

Create a css folder for your screen and print style sheets; this is where you'll store your CSS files. Add a link element to the head element of your page and create a link to your brand-new CSS file.

3. Link to a print style sheet

We've provided a ready-made print style sheet for you to link to. You can download the print style sheet (along with a number of other assets) from the following location:

> www.webstandardistas.com/13/assets.zip

Once you've downloaded these files, transfer the print.css file into your css folder and add a link to it. Remember to include a media attribute for both of your linked style sheets to inform the browser of their purpose.

4. Add a favicon

You'll see that we've provided a favicon for you, which was included with the other assets for this chapter. Referring to our example, add a link to your new favicon and test it in your browser.

13

5.   Test and troubleshoot

Using your Gordo page as an example page, test out the page using both Browsershots (www.browsershots.org) and Litmus (www.litmusapp.com). This will give you some idea of how others see it. Needless to say, we expect you to take care of any troubleshooting that might be required (you can use our checklist to assist you in this process).

As before, to help you with creating your external style sheet, we've created our own, similarly styled, page about King Kong featuring all of the additional material we covered in this chapter. You can refer to this, using your browser's View Source menu command to see how we've created our external style sheet, here:

www.webstandardistas.com/13/king_kong.html

Once you've created your external style sheet, linked to the print style sheet we supplied, and tested it out by printing your Gordo page, put the kettle on and enjoy a cup of *Assam SFTGFOP Mangalam* as you prepare yourself for the next chapter.

To paraphrase Sid Vicious (or was it Frank Sinatra?): "And now, the end is near, and so we face the final curtain . . . "

As we embark on our final chapter together, we've gathered together a number of resources that will help ensure your ongoing journey as a Web Standardista is a smooth one. To help you along on your journey, we've

- Suggested a number of web design–related topics—covering both established and emerging technologies—that you might like to consider exploring next
- Developed a free web-based resource for you where we're publishing additional content in the form of a periodical, reviewing web design–related books, and collecting additional links you'll find useful (we've even organized the links by category and provided short reviews for each)
- Highlighted some useful tools to add to your Web Standardistas' toolbox to make your life as a fully fledged web designer a little easier
- Recommended a number of books that fit well with topics you might want to cover once you've completed this book
- Suggested a number of web sites we recommend you bookmark and explore

This chapter, like the other chapters, is tightly tied to the book's companion web site where we're maintaining an up-to-date resource comprising book recommendations, links to recommended web sites and online resources, emerging tools, a periodical, and more. This resource allows us to keep you informed about new and emerging trends in a rapidly evolving medium.

Although you've reached the end of *this* book, your journey as a Web Standardista is only just beginning. Just like the journey toward nirvana, or the path to enlightenment, your Web Standardista journey is a lifelong one. With that thought in mind, think of this chapter as a map, pointing you in the right direction and giving you a clear indication of what to explore next.

So, without further ado, let's get started on the final part of our journey . . .

But really, where to from here?

Not coincidentally the title of this chapter is "Where to from Here?"—a question you're probably asking yourself now. You've almost concluded this book, you've followed all the exercises, you've diligently done all of your homework, and you hopefully have a completed Famous Primates web site. What next? Where to from here?

There are a number of additional technologies—both established and emerging trends—that you are now well and truly prepared to explore, and we cover some of them here. It's an exciting time to be embarking on a career as a web designer. The Web is maturing, technologies are evolving rapidly, and, just as importantly, the support for these technologies is becoming more dependable.

With a solid grounding in web standards you should be more than capable of integrating emerging technologies into your practice and expanding your portfolio of skills. So, what's out there? The last few years have seen a number of exciting developments, not least the following:

- The collaborative web, think Wikipedia (www.wikipedia.org), TripAdvisor (www.tripadvisor.com), and Urban Dictionary (www.urbandictionary.com)

- User-generated content, think Flickr (www.flickr.com), Newsvine (www.newsvine.com), and YouTube (www.youtube.com)

- Community-driven sites (sometimes characterized as "conversational media"), think Twitter (www.twitter.com), Facebook (www.facebook.com), and Slashdot (www.slashdot.org)

- Social-bookmarking services, think Delicious (www.delicious.com), FFFFOUND (www.ffffound.com), and Digg (www.digg.com)

- Web-based applications, think Basecamp (www.basecamphq.com), Gmail (www.gmail.com), and Harvest (www.getharvest.com)

The emergence of these services—both delivered *via the Web* and a product *of the Web*—has resulted in a rich online tapestry. The collaborative Web, user-generated content, conversational media, social- and community-driven sites, web-based applications . . . all have clear potential in isolation, but what's exciting about the Web now is the way in which these technologies are being *combined* in innovative and often unexpected ways.

The decision by many companies and developers to embrace the use of open application programming interfaces (APIs) that allow users to combine data from diverse sources and reconfigure and shape content in a variety of ways has resulted in a proliferation of web-based services and applications.

Known as **mashups**, these web-based applications combine data from more than one source, creating single, integrated tools that were unimaginable only a few years ago.

The decision of companies like Google, Amazon, Flickr, and Twitter (to name just a few) to freely open up access to their information—the core of their respective businesses—is giving rise to innovative new applications as the Web moves forward.

Figure 14-1 shows an example of this in action. Building on Google's Google Maps API and combining this with social-networking aspects allows Platial to create a web-based, shared mapping tool. As its cofounder Jason Wilson states, "Platial enables anyone to find, create, and use meaningful maps of Places that matter to them. Our dream is to connect people, neighborhoods, cities, and countries through a citizen-driven common context that goes beyond geopolitical boundaries. We are building Platial because we adore Places."

14

Figure 14-1. Platial, a social mapping service that is built on a number of APIs

Last.fm—self-styled home to "The Social Music Revolution"—proclaims the following on its home page:

Right now, all over the world . . .

433 people are listening to Ted Sulkowicz—Black Dot

43,206 people love Stephan Mathieu

4,832 people are attending Kraftwerk in Dublin

This kind of information, constantly updated, constantly changing, and pulled from the ether, where it's openly shared, suggests possibilities that perhaps even Tim Berners-Lee didn't see: particularly the unexpected manner in which information—the very fabric of the Web—can now be shaped, merged, blended, and reconfigured as the Web evolves.

So, what might you explore now?

What you've learned so far is a solid foundation on which you can build. Some things to look at might be JavaScript libraries, to add dynamic features to your site; PHP and MySQL, for the creation of dynamic, database-driven web sites; and AJAX (Asynchronous JavaScript and XML) to create web-based applications.

The Web is changing, it's rapidly evolving, and—with the solid foundation you now have—you can become a part of this rapidly evolving landscape.

JavaScript libraries

What is a JavaScript library? Essentially a collection of prewritten JavaScript functions that allow for easier development of JavaScript-based applications, JavaScript libraries have the potential to enhance web site functionality and can improve user experience considerably. Combined with well-structured XHTML markup and CSS, both of which you should by now be well acquainted with, JavaScript libraries make it easier and quicker to create truly accessible dynamic web sites.

The first thing to note is that there are a number of JavaScript libraries in existence, all with particular strengths. By now you'll be unsurprised to hear that some research is required in order to select the one that best fits your needs. Some libraries worth exploring include jQuery (`www.jquery.com`), Prototype (`www.prototypejs.org`), MooTools (`www.mootools.net`), and the Yahoo! User Interface Library (`http://developer.yahoo.com/yui`). All have extensive resources and tutorials available online.

Not only are JavaScript libraries making advanced JavaScript capabilities available to non-programmers, they are also easing and accelerating the development process. Easy to integrate into a web site, they enable mere mortals to add advanced functionality and dynamic effects to web pages that would once have been the exclusive domain of JavaScript programmer demi-gods. Figure 14-2 shows one example of a JavaScript-driven user interface in action, in this case a gallery window opening in an overlay on top of the current web page using Lokesh Dhakar's popular Lightbox plug-in.

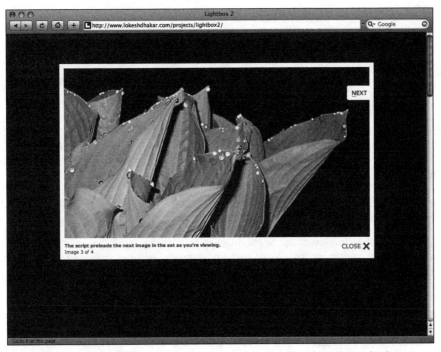

Figure 14-2. Lokesh Dhakar's Lightbox plug-in is an elegant and unobtrusive mechanism to overlay images on the current page through the power and flexibility of the Prototype framework and script.aculo.us effects library.

14

The emergence of various libraries—and equally importantly, their support in standards-compliant browsers—has positioned JavaScript as a serious contender to Flash thanks to its ability to easily create dynamic effects. They also form a basis for the emergence of AJAX.

The road map for JavaScript libraries looks set to only improve as browser manufacturers invest significant resources into this area due to the richness of user experiences that can be created using JavaScript to enhance otherwise static web sites.

Database-driven sites

When developing small web sites with only a few pages, it's fine to build each page by hand, creating and adding the content for each page as it is added to the site. If, however, your site grows substantially, possibly expanding to include multiple authors, all adding and editing content, there are more efficient ways of developing and maintaining your web site. Enter databases.

By storing your content in a database and dynamically populating your pages with content, you can build large and complex sites that have the additional advantage of allowing your content to be searched and output in a variety of ways.

One approach worth considering is a combination of PHP and MySQL, a popular choice for database-driven sites. Both are free to use and are supported via a variety of online resources.

AJAX and Rich Internet Applications

Rolling both of the preceding together—JavaScript and the seamless exchange of information between a browser and a database—*without* refreshing a web page, moves the discussion toward AJAX (Asynchronous JavaScript and XML).

AJAX is often confused with the use of JavaScript in general, with beginning developers considering the integration of dynamic, user interface effects via the use of JavaScript—in particular through the use of JavaScript libraries—to be equivalent to AJAX: "Check it out, my page is using AJAX!"

The clue to what AJAX *really* is lies in its name, suggesting the asynchronous exchange of data between a database and a web page.

AJAX enables the creation of application-like interfaces that have the ability to send and receive data to and from the server *in the background* without the need to reload the page for every exchange of data made, as is the case with normal XHTML pages.

One example of this process can be seen in Figure 14-3, which shows Google's Google Suggest feature. As you type into the search box, Google Suggest anticipates what you might be typing, offering possible search term suggestions in real time. Essentially these search results are retrieved from the server and displayed in the browser as you type, enabling you to accelerate the search process.

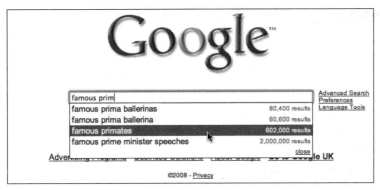

Figure 14-3. Google Suggest, an example of AJAX adding dynamic functionality to an otherwise static XHTML page

Popular micro-blogging site Twitter summarizes the benefits of an AJAX approach nicely: "Updates are now refreshed via AJAX, instead of loading the whole page, which should be faster." What this means is that parts of a web page can be refreshed dynamically by querying a database *without reloading the entire page*, resulting in more dynamic pages.

One reason for the rapid growth in interest in AJAX lies in the widespread adoption of Gmail, an application that relies heavily on the technology. AJAX, coupled with the widespread availability of faster Internet connections, has been behind the growth of a number of web-based applications that use AJAX components as a part of the fabric of their design.

Web Development Solutions: Ajax, APIs, Libraries, and Hosted Services Made Easy by Mark Norman Francis and Christian Heilmann (friends of ED, 2007) provides a comprehensive introduction to AJAX and the use of JavaScript libraries as you continue your journey.

www.webstandardistas.com

First and foremost, as you embark on your journey as a fully fledged Web Standardista, you're not alone. We've built a solid resource to assist you on your journey, which is available at the book's companion web site:

www.webstandardistas.com

What's available at the site? Well, apart from all the files you need for the Famous Primates web site and example files showing what we've covered in each chapter of the book, we've gathered together a number of other resources to make your journey from here as easy as possible.

We've organized the web site into a number of sections that not only cover tools and resources mentioned in the book, but also highlight and review new or upgraded tools as they emerge. The web site also features a periodical through which we're continuing to add to the dialog as the Web evolves—a lively and engaging resource that we hope you will keep returning to after you've put this book down.

14

The Web Standardistas' periodical

The Web is constantly changing, and to reflect this we've created a periodical section at the book's companion web site where we cover new and emerging technologies in addition to other topics that should be of interest to the aspiring Web Standardista. Some topics we're covering include usability, design, culture, and code.

The periodical section also contains interviews with internationally respected designers and developers allowing you to gain an insight into how other practitioners work and to see examples of their work.

You can follow the Web Standardistas' periodical here:

> www.webstandardistas.com/periodical

Book reviews

Although we've recommended some books in this chapter, this list is by no means comprehensive. Our reading lists for our final year interactive design students are extensive, and we've integrated them into the Web Standardistas' web site. All feature reviews that give you a concise overview of the books we recommend. We've built on those lists and included a number of other books we recommend highly.

These books aren't just restricted to those covering XHTML and CSS, but also include titles that cover a broader range of topics including usability, design, culture, and code. You can find our recommended list of books here:

> www.webstandardistas.com/reviews

Resources

As you by now know, we've listed a number of resources throughout the book. We'll be adding to this list as new resources become available. You can find the latest list at the book's companion web site:

> www.webstandardistas.com/resources

Tools

In addition to our lists of recommended plain text editors, image editors, and FTP clients, we've also included links to a number of other tools that might prove useful to the aspiring Web Standardista. You can find links to the relevant applications' web sites at the book's companion web site:

> www.webstandardistas.com/tools

Badges

We mentioned badges back in Chapter 1; we have created a number of badges for you to put on your site, proudly displaying your Web Standardista credentials for the world to see. You can find them here:

www.webstandardistas.com/badges

For those of you not satisfied with pixels, a limited edition of *real* badges have been carefully crafted and are ready to be delivered on a first come, first served basis. The details on how to obtain these rare collectibles are outlined in the "Homework" section at the end of this chapter.

Tea

Those of you who have been following along with the homework diligently will notice that each our chapters' "Homework" sections has finished with a recommended tea. Should you wish to avail yourself of these teas—perhaps you'd like to relax over a cup of *China White Monkey* or perhaps you need a refreshing pick-me-up courtesy of a cup of *China After the Snow Sprouting Reserve Organic*—you can find links to tea suppliers here:

www.webstandardistas.com/tea

Tools to make your life easier

In this section we've introduced a number of tools to make your life easier as a Web Standardista. All are either web-based or cross-platform; better still all are free or have free options.

As with our other recommended tools, you'll find links to the latest versions of these tools at the book's companion web site:

www.webstandardistas.com/tools

As a conscientious Web Standardista you'll naturally be spending a good proportion of your time testing and troubleshooting your designs. There are a number of tools that make this process easier; in this section we'll outline a few options.

Firefox Web Developer Add-on

Developed by Chris Pederick, the Web Developer Add-on for Firefox is an excellent utility that will help you considerably in your ongoing journey as a Web Standardista. Generously distributed for free under the terms of the GNU General Public License (www.gnu.org/copyleft/gpl.html), Pederick's extension is well worth installing. The Web Developer Add-on adds a toolbar to Firefox as illustrated in Figure 14-4.

14

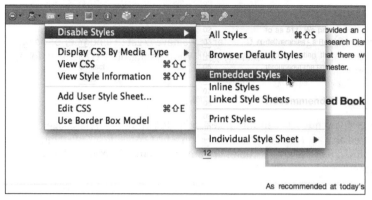

Figure 14-4. Chris Pederick's excellent Web Developer Add-on toolbar in action, disabling a web page's embedded style sheet

The Web Developer Add-on toolbar allows you to do the following:

- Visually outline the different elements on your web page, which helps considerably when creating and debugging layouts.
- View and edit your XHTML and CSS within the browser and see live previews of these edits, which is extremely useful when developing web pages and troubleshooting.
- Switch off your web page's CSS to see how it looks unstyled, as it might be seen by a mobile phone, PDA, or screen reader.
- Access the W3C's various validators via keyboard shortcuts.

This list barely scratches the surface. The best way to get a feel for the Web Developer Add-on and its extensive array of functions is to install the Add-on to your copy of Firefox and try it out. You can find out more about it and download it at Chris Pederick's web site:

http://chrispederick.com/work/web-developer/

Firebug

Firebug, shown in Figure 14-5, is another indispensable Firefox add-on, using a slightly more visual approach than the Web Developer toolbar. Created by the talented Joe Hewitt, one of the original developers of Firefox (and a classically trained kazoo player), Firebug is released as an open source project and maintained by a small team of developers. It is free to use and should occupy pride of place in any aspiring Web Standardista's toolbox.

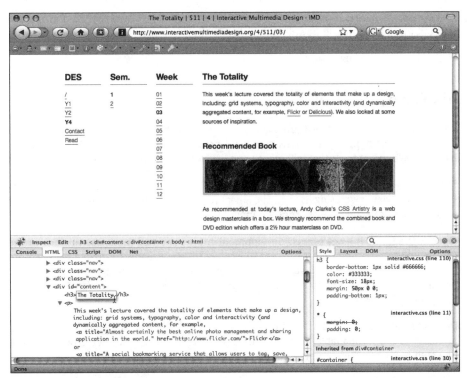

Figure 14-5. Firebug's three-pane interface allows you to edit your XHTML and CSS and see the resulting changes displayed live in the browser window.

Once installed, Firebug can be easily invoked by simply using keyboard shortcuts. Firebug allows you to do the following:

- Inspect and edit your CSS and XHTML markup, allowing you to make experimental real-time edits to the source of your page that update live in the browser as you type. (The CSS editor even features autocompletion and several tools that make editing your style sheets easier.)

- Visualize your CSS by providing previews of colors and even background images as you hover your mouse over your different CSS declarations.

- Disable individual CSS rules with a simple click of the mouse, making debugging live pages easier and faster.

- Check for errors in your CSS and XHTML markup without leaving the page. Firebug features a status indicator that immediately tells you if something isn't right, and shows you a list of possible errors.

Firebug has an array of other features, including advanced JavaScript inspectors, CSS metrics display, and much more. It even comes in a "Firebug Lite" version, a piece of JavaScript that you can install for IE, Opera, or Safari, enabling you to take some of Firebug's features with you to other browsers. As with the Web Developer Add-on, the best way to discover

14

what Firebug can do is to install the add-on to your copy of Firefox and try it out. You can find out more about it and download it at the Firebug web site:

    www.getfirebug.com

Tools for other browsers

There are a number of other tools available for exploring, debugging, and analyzing web pages, and most modern, standards-compliant browsers include some built-in or add-on-based development tools that will make your development process easier.

Safari's Web Inspector allows you to view the XHTML markup and CSS associated with any element of a web page using its Inspect Element feature, available by right-clicking within a web page and selecting the appropriate menu command.

Opera's Dragonfly is a set of web development tools built into the latest versions of the Opera browser, sporting similar features to Firebug, albeit available through a slightly more complex interface. Another feature Opera offers that's worth mentioning is its ability to display web pages using built-in accessible style sheets, including both a High Contrast and an Accessibility Layout.

Even Internet Explorer gets in on the game with the Internet Explorer Developer Toolbar, available as a downloadable extension for older versions of IE. Internet Explorer 8 goes one step further, including developer tools built into the browser itself.

Using these tools can make your life easier and save you tearing your hair out trying to determine exactly what is going wrong, if and when something on your web page isn't working the way you expected.

Basecamp

Web development isn't all about debugging web pages, however. 37signals' excellent Basecamp allows you to easily track and organize all aspects of a project in one place, making it the perfect tool to keep track of the web sites you're developing.

A web-based application, Basecamp lets you manage and track projects and quickly create resources for them, allowing you to easily create shareable to-do lists; manage user-friendly, shared project calendars that highlight project milestones and deliverables; and gather discussion about projects in a central location.

37signals offers a free plan that allows you to manage a single project with unlimited users, enabling you to try out the software fully. Find out more about Basecamp here:

    www.basecamphq.com

What else is out there?

The preceding list is a good start, although there are a great deal more resources out there. If you haven't already downloaded and installed Firefox, it's certainly worth doing so. Its open Add-ons architecture has resulted in a number of useful extensions aimed specifically at web developers including LinkChecker, EditCSS, and ColorZilla.

You can download Firefox here:

> www.mozilla.com/firefox

An open and standards-compliant browser, Firefox's Add-ons architecture allows for the easy installation of extensions to the browser that can prove invaluable in extending its use beyond a stand-alone web browser, making it a perfect environment for web development. Throughout the development of your web site you should make a point of testing your site in a variety of browsers to make sure that the site you're developing works as it should across a broad base of browsers.

As we suggested in Chapter 13, install and test your site in all the browsers available for your platform, and then get a friend using a different operating system to check your web site in the browsers available on that platform. Establishing a guerilla testing suite like this can quickly and painlessly point out browser-related issues early in the development process.

We've already recommended using Firefox as a development browser; one thing we would highly recommend *against* is using Internet Explorer as a development browser. By developing for IE first you run the risk that your XHTML markup and CSS is tailored to the bugs sadly still present in IE. The result can be a web site that only works as it should in IE.

A far better and easier approach is to build your web site the right way first, making sure it works in standards-compliant browsers, before making adjustments for less-compliant browsers.

Recommended books

When we embarked on writing this weighty tome, our intention was to create a book that would tie neatly into the list of books we already recommend to the final year interactive design students we teach at degree level and the masters students that we mentor.

To that end we've recommended a number of additional books in this section. Literally hundreds of books cover web design; however, we've focused here on books that we feel fit well with the "where to from here" approach of this chapter.

You've read this book, what next?

There are a lot of excellent books that we point our students toward: Dan Cederholm's inspiring *Web Standards Solutions*, Paul Haine's meticulous *HTML Mastery*, and Andy Budd's *CSS Mastery*, to name but a few. All are fantastic books, and we urge readers to

14

continue their learning by selecting a few and reading further. We've made a number of recommendations here.

Bulletproof Web Design

By Dan Cederholm (New Riders, 2007)

Following the success of his first book, *Web Standards Solutions* (friends of ED, 2004), another book that should be at the top of any self-respecting Web Standardista's reading list, Dan Cederholm's second book focuses on creating CSS solutions that are robust and flexible, and that degrade gracefully in worst-case scenarios.

Bulletproof Web Design, now in its second edition, follows a similar approach to *Web Standards Solutions*, applying a variety of alternative approaches to everyday web design challenges: deconstructing existing approaches and noting their potential pitfalls before proposing bulletproof alternatives using XHTML and CSS.

Bulletproof Web Design concludes with a chapter that ties together all of the case studies discussed in the book, culminating in a single, bulletproof page template.

CSS Artistry

By Andy Clarke (New Riders, 2008)

CSS Artistry is a web design masterclass in a box. Combining Andy Clarke's excellent book *Transcending CSS* with *Inspired CSS*, a 2 1/2-hour masterclass on DVD, the resulting boxed set is a resource that you can return to again and again, for inspiration and reference.

With a heavy focus on the creative design aspects of the web development process, Clarke—an internationally recognized speaker and designer who focuses on creative and accessible web design—brings his trademark charisma and unbridled enthusiasm to an excellent web design resource.

Given that the cost of a one-day masterclass with the aforementioned Mr. Clarke runs to more than ten times the cost of the combined book and DVD, *CSS Artistry* is, shall we say, a bargain.

The Zen of CSS Design

By Dave Shea and Molly E. Holzschlag (New Riders, 2005)

Driven by practical examples, *The Zen of CSS Design* is an enlightening, design-focused book that showcases the potential of CSS-based design by systematically walking through 36 of the most inspiring designs from the CSS Zen Garden (www.csszengarden.com).

By using real-world examples, Dave Shea and Molly E. Holzschlag reveal the wealth of possibilities that CSS-based design can offer. With a first chapter titled "View Source" and subsequent chapters covering, among other topics, design, layout, imagery, and typography, *The Zen of CSS Design* is the perfect book to provide inspiration for any project.

Eric Meyer, widely respected web standards advocate, states, "This is the book I've been waiting for: a combination of design theory and real-world Web Design all rolled into a beautiful package."

CSS Mastery

By Andy Budd (friends of ED, 2006)

As its title suggests, *CSS Mastery* is aimed at web designers with some experience of XHTML and CSS (after reading this book, that's you!). Andy Budd's book picks up where this book leaves off, introducing a variety of useful techniques including styling forms and tables, introducing a number of helpful hacks and filters, and troubleshooting a variety of common CSS problems.

The book closes with two case studies—imaginary real-world examples—by noted web designers Cameron Moll and Simon Collison that show the book's content in action.

HTML Mastery

By Paul Haine (friends of ED, 2006)

We were delighted when we discovered Paul Haine was assigned to be our technical reviewer. We've been recommending his book, *HTML Mastery*, to our final year interactive design students since it was published in 2006. As he states, "Markup is the fabric that holds the web together, but most people only scratch the surface of what can be achieved using (X)HTML."

It's no mistake that half of the book you're now holding in your hands and reading is dedicated to a solid understanding of XHTML. Haine's *HTML Mastery* will allow you to further that understanding, deepening your knowledge of HTML, and enabling you to create better, well-crafted, and more meaningful web pages.

Other books we recommend

We could go on, listing an extensive range of books—there are a great many that are useful to the beginning web designer; however, rather than list every book we think is useful, we recommend you focus on the core set of books we've highlighted above.

Once you've read these, we strongly recommend the following books—in no small part because they deal with everyday usability issues. You can find a full, updated list at the Web Standardistas web site.

14

- *Don't Make Me Think! A Common Sense Approach to Web Usability* by Steve Krug (New Riders, 2005)
- *Defensive Design for the Web* by 37signals (New Riders, 2004)

- *Designing with Web Standards, Second Edition* by Jeffrey Zeldman (New Riders, 2007)
- *Web Standards Creativity: Innovations in Web Design with XHTML, CSS, and DOM Scripting* by Cameron Adams et al. (friends of ED, 2007)

Recommended sites

The beauty of working on the Web is that it serves up a wealth of resources at your fingertips, all just a click of a mouse away. Better still they're all, for the most part, free. We've listed a number of recommended sites here along with short reviews, outlining what each site is about and why we think it's worth a visit.

Rather than overwhelm you with a long, unstructured list, we've broken our recommendations down and organized them by topic (think of the following organized and structured list as a parting shot in structured markup!).

We'll be updating this list to take account of the Web's constant evolution at the book's companion web site:

www.webstandardistas.com/resources

Check this link for frequent updates and recommendations.

Organizations and publications

To list every organization or publication with a bearing on the evolution of the Web would, as you can probably imagine, result in a book (or at the very least a chapter) in itself. The following organizations, however, are worth bookmarking and checking into periodically as the Web evolves.

W3C

www.w3.org

The W3C's XHTML and CSS validators aren't the only thing we have to thank our friends at the W3C for. They also maintain an extensive resource that includes the *W3C A to Z* (a comprehensive rundown covering everything you ever needed to know about web standards).

At first glance the W3C web site might seem a little dry; on closer inspection, however, it provides a wealth of information well worth tapping into.

Web Standards Project

www.webstandards.org

The Web Standards Project (WaSP) is, in their own words, "a grassroots coalition fighting for standards which ensure simple, affordable access to web technologies for all."

We have the WaSP to thank for the standards-compliant browser support we've now come to expect as a matter of course. Before it was established, standards support among browser makers was less than stellar to say the least, so thank you WaSP.

A List Apart

www.alistapart.com

As their strapline states, *A List Apart* is "For people who make websites." Its secondary strapline, in the web site's footer, adds "From pixels to prose; coding to content." Both cover it well. *A List Apart* features an excellent and diverse range of topics exploring all aspects of web development.

Better still, it has a writing team to die for: Jeffery Zeldman, Eric Meyer, Dave Shea, and Cameron Moll, to name but a few. *A List Apart* should be at the top of any self-respecting Web Standardista's list of bookmarks, no question.

Digital Web Magazine

www.digital-web.com

A great source of inspiration and web-related discussion, *Digital Web* magazine's stated goal is "to encourage designers to be creative, developers to be innovative, information architects to be strategic, and overall [for all] to be well versed in the web environment."

Digital Web magazine gathers a broad range of articles, reviews, and tutorials by a wide variety of leading writers. Covering everything from APIs to XML, *Digital Web* magazine is a fantastic resource for any aspiring Web Standardista.

Design and inspiration

There are a wealth of design-related resources online, and we've collected an extensive list of links to these resources at the book's companion web site. The following web sites are well worth a visit for inspiration and will help you develop a solid understanding of design.

Design Observer

www.designobserver.com

Subtitled "Writings on Design and Culture," *Design Observer* is a vibrant community-based web site gathering articles by an internationally respected collection of writers at the top of their form.

With articles on all manner of topics from, among others, Michael Bierut, Rick Poyner, Adrian Shaughnessy, and Lorraine Wild, *Design Observer* is an excellent resource you'll want to tap into. Covering topics as diverse as the "Aesthetics of Wind Farms" to "What Design Schools Don't Teach" *Design Observer* is the perfect source of design inspiration for web designers and non web designers alike.

14

The Elements of Typographic Style Applied to the Web

www.webtypography.net

Based on Robert Bringhurst's excellent *The Elements of Typographic Style* (Hartley and Marks Publishers, 2004), Richard Rutter's *The Elements of Typographic Style Applied to the Web* introduces a wealth of typographic resources with a specific emphasis on how typography can be used to improve the Web.

Rutter's personal web site (www.clagnut.com) is also well worth bookmarking.

Stylegala

www.stylegala.com

A "publication about web design and standards," *Stylegala* gathers together news and reviews about standards-based design including features on typography, design, standards, and style.

Stylegala's gallery is more than a generic list of screenshots, with all its entries reviewed and rated. *Stylegala's* CSS reference is also an excellent and comprehensive guide to CSS that's you'll come back to again and again.

CSS Zen Garden

www.csszengarden.com

Although now over five years old, Dave Shea's *CSS Zen Garden* was one of the driving forces behind the promotion of CSS-based design and still provides inspiration today.

With style sheets contributed by designers from all over the world, the *CSS Zen Garden* shows the power of CSS to change the visual presentation of a single, well-structured XHTML page in a multitude of ways, underlining what it's possible to achieve with CSS.

Accessibility

Throughout this book we've underlined the importance of ensuring the web pages you create are accessible to as wide an audience as possible. One by-product of the Web Standardistas' approach is the creation of well-formed, accessible web pages. The following web sites are well worth exploring to further your knowledge of accessible design.

456 Berea Street

www.456bereastreet.com

Roger Johansson's excellent web site places a heavy emphasis on accessibility and should be a first port of call for anyone wishing to improve their web site's accessibility.

456 Berea Street isn't just about accessibility, however; Johansson's writing covers a broad range of web design–related topics. This, coupled with his excellent book reviews, makes *456 Berea Street* an excellent resource.

Dive Into Accessibility

www.diveintoaccessibility.org

Although it was created by Mark Pilgrim in 2002, *Dive Into Accessibility* is still very much relevant today. Presented as a 30-day course—which is free to take—*Dive Into Accessibility* is essential reading for any aspiring web designer wishing to improve the accessibility of the web sites they create.

Did we mention that the course is free?

Joe Clark

www.joeclark.org

Joe Clark's excellent *Building Accessible Websites* (New Riders, 2002) is now available to read in its entirety online. An exhaustive introduction to accessible web design, Clarke's book is required reading for anyone wishing to improve their understanding of accessible design.

Having written for a variety of publications—from *Applied Arts* to *Bicycle Retailer and Industry News*—Clark's critical writings on design, typography, and a variety of other topics are also well worth reading.

North Temple Journal of Design

www.northtemple.com

Subtitled "A collection of original design thought, commentary, and study," *North Temple* is a web site created by a collective of designers from Salt Lake City, Utah.

On a mission to spread the good word about design, *North Temple*'s accessibility articles are both well written and well considered, and should inform any aspiring Web Standardista's approach to the creation of accessible web sites.

People

The Web is all about people. We follow too many writers to list here (check the book's companion web site for an extensive list). The following writers are not only extremely knowledgeable, but are also very good writers.

Dan Cederholm

www.simplebits.com

Dan Cederholm's books have established him as a leading voice in the field of web standards–based design. His web site is equally inspiring, gathering together a wealth of articles and links to emerging trends. It's also home to Cederholm's excellent SimpleQuiz, which formed the basis of his first book.

Cederholm's IconShoppe (www.iconshoppe.com) is also well worth visiting, home to a wealth of lovingly handcrafted royalty-free stock icons for the Web, all guaranteed to add a little sparkle to any web site.

14

John Gruber

www.daringfireball.net

Although not strictly focused on web design per se, John Gruber's *Daring Fireball* is well worth bookmarking for a daily dose of well-founded hyperbole. With a focus on "Mac Nerdery, Etc.," Gruber's eye is well and truly on the technical pulse; highlighting emerging trends, his no-nonsense posts are entertaining and thoughtful.

Gruber is also the creator of the excellent Markdown (www.daringfireball.net/ projects/markdown), a tool that allows you to write using an easy-to-read, easy-to-write plain text format, and then convert it to structurally valid XHTML.

Jon Hicks

www.hicksdesign.co.uk

Jon Hicks, the creator of Firefox's eye-catching icon and the excellent primate illustrations behind Silverback and MailChimp, gathers together a variety of writings on web development and design at his web site's journal. His openness about his design process, in particular the way in which he shows step by step how he creates his excellent illustrations, is both inspiring and educational.

He also likes tea (and cheese).

Jeffrey Zeldman

www.zeldman.com

The publisher of *A List Apart* and author of the excellent *Designing with Web Standards*, now in its second edition, Jeffrey Zeldman also cofounded the Web Standards Project in 1998. Zeldman's writing on standards, design, code, and culture at the *Daily Report* (published since 1995) are inspirational and well worth following.

Zeldman's role as an advocate for a web standards approach can't be overstated; his extensive writing has helped to promote a huge improvement in the technical and visual design, usability, and accessibility of web sites through the careful use of XHTML and CSS.

A fond farewell

So, that's it . . . Rather than wish you goodbye, however, we wish you *à bientôt*, until next time.

We hope you've enjoyed the book, and we hope you'll find the book's companion web site useful. We welcome your feedback on the book and its companion web site. Get in touch, we'd love to hear from you:

www.webstandardistas.com/hello

Thanks and good luck!

Summary

So what have we covered? In this chapter we've given you some pointers for the future, and we've suggested where you might head from here now that you have a solid understanding of XHTML and CSS.

Along the way we introduced JavaScript libraries, the benefits of database-driven web sites, and how AJAX is changing the nature of the Web. We also introduced you to a broad range of tools to help you in your ongoing journey as a fully fledged Web Standardista. Lastly, we introduced you to some emerging trends on the Web and provided you with a list of resources to help you continue your learning, all of which can be accessed from the book's companion web site.

Homework: You've earned the badges—now use them!

This chapter's homework isn't too complicated. In fact it only consists of one step: adding a badge to your Famous Primates web site. If you've made it this far, you've earned it. Well done.

1. Get a badge

In Chapter 1 we promised you we'd give you a badge if you made it to the end of the book. Would we lie to you?

We've actually created a number of Web Standardistas badges available to download at the book's companion web site. Wear them with pride on your web site and help spread the Web Standardistas' word! You can download them here:

www.webstandardistas.com/badges

As we also mentioned we've created a very limited edition of "real" badges, ones that you can pin onto the lapel of your "real" tweed jacket. All we ask you to do in order to earn the special honor of receiving one is to complete the "Homework" sections in this book and supply us with a link to your finished Famous Primates web site.

When you're ready, visit the preceding address, enter your details into the form and, once we've checked your web site validates, a badge will be hurried your way *posthaste*. We only have a limited number of these collector's items available, so please note:

First come, first served!

That's it! Once you've added your Web Standardistas' badge to your site, feel free to surf the interwebs, put the kettle on, and enjoy a cup of *ISO 3103* as you prepare yourself for your career as a fully fledged Web Standardista.

14

INDEX